FinTech, Artificial Intelligence and the Law

"The edited collection FinTech, Artificial Intelligence and the Law raises critical legal and ethical issues in the important and contemporary topic of technology in finance. Ryder and Lui's book incorporates a range of chapters on the opportunities and challenges that come with Artificial Intelligence, and contains interesting recommendations on FinTech and Law. Lui and Ryder's editing has brought together a roster of diverse contributors on topical issues, while leaving room for new perspectives that will shape the future of fintech globally. As such, this interdisciplinary collection will be beneficial to international development and non-governmental organisation practitioners, employees within the financial services sector, as well as professional services such as law, technology and corporate governance."

Ronda Zelezny-Green, PhD

This collection critically explores the use of financial technology (FinTech) and artificial intelligence (AI) in the financial sector and discusses effective regulation and the prevention of crime.

Focusing on crypto-assets, InsureTech and the digitisation of financial dispute resolution, the book examines the strategic and ethical aspects of incorporating AI into the financial sector. The volume adopts a comparative legal approach to: critically evaluate the strategic and ethical benefits and challenges of AI in the financial sector; critically analyse the role, values and challenges of FinTech in society; make recommendations on protecting vulnerable customers without restricting financial innovation; and to make recommendations on effective regulation and prevention of crime in these areas.

The book will be of interest to teachers and students of banking and financial regulation related modules, researchers in computer science, corporate governance, and business and economics. It will also be a valuable resource for policy makers including government departments, law enforcement agencies, financial regulatory agencies, people employed within the financial services sector, and professional services such as law, and technology.

Alison Lui is Reader in Corporate and Financial Law, Liverpool John Moores University, UK.

Nicholas Ryder is Professor of Law, Bristol Law School, University of the West of England, UK.

The Law of Financial Crime
Series Editor: Nicholas Ryder

Financial Crime and Corporate Misconduct
A Critical Evaluation of Fraud Legislation
Edited by Chris Monaghan and Nicola Monaghan

Corporate Liability for Insider Trading
Juliette Overland

Corruption in the Global Era
Causes, Sources and Forms of Manifestation
Lorenzo Pasculli and Nicholas Ryder

Counter-Terrorist Financing Law and Policy
An analysis of Turkey
Burke Uğur Başaranel and Umut Turksen

Integrity and Corruption and The Law
Global Regulatory Challenges
Edited by Nicholas Ryder and Lorenzo Pasculli

Regulating and Combating Money Laundering and Terrorist Financing
The Law in Emerging Economies
Nkechikwu Valerie Azinge-Egbiri

Combating Corruption in the Middle East
A Socio-Legal Study of Kuwait
Khaled S. Al-Rashidi

FinTech, Artificial Intelligence and the Law
Regulation and Crime Prevention
Edited by Alison Lui and Nicholas Ryder

For more information about this series, please visit: www.routledge.com/The-Law-of-Financial-Crime/book-series/FINCRIME

FinTech, Artificial Intelligence and the Law
Regulation and Crime Prevention

Edited by
Alison Lui and
Nicholas Ryder

LONDON AND NEW YORK

First published 2021
by Routledge
2 Park Square, Milton Park, Abingdon, Oxon OX14 4RN

and by Routledge
605 Third Avenue, New York, NY 10158

Routledge is an imprint of the Taylor & Francis Group, an informa business

© 2021 selection and editorial matter, Alison Lui and Nicholas Ryder; individual chapters, the contributors

The right of Alison Lui and Nicholas Ryder to be identified as the authors of the editorial material, and of the authors for their individual chapters, has been asserted in accordance with sections 77 and 78 of the Copyright, Designs and Patents Act 1988.

All rights reserved. No part of this book may be reprinted or reproduced or utilised in any form or by any electronic, mechanical, or other means, now known or hereafter invented, including photocopying and recording, or in any information storage or retrieval system, without permission in writing from the publishers.

Trademark notice: Product or corporate names may be trademarks or registered trademarks, and are used only for identification and explanation without intent to infringe.

British Library Cataloguing-in-Publication Data
A catalogue record for this book is available from the British Library

Library of Congress Cataloging-in-Publication Data
Names: Fintech, Artificial Intelligence and the Law (Conference) (2019 : Liverpool John Moores University) | Lui, Alison, editor. | Ryder, Nicholas, editor.
Title: Fintech, artificial intelligence and the law : regulation and crime prevention / edited by Alison Lui and Nicholas Ryder.
Description: Abingdon, Oxon ; New York, NY : Routledge, 2021. | Series: The law of financial crime | Includes bibliographical references and index.
Subjects: LCSH: Financial services industry—Law and legislation—Congresses. | Artificial Intelligence—Law and legislation—Congresses. | Financial institutions—Effect of technological innovations on—Congresses.
Classification: LCC K1066.A6 F588 2019 (print) | LCC K1066.A6 (ebook) | DDC 346.08/2—dc23
LC record available at https://lccn.loc.gov/2021003918
LC ebook record available at https://lccn.loc.gov/2021003919

ISBN: 978-0-367-89765-9 (hbk)
ISBN: 978-1-032-01246-9 (pbk)
ISBN: 978-1-003-02099-8 (ebk)

Typeset in Galliard
by codeMantra

Contents

Contributors' biographies   vii
Acknowledgements   xiii

PART 1
Introduction   1

1 Introduction—mind the gaps   3
ALISON LUI AND NICHOLAS RYDER

PART 2
The FinTech ecosystem   11

2 Automation, virtualisation, and value   13
STEPHEN RAINEY

3 InsurTech's assurance – value research through an array of ABCs   27
RUILIN ZHU

4 Improving the digital financial services ecosystem through collaboration of regulators and FinTech companies   46
SONIA SOON

5 Designing social-purpose FinTech: a UK case study   64
SHARON COLLARD, PHIL GOSSET AND JAMIE EVANS

PART 3
Regulation of cryptoassets and blockchains   83

6 Should we trade market stability for more financial inclusion? The case of crypto-assets regulation in EU   85
ILIAS KAPSIS

7 Initial coin offerings: financial innovation or scam   105
   HENRY HILLMAN

8 Cryptocurrency and crime   125
   SHERENA HUANG

9 Technology and tax evasion in the world of finance:
   an indispensable helping hand or a façade for crime
   facilitation?   144
   VIKSHA RAMGULAM AND SAM BOURTON

10 The Bank of England's approach to central bank
   digital currencies – considerations regarding a native
   digital pound and the regulatory aspects   169
   MONICA LAURA VESSIO

PART 4
Artificial intelligence and the law   191

11 AI, big data, quantum computing, and financial
   exclusion: tempering enthusiasm and offering a
   human-centric approach to policy   193
   CLARE CHAMBERS-JONES

12 Risk of discrimination in AI systems: evaluating the
   effectiveness of current legal safeguards in tackling
   algorithmic discrimination   211
   JENNIFER GRAHAM

13 Unprecedented times: artificial intelligence and the
   implications for intellectual property   230
   ANA CAROLINA BLANCO HACHÉ

14 Towards a responsible use of artificial intelligence (AI)
   and fintech in modern banking   262
   LOLA OLOLADE DURODOLA

   Index   279

Contributors' biographies

Ana Caroline Blanco Haché
Ana Carolina Blanco is the editor-in-chief of the Dominican Annual Review of Intellectual Property (http://anudopi.funglode.org) published since 2014. She is an intellectual property (IP) lecturer at various universities in the Dominican Republic. She is also a practitioner in the areas of IP, entertainment, technology and Internet law. She has been a legal adviser of the Chamber of Deputies of the Dominican Republic and belongs to the drafting committee of the Dominican Private International Law No. 544-14. She holds an LLB in commercial law from the Bristol Law School of the University of the West of England in the UK (First Class Honours) and a Magister Juris (Mjur) from the University of Oxford. She is a graduate of the executive studies of Harvard University's Kennedy School of Government in Innovation for Economic Development and International Business Law of Garrigues and the Harvard University Global Law Institute.

Sam Bourton
Sam Bourton is a lecturer in law at the University of the West of England, Bristol. She teaches on the LLB and LLM programmes, with modules including Foundations for Law, the Law of Financial Crime and Regulation, and International Financial Crime. Sam is also a PhD candidate, whose thesis aims to provide a comparative analysis of tax evasion law and its enforcement in the UK and USA. Her research primarily focuses on the law of financial crime, particularly the law pertaining to tax evasion and money laundering.

Dr Clare Chambers-Jones
Dr Clare Chambers-Jones is a senior lecturer in law at the Open University. She joined the OU from the University of the West of England. Clare has an LLB from Glamorgan University 2001; a PhD in Financial Exclusion and Banking Regulation, 2004, Bournemouth University; Financial Planning Certificates, 2004, Chartered Institute of Insurers; PGCert in Academic Practice, 2007; Fellow of the Higher Education Academy, 2007; Bournemouth University; PGCert in Research Supervision, 2008 Bournemouth University; and an MA Education in Virtual Worlds, 2014, University of the West of England.

Clare has worked in the City of London with Grant Thornton and subsequently Morgan Stanley, where she was an investment banking compliance officer for Europe.

Clare's main research area is banking and finance law and regulation. She has researched prolifically on the topics of financial crime including anti-money laundering regulations, counter terrorist financing, bribery and corruption, cyber and digital jurisdiction, and criminal actions on an international level as well as innovative technological developments in banking and finance. Clare's current research looks at exploring the regulatory side of cryptocurrencies, its regulatory application and the potential for financial crime.

Professor Sharon Collard

Sharon Collard is professor of personal finance and Research Director at the Personal Finance Research Centre, University of Bristol. With a background in social policy, she uses qualitative methods to explore the intersection between personal finance, financial services and well-being.

Lola Ololade Durodola

Lola is an experienced manager in retail banking and wealth management who consistently delivers profitable growth, leading highly motivated teams, for the last 15 years in global financial institutions. She is a PhD candidate at the Centre for Financial and Corporate Integrity (CFCI) of Coventry University, researching on artificial intelligence, its ethico-legal, corporate governance, and social responsibility perspectives.

Lola possesses an MBA passed with distinction from the University of East London. She is a Fellow of the Chartered Management Institute, a member of the Society for Business Ethics and Women Leading in AI, who also qualified with distinction in retail banking and conduct of business.

Outside of work and research, Lola loves leading sustainability projects and volunteering. She excels at coordinating events helping to mentor children at community sports workshops. Lola was a member of the Board of Trustees of Victoria Park, leading its risk and financial audit committee.

Jamie Evans

Jamie Evans is senior research associate at the Personal Finance Research Centre, University of Bristol. A human geographer, he specialises in mixed-methods policy research using quantitative methodologies. His recent work has focused on consumer vulnerability; mapping access to cash; and the role of financial services in reducing gambling harm.

Dr Phil Gosset

Dr Phil Gosset is head of innovation at Nationwide Building Society, where he recently architected and co-led the Open Bank for Good programme. Prior to this, he spent the last 25 years working in socio-technical innovation in the fields of finance, telecoms and computing with companies like Microsoft and Vodafone.

Jennifer Graham

Jennifer Graham is a PhD candidate at Liverpool John Moores University School of Law. Jennifer received both her LLB and LLM from Liverpool John Moores University. Her research focuses on the legal, ethical and regulatory aspects of artificial intelligence.

Dr Henry Hillman

Dr Henry Hillman is a senior lecturer at the University of the West of England in Bristol, leading the Commercial Law and Law of Financial Crime and Regulation modules. He has recently completed his PhD, researching the money-laundering risks posed by cryptocurrencies, and continues to research the regulatory issues surrounding cryptocurrencies. Henry's research interests are financial crime, cryptocurrencies, banking regulation and financial crises.

Dr Sherena Huang

Dr Sherena Huang is a PhD in economics and finance (Bangor University). She is the chief technical officer at Befficient Ltd and formerly a researcher at the UK's Financial Conduct Authority. Her academic credentials include LLM Research in FinTech regulation (Bangor University), MBA (Wuhan University), and BSc in computer science (Huazhong University of Science and Technology). Her professional credentials include a Futures Trading Practitioner (China Futures Association) and Advanced Python (HarkerRank). Building on her experience as a computer engineer and in international education and entrepreneurial vigour, Sherena is establishing a reputation at the intersection of finance, innovation, financial crime and regulation. She marries her academic objectives alongside running a start-up company. Recently, Sherena was invited to become an academy peer reviewer for Publons.

Dr Ilias Kapsis

Dr Ilias Kapsis holds a PhD in European Competition Law from the University of Bristol, UK. His research interests include competition and regulation in financial services, technology and artificial intelligence. In recent years, he has contributed to a number of publications and conference presentations on virtual currencies and Fintech. The aim of these contributions has been to develop ideas and proposals for adopting balanced frameworks for incorporating technological innovations into law. Current projects include: proposals for a legal framework for the regulation of virtual currencies; proposals to address in antitrust law competition issues in financial services from Fintech disruption; regulatory proposals for addressing systemic risks from artificial intelligence use in financial services.

Dr Alison Lui

Dr Alison Lui is a Reader in Corporate and Financial Law and the Associate Dean Global Engagement for the Faculty of Business and Law at Liverpool John Moores University. Alison is a Max Planck Fellow; Inner Temple Academic Fellow; Churchill Fellow; LJMU Early Career Fellow and has won several LJMU research grants. She has published a monograph with Routledge, various book chapters and many peer reviewed articles in top journals such as the Northern Ireland Legal Quarterly, Information and Communications Technology Law, Journal of Banking Regulation and Journal of Financial Regulation and Compliance. In particular, her monograph is listed as one of the best Banking Law books and one of the best-selling Banking Law books of all time.

Dr Stephen Rainey

Dr Stephen Rainey is a research fellow in the Faculty of Philosophy, University of Oxford. He is based in the Uehiro Centre for Practical Ethics working across a wide variety of interdisciplinary philosophical topics. Dr Rainey studied philosophy in Queen's University Belfast where he obtained his PhD with a thesis on rationality, especially how it interacts with linguistic understanding and communicative practices. His research interests include the philosophical implications of new and emerging technologies, such as the ethics of artificial intelligence, and the role of data in neuroscience and associated practices such as psychiatry. This interest also includes analysis of governance approaches to emerging technologies, where novel developments in science and technology challenge orthodox regulatory approaches. His main interest is currently in philosophy and neuroscience, investigating ethical dimensions of brain-computer interfaces in terms of language, cognition and action.

Viksha Ramgulam

Viksha Ramgulam is a first-class law graduate from the University of the West of England. She is currently enrolled on the Bar Training Course aspiring to become a barrister in corporate law and financial crime. Her passion for the topic of financial crime was sparked during the course of her studies when she opted to study the Law of Financial Crime and Regulation, the subject of which was the focus of her dissertation.

Nicholas Ryder

Nicholas is a Professor in Financial Crime and Head of the Global Crime Justice and Security Research Group at the University of the West of England, his research has been commissioned by the Innovate UK, Economic and Social Research Council (ESRC), LexisNexis Risk Solutions, the City of London Police Force, the Royal United Services Limited, ICT Wilmington Risk & Compliance, Universities South West, the France Telecom Group and the European Social Fund. His main research interest are financial crime and he focuses on money laundering, market manipulation and terrorism financing. Nicholas has provided counter-terrorism financing training to NATO, CEPOL, law enforcement agencies and financial services providers and has been asked to consult on numerous financial crime matters for the media including Bloomberg News, the BBC, CNBC, the Sunday Times, the Independent and the Wall Street Journal.

Sonia Soon

After obtaining her Bachelor degree in law from the University of Hertfordshire and master degree in law from Liverpool John Moores University, Sonia pursued a career within the compliance environment with businesses focused on digital financial services. Currently, she is the compliance manager of a local FinTech start-up, MyMy Payments Malaysia. Sonia is passionate about the digital financial services industry and its capabilities to disrupt the FinTech ecosystem. Sonia also possesses a genuine interest in all aspects of the legal and compliance field, given its investigative and problem-solving nature.

Dr Monica Laura Vessio

Dr Monica Vessio is Associate Lecturer at the University of the West of England (UWE) in the Department of Law, and research associate at the Centre for Banking Law at the University of Johannesburg. After practising as a commercial attorney for over 12 years, she returned to academia at the University of Johannesburg where she was module lead for the LLM in credit law. In August 2019, she moved to the UK and joined UWE in November 2019, where she is also involved in the Global Crime, Justice and Security Research Group. She has published widely in peer-reviewed journals and is co-author and co-editor for *Banking Law and Practice* (periodical/LexisNexis). She has provided consultancy services for the banking industry and has received funding from commercial firms to conduct bespoke research projects. She has presented seminars for the Black Lawyers Association in their centres in Cape Town, Johannesburg, Durban, Port Elizabeth and Limpopo. While her broad area of interest is banking law, her contemporary focus is on digital currencies (virtual assets, stablecoins and CBDCs) and smartcontracts. She actively engages in consultancy and legal opinion drafting for industry.

Dr Ruilin Zhu

Dr Ruilin Zhu's research focuses on information systems (IS), in particular, the business transformation enabled by digital innovation. Specifically, he leverages the traditional technical view through integrating behavioural, economic and legal perspectives in order to understand IS phenomena such as FinTech, digital healthcare and e-agriculture. His academic work builds on previous expertise gained from working for leading financial and banking institutions and international organisations and being a visiting scholar at a number of prominent academic institutions in the UK, the USA and Australia. He obtained his PhD from the University of Auckland and has published widely in leading journal outlets and international conferences.

Acknowledgements

Dr Alison Lui

This edited book is a collective effort of all the authors and my co-editor, Professor Nic Ryder. It has been a great pleasure working with them all. As always, it is a privilege working with Professor Ryder. I particularly appreciate his valuable insight, wisdom and hard work. My thanks to the publisher, Routledge, for giving Professor Ryder and I this opportunity to publish the edited book. I dedicate this book to Chi, my parents and sister. Their love and support are truly appreciated. Finally, I would like to thank you everyone who have encouraged and supported me throughout my career.

Professor Nicholas Ryder

I would like to thank all of the authors who have contributed towards this edited collection. I am very grateful to the lead editor for the project, Dr Alison Lui. Her dedication and hard work were a real inspiration during this project. There are two people in particular I would like to dedicate this book too, my wife Ruth and son Ethan. It is without their support and love that this collection would not have been possible. It is to them I dedicate this book.

Part 1
Introduction

1 Introduction—mind the gaps

Alison Lui and Nicholas Ryder

The global pandemic of 2020 has created opportunities for digital payments, a type of financial technology ('FinTech'). Lockdown restrictions across the world have led to a big surge in digital payments and online payment platforms globally. According to Mastercard's research in 2020, 64% of European consumers prefer to pay by tap-and-pay cards (Mastercard, 2020). ATM cash transaction withdrawals in the UK fell by 62% in late March 2020 when the lockdown restrictions were imposed. In Spain, cash withdrawals dropped by 90% (Thomas & Megaw, 2020). Countries such as Russia and the USA however have seen a brief surge in cash withdrawals due to fears of cash hoarding. Rise in the use of digital platforms will boost digital financial products and e-commerce. At the same time, however, the sharp rise in digital payments has excluded the vulnerable, especially those who are unbanked, the elderly and victims of domestic abuse. More importantly, many consumers are still wary of FinTech due to a trust gap. According to the Edelman Trust Barometer (2020), only 47% of the 33,000 individuals trust digital payments and peer-to-peer companies. Forty-eight per cent trust blockchain and crypto companies, whereas 49% trust digital health and robo-advisory firms. The main obstacles to wider public trust in FinTech include data privacy; fear of the unknown and thus continued loyalty with incumbent banks; the fast pace with which the technology is moving; and the recent FinTech scandals such as Wirecard.

Trust in algorithms was the centre of debate when the algorithm used to predict A-level students' grades in England, Wales and Northern Ireland in 2020 downgraded grades by up to 40%. Due to the pandemic, A-level exams were cancelled in the summer of 2020. To provide students with their grades, the algorithm $P_{kj} = (1 - r_j)C_{kj} + r_j(C_{kj} + q_{kj} - p_{kj})$ was used (Hern, 2020). It took into account an estimated grade; a ranking of each student compared with other students at the school within the same estimated grade boundary and the school's past performance in the previous three years in each subject. This sparked a controversial debate about the algorithm's fairness and accountability in the public sector. In private finance, algorithms are increasingly used in algorithmic trading, credit scoring, chatbot assistants and wealth management. Arguably, the importance of transparency and accountability of algorithms is even more crucial in a sector traditionally criticised for its opaqueness (Flannery, Kwan & Nimalendran, 2004; Morgan, 2002). Extant legal frameworks and regulations at national, European and international levels need to be scrutinised to see if they are effective. In light of recent developments in FinTech and artificial intelligence (AI), this chapter critically evaluates the gaps between FinTech, financial exclusion, regulation and supervision.

1 Closing the gap in FinTech and financial exclusion

FinTech aims to close the gap between the financially and digitally included on the one hand and those who are excluded on the other. FinTech is an enabler to global financial inclusion, creating a more equitable world (Bisht & Mishra, 2016). A number of scholars opine that the use of FinTech can circumvent structural and infrastructural problems to reach the poor (Al-Mudimigh & Anshari, 2020; Chinoda & Kwenda, 2019; Beck, Senbet & Simbanegavi, 2014). Globally, mobile phones have improved financial inclusion in 49 countries (Chinoda & Kwenda, 2019). The large number of internet users and FinTech companies in Southeast Asia has improved financial inclusion (Al-Mudimigh & Anshari, 2020). In Africa, Evans's research between 2000 and 2016 (Evans, 2018) reveals that the internet and mobile phones have improved financial inclusion, although Chikalipah (2017) argues that financial illiteracy is a major hurdle to financial inclusion in sub-Saharan Africa. Meanwhile in Europe, financial inclusion focuses on increasing customers' access to the credit market and balancing this with financial stability (Ozili, 2020). More studies need to be carried out with regards to customer barriers to FinTech adoption and how to reduce these barriers (Kavuri & Milne, 2019). Furthermore, innovative research methods and ways to collaborate between financial players in reducing customer barriers to FinTech adoption are much needed.

Will FinTech democratise access to financial services and reduce societal inequity? Bartlett et al.'s (2018) study shows that algorithms can reduce discrimination of ethnic minority borrowers by up to 40% compared to FinTech lenders. Lenders charge Latin/African American borrowers 7.9 and 3.6 basis points more for mortgages, costing them $765 million in aggregate per year in extra interest. In another study, predictive analytics in screening borrowers' creditworthiness is shown to reduce inequity. One of the advantages that financial intermediaries possess is information advantage in assessing borrowers' creditworthiness. Nevertheless, Berg et al.'s (2018) study proves that this advantage, and indeed the financial intermediary model, may be threatened. Utilising 250,000 observations of digital footprints from German e-commerce, Berg et al.'s research reveals that the digital footprints equal or exceed the predictive power of traditional credit bureau score. This finding has potentially far-reaching consequences for both borrowers and financial intermediaries. Predictive power of digital footprints can reduce inequity and close the information asymmetry gap between incumbent banks and FinTech players.

2 Gaps in FinTech, regulation and supervision

Studies into how FinTech can impact upon financial stability are still short in supply (Minto, Voelkerling & Wulff, 2017). The conundrum is that currently the precise impact of FinTech on financial stability remains unclear. FinTech increases diversity in the financial sector, which may increase the relevant market players' resilience to externalities. The more diverse the financial products, services and models in the financial market, the less exposed are financial providers to systemic risks (Minto et al., 2017). Schwarz (2012), however, disagrees and argues that FinTech can cause pro-cyclicality in the financial sector, concentrate risks and reduce public confidence in the financial system. Inter-connectedness of the global financial markets makes it easier for systemic risks to permeate and spread throughout the financial sector.

Asymmetric technology is widening the gulf between the huge advancement technology firms are making and the supervisors' adherence to out-of-date technology (Zeranski & Stefan, 2020). The Wirecard scandal is a good example of this. It is a hybrid digital payments company but also owed a bank. Wirecard filed for insolvency in July 2020 after its auditors discovered a £1.7 billion hole in its accounts. Its share price dropped by 100% after Wirecard went into insolvency (Hannah, 2020). Two days later, the company CEO was arrested for market manipulation and false accounting. In addition to market volatility, many UK customers had their accounts frozen since the Financial Conduct Authority ordered all regulated activity to stop. Wirecard provided payment processing services for a number of UK-based cards and apps which did not have their own banking licences. The freeze led to customers, many of whom did not know that Wirecard was involved, unable to use their cards or access their bank accounts.

This scandal provides a clear example of three points. First, the FinTech ecosystem is inter-connected where Wirecard was processing payments for UK customers without their knowledge. From a regulatory perspective, Wirecard did not hold client money nor did it engage in risky lending. However, its risk was concentrated due to the inter-connected nature of the financial market (Salway, 2020). This supports Schwarz's view that FinTech concentrates risks. Second, the Wirecard scandal demonstrates how a FinTech company can undermine financial stability and public trust in the financial system. Finally, regulators and supervisors need to innovate their strategies, rules and practice in monitoring FinTech companies. In the case of Wirecard, uncertainty and confusion arose between the German regulator BaFin and the accounting watchdog, the Financial Reporting Enforcement Panel, as to how Wirecard should have been supervised. Wirecard was regulated as a technology company rather than as a financial services operator. From a behavioural finance perspective, the German regulators may have adopted a laissez-faire approach in regulating Wirecard due to the buzz and frenzy linked to FinTech. The regulators may have seen a growing FinTech company as a sign of success in financial innovation, thus reluctant to intervene when there are looming signs of weaknesses (Zeranski & Stefan,

2020). As a result of this scandal, the EU Commission is reviewing the regulatory and supervisory mechanisms for hybrid FinTech companies. More research is required to examine country-specific regulatory and supervisory frameworks to curtail risks generated by FinTech and AI.

3 Structure of the book

The aim of this edited collection is to explore critically the interesting and emerging symbiosis of FinTech, AI and the law. As a branch of FinTech, AI is becoming increasingly popular in the financial sector. The pandemic has changed the FinTech ecosystem by accelerating the shift to digital financial products and services. Therefore, the main research objectives of the edited collection are as follows:

1 To critically analyse the roles, values and challenges of FinTech in society;
2 To critically evaluate the legal and ethical challenges in FinTech and AI;
3 To make recommendations on effective regulation of FinTech and AI.

The book is divided into four parts. In Part 1, 'Introduction—mind the gaps', the editors will set out the gaps in FinTech, financial inclusion, regulation and supervision. Whilst FinTech aims to close the gap between the financially included and excluded, the widening of current gaps between technology, regulation and supervision has to be addressed urgently. Recommendations will be made in this chapter.

Part 2 is titled 'The FinTech Ecosystem'. There are four chapters under this part. Chapter 2 opens with a thought-provoking chapter by Stephen Rainey on the roles and values of FinTech in a capitalist society. Rainey argues that the financial sector is somewhat disconnected from capitalistic interactions as it has become an autonomous sector. However, Rainey submits that FinTech has its values in our capitalistic society. In Chapter 3, Ruilin Zhu discusses a much-neglected area of FinTech, namely InsurTech. In his chapter, Zhu focuses on the apprehension of using digital innovations-empowered InsurTech on industry stakeholders in support of the development of insurance as a way to promote value research. He discusses the use of big data and AI in the insurance sector. Zhu uses two Chinese insurance companies as contextual examples, and narratives are presented for discussions aimed at identifying ways in which the insurance industries and technology sectors can achieve value proposition through InsurTech.

In Chapter 4, Sonia Soon explores the digital financial services ecosystem and the issues contributing towards its limitations, notably, the regulator's role. She adopts a comparative legal analysis method and examines the different approaches to FinTech regulation in Asia, Africa and South America. She concludes that desired outcomes can be achieved when regulators and FinTech companies collaborate to meet their shared objective, which is to flourish the FinTech ecosystem and bridge the gap in financial inclusion, all while protecting the interests of the public and the country. In Chapter 5, Sharon Collard,

Phil Gosset and Jamie Evans continue with the theme of financial inclusion and critically analyses the main financial inclusion challenges faced by individuals and households in the UK. Collard et al explore the potential for FinTech to help address these challenges and reflects on the opportunities and hurdles to make this happen. In doing so, she considers various 'FinTech for good' initiatives in the UK that aim to ensure the application of FinTech for social purposes rather than simply for profit. Using Nationwide Building Society's Open Banking for Good programme as a case study, this chapter demonstrates the potential of using a Grounded Innovation approach as a means to ensure that social-purpose FinTech is inclusively designed from the start to increase its potential to meet the needs of the financially squeezed.

Part 3 of the book examines several challenges raised by crypto-assets. Ilias Kapsis starts off the discussion in Chapter 6 by addressing the regulation of crypto-assets. He argues that a more flexible, principles-based approach to regulation of crypto-assets may be required due to the challenges posed by crypto-assets. Henry Hillman continues with this topic in Chapter 7 with a critical discussion of initial coin offerings ('ICO'). He critically analyses ICOs from four perspectives: businesses offering coins, investors, regulators (in this case, the Financial Conduct Authority) and the potential criminal. Recommendations are made on how market participants and regulators should react to ICOs. The chapter draws conclusions on the integrity of ICOs, especially whether they are a financial innovation or are pyramid schemes that have been taken to a new dimension. Financial crime is the theme of Sherena Huang's contribution to this volume in Chapter 8. She examines the role of cryptocurrency in financial crime and classifies cryptocurrency illicit activities into two categories—direct and indirect unlawful activities. By doing so, her analysis proceeds to highlight three specific flaws in financial regulation: micropayments, individual activities and jurisdictions. All these three issues exist in the current compliance measures and international cooperation. The lack of international cooperation has caused a delay in some legal proceedings of cryptocurrency crime, while the micropayments and individual activities can potentially create a grey area making the entry easy for the criminals gaming with the system.

In Chapter 9, Viksha Ramgulam and Sam Bourton investigate the role of technological innovation in the development of methods used to commit tax evasion as well as the methods used to detect and respond to this financial crime. The chapter discusses whether technological innovation ultimately helps or hinders efforts to combat tax evasion. The authors conclude by arguing that technological innovation has assisted both those who evade tax liabilities and those charged with the enforcement of those liabilities. In particular, the chapter discusses the possibilities offered by increased use of blockchain technology. In Chapter 10, Monica Vessio examines the understanding of the concept of Central Bank Digital Currencies (CBDC) both at the global level and at the prevailing national level. In this context, the chapter proceeds to examine issues of design principles and the genre of CBDC being contemplated by the Bank of England as well as the regulatory aspects that come into play when considering the introduction of a new form of money into an already existing and regulated payments system.

Part 4 concentrates on AI and the law. The section starts with Clare Chambers-Jones's evaluation in Chapter 11, especially around the central question of whether AI can be a potential solution to financial exclusion. Her chapter provides a new way of thinking about financial exclusion by breaking down existing literature and policy measures demonstrating the ineffective regulation surrounding financial exclusion. The chapter offers solutions to governments and policy makers as to the unique position they are in to draft meaningful, human-centric, understandable and useable regulations to assist AI banking include in its fold the unbanked within the UK. The chapter not only adds to the existing literature but is also unique for its contention that financial exclusion will never be eradicated and that there is no one solution to the problem. However, if broken down into smaller manageable elements, advances can be made. AI offers a possible solution if regulated in the right way.

Using a legal and ethical angle, Jennifer Graham critically evaluates the topical issues of bias and discrimination in AI in Chapter 12. She examines the effectiveness of current legal safeguards such as the General Data Protection Regulation (GDPR), the European Convention on Human Rights (ECHR) and the Equality Act 2010 in addressing bias and discrimination. In Chapter 13, Ana Carolina Blanco Haché examines the implications of AI within the intellectual property (IP) system. In particular, she discusses the patent eligibility of AI innovations and the issues concerning ownership of potential copyrightable computer-created works. The chapter highlights the interference of the user, a collective group and developer of such AI inventions to claim rights over the resulting works or whether by default those works will fall within the public domain. New challenges are emerging that will require the international IP system to adjust its policies to AI technologies and data including privacy issues, ethics, integrity and cybersecurity. Finally, in Chapter 14, Lola Ololade Durodola discusses both the benefits and challenges of AI in the financial sector as an employee in the financial industry. In particular, she addresses the #AIFear factor—challenges such as reduction of jobs and financial exclusion.

Bibliography

Al-Mudimigh, A., & Anshari, M. (2020) 'Financial technology and disruptive innovation in ASEAN', in *Financial technology and innovative financial inclusion*. IGI Global, pp. 119–129.

Bartlett, R., Morse, A., Stanton, R., & Wallace, N. (2018) Consumer-lending discrimination in the era of fintech.

Beck, T., Senbet, L. & Simbanegavi, W. (2014) 'Financial inclusion and innovation in Africa: An overview', *Journal of African Economies*, 24, pp. 3–11.

Berg, T., Burg, V., Gombovic, A., & Puri, M. (2018) On the rise of the FinTechs—Credit scoring using digital footprints. Available at: https://www.fdic.gov/bank/analytical/cfr/2018/wp2018/cfr-wp2018-04.pdf.

Bisht, S., & Mishra, V. (2016) 'ICT-driven financial inclusion initiatives for urban poor in a developing economy: implications for public policy', *Behaviour and Information Technology*, 35(10), pp. 817–832.

Chikalipah, S. (2017) 'What determines financial inclusion in Sub-Saharan Africa?', *African Journal of Economic and Management Studies*, 8, pp. 8–18.

Chinoda, T., & Kwenda, F. (2019) 'Do mobile phones, economic growth, bank competition and stability matter for financial inclusion in Africa?', *Cogent Economics & Finance*, 7, pp. 1–20.

Edelman (2020) Edelman trust barometer 2020 spring update: Trust and the Covid-19 pandemic financial services. Available at: https://www.edelman.com/sites/g/files/aatuss191/files/2020-05/2020 Edelman Trust Barometer Spring Update Financial Services.pdf.

Evans, O. (2018) 'Connecting the poor: The internet, mobile phones and financial inclusion in Africa', *Digital Policy, Regulation and Governance*, 20, pp. 568–581.

Flannery, M., Kwan, S., & Nimalendran, M. (2004) 'Market evidence on the opaqueness of banking firms' assets', *Journal of Financial Economics*, 71(3), pp. 419–614.

Hannah, F. (2020) 'What the Wirecard scandal means for your finances', *The Independent*, 14 July. Available at: https://www.independent.co.uk/money/wirecard-scandal-what-money-safe-card-access-freeze-protected-fraud-a9617576.html.

Hern, A. (2020) 'Ofqual's A-level algorithm: why did it fail to make the grade?', *The Guardian*, 21 August. Available at: https://www.theguardian.com/education/2020/aug/21/ofqual-exams-algorithm-why-did-it-fail-make-grade-a-levels.

Kavuri, A., & Milne, A. (2019) FinTech and the future of financial services: What are the research gaps? Available at: https://www.researchgate.net/profile/Anil_Kavuri2/publication/331244922_Fintech_and_the_Future_of_Financial_Services_What_Are_the_Research_Gaps/links/5e09fe8a4585159aa4a5f5c9/Fintech-and-the-Future-of-Financial-Services-What-Are-the-Research-Gaps.pdf.

Mastercard (2020) Mastercard recovery insights: the shift to digital. Available at: https://www.mastercardservices.com/en/recovery-insights/shift-digital?source=cex&cmp=us.en-us.usa.b2b.mastercard.com.cx.blg..gen.recovery-insights..shift-digital.

Minto, A., Voelkerling, M., & Wulff, M. (2017) 'Separating apples from oranges: identifying threats to financial stability originating from FinTech', *Capital Markets Law Journal*, 12(4), pp. 428–465. doi: 10.1093/cmlj/kmx035.

Morgan, D. (2002) 'Rating banks: Risk and Uncertainty in an opaque industry', *American Economic Review*, 92(4), pp. 874–888.

Ozili, P. (2020) 'Financial inclusion research around the world: A review', Forum for Social Economics, pp. 1–23.

Salway, J. (2020) 'Wirecard's collapse exposes gap in payments regulation', *Financial Times*, 30 September. Available at: https://www.ft.com/content/0e84428b-bee6-45e6-bef1-b03f6f9be335.

Schwarcz, S. (2012) 'Regulating shadow banking', *Review of Banking and Financial Law*, 31(1), pp. 619–642.

Thomas, D., & Megaw, N. (2020) 'Coronavirus accelerates shift away from cash', *Financial Times*. Available at: https://www.ft.com/content/430b8798-92e8-4b6a-946e-0cb49c24014a.

Zeranski, S., & Stefan, I. (2020) 'Digitalisation of Financial Supervision with Supervisory Technology', *Journal of International Banking Law and Regulation*, 35(8), pp. 309–329.

Part 2
The FinTech ecosystem

2 Automation, virtualisation, and value

Stephen Rainey

1 What is FinTech?

FinTech as we know it, started out in the 1990s as an initiative undertaken by Citigroup to facilitate technological innovation in financial applications (Arner et al., 2016). More generally, it might be termed "...a new financial industry that applies technology to improve financial activities" (Schueffel, 2016, p. 45). While money itself, the physical instantiation of transferable value, might be seen as an initial financial technology, more obvious technological innovations can be seen in the introduction of the telegraph for trading, credit cards, ATMs, and so on.

Contemporary FinTech can be seen especially in terms of consumer services that encompass areas including loans and investing, payments, and user interface with, for example, banks. The potential opportunities here lie not least in the micro-tailoring of financial services to the exact needs of specific consumers, whose input to an app might characterise their risk for something like a loan more precisely than traditional means of seeking finance. In redistributing responsibilities and power more widely among a web of those involved in all things financial, FinTech presents the promise of insulating against future negative financial shocks of the sort seen in 2007–2008 financial crisis. But this also brings some questions.

In one sense, for all its innovative power, FinTech can be seen as a novel means of accessing traditional financial services, such as loans and savings. For all the hopes that micro-tailoring such access to individual circumstances could stave off negative spirals in the wider economy, this could open a new front in terms of FinTech. Predatory practices played a role in the 2007–2008 financial crisis, such as those in the area of subprime mortgages and the marketing of collateralised debt obligations (CDO). With FinTech, such risks could be obviated, but replaced by naive consumer behaviour or normatively unclear practices, as algorithmic activity replaces human judgement in something like seeking a loan. Responsibility might be divested onto 'the system,' 'the algorithm,' and so on. Moreover, in being based on data, algorithm-powered FinTech is not without its own potential for causing confusion regarding objectivity and value. This chapter provides a critical point of departure for a debate on the role and values of FinTech in these and related respects.

2 A standard view of value

Thinking about finance, for the layperson at least, probably means paying attention to ideas about banks, cash, loans, and buying items like food, products, and services. This is a very material way of thinking about finance. Although most people are aware of the more arcane dimensions of financial practices, like stock market trading, leveraging assets, and so on, for the most part financial reality is far more grounded in more basic concepts. Without developing a whole philosophy of economics, or an anthropology of transaction, it's worth pursuing this idea in order to sharpen up some 'common sense' concepts relating to finance. In particular, the concept of *value* could do with some scrutiny, in order to flesh out a difference that seems to emerge between the layperson's ideas and an emerging context of technology-mediated finance. To pre-empt a little, it's possible that FinTech poses some challenges to this set of laypersons' ideas. In doing so, it may prompt a question about whether general ideas about finance ought to change in response to FinTech or whether FinTech ought to be considered some kind of risk to received financial wisdom. If we look at the language of how everyday transactions work, we can come up with a few notions straightaway that look like clues about how finance is thought of.

Contexts in which transactions are likely to arise include those where you have a skill that I lack, or I have a skill that you lack; you have a commodity I lack, or I have a commodity that you lack; to stretch this further, in another scenario, you have either of the above, and I have *currency* that you lack that serves as a proxy for skill or commodity. In any of these scenarios, it seems clear that value is derived for the skill, commodity, or currency from the context. In these simple types of transactions, value can come from context as follows: I need a fence to secure my land, and you need transport to the well. There is plenty of wood around, you are deft with your hands, and so the fence to you is little hassle. I have a vehicle and move around regularly, so transporting you is no burden for me. We easily strike a deal here. It's a simple win-win.

In trades of commodities, the same transactional framework may apply in terms of context, but value may also be derived from a commodity's functional properties. Short-lived qualities in some commodities may make those commodities more valuable in some contexts; for example, medical isotopes are partly valuable due to their use in diagnostic or clinical applications but possess no shelf-life. However, what makes their acquisition more valuable is the urgency of the need to use them in specific contexts such as diagnostic or clinical applications and/or therapeutic processes. On the other hand, things that last for the long-term may gain value in virtue of that longevity. Sturdy boots, made famous in a short discussion by Terry Pratchett on wealth, are one such example (Pratchett, 2013).[1] Here, we can see how value relates to context and to the functional properties of the commodity in question.

---

1 The so-called Boots theory of socioeconomic unfairness from Pratchett states that the rich are rich because they need to spend less money: "Take boots, for example. He earned thirty-eight

In currency-mediated transactions, we can put a number on the value, which is in part the value of money. We need not prevaricate about the relative value in terms of context or function where money is involved. If I value your commodity ten times more than possessing a single unit of my currency, you can charge ten units for your commodity and we'll each get what we want. If I prefer having 10 euros (or pounds or dollars) over what you have to offer, my decision is easy to make. We each get to keep what we already have – no harm, no foul.

These simple sorts of examples are illustrative of attitudes towards value as they pertain to a simplified form of market. Concepts like supply, demand, and scarcity constrain value in this picture of market, because the animating principle is one of material interactions. The ways in which value is understood are often connected with the way real or imagined encounters with others, and their wares, turn out. We can call this *the naïve view*, meaning the view of a pre-reflective layperson.

At a different level, such concepts can themselves be commodified, which introduces something more abstract into matters. For instance, if I sell the best apples in a market full of apple sellers, you might gain value if you can guide others my way. As a trusted person, able to point others to valuable items, your advice gains value, and you may trade upon that. This kind of *meta-value* is a value about the valuable nature of your knowledge about material things on sale. Reality here is in knowledge of trends, well-grounded predictions, and the power to sway market activity. In combination, this points to a highly complex picture. Where many people are trusted in a market place, and many wares are on offer, those out to buy items must navigate a quite complex terrain, and one a little removed from straightforward exchange and barter.

Because this is a somewhat more slippery notion than that of fences and trips to wells, or sturdy boots, there is a degree more jeopardy at play. Were you and I in cahoots, for instance, we could easily take advantage of your trusted status and ensure my substandard Granny Smiths were sold despite their unsatisfactory nature. This is where the regulation as an intuitive notion comes in. Where things like stockpiling, false advertising, or manipulated production can influence material judgements about value decisions, there is an obvious place for authority to dissuade bad practice.

Even in these very basic examples, there is an implicit normative dimension. This emerges when consideration turns to slightly more abstract ideas of value, like the meta-value of knowledgeable advice. From this, it is only a short way to go before law, policy, or other means of market governance are imagined.

---

dollars a month plus allowances. A really good pair of leather boots cost fifty dollars. But an affordable pair of boots, which were sort of OK for a season or two and then leaked like hell when the cardboard gave out, cost about ten dollars....

But the thing was that good boots lasted for years and years. A man who could afford fifty dollars had a pair of boots that'd still be keeping his feet dry in ten years' time, while the poor man who could only afford cheap boots would have spent a hundred dollars on boots in the same time and would still have wet feet."

But even in the very simple ideas of trade and barter, there are implicit ideas of fairness. After all, without a basic assumption of trust in reciprocity, the very idea of 'trade' would cease to function. 'Value,' under these conditions, would be little more than hope.

Essentially, this short trip through imagined transactions has served up a few key concepts that appear essential to structuring the idea of value in material transactions. They have included *context, skill, commodity, currency, transaction,* and how these affect *value*. The context has included more abstract entities too, that gain value as a meta-concept ranging over knowledge of the material transaction space – *expertise*. In each case, there is a structure that involves the abilities one has to reason about valuable items. Where value is at stake, one has to consider how context, skill, commodity, currency, transaction, and value interrelate so as to make decisions about what to acquire, what to retain, and what to exchange.

Might this picture of things be challenged in contexts of FinTech? By looking at how actual markets have undermined themselves in recent history, it will become clearer how abstraction from the basic picture outlined here can serve to be such a challenge.

3 Finance industry

In November 2011 in a BBC Radio Four documentary (The New Global Economics, 2011), Adair Turner bemoaned 'failures of understanding' among economic policymakers. Among this group it had become commonplace that financial services were a natural next step in the evolution of capitalism. In the same documentary Mohamed El Erian, of PIMCO, noted how the 'financial services industry' started to be referred to as the 'financial industry.' What started as a shorthand, however, brought about a reimagining of the purpose of the enterprise. On the assumption that financial services were the next step in capitalism, a policy background was constructed that could serve these services. The financial industry was assumed to have an internal logic that ought to be allowed to proceed unhindered. Actual economies might even represent such hindrances. 'Actual economies' here are just those relations among real people, retailers, banks, civic authorities, and so on, mediated by the institution of capital.

Owing to the assumptions flagged by Turner and El Erian, the financial services industry came to be an autonomous sphere of activity, encouraged by policymaking to engage in self-sufficient action unrelated to the everyday comings and goings of human plans and interests. In the name of one idea of capitalism, it disconnected from the loci of capitalistic interactions that enabled the sector to expand in the first place. A view from outside the cocoon of finance might have spotted the worrying nature of the posit – that this kind of industry has an internal logic whose unfolding must be facilitated even at the expense of relevance to real economies. But a generalist view was not available, perhaps owing to the specialisation of relevant actors into ever-more obscure financial instruments and practices. If the industry can be said to have drifted from hitherto expected assumptions of finance, it would certainly have left far behind the assumptions made by the layperson.

The gamut of interactions in financial industry terms include more than just those material interactions considered above as the received wisdom of laypeople. The idea of a Collateralised Debt Obligation ('CDO'), for instance, does not appear to have a natural home in the range of basic concepts discussed above. A CDO is a financial product sold as an investment for those operating in a secondary market related to the primary market in which loans and debts are realised. The value of CDOs is related to the attributes of other assets, such as the performance of loans or forecasts relating to payment of credit card debts. How might someone seeking a mortgage for a house, for instance, be expected to imagine their loan-worthiness was not paramount in the calculations coming from their bank, that place instead being filled by the relative position in a cascade of probabilities of returns from other debts? The differing aims of finance industry players and their customers can be seen through this lens: the view of the consumer here appears on the one hand naïve, but on the other, utterly reasonable. The industry view appears at once reasonable, in terms of a system-stabilising function, and yet completely detached from the material reality of customers.

The commodification of financial products raises questions about justice in terms of provision of access to finance versus paternalistic duties to constrain such access in avoidance of undue risk. This tracks a longstanding tension in the regulatory landscape, wherein access to markets must be provided while nonetheless striving for market stability. This tension becomes most pronounced where what's being traded in the market are items whose value is itself determined by the nature of the market. Think CDOs again, and how they have a market value relative to a set of probabilities about other debts. The buying and selling of such an entity is clearly unlike a transaction as naïvely conceived by a layperson. Such people's access and exposure to such a market ought thereby to be thoughtfully constrained.

This area – regulation – is one wherein FinTech can be seen as having positive potential. As both Arner (2016) and Magnuson (2018) discuss, the banking sector thus far has tended towards consolidation, over many years. Mainly, this has been through various mergers and so on leading to a growth in the size of institutions. With size comes clout and, hence, the emergence of the moniker *too big to fail*. Among the concrete results of this status has been the erecting of barriers to financial market entry, with a concomitant paucity of control over inequalities across the financial sector. While this is a problem within the sector, from the outside with the emergence of novel technologies, it also is a signal that the time is ripe for market entry, to remedy the worst of this. FinTech can be seen in this rectifying light, one of putting the idea of consumer back to the centre, and replacing too-big-to-fail ideas of market functionality, with service provision at the scale of individuals. This could be seen as the democratising potential in FinTech: bringing back into focus the standard view of finance.

4 FinTech revolution

Disruptive FinTech start-ups can 'start from scratch,' without the old, clunky, inherited tech setups of well-established banks. Such setups, themselves the products of various acquisitions and mergers over the years, might be seen as the de facto infrastructure of finance per se, given those banks' too-big-to-fail status. While the sector, in this sense, has required the mergers in order to retain market stability, the tech has not been directed towards clear goals. Rather, it has been taken for granted as the constraints on sectoral activity or required specific types of technical workarounds in order to generate novel opportunities. The advent of high-frequency trading, as recorded by Michael Lewis in his *Flash Boys*, contains various examples of this kind of thing. There we see finance outsiders like telecom engineers circulating among big banks, each trying to shave microseconds off trades through ad hoc tinkering with creaking hardware and software (Lewis, 2014).

FinTech can be service-specific, and customer-centred, unhindered by legacy hardware, software, hierarchies, and business practices. This tech-savvy specificity can be seen as essential to its 'revolutionary' potential (Mackenzie, 2015). Users may not be constrained by providers, just what front-ends they can find for the specific functions they require, and these can be found through simple web searches. The customer can, in principle, shop around for the 'best deal' relative to the function they require (e.g. a business loan, equity release from a mortgage). They might also tailor their experience to suit their own preferences, such as with inputting desired levels of risk when consulting an automated investment advice service or 'robo-advisor' (Magnuson, 2018, p. 1176). This means an individual can bypass conventional structural or regulatory roadblocks that might otherwise forestall their plans. This kind of opportunity is a paradigm case of FinTech as the application of technology to improve financial activity (Schueffel, 2016).

Crowdsourcing money for an idea may require no detailed plan of action, or collateral, for example, whereas applying for a loan to the bank with which one has a mortgage, and a current account, might be considerably more formal. In the latter case, the customer will have all the technical hoops to jump through about the likelihood of repaying. They will also have more social, institutional constraints, such as having to dress a certain way to portray trustworthiness to a loan manager. In terms of crowdsourcing, the cultivation of enthusiasm among a base of micro-investors is all that may be required, aided by social media and viral marketing approaches or through material incentives rewarding early contributors (Magnuson, 2018). This can be done from anywhere, in any state of dress.

This might run counter to certain goals of regulation and policymaking that would seek to promote a *level-playing field* in the financial sector. In a sense, these FinTech usurpers appear, as if from nowhere, and promise easy access to that which banks had hitherto held onto as their own (that's the nature of disruption, we might suppose). But since the concept of too big to fail already distorts the idea of a level-playing field, and structural improvement is sought, a too narrow interpretation of 'level' might serve to scupper efforts at improving matters overall (Philippon, 2016). FinTech-supplied service specificity might be in tension with regulatory aspirations for a level-playing field, yet also be less egregious than the distortions brought about by the contingent existence of banking behemoths considered too big to fail.

A new industry, with improved activities, opens clear regulatory questions. Whereas brick-and-mortar banks saw heightened regulation following the crisis, tech firm-backed start-ups escape the net of these advanced moves, exemplified by the US Dodd–Frank Act. Yet it can be argued that FinTech sees a similarly serious, if differently constituted, risk profile as those other establishments (Magnuson, 2018). Amid market turmoil, shocks, financial service reorganisation, and regulatory shakeup, how far is there a move from familiar understandings of transaction, value, and market? Do new entrants to the scene change the context or simply operate within it so as to offer novel financial products and services to consumers?

5 What's the difference?

Wider access to markets, through highly personalised means, seems a sure-fire way to benefit customers. Certainly, when a bank needn't be involved, lending can be cheaper, as can getting investment advice. But there is a change in what the customer is getting, even if the function still appears superficially the same. One area worth mentioning is that of risk.

In seeking a loan for a small business from a bank, part of the scrutiny involved is to maximise the likelihood of timely repayment. Leaving aside predatory lending, this is to protect the lender and the lendee. In this respect, market regulation is consumer protection and vice versa. After all, if loans are routinely made to those unable to repay, the lending sector as well as the consumer base are exposed to negative consequences and likely to spiral. Part of the way the FinTech context of lending works is by spreading risk among a wider pool of people, each taking on smaller amounts of risk. If a loan is provided from 100 individuals, each putting a little into the pot, then any eventual problems might represent just 1% of the fallout had all of the capital been provided by a single lender. However, the FinTech case is somewhat unlike standard loans in terms of what is presented to the lendee.

In spreading risk, the FinTech entity may not shoulder any themselves. In providing a platform for others to micro-invest, that company may merely facilitate others to take on risk – even if only a small amount – while themselves receiving benefits. In this disconnect between reward and risk, there is the incentive to act unscrupulously. At the very least, there is a road to short-termism. From a consumer point of view, this may not be apparent. In receiving a loan at all, given the naïve presumptions about value discussed above, the consumer is likely to believe they deserve that loan because of their business idea. But from another point of view, their loan is more like a bet made among micro-investors hosted on a risk-free platform.

The same might be said for investment advice, where robo-advisors replace the role of humans. Trust in robo-advice can be high because traditional advice may be seen as biased (Philippon, 2016, p. 18). With wider public awareness of dark money pools, opaque trading practices, and the incomprehensible realities of high-frequency trading, the world of investment advice can appear decidedly murky. Software, meanwhile, can be monitored more easily than human biases. Records can be kept of every element of software activity, and those logs scrutinised should the need arise. On this view, consumers are *all watched over by machines of loving grace*, in Richard Brautigan's words (Turner, 2008, pp. 38–39). But as algorithms become advanced, data interlinked, and proprietary systems sequestered behind intellectual property walls, this might prove less the case.

The potential for algorithmic bias remains high, especially such that could prompt cascades of investment advice, leading to herd-like behaviour. All algorithms of the sort envisioned here rely on descriptive data regarding past events, in order to predict future trends (Dietterich and Kong, 1995; Crawford, 2013). In a simplified sense, they can advise to invest in x at time t because x was invested in at time $t-n$. A cascade of such investment behaviour might then result at time $t+n$ and so on, because the investment in x at $t-1$, and t, appears to describe a trend. But maybe the investing itself is the trend, not the value of x.

This kind of activity may have little to do with market predictions of the sort a savvy trader might make. Yet this may be what is expected by a consumer: savvy guesses, not the application of the Pearson coefficient to a curated dataset. This is parallel with the naïve example of the market in information that can emerge, illustrated by the apples in the food market example from above. Knowledge of which apples are the best, in some respect, may have nothing to do with which apples sell most. The expertise of the apple-recommender comes from their astute sense of quality. That is where their advice gains value. A savvy investment advisor can always be asked *why* they chose to invest in what they did. They may then be judged on how good their advice was, given the basis they provide. This is not clearly available in the case of an algorithmic approach. Again, the parallel would be with judging apples on volume of sales, rather than insight to their value with respect to some intrinsic characteristics. Do we want to forget about this dimension of investment in a new paradigm of outcome-focussed, algorithm-led FinTech consumerism? Maybe so: a world beyond appreciation of *savvy*. But certainly, there is this difference in value at play in the example of robo-advice.

In these examples of micro-lending and robo-advice is the kernel of another salient issue that underlies many FinTech applications such that value is affected. This dimension of FinTech could serve to fundamentally alter the character of transactions being undertaken by consumers, certainly in contrast with the naïve views outlined above.

6 Data

Obviously, in the case of robo-advice, there is data-crunching as algorithms comb market data in order to identify trends, gaps, and opportunities to make profits. As just mentioned, this dimension of the activity likely makes what on the face of it is investment advice considerably different to what the naïve consumer might expect it to be. Micro-lending and other applications are not obviously similarly data intensive, but data play a role here too.

The data on which FinTech applications operate are themselves a commodity. By way of illustration, Plaid is a recent highly valued FinTech service whose business model is aggregating the data collected across a variety of other FinTech applications and platforms, including Venmo, and TransferWise (Rabin, 2020). Plaid deals in data on transactions, user identity, authentication, balances, and assets in order to enable developers to have access to this fine-grained information for their own platforms and other uses (Plaid in the UK | Plaid, 2020). The behaviour, and the status, of the users of various FinTech platforms are thereby data assets for other platforms and use cases. This is again in contrast with the sorts of naïve assumptions that consumers may make about their roles in marketplaces. It also suggests that in order to know how, or when, or why, to use one FinTech provider over another, 'shopping around' may not be an optimal approach.

Data on user activity are of value in optimising service provision for specific FinTech platforms. This is just to say that FinTech providers need to understand concepts like user experience and market need in order to provide their services as efficiently as possible. But because user activity also represents trends, and direction of travel for markets in terms of user demand and platform popularity, it also becomes part of the value of specific instances of FinTech as assets themselves. FinTech, while constituting parts of the market at large, is also part of its asset landscape. The popularity of a platform, for example, might inform the value of that platform as an asset to be bought and sold by market players at a level higher than the customers utilising the platform.

Understanding the FinTech sector as a whole makes essential reference to the individual parts, as the platforms and providers serve to constitute the sector. Meanwhile, through this datafication lens, the understanding of each individual part requires reference to the whole sector. The sector informs the value of the part, and the parts inform the value of the sector. This can be seen as a 'hermeneutic circle,' as it suggests a grasp of the whole in terms of parts, and parts in light of the whole, is required in order to understand the whole complex of the matter (Ormiston and Schrift, 1990).

Thankfully, we needn't explore hermeneutics too much to get the point of interest here. What is of importance is how far this kind of notion, through data, departs from any naïve notion of market participation a consumer is likely to hold. In seeking a loan from a micro-lending platform, or changing money from one currency to another, one is unlikely to expect this to contribute to a data ecosystem that can inform an array of financial activities well beyond that seemingly simple act. While it is known to be the case that, yes, all manner of financial activity is interconnected, in this datafied context, the connections can relate directly to the platforms and services the user accesses. And their use data serve to constitute that information. This means one's identity and behaviour are commodities for the platforms one utilises. This is a departure from received wisdom, for sure.

Present use data can serve to constrain possibilities for a consumer's future uses of platforms and services in the FinTech ecosystem. Imagine, for example, one uses online lending services, and online payment services. Overall, one's spending profile can be tracked and a pattern of behaviour derived therefrom. Where that profile deviates from some emergent norm, it may be taken to indicate that one ought not to be given as favourable terms, or perhaps not be given access to, loan services in the future. This is not the case with money, as cash, which can be gained via a loan and spent relatively anonymously. A deviation from received wisdom thus emerges once more; the act of using FinTech across seemingly unrelated contexts may nevertheless provide conditions for future uses. This is based in second-order data-as-commodity directing the services provided, as those very services are provided. What's more, no one need make these decisions as the algorithmic detection of trends take on the burden of data processing.

Algorithms 'decide' on a statistical basis what ought to count as normal (this raises an array of issues, discussed in boyd and Crawford, 2012; Kitchin, 2017). This provides an air of objectivity, as use data reveal 'the market' and the consumer profiles that occupy it. But there is some virtualisation going on in the representation of users, and the market, here. By 'virtualisation' is meant the generation of profiles and categories of action based in the processing of descriptive data themselves collected according to predefined categories deemed essential to characterising a market. Of relevance are 'instances of *x*,' where '*x*' needn't be an individual. Datafication means that a *gestalt* is generated as a character heading into which are fitted specific users who fit the profile more or less.

Datafication of markets and customers using FinTech serves to alter the nature of ideas like transaction, value, and market, so each now constitutes part of higher-order market determination. In combination with the ways in which risk, regulation, and algorithmic advice appear on the scene, this further detaches the realities of FinTech from the naïve assumptions consumers likely hold, derived from material interactions, in terms of *context, skill, commodity, currency,* and *transaction*. The consequences of these deformations of assumed realities affect *value*. All of the discussion so far on this has been aimed at opening these dimensions up to scrutiny. But it remains to be seen how this affects people. Why might a shift like this matter?

7 Practical reasoning

When human beings have clear goals, well-defined ends in sight, we can typically deliberate among a variety of means in order to hit upon the best means towards those ends. So, for instance, when we want to travel to some destination we can consult maps and find the most efficient route. That would serve well where the goal is to get there quickly. If instead the goal includes having a memorable journey, we might settle on a longer but more scenic route. In either case, there may be several competing options: the shortest route from A to B may also be more prone to traffic than a slightly longer route, and so we pick the longer rather than the shorter, because overall it would be faster. Or we deliberate about whether we prefer a mountain route to a valley, in terms of scenery.

One way of thinking about this kind of reasoning, drawing upon Aristotle as read by David Wiggins, is as a kind of internal weighing up of our ideal goals, and the various constraints put upon us by some given context (Wiggins, 1998, pp. 215–237). This 'weighing up' includes placing our aims against the situation as we perceive it, our 'situational appreciation,' in order to come up with a course of action that responds both to what we aim for and the possibilities afforded us by that situation.[2] This can be seen as a sort of means–end reasoning that is familiar. It can be seen as implicit in the naïve concepts of market behaviour laid out above, for example, as we imagine decisions about transporting fence-makers, exchanging currency for goods, and taking advice on apples. All of those simple cases involved appraisal of contexts, costs, and means, in the light of goals.

Markets in general do appear to be cases wherein the means–end reasoning is particularly applicable. In such contexts, we have fixed resources, some ends in sight, and a variety of options available to secure them. But having seen some of the ways in which, while superficially similar to standard markets, FinTech contexts depart from received wisdom, we can question how this affects our ability to practically reason about means and ends. Where this has an effect, it can serve as a reason to reappraise important dimensions of both FinTech markets and our ways of valuing within them.

Can we make sense of situational appreciation in terms of FinTech? The example of CDOs, above, served to suggest that in the 2007–2008-era market realities had departed from any reasonable conception consumers were likely to have of the products and services they were seeking to buy. Instead of a mortgage, based on an assessment of the lendee's likelihood of repaying, consumers found themselves as an element in a very broad portfolio of bets on a range of probabilities of unrelated defaults. But in FinTech contexts such as micro-lending, the securing of capital from a base of lenders is only one element of a general data market in which the customer's behaviour is the asset. And this unusual circumstance can go on to constrain that customer's future access to subsequent services, in being datafied and processed by algorithms.

Where investment advice is sought from apparently unbiased robo-advisors, the customer can again find themselves not in the relation of layperson-to-expert that might be expected. Instead, a general algorithm may be 'advising' on the basis of a trend that its own advice is serving to perpetuate. This makes the customer a data-point in an impersonal strategy, not the receiver of wisdom from

---

2 Wiggins puts it like this: "...if there is no real prospect of an ordinary scientific or simply empirical theory of all of action and deliberation as such, then the thing we should look for may be precisely what Aristotle provides – namely, a conceptual framework which we can apply to particular cases, which articulates the reciprocal relations of an agent's concerns and his perception of how things objectively are in the world; and a schema of description *which relates the complex ideal the agent tries in the process of living his life to make real to the form that the world impresses, both by way of opportunity and by way of limitation, upon that ideal*" (p. 237).

some savvy agent. What's more, and parallel with the lending example, all of this data can further be processed and sold on by companies like Plaid to inform future iterations of platforms the customer may go on to use.

These, and a range of other examples, should serve well enough to cast doubt on the possibility that situational appreciation can survive a FinTech revolution unscathed. Yet on the face of it, little changes: getting a loan, exchanging currency, seeking investment advice, are still available services which on a superficial description remain the same, i.e. one can get the loan, change the money, or invest in recommended ways. What changes is that patterns of statistical inference, not reasons-driven behaviour, drive the novel enterprises. This is enough to ground the idea that there is an effect on practical reasoning.

A consumer may still deliberate over which of a variety FinTech services, or platforms, they wish to use. In this sense, there is little impact upon the means–end reasoning. But these deliberations will concern immediate issues of, say, the interest on a loan, or the cost of robo-advice versus the person-to-person equivalent. What is not available to the consumer is a sense of all that is implicated in the use of the service or platform, in terms of what's on offer, the data collected and processed, and the wider implications of that data processing. When the loan is not a loan in any familiar sense, in that it's better described as a distributed bet among micro-lenders facilitated risk-free by a platform, the customer can't fully deliberate about their actual loan-worthiness. Is the loan granted because the enthusiasm for its purpose genuinely reflects that purpose's viability? Or is it just not sufficiently risky for each micro-lender to particularly care about its chances of failure? Whatever way it's spun, the loan in this context is unlike the loan from a standard context – the temporary release of funds from one party to another, based on an assessment of likelihood of repayment, represented by an interest rate. This presents a foreshortened context of deliberation.

The situational appreciation the consumer is hoping to acquire in order to inform practical reasoning is complicated because the context shifts in response to the actions of that consumer. The hermeneutic circle, requiring that the parts be understood in terms of the whole and vice versa, turns based upon the behaviour of the consumer (and every other consumer). It also responds to other market factors, meaning that an apparently stable, significantly inert, context is in fact dynamic, and reactive to a set of factors wholly out of the possible grasp of any given consumer.

It must further be asked how one can conceptualise value where it is a moving target in a datafied market? Where the loans, exchanges, and advice received are of a significantly – albeit subtly – different character to standardly available products and services, how can their desirability be assessed as valuable or not? Where naïve concepts of *context*, *skill*, *commodity*, *currency*, and *transaction* are altered in the FinTech paradigm, the idea of value becomes very murky with it, and practical reasoning forestalls.

8 Conclusions

The democratising potential within FinTech has hidden dimensions. The mis-characterisation of 'the financial' is possible by technologisation, virtualisation through data, and the opaque manipulations of algorithms. This can serve to render financial services significantly unintelligible from a consumer perspective. In effect, this might mean that FinTech services and platforms essentially replay the eventualities flagged by Turner and El Erian. The FinTech paradigm asserts a novel, standalone, financial services industry that ultimately is loosened from the usual tethers expected upon activity in the financial sector. If this is so, what is required from FinTech providers, and their users?

On the one hand, vigilance to avoid unexpected outcomes might be prudent. Greater digital literacy among consumers might ensure they can make more informed, and hopefully better, decisions about FinTech in their wider financial activities. If their 'loan' might better be thought of in terms of a range of micro-lender bets, it is better that the consumer decides for or against taking it on those terms. On the other hand, though, perhaps the kind of discussion that would lead to increased digital literacy might lead to more widespread agreement to embrace this paradigm shift. Perhaps the opportunities, at least in terms of overcoming older paradigms of too-big-to-fail institutions, outweigh the risks in terms of FinTech.

With eyes open, it could be the case that established ways of doing things ought to yield to the new. If there is such a decision to be made, however, it ought to be made in public, framed in policy, and enacted overtly. It ought not to simply emerge, as internal practices change within service providers. One central reason for this is the impact upon ideas of value, and what that means for practical reasoning.

References

Anon (2020) *Plaid in the UK | Plaid* [online]. Available at: https://plaid.com/uk/ [Accessed 19 March 2020].

Arner, W., Barberis, J.N. and Buckley, R.P. (2016) The evolution of FinTech: A new post-crisis paradigm? *Georgetown Journal of International Law* 47, p. 51.

boyd, danah and Crawford, K. (2012) Critical questions for big data. *Information, Communication & Society* [online] 155, pp. 662–679. Available at: http://dx.doi.org/10.1080/1369118X.2012.678878 [Accessed 20 February 2017].

Crawford, K. (2013) The hidden biases in big data [online]. *Harvard Business Review*. Available at: https://hbr.org/2013/04/the-hidden-biases-in-big-data [Accessed 21 February 2017].

Dietterich, T.G. and Kong, E.B. (1995) *Machine learning bias, statistical bias, and statistical variance of decision tree algorithms.* Technical report, Department of Computer Science, Oregon State University, Corvallis, OR.

Kitchin, R. (2017) Thinking critically about and researching algorithms. *Information, Communication & Society* [online] 201, pp. 14–29. Available at: https://doi.org/10.1080/1369118X.2016.1154087 [Accessed 4 December 2017].

Lewis, M. (2014) *Flash boys: A Wall Street revolt.* 1st edition. New York: W. W. Norton & Company.

Mackenzie, A. (2015) The FinTech revolution. *London Business School Review* [online] 263, pp. 50–53. Available at: https://onlinelibrary.wiley.com/doi/abs/10.1111/2057-1615.12059 [Accessed 17 March 2020].

Magnuson, W. (2018) Regulating FinTech. *Vanderbilt Law Review* [online] 714, p. 1167. Available at: https://scholarship.law.vanderbilt.edu/vlr/vol71/iss4/2.

Ormiston, G.L. and Schrift, A.D. (1990) *The hermeneutic tradition: From Ast to Ricoeur.* New York and Albany: SUNY Press.

Philippon, T. (2016) *The FinTech opportunity* [online]. Cambridge, MA: National Bureau of Economic Research, p. w22476. Available at: http://www.nber.org/papers/w22476.pdf [Accessed 24 February 2020].

Pratchett, T. (2013) *Men at arms.* London: Random House.

Rabin, K. (2020) The new age of FinTech – What you need to know about data aggregators. *Finextra Research.* Available at: https://www.finextra.com/blogposting/18444/the-new-age-of-FinTech---what-you-need-to-know-about-data-aggregators [Accessed 19 March 2020].

Schueffel, P. (2016) Taming the beast: A scientific definition of FinTech. *Journal of Innovation Management – The International Journal on Multidisciplinary Approaches on Innovation* [online] 44, pp. 32–54. Available at: https://repositorio-aberto.up.pt/handle/10216/102610 [Accessed 17 March 2020].

The New Global Economics (2011) [Radio] *The Shock.* London: BBC. 14 November. Available at: https://www.bbc.co.uk/programmes/b0174f04 [Accessed 19 November 2019].

Turner, F. (2008) *From counterculture to cyberculture: Stewart Brand, the Whole Earth Network, and the Rise of digital utopianism.* 60265th edition. Chicago, IL: University of Chicago Press.

Wiggins, D. (1998) *Needs, values, truth essays in the philosophy of value.* 3rd edition. Oxford: Oxford University Press.

3 InsurTech's assurance – value research through an array of ABCs

Ruilin Zhu

1 Introduction

The insurance industry is approximately five years behind the digital maturity curve (Liu and Xiong, 2016); indeed, the very foundations of the sector are under siege from digital innovation. While un-serviced or under-serviced areas in banking sectors, such as payment and saving, are intensively targeted by FinTech, it is now the turn of insurance companies to confront InsurTech. However, state-of-the-art technologies such as artificial intelligence (TA), big data (TB), and cloud computing (TC) have the potential to reshape the industry with forward-thinking strategies and cutting-edge business models (Fisk *et al.*, 2010). InsurTech aims to rid the industry of its value proposition for stakeholders by introducing new distribution structure of agents (SA), enabling business transformation (SB) and changing customer expectations (SC).

Every insurance innovation involves rearranging entities – objects and/or persons – to allow value and value practices to be standardised (Stoeckli *et al.*, 2018), and InsurTech is no exception. It dislodges incumbents allowing insurance transactions to be specifically value-oriented. In doing so, InsurTech is actively leveraging digital innovations through technology-intensive activities surrounding TA, TB, TC, and more, for reorganising value chains to the target market. It is the insurance companies' goal to address the efforts in the achievement of an optimised situation in which persons and objects are squarely arranged in a transformative but opportunistic context that remains partially understood to the industry.

Specifically, with the insurance products and information being readily available through digital medium, the sector expertise and sale acumen provided by the agents nestled on the traditional distribution structure will be firstly challenged. The new structure purports to divert the vested interests of agents that are historically embedded within the industry by resorting to digital innovation. Similar to the sweeping trend diffused in banking sector worldwide of diminished counter services, unstaffed branches, and virtual branches, the insurance industry will have to witness a fundamental shift that may uproot the agent model given the current trend of an increasing number of insurance products becoming standardised and commoditised due to the technology advance. The agent distribution structure is more severely threatened by the introduction of innovative insurance policies. Mutual insurance, for instance, is not a brand new concept but has re-entered the spotlight as InsurTech has revitalised its applicability especially in some underinsured emerging countries, such as China. It is evidenced by the resounding success of the Xianghu Bao (meaning mutual insurance in Chinese), a latest insurance trial orchestrated by the Ant Finance, the highest valued FinTech company in the world, on 16 October 2018, attracting more than 50 million users within six months (Wang, 2019). It sensibly bypassed the traditional agents by platformising the sale of product through its extensive channels, suggesting the established distribution structure through which the value is transmitted needs to be reconsidered.

As the insurance policy starts to be tailored for the specific needs of particular groups, the underserved niche markets – particularly micro, small, and medium-sized enterprises among the corporate clients or business – have emerged to encourage further industry engagement. The situation is complicated by the incorporation of new economy companies that reshuffled the business nature and manifestation. Accompanying the rise of the sharing economy facilitated by digital innovation, businesses have constantly evolved to become adaptive to dynamic market needs that are not compatible with traditional insurance services. For example, Uber may disagree with the description that Uber drivers are a "private hire taxi service"; however, this is a generally held view among UK car insurance companies. This disjuncture indicates that while Uber drivers will be required to obtain the appropriate taxi insurance policy, the normal car or van insurance is inherently not suitable for them. The development of business nature that is embodied in different commercial activities, such as online-to-offline takeaway or bike-sharing, necessitates the scope extension of insurance, which thus become able to provide more inclusive coverage to those who are previously uninsured or underinsured. To this end, the strategies towards business in the digital era where the value is contextualised have to be redesigned.

In addition, customers, the millennial generation in particular, are increasingly valuing speed and simplicity of use over established conventions and connections with legacy insurance companies. Traditionally, insurance is often purchased begrudgingly; in other words, the linkage between insurers and customers is generally sporadic and distant, featured with infrequent contact. However, with the advent of digital innovation, customers desire personalised products, unrestricted access and assistance, and frequent and tangible benefits. Further worsening matters is the increasing affinity for technology and thirst for transparency along with a propensity to quickly adopt and accept changes. As a result, instead of assuming that customer familiarity and brand loyalty will sustain in the wake of digital technologies, insurance companies must accept that connections with customers will be, or even have already been, fundamentally changed as the customers progressively take a more proactive and predominate role.

In view of this trend, incumbent insurers are expected to provide 'added value' to the insured as the diversified customers' needs are due to be reinvestigated. Indeed, China witnesses a distinctive picture where it leads the digital innovation in insurance with incumbent companies exerting strengths on the InsurTech arena, whereas the traditional insurance is also experiencing a vibrant supplement from InsurTech start-ups. The two-pronged development route is research-worthy and thought-provoking, suggesting that if two developmental paths can be readily oriented in a joint effort, mutual benefits will be envisaged.

The chapter focuses on the apprehension of using digital innovations-empowered InsurTech on industry stakeholders in support of the development of insurance as a way to promote value research. The situation in China is generally taken as the contextual example, and narratives are convened for discussions aimed at identifying ways in which the insurance industries and technology sectors can achieve value proposition through InsurTech.

The chapter aims to shed light on three overarching questions facing the insurance industry: (1) Which of, and how, the technologies (TA, TB, and TC) should be leveraged for value recreation to designated stakeholders and across the industry? (2) Where do we position an insurance company among SA, SB, and SC as an overarching strategy for value discovery? (3) Who should take the lead in InsurTech (start-ups or incumbent companies) for value realisation? I wish to re-examine the values that have been dislocated, downplayed, or disregarded. To this end, the insurance community must possess a growth mind-set by combing and charting the relationships between TA, TB, and TC, and SA, SB, and SC.

The remainder of the chapter proceeds as follows. The next section details the unwavering potentials of TA, TB, and TC in promoting insurance industry before leading the discussion on SA, SB, and SC in Section 3. I discuss the role of start-up and incumbent company in Section 4, while implications are presented thereafter to conclude the chapter.

2 Overview of InsurTech

InsurTech, as the name suggests, is the synergy of insurance and technology. Despite various definitions (e.g., Sen and Lam, 2016; Schueffel, 2017; McFall and Moor, 2018), it is generally believed that the manifestation of InsurTech has been progressing further afield with the disruptive nature transforming contemporary products, services, processes, and strategies. The term did not make inroads in the sector until 2011 and came under spotlight in late 2015 (Yan et al., 2018). Technology, however, has always influenced insurance industry, with advancements permeating operation and management through the sector.

China's insurance industry, so far, has witnessed primarily three stages of development enabled by technologies, which were leveraged to promote its business fronts. The first stage relates to *digital insurance*, which features digitisation of main operational units and managerial sections from 1999 to 2008. During this period, management systems across organisations and industry were established, and transaction data were progressively aggregated at the organisational level in a bid to feed the strategy. With the introduction of Web 2.0, the industry was pushed forward onto the next stage – *internet insurance*. It refers to the upward trend of insurance fuelled by the massive utilisation of internet and mobile devices from 2008 to 2016. It marked the diversified transaction channels that are facilitated by the internet, in particular the mobile internet, through official webpage, e-business websites, and apps, ushering in an era when transaction data

30 *Ruilin Zhu*

started to contextualise upon scenarios with a meteoric rise in the internet insurance market (Figure 3.1). More importantly, not only did internet insurance foster the market expansion, but it also led the campaign of harvesting the benefits of technology adoption in the sector: it enriched insurance scenarios by tailoring the technology to meet the growing needs while strengthening the efforts on harnessing advanced technical innovations. As the technology permeates insurance industry from the front-end to back-end and from operation management to value establishment, it became evident that internet insurance is insufficient in capturing the whole picture as it is attributed more exclusively to the innovation in sales operations driven by the internet in the insurance sector. More recently from 2016, as a result, *InsurTech* has dominated the industry attention by highlighting the possibility of automation and intelligence. It is anticipated to further augment the capability of management and operation, laying a solid foundation for sustainable development. It will also restructure the business process by shifting the focus from broadening the sale channels to deepening the values. Specifically, the business processes are expected to be shaped by the adoption of artificial intelligence (AI), big data, and cloud computing. Throughout the next section, I discuss how technology may enable insurance industry to cope with the challenges and sustain the steady developments.

3 The array of technological ABC

3.1 *Cloud computing*

Cloud computing is defined by the US National Institute of Standards and Technology as "a model for enabling ubiquitous, convenient, on-demand

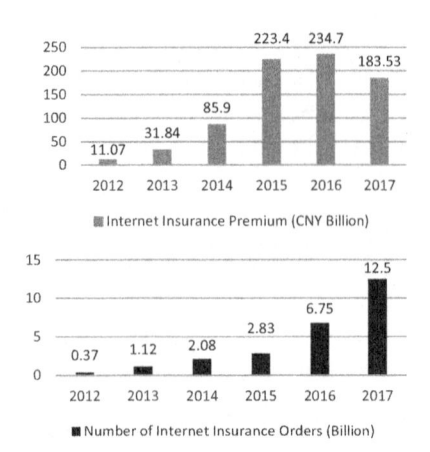

Figure 3.1 Increase in the internet insurance market in China.[1]

---

1 Data from Insurance Associate of China (2018): http://www.iachina.cn/col/col41/index.html (in Chinese) [Accessed 26 June 2020].

network access to a shared pool of configurable computing resources that can be rapidly provisioned and released with minimal management effort or service provider interaction" (Mell and Grance, 2011). It entails the development and deployment of transformational strategies for digitising, designing, developing, and deploying business activities. The rise of cloud computing is a result of the confluence between declining per-unit cost of exponentially powerful computing capabilities and increasing transactional demand of a complicated business sector like insurance. On the one hand, computing power continues to grow rapidly to the extent that it is deemed as a standardised commodity (Lasica, 2009). On the other hand, a large and heterogeneous collection of business processes are highly entwined in organisations; this scenario is further complicated by the adoption of disparate IT infrastructure and distributed data, suggesting that robust computing is necessary for the insurance sector to thrive (Roehrig, 2008). Cloud computing stands satisfactorily at the junction of the two trends as it is aimed at delivering a wide range of technological functionalities and services at much more reasonable costs without imposing hefty investment burdens on organisations (Asadi et al., 2017). Thus, cloud computing represents a momentum in driving the business towards a united front that comprises information technology and business development. During this upward trend, cloud computing highlights an efficient utilisation of modern technologies through scalable and flexible hardware and software resources while underlining an effective establishment of competitive business analytics and applications through agile business adaptions (Trziszka, 2019).

This is particularly important for insurance industry in China. The tradition of "a good start" amongst China's insurance companies that takes place during the first quarter typically accounts for approximately 50% of the annual premiums (Jiang and Zhou, 2020), suggesting significantly uneven demands for technical supports throughout the year. According to the latest report released by Wheatley (2019), the average server usage rate in corporate data centres is only 18%, signalling an alarming trend that shows that a majority of IT investments have become redundant or were wasted. To this end, the development of insurance industry has to encounter two issues – the fluctuation in IT usages and the lack of efficiency in the utilisation of IT resources; this is where cloud computing can step in to cope with the challenges in the sector.

Generally, there are three dominant service models of cloud computing: Infrastructure as a Service (IaaS), Platform as a Service (PaaS), and Software as a Service (SaaS) (Jansen and Grance, 2011), each representing a different arrangement of technical resources (Table 3.1). IaaS is the most basic offering as customers are able to purchase "processing, storage and network services and then build their own systems on top of this infrastructure" (Mell and Grance, 2011). In other words, in the situation of IaaS, customers employ cloud computing when the hardware deficiency emerges in a bid to maintain the smooth operation of core business. In addition, given the nature of cloud computing, customers are not directly involved in the responsibility of hardware management, which allows them to meaningfully concentrate on their core business.

As a step-up, PaaS enables the provision of preconfigured middleware and run-time (He *et al.*, 2015) in addition to the hardware support. It serves those customers whose technical needs are generally standardised at both software and hardware levels. This is highly helpful for insurance companies that largely possess some legacy information systems as PaaS has the potential to help them to both retain control over their own outdated systems and avail the more up-to-date services provided by advanced computing power.

In contrast, SaaS, on top of PaaS and IaaS, provides all-in-one applications functionality through the media of the internet as a service (Sultan, 2011), which is considered as a segment of cloud computing with the most potential (Wu *et al.*, 2011) that may lead to various benefits for organisations with profound consequences in improving performance (Catteddu and Hogben, 2009). SaaS emancipates customers from performing technical routines, such as installing and operating software and maintaining hardware. Considering that experienced vendors shoulder the responsibility of managing IT infrastructure and processes required for customers to deliver essential operations, customers can make most use of vendors' expertise and experiences to develop their own business (Bhardwaj *et al.*, 2010).

In this regard, IT resources, in particular computing power, facilitated by cloud computing, become public services in the format of IaaS, PaaS, or SaaS, providing solid technical support to end-users. It thus diminishes organisations' reliance on supporting technologies thereby enabling them to invest proportionately on business aspects, paving the way towards sustainable development.

3.2 Big data

Amongst various definitions, the most well-accepted one comes from Gartner (n.d.), who defines big data as "high-volume, high-velocity and high-variety information assets that demand cost-effective, innovative forms of information processing for enhanced insight and decision making" (Figure 3.2). This descriptive approach has attached three dimensions to the concept (Hartmann *et al.*, 2014). To start with, it expanded the scope of "being big" from volume-only to volume-velocity-variety as a whole, suggesting in a nutshell big data must be understood from a holistic perspective rather than being measured by its size. In addition, the definition specified big data as "information assets" of organisations, highlighting its unfolding potential and foreseeable values to business. It also posited that the reason big data is able to assist organisation is because it can provide "cost-effective and innovative" solutions.

Speaking from the insurance industry's perspective, the most salient impacts are surrounding the following two aspects – enhanced insight into customer mind-sets and behaviour and choices (Erevelles *et al.*, 2016) and enhanced prevention from fraud (Chen *et al.*, 2015). According to the arguments of the Organisation for Economic Co-operation and Development (OECD, 2020) and Mizgier, Kocsis, and Wagner (2018), one of the most inspiring features of big data for insurance is the ability to leverage accumulated data to step up insurance

Table 3.1 Comparison of different cloud computing services

Traditional IT	IaaS	PaaS	SaaS
Application (Self-management)	Application (Self-management)	Application (Self-management)	Application (Vendor management)
Data	Data	Data	Data
Runtime	Runtime	Runtime (Vendor management)	Runtime
Middleware	Middleware	Middleware	Middleware
Operating systems	Operating systems (Vendor management)	Operating systems	Operating systems
Virtualisation	Virtualisation	Virtualisation	Virtualisation
Storage	Storage	Storage	Storage
Network	Network	Network	Network

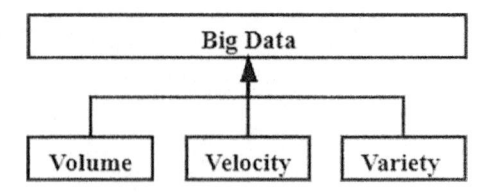

Figure 3.2 Visualisation of big data definition.

companies' understanding of customers. It thus provides an opportunity for them to actively enhance their endeavours in customer engagement and proactively improve their efforts to boost customer satisfaction. For instance, big data can help derive insight by making most sense from unused or underused data, such as unstructured data.

Big data is also highly useful in shielding insurance companies from individual and/or organisational fraud. Due to the increasing sophistication and complexity of swindles, the traditional approach to detect and identify fraud has become less effective (Fernando, 2015), leading to failures and/or negligence in spotting certain fraudulent activities. However, with the adoption of big data, insurance companies are now able to obtain larger data sources and analyse them to flag up suspicious incidents, helping to minimise the possible exposure to such avoidable risks.

In order to achieve these benefits, drawing on the concept of "as-a-service" form of cloud computing, a few scholars (Chen *et al.*, 2011; Stipic and Bronzin, 2012; Delen and Demirkan, 2013) proposed Data-as-a-Service (DaaS) and Analytics-as-a-service (AaaS) for big data services. DaaS refers to the aggregation and provision of a wide range of data through collection, procurement, and partnership for a data-driven and evidenced-based service. AaaS relates to the analysis of numerous types of data through integrated and customised modelling for a predictive and/or prescriptive service.

3.3 Artificial intelligence

Artificial intelligence (AI) is a general term that implies the use of a computer to model intelligent behaviour with minimal human intervention (Gent, 2019). AI is particularly data-reliant (Quan and Sanderson, 2018) in order for it to function reasonably and meaningfully by employing effective algorithms, such as natural language processing (Doszkocs, 1986), machine learning (Ongsulee, 2017), and deep learning (Iriondo, 2018) to build inner logics and processing structure.

The advantages of AI in insurance industry are multi-fold. Empowered by big data, it is able to identify previously unknown patterns and discover insightful observations from vast data sources in different types over time. AI's attributes of scalability (Long and Gupta, 2008), longevity (Akerkar, 2019), and evolvability (Sloman and Logan, 2000) have unlocked the potential of self-learning models, which allow insurance companies to promptly adapt their business strategies to

```
                    ┌──────────────┐
                    │   Internet   │
                    └──────┬───────┘
                     ┌─────┴─────┐
                     ▼           ▼
              ┌──────────┐   ┌──────┐
              │ Big Data │──▶│  AI  │
              └──────────┘   └──────┘
                     ▲           ▲
                     └─────┬─────┘
                    ┌──────┴───────┐
                    │Cloud Computing│
                    └──────────────┘
```

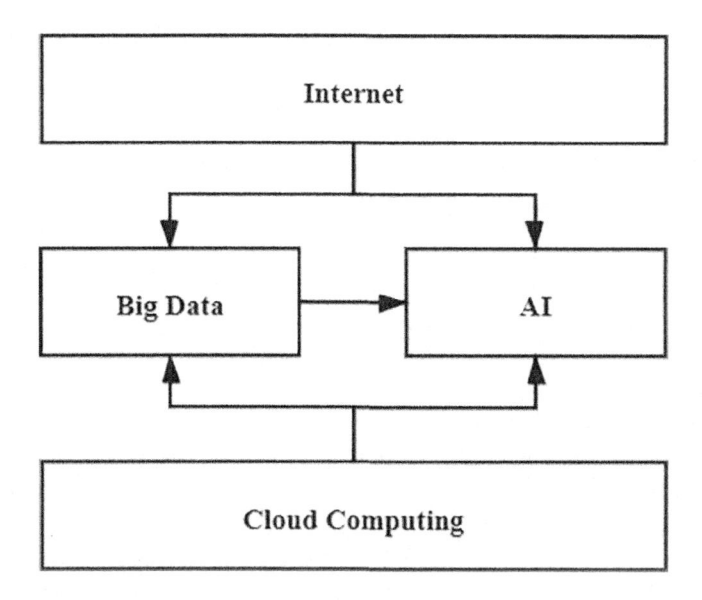

Figure 3.3 The array of technological ABC.

underlying market conditions. Ultimately, AI aims at providing value-enriched business models by accelerating innovations in product, process, and strategy through the utilisation information assets that are produced by cloud computing and big data.

In sum, these three leading technologies together have exerted concerted efforts as InsurTech on insurance industry with the hope for its attainable and sustainable development (Figure 3.3). To be specific, cloud computing ensures the possession and deployment of fundamental computing capabilities that are essential to foster technical resources and business data. In the follow-up stage, big data captures various data sources and mines through vast available data to identify the latent values that remained unknown previously. Based on mounting computing power and aggregative information assets, AI unleashes productivity by assisting or replacing manpower to realise the embedded values. In this sense, InsurTech is a cumulative process that purposefully connects critical technologies by digitising possible activities and digitalising essential strategies in insurance industry for a series of evidenced and valued targets.

4 The array of stakeholder ABC

4.1 *Customer*

The insurance industry is customer-oriented in nature since insurants, formulating the business foundation, are viewed as the driving power for companies' development. This is echoed by the observation from Peng *et al.* (2007), who suggested that customers are of great importance in the insurance sector. Given the fact that the premiums of customers are the primary profits and the settlement of claims from customers are the major expenditures, Fang *et al.* (2016) recommended that it is necessary for insurance companies to fully understand customers. InsurTech is believed to demonstrate a high potential in achieving this target primarily through the following three aspects – customer profiling, customer interaction, and customised products.

With the assistance from TA, TB, and TC, customer data will not serve in a standalone manner but will be aggregated for a holistic profiling that describes the client from multiple dimensions (Hu and Tracogna, 2020). Amongst those, demographic information (Huang *et al.*, 2011) and behavioural information (Ayuso *et al.*, 2019) associated with focal customer or customer group are particularly important as they will help differentiate customers and establish a concrete model to more accurately evaluate the possible premium and expected expenditure. They will also give rise to the transition from classic insurance pricing to dynamic insurance pricing, such as telematics pricing (Roel *et al.*, 2017).

InsurTech will enhance customer interaction to not only foster reciprocal communication but also help insurers track and guide customers' behaviour and rationales in choosing policies and nurture and demonstrate a more responsible behaviour towards their customers (Meyers and Hoyweghen, 2020). Being more accessible for customers through various digital means indicates the possibility of maintaining close contact with clients without being recognised as intrusive. More importantly, it will help insurance companies proactively liaison with customers as a way to progressively detect risk events and cultivate accountable behaviours.

In further profiling customers and better tracking their behaviours, InsurTech promises the reduction of insurance risk and the uptick of customised pricing for bespoke products and premiums. Traditional actuarial science is mainly based on the sample risk data and historical claim data, whereas InsurTech expanded the extant limited datasets into population risk data and real-time data, supplemented by external data, health data, behavioural data, and so on. The customised pricing thus becomes possible and available (Cappiello, 2018). To this end, InsurTech has redeveloped value by better serving customers.

4.2 Business

InsurTech's revolutionary impacts can also be witnessed at the business end in terms of both operational cost reduction and fraud detection. AI has been extensively deployed in the areas of smart underwriting (Balasubramanian *et al.*, 2018), smart claim handling (Corea, 2019), smart customer service (Grosz, 2018), and significantly deceasing labour force and thus lowering human resources cost. This is in line with the claim made by Lamberton *et al.* (2017) that the manual operation cost can be reduced by 25–50% or more. Considering InsurTech is more mature and dependable, pay-outs can be calculated by digital systems more quickly than staffed claims departments (Kiron, 2017).

Consequently, the return on InsurTech investment becomes more sensible and reasonable; for example, Fukoku Mutual Life Insurance made 34 employees redundant by replacing them with IBM's Watson Explorer AI (McCurry, 2017). Through this move, the company could save 140 million yen per year whilst increasing productivity by 30%.

According to the research by Lin and Chen (2020), InsurTech promises substantive benefits for the insurance sector by enabling insurers to quickly spot scams or frauds and act more effectively in detecting and preventing such frauds. To be specific, cloud computing offers greater calculation and processing capability to model the operational risks by specifying the possibility of insurance fraud or such; big data entails more precise measurements of underlying insurance risks as beforehand preventions to eliminate the information asymmetry between customers and companies, and AI refines insurers' strategic activities to avoid systematic risks. In short, InsurTech has enlarged value by diminishing business costs and risks.

4.3 Agent

Due to the increasingly diversified channels enabled by InsurTech, insurance companies are now closer to customers than ever before (Andrews, 2018), posing a great threat to traditional agents who routinely broker contacts between the two stakeholders – the insurer and the insurant. This threat is exemplified by two different but connected trends – *de-agent* and *re-agent*. De-agent describes a situation where the agent is displaced by InsurTech in an effort to save considerable labour costs and agent commissions. Traditionally, insurance application involves multiple visits to physical offices or rounds of phone calls with agents featuring long turnaround and lengthy paperwork. Aided by InsurTech, standardised policies can be sold more quickly and easily without the involvement of agents (Holliday, 2019). In these cases, the prevalence of agents is overshadowed by the rise of InsurTech.

However, in the meantime, agents are becoming particularly important in handling non-standardised policies, which are readily provided by InsurTech-enabled personalised services. Those bespoke services are carefully designed and developed to meet the needs of certain group of customers in a specific context, which thus calls for hands-on expertise and experience to ensure timely and accurate service delivery to clients (Shankar, 2017). This scenario is exceptionally obvious in the case of life insurance due to its complex and tailored nature. To this end, the importance of agents is unveiled by InsurTech. In brief, InsurTech has reconfigured value by shifting the role of agents.

5 Who should take the lead?

Speaking from an InsurTech perspective, innovations typically are nurtured and promoted by start-ups, whereas incumbent companies, such as Ping An Insurance and Ant Finance, provide the main impetus behind the scene in China. To this end, a well-informed understanding towards both scenarios is indispensable given the complexity of the leading role in InsurTech. It thus calls for integrated and concerted efforts from different sources – any monolithic attempt would lead to lopsided and inconclusive results that are less feasible in action and too generic in engagement. As a result, a closer look at the exemplary cases from both sides is not only desirable but also essential.

5.1 Ping An Insurance

Literally meaning "safe and well", Ping An, a Chinese holding conglomerate, is one of the most valuable financial groups worldwide, with subsidiaries providing a full range of financial services, such as insurance, banking, and asset management. Within the group, Ping An Insurance, the founding company, was the first Chinese life insurer established in 1988[2] and currently firmly holds the position as the China's biggest insurer, with $94 billion in premium revenue (Chen, 2018).

Leading in life and general insurance in China, Ping An Insurance is also investing aggressively in technology to transform itself into a tech-empowered insurance giant. According to Kapadia's report (2020),[3] it poured $7 billion during the past decade and has plans for investing an additional $15 billion over the coming decade. Recognised as one of the most technologically advanced insurance companies globally, Ping An Insurance has unparalleled advantages in mobile apps and underlying technologies based on AI and cloud computing.

Specifically, Ping An Insurance has primarily developed two technology clusters – AI and cloud computing – that sustain its both short-term and long-term business targets. It developed the cloud computing platform – Ping An Cloud – providing effective and efficient services for 500 million users from a wide range of industries, such as finance, healthcare, real estate, automotive, and smart city (Liu, 2018).

Aiming to enhance its ability to understand customers and risks, Ping An Insurance has extensively employed AI and started to embed it organically into the existing business processes. In the example of the latest AI-enabled "smart motor insurance claims" system, motorists are able to conduct self-assessment of external vehicular damage via a dedicated mobile App, which significantly accelerated the insurance process for minor accidents. Only four steps are needed to settle claims (Olano, 2019): after inputting the repair amount, the user will be prompted to confirm the accident information and then upload photos, before completing the process by supplying payment information. Typically, the system will finalise the process in no more than 3 minutes.

---

2 Ping An Insurance Website: https://www.pingan.cn/m/en/about/history.shtml [Accessed 26 June 2020].
3 Chinese Insurer Ping An Is Betting Big on Tech. Here's How That Will Boost Its Stock: https://www.barrons.com/articles/chinese-insurer-ping-an-is-betting-big-on-tech-heres-how-that-will-boost-its-stock-51578076483 [Accessed 26 June 2020].

Notably, the system utilises image recognition technology for an accurate recognition of pictures and leverages AI on the risk leakage rules to finalise loss assessment and pricing more efficiently. Drawing on the benefits of big data collected through the financial ecosystem within Ping An Group, such as credit history, driving data, and claim history, the insurance company built a customer white list to formulate a base for effective decision-making. On top of that, Ping An Insurance further utilises adequate and necessary information to establish data-supported and trust-based quotas that are designed for the specific motorist regarding the claims settlement.

In short, Ping An Insurance deems InsurTech as the fundamental strategy that coherently and consistently connects its internal and external processes. To be specific, InsurTech facilitates internal operations primarily by enhancing efficiency (AI), reducing cost (AI and cloud computing), improving experience (big data), and strengthening risk management (AI and big data). On the external end, InsurTech helps Ping An Insurance to supply bespoke services and create value chains. This is achieved by synergic efforts of AI, big data, and cloud computing to establish the so-called Ping An ecosystem (Greeven et al., 2019). Departing from its existing large user base accumulated through insurance and banking services over the years, Ping An Insurance firstly leverages its cloud computing platform to reach as many industries as possible, an effort to further expand the direct and indirect customer base. The move also extends its influence from the financial domain to other areas, such as healthcare and automotive, so as to diversify customer data and develop its chief asset – customer information. So far, Ping An Insurance has successfully established five sub-ecosystems within its realm – financial service, healthcare, auto service, real estate, and smart city (Prakash, 2020). These five pillars, on the basis of cloud computing, together further feed its AI and big data capabilities with rich scenarios and detailed data – a strategy Ping An named as "initiating engagement with one service, extending the scope to multiple services, then to multiple products" (Ping An, 2016).

5.2 Zhong An Insurance

Zhong An Insurance, the first and only company in China that possesses an internet insurance licence, has been providing services to a large client pool of 150 million customers with over 630 million insurance policies issued within one year after the debut (Lloyd-Jones, 2018). It attracts largely the millennial market due to its nearly real-time claims process with 60% customers aged between 25 and 30 who are mostly city-dwellers (Littlejohns, 2019). Aiming at revolutionising traditional insurance by applying digital mind-set across the insurance value chain from product to process, Zhong An Insurance advantages lower operating and distribution costs chiefly through AI.

Zhong An Insurance particularly adopted AI applications for 70% of online customer services to considerably reduce manual labour costs, leading to a 63.7% decrease in staff number (Efrat, 2019). This is convincingly corroborated by the fact that the automation rate of the underwriting and claim settlement services reached 99% and 95%, respectively, through the implementation of intelligent underwriting, claim management, and automatic processing (Tan, 2020). In addition, the company has devoted to improve customer communication by introducing AI-enabled chat bots to serve 97% of its clients (Yeung, 2017). This approach made the interaction between customers and company informative, convenient, and prompt, substantively increasing the level of customer satisfaction. AI has been purposefully exploited in Zhong An Insurance, where product innovation is fast-tracked. It initiated a scheme of "product innovation group" to provide a wide range of products that are carefully designed and specifically developed for niche markets. A portfolio of more than 200 products is closely linked to customer's daily life and relatively easy to understand for the majority of customers (Griffith, 2017), securing a favourable acceptance in local market. Such a wave of popular products has been structured by utilising AI. AI analysed consumer data for product pricing, underwriting rules, and risk management and later formulated strategies for product orientation and segmentation.

As such, AI, being an instance of InsurTech, has been deeply and extensively embedded within Zhong An Insurance's major business processes (e.g., product, customer, and claim service) and has started to conflate the values from different aspects into an integrated picture – an insurance-based ecosystem (Peverelli and Feniks, 2018). It is worth noticing that the ecosystem of Zhong An Insurance is different from that of Ping An Insurance as discussed above. While Ping An Insurance has stretched its efforts to almost all corners of financial markets as well as other primary sectors, Zhong An Insurance generally concentrates on its own backyard of insurance only. Given that Zhong An Insurance is a medium-sized start-up, it would be difficult, if not impossible, for it to implement a full-scale campaign; instead, by employing AI with numerous selective products targeting different clients, it has rapidly aggregated user data and enriched the applicable scenarios as the starting point to form a virtuous circle. In other words, Zhong An Insurance proactively utilised InsurTech to make up for its lack of initial customer base and data sources, a common issue facing start-ups; it then swiftly made most use of the collected data to incessantly ameliorate its following rounds of products and services, an effort to cause ripple effect. Since AI has reasonably increased the efficiency and comfortably decreased the operational and human resource costs, Zhong An Insurance has been able to outmanoeuvre other competitors by making more resources available for its client base and keep itself ahead of the game.

In summary, InsurTech has been fully leveraged in both powerful incumbent and competitive start-ups with different focuses. The incumbent, such as Ping An Insurance, endeavours to *retain* customers within its multi-layered ecosystem through the provision of products covering a wide range of aspects at and beyond insurance level, whereas the start-up, for instance Zhong An Insurance, strives to *attract* customers to its concentrated ecosystem through the supply of products for designated scenarios at the insurance level. To this end, incumbent is more concerned about the role of InsurTech in systematically transforming the underlying and underpinning businesses, and the start-up is more inclined to utilise the capability of InsurTech to constructively convert digital innovations into products and data. In this regard, they both lead the game on different raceways, but coordinated and concerted efforts are envisaged if InsurTech is going to be bourgeoning throughout the industry.

6 Conclusion

Slowly but substantively, InsurTech has made its footprint in the insurance industry. Different from its predecessors, such as informationalisation and internetalisation, InsurTech intends to transform the insurance sector's landscape in relation to both technology and value creation. The three underpinning technologies – AI, big data, and cloud computing – together redefined the roadmap that insurance companies pursue to allocate resources, organise activities, and manoeuvre strategies to achieve optimum lower operational cost, larger customer base, and adaptive tactics. These upturns in insurance business will then result in a redistribution of value born with the sector amongst its three key stakeholders – agents, business (operators), and customers. Mediated by InsurTech through three leading technologies, the value is reconfigured with agents, enlarged at business, and redeveloped for customers. Considering the huge but untapped benefits of InsurTech, both incumbents and start-ups are aggressively racing for it. Despite the distinctive InsurTech strategies and orientations, they are at the helm of their own domains in leveraging technologies that can be synergised for a better understanding and utilisation of it. In this regard, InsurTech will play an increasingly important role in the sector in the future and has already demonstrated its potential sufficiently in delivering value through proper means to the right places.

Acknowledgement

Special thanks goes to Mr Sanyang (Steve) Liu from Aviva-COFCO for his topical insights. Many thanks to Mr Jinyuan (Daniel) Zhang, the Research Assistant, for his efforts on literature and in-text figures.

References

Akerkar, R., 2019. *Artificial intelligence for business.* Cham: Springer.
Andrews, D.L., 2018. InsurTech: the next disruptor to the insurance industry. *Predictive Analytics and Futurism*, 18, pp. 22–25.
Asadi, S., Nilashi, M., and Yadegaridehkordi, E., 2017. Customers perspectives on adoption of cloud computing in banking sector. *Information Technology and Management*, 18(4), pp. 305–330.
Ayuso, M., Guillen, M., and Nielsen, J.P., 2019. Improving automobile insurance ratemaking using telematics: incorporating mileage and driver behaviour data. *Transportation*, 46(3), pp. 735–752.
Balasubramanian, R., Libarikian, A., and McElhaney, D., 2018. *Insurance 2030 – the impact of AI on the future of insurance.* New York: McKinsey & Company.

Bhardwaj, S., Jain, L., and Jain, S., 2010. An approach for investigating perspective of cloud Software-as-a-Service (SaaS). *International Journal of Computer Applications*, 10(2), pp. 40–43.

Cappiello, A., 2018. Digital disruption and InsurtTech start-ups: Risks and challenges. In *Technology and the insurance industry* (pp. 29–50). Cham: Palgrave Pivot.

Catteddu, D., and Hogben, G., 2009. Cloud Computing: benefits, risks and recommendations for information security. European Network and Information Security Agency (ENISA) (pp. 1–125).

Chen, J., Tao, Y., Wang, H., and Chen, T., 2015. Big data based fraud risk management at Alibaba. *The Journal of Finance and Data Science*, 1(1), pp. 1–10.

Chen, S.-C.J., 2018. Chinese Giant Ping An looks beyond insurance to a Fintech future. *Forbes*. Available at: https://www.forbes.com/sites/shuchingjeanchen/2018/06/06/chinese-giant-ping-an-looks-beyond-insurance-to-a-fintech-future/#3c3cdeca48f3 [Accessed 26 Jun. 2020].

Chen, Y., Kreulen, J., Campbell, M., and Abrams, C., 2011. Analytics ecosystem transformation: a force for business model innovation. SRII Global Conference 2011 San Jose, CA (pp. 11–20).

Corea, F., 2019. How AI is changing the insurance landscape. In *Applied artificial intelligence: where AI can be used in business* (pp. 5–10). Cham: Springer.

Delen, D., and Demirkan, H., 2013. Data, information and analytics as services. *Decision Support Systems*, 55(1), pp. 359–363.

Doszkocs, T. E., 1986. Natural language processing in information retrieval. *Journal of the American Society for Information Science*, 37(4), pp. 191–196.

Efrat, Z., 2019. ANZIIF: Artificial intelligence real problems. Australia and New Zealand Institute of Insurance and Finance. Available at: https://anziif.com/members-centre/the-journal-articles/volume-42/issue-2/artificial-intellegence-real-problems [Accessed 26 Jun. 2020].

Erevelles, S., Fukawa, N., and Swayne, L., 2016. Big data consumer analytics and the transformation of marketing. *Journal of Business Research*, 69(2), pp. 897–904.

Fang, K., Jiang, Y., and Song, M., 2016. Customer profitability forecasting using Big Data analytics: a case study of the insurance industry. *Computers & Industrial Engineering*, 101, pp. 554–564.

Fernando, S., 2015. Fraud detection and prevention: A data analytics approach. Available at: http://wso2.com/whitepapers/fraud-detection-and-prevention-a-data-analytics-approach/ [Accessed 26 Jun. 2020].

Fisk, R., Grove, S., Harris, L.C., Keeffe, D.A., Daunt, K.L., Russell-Bennett, R., and Wirtz, J., 2010. Customers behaving badly: a state-of-the-art review, research agenda and implications for practitioners. *Journal of Services Marketing*, 24(6), pp. 417–429.

Gartner n.d. Big data. Information technology glossary. Available at: https://www.gartner.com/en/information-technology/glossary/big-data [Accessed 26 Jun. 2020].

Gent, E., 2019. Why AI won't replace human investors. Available at: http://www.raconteur.net/business-innovation/innovation-automation [Accessed 26 Jun. 2020].

Greeven, M., Duke, L., Yang, J.A., and Wei, W., 2019. The role of Ping An Technology in Ping An Group's digital ecosystem. *IMD Business School*. Available at: https://www.imd.org/research-knowledge/for-educators/case-studies/The-role-of-Ping-An-Technology-in-enabling-Ping-An-Groups-digital-ecosystem/ [Accessed 26 Jun. 2020].

Griffith, S., 2017. Eight things you need to know about Zhong An. *Oxbow Partners*. Available at: https://oxbowpartners.com/blogs/zhong-an/ [Accessed 26 Jun. 2020].

Grosz, B.J., 2018. Smart enough to talk with us? Foundations and challenges for dialogue capable AI systems. *Computational Linguistics*, 44(1), pp. 1–15.

Hartmann, P.M., Zaki, M., Feldmann, N., and Neely, A., 2014. *Big data for big business? A taxonomy of data-driven business models used by start-up firms.* Cambridge Service Alliance Working Paper. Available at: https://cambridgeservicealliance.eng.cam.ac.uk/resources/Downloads/Monthly%20Papers/2014_March_DataDrivenBusinessModels.pdf [Accessed 26 Jun. 2020].

He, P., Wang, P., Gao, J., and Tang, B., 2015. City-wide smart healthcare appointment systems based on cloud data virtualization PaaS. *International Journal of Multimedia and Ubiquitous Engineering*, 10(2), pp. 371–382.

Holliday, S., 2019. *How Insurtech can close the protection gap in emerging markets* (No. 32366). The World Bank.

Hu, T.I., and Tracogna, A., 2020. Multichannel customer journeys and their determinants: Evidence from motor insurance. *Journal of Retailing and Consumer Services*, 54, p. 102022.

Huang, Y., Hannon, P.A., Williams, B., and Harris, J.R., 2011. Workers' health risk behaviors by state, demographic characteristics, and health insurance status. *Preventing Chronic Disease*, 8(1), p. A12.

Iriondo, R., 2018. Machine learning vs. AI and their important differences. *Medium*. Available at: https://medium.com/towards-artificial-intelligence/differences-between-ai-and-machine-learning-and-why-it-matters-1255b182fc6 [Accessed 26 Jun. 2020].

Jansen, W., and Grance, T., 2011. *Draft NIST special publication guidelines on security and privacy in public Cloud computing.* Computer Security.

Jiang, P., and Zhou X., 2020. Why will insurance get off to a good start in 2020 (in Chinese). *YiCai*. Available at: https://www.yicai.com/news/100475954.html [Accessed 26 Jun. 2020].

Kiron, D., 2017. What managers need to know about artificial intelligence. *MIT Sloan Management Review*. Available at: https://sloanreview.mit.edu/article/what-managers-need-to-know-about-artificial-intelligence/ [Accessed 26 Jun. 2020].

Lamberton, C., Brigo, D., and Hoy, D., 2017. Impact of Robotics, RPA and AI on the insurance industry: challenges and opportunities. *Journal of Financial Perspectives*, 4(1), pp. 8–20.

Lasica, J.D., 2009. *Identity in the age of cloud computing: the next-generation Internet's impact on business, governance and social interaction.* Washington, DC: Aspen Institute.

Lin, L. and Chen, C.C., 2020. The promise and perils of InsurTech. *Singapore Journal of Legal Studies*, 1, pp. 115–142.

Littlejohns, P., 2019. What is Zhong An Insurance? China's digital-only policy provider. NS Insurance. Available at: https://www.nsinsurance.com/news/what-is-zhong-an-insurance/ [Accessed 26 Jun. 2020].

Liu, T. and Xiong, X., 2016. An analysis of the maturity index of China's insurance industry. *Shanghai Management Science*, 38(6), pp. 13–17.

Liu, Y., 2018. Insurer Ping An targets banks, hospitals with new cloud service. *South China Morning Post*. Available at: https://www.scmp.com/business/companies/article/2169023/chinese-insurance-giant-ping-launches-cloud-service-aimed-banks [Accessed 26 Jun. 2020].

Lloyd-Jones, T., 2018. The digital platform economy and global technology infrastructure developments for insurance. *Insurance Insights*. Available at: https://blogs.lexisnexis.com/insurance-insights/2018/10/the-digital-platform-economy-and-global-technology-infrastructure-developments-for-insurance/ [Accessed 26 Jun. 2020].

Long, L.N. and Gupta, A., 2008. Scalable massively parallel artificial neural networks. *Journal of Aerospace Computing, Information, and Communication*, 5(1), pp. 3–15.

McCurry, J., 2017. Japanese company replaces office workers with artificial intelligence. *The Guardian*. Available at: https://www.theguardian.com/technology/2017/jan/05/japanese-company-replaces-office-workers-artificial-intelligence-ai-fukoku-mutual-life-insurance [Accessed 26 Jun. 2020].

McFall, L., and Moor, L., 2018. Who, or what, is insurtech personalising? Persons, prices and the historical classifications of risk. *Journal of Social Theory*, 19(2), pp. 193–213.

Mell, P., and Grance T., 2011. *The NIST definition of cloud computing*. Gaithersburg: National Institute of Standards and Technology.

Meyers, G., and Hoyweghen, I.V., 2020. 'Happy failures': Experimentation with behaviour-based personalisation in car insurance. *Big Data & Society*, 7(1), p. 2053951720914650.

Mizgier, K., Kocsis, O., and Wagner, S., 2018. Zurich insurance uses data analytics to leverage the BI insurance proposition. *Journal on Applied Analytics*, 48 (2), pp. 94–107.

OECD, 2020. The impact of big data and artificial intelligence (AI) in the insurance sector. Available at: www.oecd.org/finance/impact-Big-Data-AI-in-the-Insurance-Sector.htm [Accessed 26 Jun. 2020].

Olano, G., 2019. AI to be more deeply integrated into insurance – Ping An. *Insurance Business Asia*. Available at: https://www.insurancebusinessmag.com/asia/news/breaking-news/ai-to-be-more-deeply-integrated-into-insurance--ping-an-190507.aspx [Accessed 26 Jun. 2020].

Ongsulee, P., 2017. Artificial intelligence, machine learning and deep learning. *15th International Conference on ICT and Knowledge Engineering (ICT&KE)* (pp. 1–6). Bangkok: IEEE.

Peng, Y., Kou, G., Sabatka, A., Matza, J., Chen, Z., Khazanchi, D., and Shi, Y., 2007. Application of classification methods to individual disability income insurance fraud detection. *In International Conference on Computational Science* (pp. 852–858). Berlin, Heidelberg: Springer.

Peverelli, R. and Feniks, R. de, (2018). Thinking ecosystems is the secret behind Zhong An. Digital Insurance Agenda, Accelerate Innovation in Insurance. Available at: https://www.digitalinsuranceagenda.com/267/thinking-ecosystems-is-the-secret-behind-zhongan/ [Accessed 26 Jun. 2020].

Ping An, 2016. Annual report 2015. Ping An Insurance (Group) Company of China. Available at: http://www.pingan.com/app_upload/images/info/upload/8a7f95f7-38f2-4ad1-8313-9d1eca0cce80.pdf [Accessed 26 Jun. 2020].

Prakash, A., 2020. The Ping An Ecosystem— how an insurance company reached the Forbes top 10 ranking. *Medium*. Available at: https://medium.com/@arun_prakash/the-ping-an-ecosystem-how-an-insurance-company-reached-the-forbes-top-10-ranking-df3136ff41c [Accessed 26 Jun. 2020].

Quan, X.I. and Sanderson, J., 2018. Understanding the artificial intelligence business ecosystem. *IEEE Engineering Management Review*, 46(4), pp. 22–25.

Roehrig, P., 2008. New market pressures will drive next-generation IT services outsourcing. *Global Services*, 3(35), pp. 22–23.

Roel, V., Antonio, K. and., and Claeskens, G., 2017. Unraveling the predictive power of telematics data in car insurance pricing. Available at: SSRN 2872112.

Schueffel, P., 2017. Taming the beast: A scientific definition of Fintech. *Journal of Innovation Management*, 4(4), pp. 32–54.

Sen, A., and Lam, D., 2016. *Insurtech: Disruptions and opportunities in the insurance industry*. PineBridge Investment.

Shankar, S., 2017. Insurance agent role will transform but continue to be valuable in digital era. *Insurance Insights*. Available at: https://blogs.lexisnexis.com/insurance-insights/2017/04/insurance-agent-role-will-transform-but-continue-to-be-valuable-in-digital-era [Accessed 26 Jun. 2020].

Sloman, A., and Logan, B., 2000. *Evolvable architectures for human-like minds. Cognitive Science Research Paper*. University of Birmingham CSRP.

Stipic, A., and Bronzin, T., 2012. How cloud computing is (not) changing the way we do BI. *Proceedings of the 35th International Convention MIPRO 2012*, pp. 1574–1582.

Stoeckli, E., Dremel, C., and Uebernickel, F., 2018. Exploring characteristics and transformational capabilities of InsureTech innovations to understand insurance value creation in a digital world. *Electron Markets*, 28, pp. 287–305.

Sultan, N.A., 2011. Reaching for the "cloud": how SMEs can manage. *International Journal of Information Management*, 31(3), pp. 272–278.

Tan, L., 2020. Zhong An Premium increased 30% last year. *China Banking and Insurance News*. Available at: http://xw.sinoins.com/2020-03/25/content_336124.htm [Accessed 26 Jun. 2020].

Trziszka, M., 2019. Agile management methods in an enterprise based on cloud computing. *International Conference on Applied Human Factors and Ergonomics* (pp. 122–129). Cham: Springer.

Wang, B., 2019. Xianghubao is drawing attention for getting 50 million users within 6 months. *Equal Ocean*. Available at: https://equalocean.com/analysis/201904161808.

Wheatley, M., 2019. AWS says businesses should move to its cloud to lower their carbon footprint. *SiliconAngelSiliconAngle*. Available at: https://siliconangle.com/2019/11/26/aws-says-businesses-move-cloud-lower-carbon-footprint/ [Accessed 26 Jun. 2020].

Wu, W.W., Lan, L.W., and Lee, Y.T., 2011. Exploring decisive factors affecting an organization's SaaS adoption: A case study. *International Journal of Information Management*, 31(6), pp. 556–563.

Yan, T.C., Schulte, P., and Chuen, D.L.K., 2018. InsurTech and FinTech: banking and insurance enablement. *Handbook of Blockchain, Digital Finance, and Inclusion*, (Volume 1, pp. 249–281). London: Academic Press.

Yeung, K., 2017. Zhong An uses artificial intelligence to improve its products. *South China Morning Post*. Available at: https://www.scmp.com/business/investor-relations/stock-quote-profile/article/2117527/online-insurer-zhongan-uses [Accessed 26 Jun. 2020].

4 Improving the digital financial services ecosystem through collaboration of regulators and FinTech companies

Sonia Soon

1 Introduction

Undoubtedly, the central activation and innovation component of FinTech is regulation (Goo and Heo, 2020). Hence, the overall aim of this chapter is to critically examine the current regulatory outlook and the challenges FinTech in the DFS environment are faced with in today's world. The chapter will cover the hurdles faced in bridging the gap for financial inclusion, the lack of communication between regulators and FinTech companies, and what regulatory bodies should do in order to allow for the FinTech ecosystem to flourish and develop innovative solutions. In addition, I will explore what different regions do in support of the FinTech ecosystem in order to better understand what works, where the gaps are and how to start conversations between regulators and FinTech companies.

1.1 About FinTech

Financial technology, or "FinTech", encompasses a wide range of ever-evolving financial innovation in the digital financial services (DFS) environment (Scott, 2020). Examples of these include mobile payments, digital banks, insurance, cryptocurrency, blockchain, crowdfunding platforms and so on. The aim is to challenge the common and traditional methods used in the current DFS environment (Howat, 2020). However, looking at FinTech holistically, one will find that FinTech also involves the digitisation and datafication of the global financial markets (Arner, Barberis and Buckley, 2017).

DFS has shaped how we perceive finance today, stemming from the financial crisis of 2007–2009, where we witnessed the power of technology and opportunities coinciding. FinTech may seem daunting to many due to the rise of new DFS such as digital currencies, digital banks and so on. However, the automatic teller machine (ATM), for example, was considered a form of financial technology back in the day (Eshraghi, 2019). As daunting as it may seem, we as a society have been progressing towards a digital financial landscape for decades without even realising it. The fear presumably may derive from the fact that most financial technologies cannot be seen or felt like an ATM. Other aspects of fear derive from consumers' uncertainty on data collection and sharing, their lack of awareness and their fear of being a victim of cyberattack.

Whether we like it or not, technology has played and will continue to play a vital part in our daily lives. Those who fail to adapt may be left behind (Georg, 2018), as the way businesses intended to function would be dominated by technology, machine learning and artificial intelligence (Howat, 2020). Having said that, FinTech development will not be able to go far if the regulation that surrounds the different types of DFS does not accommodate them. Rapid growth does not equate rapid adoption from regulators, who are obligated to put the interests of the country and consumers first.

Regulators are mindful of the need for technology innovation and thus aim to endorse and encourage the FinTech ecosystem. However, they would not want to make room for the current threats, in particular cyber security, and fraud to evolve whilst supporting FinTech developments (Phillips, 2019). The increasing momentum is creating a double-edged implication of modernising financial ecosystems and spurring improvements in customer and industry behaviour while undermining existing employers, business models and regulatory frameworks (Nicoletti, 2017).

2 What are the issues?

As technological integration has become more complex and widespread, regulatory issues have increased making financial services one of the world's most regulated markets. In addition to that, as it targets new markets and provides new audiences with financial tools, FinTech frequently operates in spaces where regulatory guidance is limited. As a result of this, FinTech companies are frequently being held on a tight leash to be closely monitored and controlled by regulators (Mention, 2019).

In addition, as the industry is moving beyond the basic DFS to an extended bouquet of services and business models leveraging the use of data in product design, we see the deepening of DFS (Alliance for Financial Inclusion, 2020b). However, FinTech companies offering DFS to this day are still facing challenges which are hampering their innovative growth.

The industry is regulated by the government in many respects; thus, there are unforeseen issues when it comes to the regulations and most of the pushback faced by the industry, especially amongst the start-up industry, that are contributed by licensing regimes (Singh, 2019). Some of these regulations were not up to date to meet the different DFS needs, which is then followed by amendments that do not consider the likely domino effects they may have on a business's financial and operational capacity to meet the changes. For instance, in Malaysia, the licensing regime surrounding E-Money was issued to quite a number of DFS businesses who started putting out products and services that were governed by vague regulations and guidelines. As DFS covers a multitude of products and services, its definition is wide and the lack of consideration of that factor created a number of gaps in the industry. As years went by and regulations had to be modified to fit reported gaps, most of the companies either went dormant or were unable to carry out changes within the company to meet newly introduced guidelines causing the company to lose the trust of its customers.

In addition, Bank Negara Malaysia (BNM), Malaysia's central bank, took an approach to consider feedback as part of the contributions towards their regulatory amendments as expected in the FinTech ecosystem (Harroch, 2019). This caused some confusion amongst FinTech businesses, since they were bound by regulatory feedback based on specific types of services and products; however, not all DFS operate in the same way.

The uncertainty, delayed response and lack of clarity to the existing regulatory regime aimed at FinTechs, specifically start-ups, who are the main players in the FinTech ecosystem, caused the process to slow down and discouraged start-ups such as home-grown e-hailing companies, for example, Grab. As a result of these frustrations, Grab made the decision to move its operations to Singapore, which can be seen as an economic loss to Malaysia (*The Independent Singapore*, 2017).

The United States provide another example as to how the licensing regime hinders the FinTech ecosystem. FinTech companies must comply with both federal laws and a patchwork of state laws. Although certain federal agencies and state regulators have voiced support for promoting FinTech innovation by simplifying the applicable regulatory regime, in the near term, FinTech companies should expect to engage specialised legal counsel experienced in navigating the morass of laws, regulations and court decisions that could apply (Harroch, 2019).

Singh (2019) submits that it is only ethical to view regulation in a positive light because as long as the regulations are equal for all and do not disrupt the industry, they could create healthy competition in the ecosystem. However, rigid and excessive regulation can often adversely affect the ability of a business to develop and gain competitive advantages. To illustrate this further, Korea's domestic FinTech industry growth rate was slow despite it being an IT-powered nation due to an immature market and a lag in fostering competition. As of January 2019, Toss, a Korean FinTech company, was the only Korean unicorn company amongst the 39 global FinTech unicorn companies (Young-sil, 2019). The regulatory hindrance made it challenging for Korean FinTech firms to push their businesses forward (Goo and Heo, 2020).

Hindrance is apparent when a DFS attempts to reach out to the underserved and underbanked communities but face challenges when meeting regulator's requirements of the onboarding process where there is a need to mimic equally what is done to onboard users who have official proof of identification (The World Bank, 2018). Globally, 1.7 billion individuals have no access to bank accounts, and SMEs (95% of companies worldwide) provide more than 60% of employees with jobs who are struggling for financial access (Sahay et al., 2020).

Though it is an effort towards mitigating financial crime, consideration for reasonable leeway needs to be applicable in such circumstances. Hindrance as such would possibly lead the underserved and underbanked communities back to their old financial habits. These can be costly, risky, inconvenient and even illegal (Karamousali, 2019). In addition, many of the countries with these underserved and underbanked communities do not necessarily have reliable internet connectivity or infrastructure that may be required for them to utilise the FinTech services, which is another roadblock faced by the industry (Friedline, Naraharisetti and Weaver, 2019).

Existing regulatory mechanisms need to be enhanced to accommodate the deepening and dynamic existence of DFS and minimise the occurrence of sporadic, ad hoc and "catch-up" approaches to managing both existing and potentially new DFS-related risk concerns (AFI, 2020b). Having said that, regulators are taking the necessary initiatives to revise current legislation to incorporate technology-specific elements to current legislations, regulations or guidance for enabling technologies. There has been active engagement in application programming interfaces (APIs), cloud computing and identification and authentication based on biometrics. In comparison, regulators have not gone beyond conducting performance evaluations and providing general guidelines for artificial intelligence, machine learning and, to some degree, distributed ledger technology (Ehrentraud and Ocampo, 2020).

FinTech policy responses will need to consider various policy goals. Applying emerging technology to the financial system with an open mind would undoubtedly remain a desirable outcome of regulatory action. Concurrently, the preservation of financial stability, business and financial integrity, competitiveness and consumer safety must be aligned with policy actions (Ehrentraud and Ocampo, 2020). In addition, the prevention of regulatory arbitrage and the promotion, where necessary, of a level-playing field may be pursued while retaining adequate control over businesses with a greater potential for systemic risk development (Ehrentraud and Ocampo, 2020).

3 FinTech and financial inclusion

The FinTech industry has great potential to modernise the financial world; however, the main focus of its potential is exemplified through its capacity to close the gap in financial inclusion. (AFI, 2020d.). In addition to FinTech's growth towards its financial innovation contribution, it is also a contributor to the growth of financial inclusion in many parts of the world. Financial inclusion is a cornerstone for both poverty eradication and economic development opportunities, and access to DFS in the underserved environment is vital for a successful digital economy (The World Bank, 2018).

FinTech surrounding DFS can contribute towards improving the design of transaction accounts and payment products and, with enhanced user interface and knowledge, make them widely accessible (Pazarbasioglu et al., 2020). Services can be more efficient, and barriers to entry into the market can be lowered. Still, in terms of operational and cyber resilience, consumer fund security, data protection and privacy, digital exclusion and market concentration, these potential benefits can also present threats. If these threats are not appropriately managed, they could undermine financial inclusion (The Bank for International Settlements, 2020).

One of the vulnerabilities of a DFS is a social engineering attack. Users would be deceived into revealing sensitive information or prompted to download types of malware that would provide the cybercriminal with access into the user's physical locations, systems or networks. Consequently, DFS providers from Ghana, Kenya, Tanzania, Uganda and Zambia have reported that their employees fell victim to such criminal activity. However, the consequence was much more intensified as the information shared was of their own company user login details which enabled the criminal to access the corporate information systems (Baur-Yazbeck, 2018).

The traditional financial methods have its benefits, but for those who are from rural areas, for example, the accessibility and opportunity to even open a bank account may not even be possible. Providing access to financial services such as payments, deposits, insurance and credit to these individuals helps them handle their financial commitments and enhance their livelihoods while fostering widespread economic growth, prosperity and reduction in poverty (Koonprasert and Mohammad, 2020). Hence, this is why financial inclusion should always be a topic of discourse amongst FinTech companies and regulators. The discourses should then be followed by collaborative initiatives like a regulatory sandbox to set the stage for financial innovation as exemplified by the Philippines regulators, Bangko Sentral ng Pilipinas, whose aim is to encourage FinTech companies who can cater the underserved and underbanked (Duran and Tupaz, 2020). Regulators would need to be proactive and effective to encourage potential businesses and to create a dialogue amongst the public to instil confidence in the businesses being licensed.

In addition, in support of FinTech companies offering DFS, a recent and viable example that displays its true potential is exemplified throughout the recent COVID-19 pandemic. A global crisis as such imposes significant effects on the economic and financial markets; however, it allows for DFS to serve a functional role in promoting transactions beyond cash (AFI, 2020b). Not only have these types of DFS supported swift and reliable financial resources for "hard-to-reach" individuals and businesses, they have also minimised economic consequences and greatly enhanced the recovery journey (Eriksson von Allmen et al., 2020).

The FinTech industry has proven itself to be an important aspect of building a cashless society and appears to serve as a catalyst in enabling financial inclusion (FinSMEs, 2020). During lockdowns, governments turned to DFS such as M-Pesa for its credibility in delivering mobile money transfer facilities to millions of people in Africa that have a mobile phone but do not have access, or have only restricted access, to a bank account.

4 Regulator's perspective and responsibilities

Regulators' decisions and regulatory measures will ultimately influence the degree to which FinTech will have an impact on financial stability in the years to come (Gray and Leibrock, 2017). Regulations could hinder effective innovation if they are too rigid, but if they are too relaxed, they may fail to safeguard themselves against the adverse effects of technology (McQuinn, 2019).

The way DFS is designed is gradually being changed by technical advances in financial services. This transition opens up opportunities, as well as pose negative impacts, such as magnifying cybersecurity vulnerabilities or amplifying third-party threats (Gray and Leibrock, 2017). These possible threats affect consumers and investors and, more generally, financial stability, the market structure in financial services (Vučinić, 2020) and credibility that financial regulation intends to protect.

It is vital to monitor the resilience of DFS businesses because whether or not emerging vulnerabilities may adversely affect financial stability it would ultimately depend on resilience. Data are critical in evaluating such detrimental effects, as it involves an understanding of how vulnerabilities occur and how they evolve over time, along with the better understanding on how DFS may act as a means for structural change in the FinTech ecosystem and influence the risk-stability trade-off (Buch, 2019).

As existing statistical frameworks have little data for the systematic monitoring of these patterns, it is ideal for international cooperation to bridge this need, since it plays a key aspect in protecting the financial stability within the DFS environment (Buch, 2019).

FinTech offerings need to be analysed on a case-by-case basis given the wide range of underlying applications, each with their own characteristics and their own specific context (Gray and Leibrock, 2017). To date, the impact of FinTech on financial stability still appears to be minimal. However, given FinTech's rapid and unpredictable growth, this could change quickly. As such, it is important to carefully monitor FinTech developments. As new FinTech offerings continue to evolve at breakneck speed, the remit of the risk management function must keep pace in order to identify emerging threats on a timely basis (The WFE Focus Team, 2017).

Regulations have, in most cases, concentrated on minimising the risk that is associated with the use of a technology. More specifically, as regulated financial organisations are increasingly using cloud computing, the regulators have since developed standards (as in Brazil) or issued guidelines (as in the EU) to monitor and manage the operational risks involved. Some authorities, such as in Luxembourg and Singapore, are tackling the risks raised by the misuse of artificial intelligence and machine learning algorithms. Papers have been published to illustrate the risks resulting from insufficient management of personal data, poor governance, lack of openness, and corrupt practices (Restoy, 2019).

On the bright side, we can see that innovative developments have encouraged regulators to keep up to avoid hindering its growth. However, regulators are also mindful of the emerging risks and challenges resulting from unclear data protection practices or structural vulnerabilities from cybersecurity threats due to the growth of DFS and FinTech products (Koonprasert and Mohammad, 2020). In addressing the gaps and overlaps among jurisdictions (Koonprasert and Mohammad, 2020) and in ensuring stability of the financial ecosystem, consistency is important. Based on that, it is best for regulators to look at different approaches and initiatives regulators of different countries apply in order to come up with similar approaches when handling the growth of FinTech (Pazarbasioglu et al., 2020).

5 Objectives

5.1 Regulatory overview

To date, it appears that regulations in emerging FinTech ventures and technologies have centred more on reducing risks in information security and operational flexibility with minimal improvement directed towards prudential safeguards. The frameworks would still need to be more responsive to fast-evolving economic conditions in maintaining the resilience of FinTech, whilst providing an environment conducive for financial innovation and growth. This limitation affects the ability for advances in technology to disrupt the financial system (Restoy, 2019).

Prudential safeguard, consumer security and market integrity remain largely unchanged (Ehrentraud and Ocampo, 2020). DFS faces restrictions when it comes to safeguarding customers' funds, mainly when they are allowed to accept cash from the public. Examples of this are reflected where the maximum limit in Switzerland is up to CHF 100 million cap for FinTech licence holders, or ample liquidity coverage such as the 100% reserve requirements for outstanding client balances (the float) in Brazil and China. As a result, any operation requiring a significant risk transformation of public funds often requires a banking licence (Restoy, 2019).

As the FinTech industry comprises all sorts of different financial services, we need to examine the regulation surrounding FinTech in a wider stance, where it is targeted not only towards the forefront of the service but also towards the regulations that handle the backend portion of the product and service as well (Restoy, 2019). While several countries in the Southeast Asia, East Africa and Latin America regions have begun to address basic enabling factors for DFS to achieve a sustainable level, DFS needs a more comprehensive set of enabling factors. These include better internet connectivity that can encourage better mobile-phone adoption, exploring methods to onboard users who do not have relevant identification in order to roll out digital and biometric ID systems and so on. This is to ensure there is financial integrity, stability and competitiveness (Pazarbasioglu et al., 2020).

FinTech-related policy initiatives can be usefully divided into three groups. First, those that specifically regulate FinTech activities; second, those that lay emphasis on the meaning of technological innovations in the provision of financial services; and, lastly, those that promote DFS more specifically (Restoy, 2019).

Internationally, regulators seek to tackle emerging threats and establish mechanisms to facilitate a coordinated regulatory response to global challenges. This should be highlighted in view of the wide variety of technology emerging for the delivery of financial services and the possible scale for such services, in particular when companies with a large customer base enter the market (Ehrentraud and Ocampo, 2020). As an example of an internationally coordinated response to emerging threats, the Digital Financial Services Working Group (DFSWG) and the Consumer Empowerment and Market Conduct Working Groups (CEM-CWG) partnered together to produce codified key policy guidelines from applicable data sources developed over the decade. They paired with industry practices within the AFI network in the Consumer Protection for DFS (CP4DFS) framework to tackle consumer protection (CP)-related risks (AFI, 2020b). In parallel with their initiatives, the goal is to synthesise and harmonise learnings, best practices and policies from their respective data sources and around the network into a recognised policy model (AFI, 2020b).

In addition, reports by the Financial Action Task Force (FATF) have found a spike in illegal activities during the peak of DFS adoption due to the pandemic. Some of the activities include the abuse of online financial services deriving from potential bribes within government stimulus funding and so on (Crisanto and Prenio, 2020).

As a result, security officials between the United Kingdom and the United States collaboratively issued a joint statement. The statement prompts individuals and organisations to establish an enhanced level of security. It also informs them on threats linked to scam email and messages that mask themselves as a credible source, such as the World Health Organisation, for example, to offer assistance to combat the pandemic (Crisanto and Prenio, 2020).

5.2 Examples where regulatory bodies and regulation support FinTech development

In order to adapt to financial and technological development, it is advisable to assess existing organisational structures to determine whether current structures can provide adequate support for the regulation of innovations in the FinTech industry. Some regulators and supervisory authorities have started to adapt their organisational structures in order to better align themselves with the increasingly changing financial services environment by incorporating FinTech or innovation units (Koonprasert and Mohammad, 2020). Let us take the example of the Malaysian financial regulator BNM's approach to FinTech. Currently, the Malaysian regulators have taken an activity-based approach taking into account the kinds of businesses that the financial companies conduct (Fintech News Malaysia, 2020). This method provides clarity to the businesses to know whether or not they fall under the purview of BNM or whether they need to have a discussion with the Securities Commission of Malaysia, or both (Fintech News Malaysia, 2020). In relation to their approach to FinTech regulation, BNM relies on three principles they have been following, which are parity, proportionality and neutrality. The goal is to ensure they provide a level-playing field for the businesses in similar environments whilst keeping an open mind towards new innovative ideas that would require the BNM to consider the requirements relevant in meeting their innovative needs (Fintech News Malaysia, 2020).

While regulators generally aim to be technology-neutral, some jurisdictions such as Latin America and Europe have taken steps to remedy both the constructive consequences and the dangers involved with the application of specific innovations. As an example of policy support, the use of APIs has been expressly endorsed to encourage open banking (Restoy, 2019). In Mexico, for example, the National Banking and Securities Commission (CNBV) published in the Official Gazette of the Federation the general provisions in relation to computer APIs standardisation. The provision was issued pursuant to the Law for the Regulation of Financial Technology Institutions ("Fintech Law") (Garrigues, 2020). Speaking of Mexico, they have been seen as the leading country in Latin America that is leading the path (Pazarbasioglu et al., 2020) for FinTech regulation after introducing the Financial Technology Institutions Law (FinTech Law) framework in 2018 which covers a wide range of FinTech activities in one piece of legislation. The objective is to bring new financial business models into the regulatory framework, such as crowdfunding and e-money operations (Koonprasert and Mohammad, 2020). The legislation has been motivated by the rapid growth of these activities in recent years.

The Mexican authorities expect deeper financial inclusion, increased competition, improvements in organisational efficiency and changes in customer behaviour to be seen with the creation of a legal and regulatory structure for FinTech. In essence, the Mexican regulatory approach towards FinTech is similar to Malaysia's. However, the same results cannot be produced in Mexico due to a drop in their financial inclusion rate. A number of factors contribute to this lack of adoption rates, including a large unbanked population (Aldaya, 2020), poor penetration of internet subscribers and lack of smartphone usage (Herrera, Gonzáles and Camargo, 2020).

Though FinTech companies have been rapidly growing throughout the pandemic, Mexico is still unable to bridge the gap for financial inclusion and may not be able to retain the banked population post pandemic. The regulator's initiatives have been commendable; however, there is room for improvement, and collaboration is the key. The lack of collaboration between Mexico's government and FinTech companies that impedes the process of distributing emergency aids and loans displays how important it is for collaboration to exist between both parties, especially in order for the financial ecosystem to grow and address gaps where needed. Though regulators have taken steps towards the betterment of the industry, if FinTech entities fail to avail when the right opportunities, arise in the financial ecosystem that could be markedly beneficial for all-around growth, it defeats the whole purpose of FinTech's existence (Aldaya, 2020).

Meanwhile, in Tanzania, they have demonstrated major success in relation to the use of DFS. Tanzania has undergone exponential growth since the service was first launched in 2008 and has continued to do so in a fiercely competitive and collaborative environment (Pazarbasioglu et al., 2020). The government has taken measures to support financial sector businesses. One example of the government's initiative is the convergence of all mobile-money networks through the Tanzania Communications Regulatory Authority's (TCRA) National Transfer

Interoperability Agreement. This helps provide businesses with the accessibility to their consumers from various mobile wallets to transfer funds from one mobile wallet to another (African Legal Network, 2018).

The national strategy in this sector has ensured that regulators are open to digital innovations. The financial sector is traditionally heavily regulated in Tanzania, with rigid, time-consuming and costly licencing applications. The Bank of Tanzania (BoT) is the regulator of the financial sector and so is the TCRA, depending on the service offering. As the saying goes, "too many cooks spoil the broth", typically having multiple regulators can be a formula for instability and inefficient service delivery, but this was not the case in Tanzania as each of the regulators involved has a specific role, making it easier to know who is in charge of what.

This approach is quite similar to the Malaysian regulator's approach, where potential FinTech companies or new innovations that plan to penetrate the market have clarity as to which relevant regulator will assess matters on consumer protection, market stability and prevention of money laundering and fraud. Given this, all necessary information receives necessary consultation, and all of the relevant clearances are obtained (African Legal Network, 2018) along with the convenience of faster communication between the regulatory departments.

In addition, the BoT's decision to allow electronic funds transfer systems to run until a proper juridical system was developed back in 2008 is a clear example of idealism. However, the BoT had a clear tool and process for evaluating consumer safety, economic stability and prevention of money laundering and fraud when the FinTech business was looking to launch a new product (African Legal Network, 2018).

5.3 *How does FinTech regulation help bridge the gap in financial inclusion?*

Financial inclusion can promote economic development targets, balance income distribution gaps and empower people to invest in the market along with the DFS offered by nonbank entities that empower communities. This encourages the continuous use of FinTech-driven innovations (Ulbrich, 2020).

The leading organisation involved in devising financial inclusion policies and regulations, the Alliance for Financial Inclusion (AFI), emerged as a result of the rise in digital innovation. One of the initiatives they had persisted on in aid of financial inclusion is displayed in the Maya Declaration, which is the first global and measurable set of commitments, by developing and emerging country policymakers to unlock the economic and social potential of the 2.5 billion poorest people through greater financial inclusion (AFI, 2020a).

Through the Maya Declaration, they ensured the significant dedication managed to bring on board its member institutions committing to harnessing their ability to advance financial inclusion. AFI members from Russia, Malaysia, Philippines, Brazil, Thailand and Mexico are already at the forefront of using FinTech for financial inclusion in their own countries (AFI, 2020e). The Maya

Declaration is important as it not only raises the profile of a major global issue but also provides the public visibility needed to ensure that policymakers are held accountable for their commitments and make tangible progress (AFI, 2020c).

In addition, with a strategic architecture of underlying infrastructures, policy and regulatory climate that can help digital financial development, FinTech can realise its full potential for financial inclusion. According to a report by the AFI, it shows that the best approach is staged and progressive, focusing on four main pillars (Arner et al., 2018), based on experience in a number of developing, emerging and developed countries. The four pillars include the basis for digital financial transformation and financial inclusion. The first pillar is the development of digital identification and e-KYC systems to facilitate access to the financial system. Digital payment systems and decentralised electronic payment systems are the second pillar and are the primary strategy to promote digital financial flows in an economy. In the third pillar, the fostering of account opening and access is combined with the electronic provision of government services, specifically for public transfers and payments. The fourth and final pillar, the digital financial markets and systems architecture, builds on the first three to facilitate wider access to finance and investment by promoting use cases such as bond trading, clearing and settlement, and other more comprehensive banking functions (Arner et al., 2018). As exemplified by the countries above, regulators should collaborate and use guidelines by organisations such as the AFI that have dedicated research and proposed guidelines to meet regulator's goals towards closing the gap between DFS and financial inclusion.

ASEAN member-states have done significant work to achieve financial inclusion. As a few examples, we see how some FinTech companies, with the goal of reinventing customer buying, saving and investing throughout the country, are taking financial services to the unbanked communities of Southeast Asia. Julo, which is headquartered in Jakarta, uses patented credit assessment technology that leverages machine learning and sophisticated credit analytics to determine the creditworthiness of the community that is frequently ignored by traditional institutions. MyCash is another example where foreign workers, who are a big unbanked and underbanked community, are being served. Based in both Malaysia and Singapore, MyCash Online is a marketplace that provides fast, reliable and flexible digital services, including bus fares, air tickets and mobile top-up sales, international reloads, bill payments and mobile remittances (Fintechnews Singapore, 2020).

Having looked into the potential of digital finance services in bridging the gap for financial inclusion, the chapter looks into this subject based on the current COVID-19 pandemic that has affected the entire world. Most of the strategies and recommendations were made before anyone could have predicted that a pandemic in 2020 could disrupt the economy. However, as discussed above, we do see the light at the end of the tunnel in relation to the benefits of digital finance services offered in this crucial time.

DFS were available throughout the COVID-19 pandemic (Sahay et al., 2020), enabling a cashless society whilst minimising physical contact. Where digital financial inclusion has evolved, it helps promote the successful and accelerated implementation of government assistance initiatives, particularly for impacted persons and organisations by the pandemic. However, it is essential to address and provide extra attention in ensuring that women are a part of a DFS conversation for financial inclusion and are not left behind in times of a pandemic. Although it seems like FinTech has narrowed gender disparities, organisations recognised that some constraints to DFS inclusion are more prominent for women, such as access to services (mobile phones, the internet), cultural or social values, and technical and financial literacy (AFI, 2019).

Adding to the point where DFS does provide a path towards financial inclusion for women, statistics show that 140 million women globally opened their first bank account for better accessibility in obtaining public sector salaries, pensions and protection net transfers; this was the case even before the pandemic (Miller et al., 2020).

The combination of the rapid pace of innovation in financial services technology and the commitment to financial inclusion of an unprecedented number of leading policymaking institutions in developing and emerging countries is a unique opportunity to resolve some of the most intractable challenges for financial inclusion (AFI, 2020d).

5.4 What can regulators do to avoid hindering the FinTech ecosystem?

Regulators should foster the orderly adaptation of the industry's structure to a new environment characterised by new technology, new players and new activities for the regulation of financial services. This however is a key component of the current regulatory debate. A generally accepted idea, and one that inspires many of the recent regulatory innovations, is that policy action should aim to minimise the potential of regulatory arbitrage (Restoy, 2019).

Technological innovation enables new players to carry out operations that have historically been carried out only by heavily regulated institutions. Regulation should also be tailored to discourage risk-generating business practices from moving between organisations in search of lighter regulatory control (Restoy, 2019). In order to better govern FinTech, regulators would need to apply the enigmatic combination of prudence and commitment that is so often needed in policymaking. Prudence is required to avoid discouraging developments that may potentially favour society, and also to discourage core public interests, such as financial stability or consumer fairness, from playing second fiddle to short-term industrial policy priorities (Restoy, 2019).

Businesses such as Kenya's M-Pesa, or West Africa's MTN Mobile Money, can address financial inclusion among women more significantly than traditional banking services. Regulatory policy to encourage ownership of mobile phones amongst women should be supported as it will help bridge the technology and financial inclusion gap in regions like the Middle East and North Africa, where an estimated 65 million women who do not have bank accounts have mobile phones; this is a "ready-made" opportunity to deploy DFS (Miller et al., 2020). As far as commitment is concerned, this consists largely of taking steps to combat growing threats as soon as they are identified. However, the commitment would also be required to maintain the appropriate collaboration between agencies in various fields and jurisdictions (Restoy, 2019).

5.4.1 Collaboration

Collaboration is a key tool for a FinTech's success (Mention, 2019). Dialogues with regulators, FinTech groups, FinTech accelerators and incubators in the AFI network and beyond should be a natural habit practiced in the FinTech ecosystem. This not only encourages all of these entities to share industry knowledge and solutions but also helps regulators to gain a better insight as to how they can tackle current issues surrounding FinTech innovation and how to manage existing issues in harnessing its innovative potential.

5.4.2 Implementing a sandbox environment

Besides collaboration, providing a safe environment for FinTech companies to test their innovations and technologies plays a vital role for regulators, as it offers an essential learning experience which can shift conventional trends, since the market views the regulator as an organisation that can help them solve regulatory challenges (Mention, 2019).

FinTech companies tend to evaluate, customise and build frameworks that incorporate diverse and typically heterogeneous technology in the production of their technological platforms. Hence, live simulation testing and practical working environments are a critical part of the production phase. Unfortunately, these activities include strategic cooperation and a favourable regulatory climate, which is why it is important for regulators to consider regulatory alternatives that would harness the innovative potential rather than discourage the FinTech company (Mention, 2019).

In a sandbox environment, regulators will be able to assess the impact of new solutions and thus decide if they are detrimental to current regulations. If there is a need to relax the rules, regulators will be able to reasonably mitigate the regulations. As a result, these regulatory sandboxes could potentially overcome the issue of delayed market launch due to regulatory uncertainties. In addition, it can result in significant savings and innovative development (Goo and Heo, 2020).

Research shows that the adoption of regulatory sandboxes has an impact that encourages the investment of venture capital in the FinTech industry, which is essential in the early stages of every FinTech business. In addition, research suggests that it serves to decrease legal and institutional risks by removing ambiguity through adopting scalable and inclusive business models by FinTech companies (Goo and Heo, 2020).

6 Conclusion

Regulation constantly puts players in the industry on their toes by pushing them to get creative in their compliance measures (Serna, 2020). Regulation should not be a taboo word that scares everyone. Despite its reputation, regulations do play an important role in the prevention of financial crime, monopolisation of the market and the protection of the consumers. Having said that, the FinTech industry needs more from regulators to follow its pace, or at least to find a middle ground where both parties can benefit.

Moving forward, regulators will have to face the fact that there will be greater challenges as technology is constantly being pushed to see where its limits lie. Ongoing efforts by regulators would be expected to understand the emerging business models and their potential risks, to develop or retain skills and capabilities in order to better assess the possible impact on financial markets and to evolve their regulatory responses in an efficient way. As we have identified, only with adequate information and access to timely and accurate information would the regulators be able to steer innovation in a favourable direction, thus mitigating possible risks to the financial ecosystem (Ehrentraud and Ocampo, 2020).

Breaking the communication barriers between regulators and FinTech companies needs to happen in order for there to be an effective solution (Arner, Barberis and Buckley, 2017). FinTech companies do have something to offer regulators, which is why collaboration is vital to initiate conversations surrounding solutions. Besides, consumers are more likely to trust companies that are regulated; hence, awareness and education go hand in hand. If the regulators show their understanding and acceptance for FinTech through public forums and events, it would produce fruitful results for the FinTech ecosystem. If regulators strike the right balance between regulation and innovation, the possibilities for the FinTech ecosystem is limitless. FinTech will be able to better optimise financial inclusion, boost financial access to customers and maximise efficiency (McQuinn, 2019).

In conclusion, in order to steer clear from hindering innovation growth within the FinTech ecosystem and to bridge the gap for financial inclusion, regulators need to provide a safe space for innovation to be tested and to allow room for open collaborative conversation. Both regulators and FinTech companies need to harness each other's strengths and resources to better serve and protect the economy and its consumers.

Bibliography

African Legal Network (2018). Encouraging Fintech Innovation in Tanzania. Africa Legal Network. Available at: https://www.africalegalnetwork.com/feature-article-encouraging-fintech-innovation-in-tanzania/#:~:text=Financial%20technology%20(fintech)%20has%20been [Accessed 13 August 2020].

Agur, I., Peria, S.M. and Rochon, C. (2020). Digital Financial Services and the Pandemic: Opportunities and Risks for Emerging and Developing Economies, IMF COVID-19 Special. Available at: https://webcache.googleusercontent.com/search?q=cache:GUi J8iw2HIsJ:https://www.imf.org/~/media/Files/Publications/covid19-special-notes/en-special-series-on-covid-19-digital-financial-services-and-the-pandemic. ashx+&cd=1&hl=en&ct=clnk&gl=my [Accessed 19 October 2020].

Aldaya, F.M. (2020). COVID Spurs Greater Fintech Use in Mexico, but Financial Inclusion Lags. Available at: https://www.spglobal.com/marketintelligence/en/

news-insights/latest-news-headlines/covid-spurs-greater-fintech-use-in-mexico-but-financial-inclusion-lags-58871441 [Accessed 15 October 2020].

Alliance for Financial Inclusion (2019). Policy Framework for Women's Financial Inclusion Using Digital Financial Services. Alliance for Financial Inclusion. Available at: https://www.afi-global.org/sites/default/files/publications/2019-09/AFI_DFS_Women%20FI_AW_25.09.19_digital.pdf [Accessed 28 August 2020].

Alliance for Financial Inclusion (2020a). General FI. Available at: https://www.afi-global.org/policy-areas/general-fi [Accessed 30 October 2020].

Alliance for Financial Inclusion (2020b). Policy Model on Consumer Protection for Digital Financial Services. Alliance for Financial Inclusion. Available at: https://www.afi-global.org/sites/default/files/publications/2020-10/AFI_CEMC%2BDFS_PM_AW2_digital.pdf [Accessed 20 October 2020].

Alliance for Financial Inclusion (2020c). A Quick Guide to the Maya Declaration on Financial Inclusion. Available at: https://www.afi-global.org/sites/default/files/publications/afi_maya_quick_guide_withoutannex_i_and_ii.pdf [Accessed 16 October 2020].

Alliance for Financial Inclusion (2020d). FinTech for Financial Inclusion; Enabling FinTech Regulation in Emerging & Developing Countries. Available at: https://www.afi-global.org/fintech-financial-inclusion [Accessed 10 August 2020].

Alliance for Financial Inclusion (2020e). Maya Declaration. Alliance for Financial Inclusion. Available at: https://www.afi-global.org/maya-declaration [Accessed 10 September 2020].

Arner, D., Barberis, J. and Buckley, R. (2017). FinTech, RegTech, and the Reconceptualization of Financial Regulation. *Northwestern Journal of International Law & Business*. Available at: https://scholarlycommons.law.northwestern.edu/cgi/viewcontent.cgi?article=1817&context=njilb [Accessed 3 September 2019].

Arner, D.W., Buckley, R.P., Zetzsche, D.A., Newnham, R. and Mohammad, A.G. (2018). FinTech for Financial Inclusion: A Framework for Digital Financial Transformation. Malaysia: Alliance for Financial Inclusion, pp. 1–28. Available at: https://www.afi-global.org/publications/2844/FinTech-for-Financial-Inclusion-A-Framework-for-Digital-Financial-Transformation [Accessed 2 August 2020].

Baur-Yazbeck, S. (2018). 4 Cyber Attacks That Threaten Financial Inclusion. Consultative Group to Assist the Poor. Available at: https://www.cgap.org/blog/4-cyber-attacks-threaten-financial-inclusion [Accessed 18 October 2020].

Buch, C. (2019). Digitalization, Competition, and Financial Stability. Bank of International Settlement. Deutsche Bundesbank Eurosystem. Available at: https://www.bis.org/review/r190820a.pdf [Accessed 20 October 2020].

Cho, W.H., Lee, H.I. and Han, H. (2020). Fintech Korea. Global Legal Insights. Available at: https://www.globallegalinsights.com/practice-areas/fintech-laws-and-regulations/korea [Accessed 14 October 2020].

Crisanto, J. and Prenio, J. (2020). Financial Crime in Times of Covid-19- AML and Cyber Resilience Measures. Bank of International Settlement. Bank of International Settlement. Available at: https://www.bis.org/fsi/fsibriefs7.pdf [Accessed 22 October 2020].

Duran, K.P. and Tupaz, E.F. (2020). Regulatory Sandboxes: Initiatives for Innovation and Inclusion in the Philippines. Available at: https://www.jurist.org/commentary/2020/09/duran-tupaz-regulatory-innovation-philippines/#:~:text=To%20incentivize%20innovation%20in%20the [Accessed 30 October 2020].

Ehrentraud, J. and Ocampo, D. (2020). Policy Responses to Fintech: A Cross-Country Overview. Bank for International Settlements. Available at: https://www.bis.org/fsi/publ/insights23.pdf [Accessed 16 September 2020].

Eriksson von Allmen, U., Khera, P., Ogawa, S. and Sahay, R. (2020). Digital Financial Inclusion in the Times of COVID-19. International Monetary Fund Blog. Available at: https://blogs.imf.org/2020/07/01/digital-financial-inclusion-in-the-times-of-covid-19/ [Accessed 14 October 2020].

Eshraghi, A. (2019). Fintech and the Future of Finance. TedTalks. Available at: https://www.youtube.com/watch?v=DiWyf_RtIYM&ab_channel=TEDxTalks [Accessed 20 August 2020].

FinSMEs (2020). How the Pandemic Helps Advance Financial Inclusiveness. FinSMEs. Available at: https://www.finsmes.com/2020/07/how-the-pandemic-helps-advance-financial-inclusiveness.html [Accessed 27 August 2020].

Fintech News Malaysia (2020). BNM Director Suhaimi Ali Explains Fintech Regulation in Malaysia. Fintech News Malaysia. Available at: https://fintechnews.my/24573/various/bnm-director-suhaimi-ali-explains-fintech-regulation-in-malaysia/ [Accessed 2 September 2020].

Fintechnews Singapore (2020). 7 Fintechs in South East Asia That's Making Financial Inclusion Its Mission. Fintech Singapore. Available at: https://fintechnews.sg/40762/financial-inclusion/7-fintechs-in-south-east-asia-thats-making-financial-inclusion-its-mission/ [Accessed 13 August 2020].

Friedline, T., Naraharisetti, S. and Weaver, A. (2019). Digital Redlining: Poor Rural Communities' Access to Fintech and Implications for Financial Inclusion. Taylor and Francis Group. Available at: https://www.tandfonline.com/doi/full/10.1080/10875549.2019.1695162?scroll=top&needAccess=true [Accessed 22 September 2020].

Garrigues (2020). Fintech: New General Provisions Regarding APIs in Mexico. Available at: https://www.garrigues.com/en_GB/garrigues-digital/fintech-new-general-provisions-regarding-apis-mexico [Accessed 20 October 2020].

Georg, C.-P. (2018). Financial Regulation in Emerging Markets and the Rise of Fintech Companies. University of Cape Town. Available at: https://www.youtube.com/watch?v=uAHcfTjBaoo&ab_channel=UCTCILT [Accessed 15 September 2020].

Goo, J.J. and Heo, J.-Y. (2020). The Impact of the Regulatory Sandbox on the Fintech Industry, with a Discussion on the Relation between Regulatory Sandboxes and Open Innovation. *Journal of Open Innovation: Technology, Market, and Complexity*, 6(2). Available at: https://www.mdpi.com/2199-8531/6/2/43 [Accessed 12 September 2020].

Gray, A. and Leibrock, M. (2017). Fintech and Financial Stability; Exploring How Technological Innovations Could Impact the Safety & Security of Global Markets. The Depository Trust & Clearing Corporation. The Depository Trust & Clearing Corporation. Available at: https://www.dtcc.com/news/2017/october/16/dtcc-unveils-framework-for-assessing-fintechs-impact-on-financial-stability-in-new-white-paper [Accessed 14 October 2020].

Harroch, R. (2019). 10 Key Issues for Fintech Startup Companies. Forbes. Available at: https://www.forbes.com/sites/allbusiness/2019/10/12/fintech-startup-companies-key-challenges/#7d3c9e0d3e45 [Accessed 14 October 2020].

Herrera, R.B., Gonzáles, H.A.C. and Camargo, M.C. (2020). Fintech Laws and Regulations Mexico. Global Legal Insights International. Available at: https://www.globallegalinsights.com/practice-areas/fintech-laws-and-regulations/mexico#:~:text=Let%20us%20put%20this%20into [Accessed 18 October 2020].

Howat, E. (2020). What Is Fintech? Available at: https://www.fintechmagazine.com/fintech/what-fintech [Accessed 18 August 2020].

Karamousali, V. (2019). What Are Hawala Transactions and How Do They Work? Pideeco. Available at: https://pideeco.be/articles/hawala-business-compliance-meaning/ [Accessed 8 August 2020].

Koonprasert, T. and Mohammad, A.G. (2020). Creating Enabling Fintech Ecosystems: The Role of Regulators. Malaysia: Alliance for Financial Inclusion, pp. 1–32. Available at: https://www.afi-global.org/sites/default/files/publications/2020-01/AFI_FinTech_SR_AW_digital_0.pdf [Accessed 12 August 2020].

Lawrence, J. (2019). Singapore and London: FinTech Regulation Report. K & L Gates. Available at: https://www.fintechlawblog.com/2019/01/singapore-and-london-fintech-regulation-report/ [Accessed 15 September 2020].

McQuinn, A. (2019). Supporting Financial Innovation through Flexible Regulation. Information Technology & Innovation Foundation. Available at: https://itif.org/publications/2019/11/04/supporting-financial-innovation-through-flexible-regulation [Accessed 8 September 2020].

Mention, A.-L. (2019). The Future of Fintech. Research Technology Management, 62(4), pp. 59–63. Available at: https://www.tandfonline.com/doi/full/10.1080/08956308.2019.1613123 [Accessed 15 August 2020].

Miller, M., Klapper, L., Gamser, M. and Teima, G. (2020). How Can Digital Financial Services Help a World Coping with COVID-19? World Bank Blogs. Available at: https://blogs.worldbank.org/psd/how-can-digital-financial-services-help-world-coping-covid-19 [Accessed 13 October 2020].

Monetary Authority of Singapore (2020). Fintech and Innovation Group. Available at: https://www.mas.gov.sg/who-we-are/Organisation-Structure/Fintech-and-Innovation [Accessed 13 August 2020].

Nicoletti, B. (2017). The Future of FinTech. Cham Springer International Publishing. Available at: https://link.springer.com/book/10.1007%2F978-3-319-51415-4 [Accessed 15 August 2020].

Pazarbasioglu, C., Mora, A., Uttamchandani, M., Natarajan, H., Feyen, E. and Saal, M. (2020). Digital Financial Services. Available at: http://pubdocs.worldbank.org/en/230281588169110691/Digital-Financial-Services.pdf [Accessed 25 September 2020].

Phillips, M. (2019). The Evolution of Fraud and Security - Is It a Numbers Game or Can It Be Calculated? Finextra Research. Available at: https://www.finextra.com/blogposting/18021/the-evolution-of-fraud-and-security---is-it-a-numbers-game-or-can-it-be-calculated [Accessed 29 October 2020].

Restoy, F. (2019). Regulating Fintech: What Is Going on and Where Are the Challenges? Chairman, Financial Stability Institute, Bank for International Settlements ASBA-BID-FELABAN XVI Banking Public-Private Sector Regional Policy Dialogue "Challenges and Opportunities in the New Financial Ecosystem". Available at: https://www.bis.org/speeches/sp191017a.pdf [Accessed 13 August 2020].

Sahay, R., Eriksson von Allmen, U., Lahreche, A., Khera, P., Ogawa, S., Bazarbash, M. and Beaton, K. (2020). The Promise of Fintech: Financial Inclusion in the Post COVID-19 Era. International Monetary Fund, No. 20/09. Available at: https://www.imf.org/en/Publications/Departmental-Papers-Policy-Papers/Issues/2020/06/29/The-Promise-of-Fintech-Financial-Inclusion-in-the-Post-COVID-19-Era-48623 [Accessed 20 September 2020].

Scott, A.P. (2020). Fintech: Overview of Financial Regulators and Recent Policy Approaches. Congressional Research Service. Available at: https://fas.org/sgp/crs/misc/R46333.pdf [Accessed 16 August 2020].

Serna, R. (2020). Why Smart Regulation Leads to Fintech Innovation. Forbes. Available at: https://www.forbes.com/sites/forbestechcouncil/2020/04/17/why-smart-regulation-leads-to-fintech-innovation/#3243c9aa5341 [Accessed 16 August 2020].

Singh, N. (2019). What's Hindering the Growth of Fintech Industry? Entrepreneur. Available at: https://www.entrepreneur.com/article/325714 [Accessed 16 September 2020].

The Bank for International Settlements (2020). How Fintech Can Promote Financial Inclusion - A New Report on the Opportunities and Challenges. Available at: https://www.bis.org/press/p200414.htm [Accessed 16 September 2020].

The Independent Singapore (2017). Grab Leaving Malaysia Is Kuala Lumpur's Loss to Singapore. The Independent Singapore. Available at: https://theindependent.sg/grab-leaving-malaysia-is-kuala-lumpurs-loss-to-singapore/ [Accessed 14 October 2020].

The WFE Focus Team (2017). Fintech and Financial Stability. Available at: https://focus.world-exchanges.org/articles/fintech-and-financial-stability [Accessed 13 October 2020].

The World Bank (2018). UFA2020 Overview: Universal Financial Access by 2020. The World Bank. Available at: https://www.worldbank.org/en/topic/financialinclusion/brief/achieving-universal-financial-access-by-2020 [Accessed 20 September 2020].

Ulbrich, S.E.K. (2020). Beyond Digital Banking: Closing the Service Gap through Financial Inclusion. Foundation LHoFT. Available at: https://www.lhoft.com/en/insights/beyond-digital-banking-closing-the-service-gap-through-financial-inclusion [Accessed 15 September 2020].

Valdez, Y.D., Branch, R.O. and Mainero, D.G. (2020). Mexico Issues First License under New FinTech Law. Available at: https://www.lexology.com/library/detail.aspx?g=e54d449f-c4fa-4408-b1a5-5326f3a1cdd0 [Accessed 16 August 2020].

Vučinić, M. (2020). Fintech and Financial Stability Potential Influence of FinTech on Financial Stability, Risks and Benefits. *Journal of Central Banking Theory and Practice*, 9(2), pp. 43–66. Available at: https://www.researchgate.net/profile/Milena_Vucinic_Former_Jovovic/publication/341948891_Fintech_and_Financial_Stability_Potential_Influence_of_FinTech_on_Financial_Stability_Risks_and_Benefits/links/5ede3f4492851cf138690883/Fintech-and-Financial-Stability-Potential-Influence-of-FinTech-on-Financial-Stability-Risks-and-Benefits.pdf?origin=publication_detail [Accessed 12 October 2020].

Young-sil, Y. (2019). Korea's Fintech Industry Growing at Snail's Pace. Business Korea. Available at: http://www.businesskorea.co.kr/news/articleView.html?idxno=32647#:~:text=The%20growth%20of%20the%20fintech%20industry%20in%20Korea%20is%20slower [Accessed 30 October 2020].

5 Designing social-purpose FinTech
A UK case study

Sharon Collard, Phil Gosset and Jamie Evans

1 Introduction

Magnuson (2018) defines financial technology (FinTech) as a new breed of companies that specialise in providing financial services primarily through technology-enabled mobile and online platforms. In the UK, politicians and others see FinTech as a potential solution to stubborn social problems, including how to improve people's access to financial services while at the same time increasing their financial capability and boosting their financial resilience. This chapter explores the idea of 'social-purpose FinTech' that aims to support innovative ideas for products and services that have a social purpose such as increasing financial well-being or addressing access issues which might otherwise struggle to attract commercial backing.

The first part of the chapter sets the context, providing an overview of UK government policy around access to financial services (Section 2) and considering its impact (Section 3) before outlining some of the contemporary access issues faced by people in the UK (Section 4).

The second part of the chapter starts with a brief description of financial technology or FinTech (Section 5) before looking in Section 6 at the recent emergence of 'social-purpose FinTech' initiatives in the UK. In Section 7, using qualitative data from a formative (process) evaluation of Nationwide Building Society's Open Banking for Good (OB4G) programme (Collard and Evans, 2019), we explore the use of grounded innovation as a means to ensure that social-purpose FinTech is inclusively designed from the start in order to increase its potential to meet the needs of its target audience. We set out our conclusions in Section 8.

2 UK government policy around access to financial services: a potted history

Globally, access to regulated financial services is a common feature of high-income economies and becoming more common among lower- and middle-income economies. There is, for example, near-universal account ownership[1] (94%) in high-income economies, while in low- or middle-income economies the figure is 63% (Demirgüç-Kunt et al., 2018). Since 2010, the G20 international

---

1 The 2017 Global Findex database defines account ownership as having an individual or jointly owned account either at a financial institution or through a mobile money provider.

forum (of which the UK is a member) has included financial inclusion as a key target of its Development Agenda (World Bank & OECD, 2013).

In the UK, access has been defined as the ability of people to engage with and use the financial products and services they need over their lifetime (Collard et al., 2016). Over the past 20 years, UK governments have demonstrated varying degrees of interest in, and commitment to, addressing the problems that people face accessing financial services.

The period from 1999 to the 2007 global financial crisis was arguably the heyday of financial inclusion policy in the UK. It saw successive Labour governments design policies and fund interventions to bring more people into mainstream financial services and to grow the non-profit 'responsible finance' sector which comprises credit unions and community finance development institutions (CDFIs). This led to a rapid growth in financial inclusion initiatives supported by various government departments and statutory bodies (Mitton, 2008).

Between 2010 and 2015, in the aftermath of the global financial crisis, financial inclusion was absent from the Conservative-led coalition government's agenda as it pursued its programme of ideological austerity (Alston, 2019). Efforts by campaigners to draw political attention to the access issues facing the UK around the time of the 2015 general election gained traction and by 2018 the Conservative government had established a Financial Inclusion Policy Forum that *"brings together leaders from industry, the third sector, ministers and the regulator, to ensure collaboration across government and with the sector on financial inclusion"* (HM Treasury, 2020). The forum meets twice yearly and is jointly chaired by the Economic Secretary to the Treasury (who leads the government's agenda on financial inclusion) and the Minister for Pensions and Financial Inclusion. There is, however, no UK-wide financial inclusion strategy or any official metrics to measure progress towards financial inclusion.

In 2019 the government pledged to build *"an economy where everyone, regardless of their background or income, can access the financial services and products they need"* (HM Treasury & DWP, 2019, p. 2). A new entity (Fair4AllFinance) was also established with a fund of £55 million to discharge the government's commitment to allocate dormant assets money to financial inclusion initiatives, with an initial focus on 'affordable credit'[2] (Fair4AllFinance, 2020a). In May 2020 (during the COVID-19 pandemic) it received another £65 million *"to increase access to fair, affordable and appropriate financial products and services"* (Fair4AllFinance, 2020b).

2.1 Financial inclusion in the devolved nations

The UK picture is complicated by the fact that the devolved legislatures and administrations in Scotland, Wales and Northern Ireland have had their own policies to promote financial inclusion (Kempson and Collard, 2012; Mitton, 2008), leading to calls for greater collaboration and coordination to create a cross-UK response to financial exclusion (House of Lords, 2017).

---

2 Restrictions on Fair4AllFinance's funding means it can only support credit unions and community lenders that have most of their operations and lending in England.

At the time of writing, the Welsh Government appears to be the only devolved nation with a current national strategy for financial inclusion. This strategy was published in 2016 along with a five-year delivery plan (Welsh Government, 2016a, 2016b). It focuses on affordable credit, access to financial information including debt advice, and building financial understanding and capability. While the Scottish Government does not have a current national strategy, access to affordable credit does feature in its Fairer Scotland action plan, and there have been government-backed initiatives such as the Affordable Credit Loan Fund (Scottish Government, 2019a) and the Credit Union Investment Fund (Scottish Government, 2019b). Meanwhile, Northern Ireland's financial inclusion strategy has been the responsibility of its Housing Executive, which is the public housing authority for Northern Ireland and its largest social housing landlord. Its last three-year strategy (which came to an end in 2019) focused on helping its tenants understand and respond to welfare reforms and maintain their tenancies (Housing Executive, 2016).

It is also worth noting that access to financial services forms a small part of the ten-year UK Strategy for Financial Well-being overseen by the Money and Pensions Service (MaPS, 2020). Running from 2020 to 2030, the strategy has (among other things) individual action plans for England, Scotland, Wales and Northern Ireland.

3 What has been the impact to date of policies to improve access to financial services?

Regardless of their politics, there have been two common themes in government policymaking around improving access to financial services:

- A focus on people who are financially excluded (i.e. they have serious problems accessing and/or using financial services), which is highly correlated with having a low income and so impacts heavily on people who are, for example, unemployed, unable to work through sickness or disability, single parents, social housing tenants and in African-Caribbean, Pakistani or Bangladeshi households (Bermeo and Collard, 2018; Kempson and Collard, 2012; Mitton, 2008).
- A focus on certain financial products, notably bank accounts for everyday money management plus consumer credit and (to a lesser degree) cash savings and home contents insurance which represent ways of dealing with periodic costs that might be anticipated (like Christmas) or unexpected (such as burglary or broken white goods).

While no attempt has been made to quantify the total investment in financial inclusion policy and practice, it is likely to be in excess of £408 million. The largest single injection of government funding came through the Financial Inclusion Fund, which invested £250 million in banking, credit and debt advice over the period 2004–2011; with a further government investment of £38 million to expand the credit union sector in 2012 (Barnard and Henson Grič,

2020). More recently, as noted above, £120 million was allocated to financial inclusion through the new entity Fair4AllFinance. Other major investors in financial inclusion include the Scottish Executive, Welsh Assembly Government, local authorities, housing associations, the financial services industry and charitable foundations (Kempson and Collard, 2012).

To what extent did such initiatives improve people's access to financial services? The clearest success relates to banking where the number of people without a bank account fell from 2.1 million in 1999 to 1.23 million in 2018 (HM Treasury/Department for Work and Pensions, 2019). This is largely thanks to the introduction of basic bank accounts which were designed to better suit the needs of people with modest finances, coupled with a shift by government to pay social security benefits directly into a bank or building society account rather than by order book or giro cheque (Kempson and Whyley, 2001).

Consumer credit has been another major focus of government policy, motivated by a desire to significantly scale up lower-cost alternatives to high-cost credit products like payday loans and home credit loans. While large-scale government investment certainly generated a short-term boost to lending by 'responsible finance' providers to people who might otherwise have used high-cost credit (Collard et al., 2011), this growth does not seem to have been sustained. While high-cost short-term lenders are estimated to originate loans worth £3 billion every year, the equivalent is just £250 million for 'responsible finance' providers (Fair4AllFinance, 2020b). Fair4AllFinance's stated aim is to tackle this so-called 10 times challenge.

Compared with banking and credit, efforts to encourage more people on lower incomes to put money into savings and to take out home contents insurance were relatively late additions to the UK's financial inclusion policy (Kempson and Collard, 2012). While some promising ideas were researched and tested, it has proved challenging to encourage the take-up of products that people feel they cannot afford or in which they do not perceive much utility or value (as with home contents insurance). The planned roll-out of a national matched savings scheme was cancelled in 2010 because the coalition government considered it unaffordable in the wake of the global financial crisis (see, for example, Insley, 2010). A similar scheme was, however, launched in 2018 by the Conservative government (GOV.UK, 2018a). By January 2020, 162,950 of these new Help to Save accounts had been opened (GOV.UK, 2020), representing around 5% of the 3.5 million people eligible for one. Meanwhile, despite product innovation to make home contents insurance better value-for-money for lower-income households, the number of UK households without home contents insurance has grown from 25% of the population in 1999 to 40% in 2017 (Barnard and Henson Grič, 2020).

4 What are the contemporary access issues faced by people in the UK?

While it is easy to take financial services for granted in high-income economies like the UK, a surprising number of people experience access problems that can leave them shut out of modern life. These problems come in a range of guises that arguably transcend the government's traditional approach to financial inclusion policy (described above) and potentially affect a wide range of people. For example:

- 1.23 million UK adults (about 2% of the adult population) still **do not have a bank account** (HM Treasury/Department for Work and Pensions, 2019). Here, the problem can be that people do not have the typical standard documents (a passport or driving licence) used by banks to verify identity (Collard et al., 2016).
- 3.1 million UK adults (about 6% of the adult population) **have used high-cost credit** in the past year (Financial Conduct Authority, 2017). Here, people may struggle to satisfy the automated decision-making processes that might enable them to access lower-cost credit because they have a 'thin' credit record or they can't easily verify their personal details (e.g. if they move home often) (Collard et al., 2016).
- Five million UK adults (about 10% of the adult population) **are in low-paid and insecure work** (Martin, 2019). Varied and irregular income can make it difficult to meet regular fixed monthly bills, like rent or utilities. This in turn can lead to a cycle of borrowing money to pay fixed costs in leaner months.
- 12.3 million UK adults (almost a quarter of all adults) **do not feel confident about financial matters**, which means they may stick with brands they know even if they could get a better deal elsewhere and might be a factor in the low numbers of people with insurance, protection and pension products (Financial Conduct Authority, 2017).
- As banking and financial services continue to move online, digital connection has become a significant access issue. For example, while 90% of UK adults **used the internet** in 2018, this falls to 67% among people with a disability. The gap in **smartphone use** is even bigger, with 78% of UK adults saying they personally use a smartphone compared with **just 45% of adults with a disability** (Ofcom, 2019)

At a personal level, the implications of access issues are serious in an economy where individuals and households are increasingly expected to take responsibility for their own financial well-being (Collard et al., 2016; Kempson et al., 2000). From a macroeconomic perspective, access to regulated financial services is also considered important to financial stability and market integrity (Bholat, Kowalski and Milward, 2016; Mehrotra and Yetman, 2015). Greater use of formal savings and credit products, for example, is likely to increase the effectiveness of interest rates as it expands the number of people directly affected by monetary policy (Bholat, Kowalski and Milward, 2016; Mehrotra and Yetman, 2015). At the same time, greater financial inclusion could potentially disrupt the stability of a financial system if it results from rapid consumer credit growth and excessive risk-taking by lenders (Bholat, Kowalski and Milward, 2016) or if relatively unregulated parts of the financial system grow quickly (Mehrotra and Yetman, 2015).

Designing social-purpose FinTech 69

The ongoing problems that people face accessing financial services in the UK combined with halting progress in financial inclusion policy (as discussed earlier) have prompted policymakers to consider new approaches to making the UK more financially inclusive, most notably in the shape of financial technology (FinTech). The UK government is a fervent supporter of FinTech in general but also sees it as an innovative way to improve access to financial services. In a 2018 speech, the Conservative City Minister stated that *"Fintech has enormous potential to transform financial inclusion through the democratic power of information and universal connectivity"* (GOV.UK, 2018b). A later government report also situated FinTech as something that *"offers opportunities for firms to develop innovative ways to increase consumer access to and use of financial services, delivering big benefits such as lower prices, increased choice, and better service to all, including the disadvantaged and vulnerable"* (HM Treasury/Department for Work and Pensions, 2019, p. 14).

Below we provide a brief description of FinTech before looking at social-purpose FinTech initiatives in the UK that support innovative ideas for products and services that have a social purpose, such as increasing financial well-being or addressing access issues.

5 What is financial technology (FinTech)?

Magnuson (2018) defines financial technology (FinTech) as a new breed of companies that specialise in providing financial services primarily through technology-enabled mobile and online platforms. The UK is seen as a global FinTech leader, with around 1,600 FinTech firms in 2019 and USD 20.7 billion investment in UK FinTech, which represents over half of total FinTech investment across Europe (Department for International Trade, 2019).

Consumer adoption of FinTech services (such as digital-only bank accounts, payment services, budgeting and financial planning, savings and investments) rose from 42% of the UK's digitally active population[3] in 2017 to 71% of its digitally active population in 2019 (EY, 2019). This increase was largely driven by more incumbent banks and financial services firms starting to offer FinTech products and services (rather different to the new breed of firms envisaged by Magnuson). A new generation of open banking products and services – conceived by UK regulators as a way to disrupt anti-competitive behaviour among the big banks – is powered by financial technology that allows consumers to securely share their bank transaction data with third-party providers that use it to provide personalised financial services (see, for example, Leong and Gardner, 2020; Reynolds and Chidley, 2019).

FinTech has been widely lauded – including by the UK government – as a potentially transformative force that will positively disrupt the 'old world' of financial services for the benefit of consumers. While consumer advocates cautiously

---

3 EY defined its survey respondents as 'digitally active' because they completed the survey online.

agree there may be some consumer benefits, they are concerned about the potential risks and harms to consumers. At a product level, some of their key concerns are around automated and data-driven 'black box' processes for risk profiling and personalised pricing that can result in discrimination and exclusion (BEUC, 2017; Financial Inclusion Centre, 2018; Financial Services Consumer Panel, 2017, 2018a, 2019; Klein, 2020). In the US, for example, there is evidence that the use of education data in credit underwriting could reinforce systemic barriers to financial inclusion for Black and Latinx consumers (Student Borrower Protection Center, 2020). There are also fears about business models that rely heavily on the monetisation of data that are shared by consumers who consent to the use of such data without knowing their value or how they are traded (Financial Inclusion Centre, 2018; Financial Services Consumer Panel 2018b; Reynolds, 2017). At a regulatory level, there are concerns that consumers will find it difficult to exercise their rights and get redress because of opaque automated decision-making processes or where consumer protection is split across multiple regulators (BEUC, 2017; Financial Inclusion Centre, 2018; Reynolds, 2017).

6 Social-purpose FinTech initiatives

A lot of financial technology innovation is business-to-business rather than business-to-consumer (see, for example, CB Insights, 2018). Where consumers are the target audience, the focus is usually the better-off, a good example being wealth management FinTech.

In efforts to promote more inclusive consumer FinTech, recent years have seen the emergence of 'social-purpose FinTech' initiatives in the UK funded by government and others. These initiatives aim to support innovative ideas for products and services that have a social purpose, such as increasing financial well-being or addressing access issues which might otherwise struggle to attract commercial backing. While carried out behind closed doors, there is a tacit assumption that the due diligence performed by funders weeds out any business models or business practices that are potentially harmful or exploitative.

The UK's social-purpose FinTech initiatives take different forms, including government-backed challenge funds, social investment and public-private innovation partnerships.

6.1 Government-backed challenge funds

The UK government-backed challenge funds generally offer grant funding for innovators to develop new ideas, plus a prize fund for the winners. They may also offer in-kind support such as pro bono legal advice or office space. The Rent Recognition Challenge, for example, was launched in 2017 with a focus on helping renters boost their credit score. This competition saw six start-ups or entrepreneurs receive grant funding to develop their ideas into workable products. The three eventual winners of the challenge shared a prize fund of £2 million designed to help them scale their products (GOV.UK, 2018c).

A subsequent Affordable Credit Challenge was designed to increase access to affordable, responsible credit. Three partnerships between community lenders and FinTechs secured a cash prize of £200,000 each (NESTA, 2020).

6.2 Social investment

Social investment is the use of repayable finance to help an organisation achieve a social purpose (Good Finance, no date). Financed by grant funding and social investment from several partners, the Fair by Design Fund is a social investor that provides loans and equity funding to start-up businesses that aim to tackle the extra costs (or Poverty Premium) paid by people on lower incomes. Some of the ventures supported by the Fair by Design Fund address specific access problems, such as a challenger credit bureau that aims to assess people's creditworthiness in a fairer way, and a FinTech that offers earnings drawdown to employees to reduce their need for high-cost credit (Fair By Design, 2019).

6.3 Public-private innovation partnerships

Public-private innovation partnerships offer a third model of supporting social-purpose FinTech, of which our case study OB4G is an example.

OB4G was a £3 million two-year programme funded and led by Nationwide Building Society with support from Accenture (which runs the London Fintech Innovation Lab), doteveryone (a responsible technology think tank that operated from 2015 to 2020) and the innovation charity NESTA. It was part of the government's Inclusive Economy Partnership (IEP), which brings together businesses, civil society and government departments *"to solve some of society's toughest challenges, to help all communities and everyone within them feel they belong to and can participate in the UK economy"* (HM Government, no date). The Chief Executive of Nationwide Building Society was on the IEP Advisory Board and co-chair of its Financial Inclusion and Capability flagship challenge (of which OB4G is one initiative).

As we go on to explore in Section 7, a novel feature of OB4G is its grounded innovation approach which aimed to ensure that social-purpose FinTech was inclusively designed from the start in order to increase its potential to meet the needs of its target audience.

7 Open banking for good: a case study of inclusively designed social-purpose FinTech

Our case study of Open Banking for Good (OB4G) draws on a formative (or process) evaluation that was carried out between January and July 2019, funded by Nationwide Building Society (Collard and Evans, 2019). The purpose of the evaluation was to capture learning about the programme's design and early implementation, primarily through qualitative research with the different actors that participated in the programme.

In this case study, we focus specifically on OB4G's use of grounded innovation as a means to ensure that social-purpose FinTech is inclusively designed from the start in order to increase its potential to meet the needs of its target audience. Our purpose is to help build an evidence base on this issue where there has been a lot of interest but little in the way of independent evaluation or published information about how these processes work in practice.

We start with a brief description of the OB4G programme, before considering its conceptual foundation in the idea of grounded innovation. We then look at how grounded innovation was operationalised in the OB4G programme and the lessons it offers for the future.

7.1 OB4G: an overview

The OB4G programme aimed to create and scale open banking-enabled apps and services in order to help the one in four UK working-age adults (roughly 12.7 million people) who are *'financially squeezed'*, who tend to be in full-time work but have significant financial commitments and little provision to cope with income shocks (CACI, 2016). OB4G focused on three challenges that experts agreed were pressing issues for the *'financially squeezed'* and which resonate with the contemporary access issues described in Section 4:

- Helping the growing number of people who have irregular or unpredictable income to manage their regular outgoings
- Making it easier for someone to produce an accurate statement of their income and expenditure
- Helping people to practice and maintain good money habits.

In October 2018, Nationwide invited applications to OB4G for innovative products to tackle these three challenges. Although the competition was open to any individual or organisation, most of the 39 applicants and all seven successful applicants were FinTechs.

The successful applicants received funding and support from Nationwide to develop and test their ideas and prototypes. They were also assigned a charity partner that could bring the user perspective into the innovation process through collaborative working and co-creation. Three of the four charity partners were organisations that delivered advice and guidance services to people likely to be *'financially squeezed'*, while the fourth conducted research and advocacy around money and mental health. Our evaluation data show that, for OB4G applicants, collaborating with charity partners was an attractive feature of the programme; constructive engagement with charity partners was also a contractual condition of staying in the programme.

7.2 Grounded innovation: a conceptual foundation

Grounded innovation describes an approach that uses innovation to solve real and grounded challenges (Holmquist, 2012), where 'real' means evidenced challenges that exist and 'grounded' means involving both experts that understand the challenge and users that regularly face it. This approach then seeks to develop and deploy solutions to such challenges. It is in marked contrast with the more commonly considered approach of using innovation as a way of encouraging blue-sky thinking to 'invent the future' which risks innovators having to justify their work by retrospectively inventing challenges that their innovative solution can solve. The distance between these invented challenges and the real, day-to-day challenges that people face means that such solutions rarely land successfully or do not have any impact.

Grounded innovation as used within the OB4G programme grew out of an approach developed within the cross-disciplinary Socio-Digital Systems (later Human Experience and Design) group at Microsoft Research under Professors Abigail Sellen and Richard Harper[4] who specialise in Human-Computer Interaction (see, for example, Ylirisku et al., 2016). As well as computer scientists, Microsoft's Socio-Digital Systems group comprised social scientists (to ensure the work was always built on deep insight into the challenges, desires and needs of real people) and designers (to ensure the solutions were well thought through and appropriately usable).

At a high level, grounded innovation is the process whereby user experts, solution experts and process experts are brought together to form an agile team to solve a specific challenge. The process is composed of two main phases. The first phase, Explore, is an exploration of the challenge such that both the user and solution experts develop their understanding of the challenge and what good looks like in the solution space through a process of co-creation. The output of this phase is a prototype solution that meets the challenge and is scalable, usable and affordable. The second phase, Build, is one where the solution experts instantiate the prototype and build out the solution, constantly testing the solution with the user experts. This approach minimises the risk of failing while maximising the utility of the solution as the suitability and viability of the solution is constantly tested.

This approach to grounded innovation promotes learning while minimising the pressure of rushing towards a solution, which are both important factors in successful innovation (Holmquist, 2012). The process engenders collaborative, mutual learning because the experts co-create the solution. By contrast, in a purely competitive environment, the ideas that are submitted at the start have little opportunity to evolve through input from the experts across the development cycle, with the user experts often only consulted during the testing phase at the end. The grounded innovation approach clearly allows the solution experts to learn about the challenge space, whilst the user experts also learn about the solution space and possible approaches. To allow the experts to spend time learning also requires them to be supported throughout the process.

---

4 Dr Phil Gosset was an Innovation Consultant with Microsoft Research's Socio-Digital Systems/Human Experience and Design group between 2006 and 2016.

7.3 How was grounded innovation operationalised in the OB4G programme?

From our evaluation data, we identify three ways in which grounded innovation was operationalised in the OB4G programme:

- It tackled real and grounded challenges
- It created time and space for innovation
- It fostered collaborative learning through a process of co-creation.

We describe each of these in the following sections and look at how they worked in practice. It is worth noting that six smaller, start-up FinTechs in the OB4G programme were allocated to an 'Explore and Develop' pathway (roughly equivalent to the 'Explore' phase described in Section 7.2) that provided three months funding to work up early-stage ideas and concepts. The seventh FinTech in the programme (which was larger and already well-established) was allocated to an 'Accelerate' pathway (roughly equivalent to the 'Build' phase described in Section 7.2) that provided six months funding to develop and test a viable concept.

7.3.1 Real and grounded challenges

The crux of grounded innovation is to bring together user experts, solution experts and process experts to solve real and grounded challenges. In keeping with this, the OB4G programme sought to ensure that it tackled real and grounded challenges faced by its target audience of working-age adults who are *'financially squeezed'*.

To do this, prior to the official launch of the programme Nationwide's three-person OB4G team (who in grounded innovation terms were the process experts) 'leaned in' to relationships with charities and other external stakeholders that are already existing across the building society, to ask them the question, *'what are the key problems that people face when they are "financially squeezed"?'* These relationships included charities locally where Nationwide staff worked as volunteers; Nationwide's corporate charity partners; and professional links with money and debt charities that had been built over several years.

There were conversations with a wide range of charities (around 18 in total), research organisations and academics which generated a long list of diverse potential use cases for the OB4G programme. From this long list, the OB4G team provisionally shortlisted three challenges (described in Section 7.1) on the basis that:

- The use case focused on people who were *'financially squeezed'*
- It was a challenge where open banking financial technology could make a difference
- The challenges were not solely about managing debt problems (i.e. crisis intervention) but also helped people to develop and maintain good money habits.

Designing social-purpose FinTech 75

Consistent with a grounded innovation approach, the OB4G team went back to the same charities (in their capacity as user experts) in a second round of engagement to discuss the three short-listed challenges. Their feedback was positive and supportive, and so the three challenges were taken forward. From the perspective of FinTechs who participated in the programme (who in grounded innovation terms were the solution experts), framing OB4G around three real challenges created an *'innovation cage'*[5] (in the words of one FinTech) where they could work to address well-defined problems for a specific target audience. These innovative boundaries, it was felt, helped keep the FinTechs focused on the social purpose of OB4G.

7.3.2 Creating time and space for innovation

Unlike in a competitive environment, a grounded innovation approach means that innovators are given time and space to gain a deep understanding of the problem they want to solve and to ideate possible solutions. In OB4G, this was achieved primarily in the way the programme funded its successful applicants. In the minds of the FinTech participants, OB4G stood out from other initiatives (such as FinTech accelerator or incubator programmes)[6] because it offered *'money on the table'* for them to research, design and develop their own propositions rather than, say, taking an equity stake in the business or offering a cash prize. As one FinTech interviewee described:

> the financial freedom for a start-up like us was massive, right, the kind of sums of money that we were talking about with OB4G were things that really allowed us to do a lot.

This funding model meant the FinTechs had a *"safe environment for ideas"* that were socially innovative rather than having to pivot their propositions to what funders or potential investors wanted, with the risk of diluting their social purpose for short-term commercial gain. As one charity partner interviewee commented:

> What sets it apart, it's kind of led by the social value as opposed to it being added on.

OB4G was also unusual because the successful applicants retained ownership of their pre-existing intellectual property (IP),[7] together with any IP they created in the programme.

---

5 Italic phrases in parentheses are verbatim quotes from evaluation participants.
6 For an explanation about these programmes see, for example, Forrest, 2018.
7 Intellectual property is a term used in property law. It concerns the ownership of an idea or design by the person who came up with it. It gives that person certain exclusive rights meaning that nobody else can copy or reuse that creation without the owner's permission.

7.3.3 Collaborative learning through a process of co-creation

Grounded innovation is intended to engender collaborative, mutual learning because the user experts (i.e. charity partners), process experts (i.e. Nationwide's OB4G team) and solution experts (i.e. FinTechs in the programme) co-create a solution. With its origins in business strategy, co-creation is defined as the active involvement of end-users in various stages of the production process in order to create value (Prahalad and Ramaswamy, 2000). In the words of one successful OB4G applicant, this co-creation approach helped overcome the risk of "*hipsters designing for hipsters.*"

Our evaluation data show that, for Nationwide's OB4G team, the aim of co-creation was to bring together user experts (i.e. charity partners) and FinTech firms to work collaboratively in teams, in order to break down powerful sectoral barriers they felt hampered co-creation. They wanted charity partners to be in the driving seat rather than a 'tick box' to be checked at the end of the development process. In turn, they saw themselves as translators and navigators between the FinTechs and the charity partners to make sure this co-creation happened.

For the FinTechs, one of the attractions of OB4G was the opportunity to have an allocated charity partner. The main benefit from their perspective was to gain deep insight into the '*financially squeezed*' population from their charity partner and potentially broker access to members of the target audience to participate in user research and testing.

For charity partners, two common points of differentiation set OB4G apart from their other interactions with the FinTech sector. First, the OB4G team brought charity partners "*in on the ground floor*" at the programme's conception in order to shape it and help select the successful applicants, as well as work with successful applicants over the life of the programme. Second, as an integral part of the programme, charity partners felt valued as experts, which was reinforced by their close involvement in the design (and in some cases testing) of the FinTech's propositions. As one charity partner interviewee described it:

> we're really at the heart of it, at the pivotal moment rather than being like an add on expert interview at the side, that's when we're able to have the biggest impact with the time that we've got.

Examples of co-creation activities in the early phase of OB4G included 'discovery meetings' between the FinTechs and their charity partners; the FinTechs visiting advice helplines run by charity partners to listen to incoming calls and develop a deeper understand of the money and other issues faced by people who are '*financially squeezed*'; and charity partners providing feedback on prototype products and services.

7.4 Lessons for the future

Our evaluation data indicate that, overall, the grounded innovation approach to OB4G achieved its aims and generated valuable collaborative learning through co-creation, which shaped the products and services developed by the FinTech participants. By working with charity partners, the FinTechs were better able to empathise with the target audience and define and ideate around the challenges to produce socially useful concepts and prototypes. The evaluation highlighted that, among charity partners that delivered services to the public, it was useful to have both operations and policy people involved in co-creation activities.

For the charity partners, a grounded innovation approach meant they gained a valuable close-up view of FinTech design and development and its potential benefit to their organisations and service users and gave them the knowledge and confidence to engage with the FinTech sector on a more equal footing, which they felt would foster better-quality conversations and discussions. As one charity partner commented:

> [OB4G is] something tangible that we could use to actually gain a bit more of an organisational knowledge about open banking for ourselves.

From the perspective of the FinTechs and charity partners, Nationwide's OB4G team was *"pivotal"* to the co-creation process. Between them, the OB4G team members were felt to bring experience, commitment, responsiveness and an enabling, innovative mentality. They worked to ensure that user experts were at the heart of OB4G from the very beginning. Once the programme launched, the team acted as facilitators, translators and navigators between the FinTechs and the charity partners, which had very different ways of working.

Indeed, a key learning from the evaluation is how different ways of working among the co-creation partners must be recognised, taken account of and accommodated, within this type of programme. Three examples of this in OB4G relate to organisational remit, resource and access to data and user testers.

7.4.1 Organisational remit

Under pressure to attract investment, FinTech firms are incentivised to rapidly develop and test ideas and prototypes to come up with a viable product. Used to this way of working, OB4G FinTechs were keen to collaborate with their charity partners as soon as the programme got underway. By contrast, charities work to a tightly defined remit to which they are held accountable by trustees and regulators. This can circumscribe the ways in which they work with commercial organisations – something which some charity partners had to work through before they could collaborate with their FinTech partners in the OB4G programme.

7.4.2 Resource

Charity partners had limited resources to devote to the OB4G programme. With no real capacity to increase those resources in the short term, it was a case of them fitting OB4G co-creation activities around their 'day jobs'. Some charity partners requested (and received) funding from Nationwide, which meant they could dedicate proper resource to OB4G. Others did not request funding (possibly due to their charity's governing rules around funding).

Issues with organisational remit and resource meant that the start of the co-creation process was delayed. As the programme got into its stride, Nationwide's OB4G team helped manage the FinTech participants' expectations around the capacity of their allocated charity partners. In some cases, the team brokered contact between FinTechs and other charity partners that had more capacity.

7.4.3 Access to data and user testers

The early co-creation activities with their charity partners– such as discovery meetings, call listening with frontline advisers, and prototype feedback – gave FinTechs valuable 'big picture' insights that informed their ideation and prototype design.

Charity partners were less able to help their FinTech partners with detailed and specific questions around their propositions, which really required user research with the target audience. It was generally not possible for FinTechs to have access to charity partners' service users as research participants and user testers, for example due to issues around client consent to share their details with the FinTechs.

Creative workarounds to get user views included testing prototypes with charity partner volunteers and associates (where they shared characteristics with the target audience); linking FinTechs with charity partners other than the one they had originally been allocated; and talking to other charities about getting their workers and/or clients involved in user testing. FinTechs also recruited user testers themselves in a variety of ways, such as via professional recruiters or their own networks.

8 Conclusion

In the UK, politicians and others see FinTech as a potential way to improve people's access to financial services, which is important in an economy where individuals and households are increasingly expected to take responsibility for their own financial well-being.

Using Nationwide Building Society's OB4G programme as a case study, this chapter has demonstrated the potential to use a grounded innovation approach as a means to ensure that social-purpose FinTech is inclusively designed from the start in order to increase its potential to meet the needs of its target audience. Put simply, we have shown how a grounded innovation approach that facilitates collaborative learning through co-design can help overcome the risk of "*hipsters designing for hipsters*," a model that will almost inevitably fail to address the real, day-to-day challenges that people face.

The chapter also makes a valuable contribution to knowledge by drawing out lessons for the future application of grounded innovation to stubborn social problems. It highlights how funding can be designed to create time and space for innovation and the importance of properly resourcing the input of user experts (in the case of OB4G, the charity partners). It also underlines the crucial role of process experts (i.e. Nationwide's OB4G team) to act as facilitators, translators and navigators especially where the other expert partners have very different organisational remits and ways of working.

References

Alston, P., 2019. *Visit to the United Kingdom of Great Britain and Northern Ireland. Report of the Special Rapporteur on Extreme Poverty and Human Rights.* [pdf] Available at https://digitallibrary.un.org/record/3806308?ln=en [Accessed 18 June 2020].

Barnard, B. and Henson Grič, J., 2020. *FinTech for All.* [pdf] Available at https://policyexchange.org.uk/wp-content/uploads/Fintech-for-All.pdf [Accessed 19 June 2020].

Bermeo, E. and Collard, S., 2018. Women and High Cost Credit: A Gender Analysis of the Home Credit Industry in the UK. *Women's Studies International Forum*, 71, pp. 85–94.

BEUC, 2017. *Fintech: A More Competitive and Innovative European Financial Sector. BEUC Response to Commission Consultation.* [pdf] Available at http://www.beuc.eu/publications/beuc-x-2017-073_fintech_a_more_competitive_and_innovative_eu_financial_sector.pdf [Accessed 24 June 2020].

Bholat, D., Kowalski, J. and Milward, S., 2016. *Financial Inclusion and Central Banks.* [online] Available at https://blogs.lse.ac.uk/ipa/2016/02/11/1341/ [Accessed 2 September 2020].

CACI, 2016. *Market Segmentation: An Overview.* [pdf] Available at https://masassets.blob.core.windows.net/cms/files/000/000/568/original/Market_Segmentation_report_An_overview.PDF [Accessed 7 April 2021].

CB Insights, 2018. *The Fintech 250: The Top Fintech Startups of 2018.* [online] Available at https://www.cbinsights.com/research/fintech-250-startups-most-promising/ [Accessed 25 June 2020].

Collard, S., Coppack, M., Lowe, J. and Sarkar, S., 2016. *Access to Financial Services. FCA Occasional Paper 17.* [pdf] Available at https://www.fca.org.uk/publication/occasional-papers/occasional-paper-17.pdf [Accessed 16 June 2020].

Collard, S. and Evans, J., 2019. *Open Banking for Good: Moving the Dial?* [pdf] Available at https://static1.squarespace.com/static/5b3b35d95b409b6cfd1c9ad6/t/5dfb93a26bc56420bffec1d8/1576768422751/Moving-the-dial+PFRC+evaluation.pdf [Accessed 25 June 2020].

Collard, S., Hale, C. and Day, L., 2011. *Evaluation of the DWP Growth Fund.* [pdf] Available at http://www.bris.ac.uk/geography/research/pfrc/themes/finexc/growth-fund.html [Accessed 22 June 2020].

Department for International Trade, 2019. *UK FinTech. State of the Nation.* [pdf] Available at https://assets.publishing.service.gov.uk/government/uploads/system/uploads/attachment_data/file/801277/UK-fintech-state-of-the-nation.pdf [Accessed 17 June 2020].

Demirgüç-Kunt, A., Klapper, L., Singer, D., Ansar, S. and Hess. J., 2018. *The Global Findex Database 2017: Measuring Financial Inclusion and the Fintech Revolution.* [pdf] Available at https://openknowledge.worldbank.org/handle/10986/29510 [Accessed 16 June 2020].

EY, 2019. *Global FinTech Adoption Index 2019*. [pdf] Available at https://www.ey.com/en_gl/ey-global-fintech-adoption-index [Accessed 17 June 2020].

Fair4AllFinance, 2020a. *About Us*. [online] Available at https://fair4allfinance.org.uk/about-fair4all/ [Accessed 18 June 2020].

Fair4AllFinance, 2020b. *£65 Million in Dormant Assets Funding Released to Fair4All Finance to Scale Access to Fair, Affordable and Appropriate Financial Products and Services*. [online] Available at https://fair4allfinance.org.uk/news/65-million-dormant-assets-released/ [Accessed 19 June 2020].

Fair by Design, 2019. Fair by Design Portfolio. [online] Available at https://fairbydesign.com/latest-fund-investments/ [Accessed 25 June 2020].

Financial Conduct Authority, 2017. *Understanding the Financial Lives of UK Adults. Findings from the FCA's Financial Lives Survey 2017.* [pdf] Available at http://www.fca.org.uk/publication/research/financial-lives-survey-2017.pdf [Accessed 16 June 2020].

Financial Inclusion Centre, 2018. *Fintech –Beware of 'Geeks' Bearing Gifts?* [pdf] Available at http://inclusioncentre.co.uk/wordpress29/wp-content/uploads/2018/01/Fintech-Beware-of-geeks-bearing-gifts-FIC-Discussion-Paper-Summary.pdf [Accessed 24 June 2020].

Financial Services Consumer Panel, 2017. *Financial Services Consumer Panel's Response to the European Commission Consultation on FinTech*. [pdf] https://www.fs-cp.org.uk/sites/default/files/fscp_fintech_consultation_response.pdf [Accessed 24 June 2020].

Financial Services Consumer Panel, 2018a. *Financial Services Consumer Panel (The Panel) Response to the Treasury Committee Inquiry on Consumers' Access to Financial Services*. [pdf] Available at https://www.fs-cp.org.uk/sites/default/files/fscp_treasury_committee_response_to_access_to_financial_services_final_20181214.docx_.pdf [Accessed 24 June 2020].

Financial Services Consumer Panel, 2018b. *Consenting Adults? Consumers Sharing Their Financial Data*. [pdf] Available at https://www.fs-cp.org.uk/sites/default/files/final_position_paper_-_consenting_adults_-_20180419_0.pdf [Accessed 3 September 2020].

Financial Services Consumer Panel, 2019. *GC 19/3 Guidance Consultation - Guidance for Firms on the Fair Treatment of Vulnerable Customers*. [pdf] Available at https://www.fs-cp.org.uk/sites/default/files/fscp_response_guidance_on_fair_treatment_of_vulnerable_customers_20191004.docx_.pdf [Accessed 24 June 2020].

Forrest, C., 2018. *Accelerators vs. Incubators: What Startups Need to Know*. [online] Available at https://www.techrepublic.com/article/accelerators-vs-incubators-what-startups-need-to-know/ [Accessed 26 June 2020].

Good Finance, no date. *What Is Social Investment?* [online] Available at https://www.goodfinance.org.uk/understanding-social-investment [Accessed 25 June 2020].

GOV.UK, 2020. *Help to Save Tables: August 2020*. [online] Available at https://assets.publishing.service.gov.uk/government/uploads/system/uploads/attachment_data/file/964749/Tables_August_2020.ods [Accessed 7 April 2020].

GOV.UK, 2018a. *Savers to Earn 50p for Every £1 Saved Thanks to Help to Save*. [press release] 12 September 2018. Available at https://www.gov.uk/government/news/savers-to-earn-50p-for-every-1-saved-thanks-to-help-to-save [Accessed 22 June 2020].

GOV.UK, 2018b. *City Minister: Innovate Finance Global Summit Speech*. [online] 19 March 2018. Available at https://www.gov.uk/government/speeches/city-minister-innovate-finance-global-summit-speech [Accessed 22 June 2020].

GOV.UK, 2018c. *Tech Firms Win Prize to Help UK's Renters onto the Housing Ladder*. [online] 15 August 2018. Available at https://www.gov.uk/government/news/tech-firms-win-prize-to-help-uks-renters-onto-the-housing-ladder [Accessed 25 June 2020].

HM Government, no date. *Inclusive Economy Partnership*. [pdf] Available at https://assets.publishing.service.gov.uk/government/uploads/system/uploads/attachment_data/file/807650/B6150-IEP-brochure-2019_v05-3-4.pdf [Accessed 26 June 2020].

HM Treasury, 2020. *Summary of Financial Inclusion Policy Forum Meetings*. [online] Available at https://www.gov.uk/government/collections/summary-of-financial-inclusion-policy-forum-meetings [Accessed 18 June 2020].

HM Treasury/Department for Work and Pensions, 2019. *Financial Inclusion Report 2018–19*. [pdf] Available at https://assets.publishing.service.gov.uk/government/uploads/system/uploads/attachment_data/file/789070/financial_inclusion_report_2018-19_web.pdf [Accessed 16 June 2020].

Holmquist, L.E., 2012. *Grounded Innovation. Strategies for Creating Digital Products*. DOI https://doi.org/10.1016/C2010-0-67726-1

House of Lords, 2017. *Tackling Financial Exclusion: A Country That Works for Everyone?* [pdf] Available at https://publications.parliament.uk/pa/ld201617/ldselect/ldfinexcl/132/132.pdf [Accessed 2 September 2020].

Housing Executive, 2016. *Financial Inclusion Strategy 2016–2019*. [pdf] Available at https://niopa.qub.ac.uk/bitstream/NIOPA/6798/1/financial_inclusion_strategy_2016-19%20%281%29.pdf [Accessed 1 September 2020].

Insley, J., 2010. Budget: Saving Scheme for Low Earners Scrapped. *The Guardian*. [online] 24 June. Available at https://www.theguardian.com/money/2010/jun/24/budget-gateway-saving-scrapped [Accessed 22 June 2020].

Kempson, E. and Collard, S., 2012. *Developing a Vision for Financial Inclusion*. [pdf] Available at http://www.bris.ac.uk/media-library/sites/geography/migrated/documents/pfrc1205.pdf [Accessed 18 June 2020].

Kempson, E. and Whyley, C., 2001. *Payment of Pensions and Benefits: A Survey of Social Security Recipients Paid by Order Book or Girocheque*. Leeds: Corporate Document Services.

Kempson, E., Whyley, C., Caskey, J. and Collard, S., 2000. *In or out? Financial Exclusion: A Literature and Research Review*. [pdf] Available at http://www.bris.ac.uk/media-library/sites/geography/migrated/documents/pfrc0002.pdf [Accessed 16 June 2020].

Klein, A., 2020. *Reducing Bias in AI Based Financial Services*. [online] Available at https://www.brookings.edu/research/reducing-bias-in-ai-based-financial-services/ [Accessed 3 September 2020].

Leong, E. and Gardner, J., 2020. Open Banking in the UK and Singapore: Open Possibilities for Enhancing Financial Inclusion. *Journal of Business Law*. doi:10.17863/CAM.55421.

Magnuson, W., 2018. Regulating Fintech. *Vanderbilt Law Review*, 71(4), pp. 1167–1226.

Martin, A., 2019. *Insecure work – are we at tipping point?* [online] Available at https://neweconomics.org/2019/06/insecure-work-are-we-at-tipping-point [Accessed 7 April 2021].

Mehrotra, A. and Yetman, J., 2015. Financial Inclusion - Issues for Central Banks. *BIS Quarterly Review*, March 2015, pp. 83–96. [pdf] Available at http://www.bis.org/publ/qtrpdf/r_qt1503h.pdf [Accessed 16 June 2020].

Mitton, L., 2008. *Financial Inclusion in the UK: Review of Policy and Practice*. [pdf] Available at https://www.jrf.org.uk/report/financial-inclusion-uk-review-policy-and-practice [Accessed 19 June 2020].

Money and Pensions Service, 2020. *The UK Strategy for Financial Wellbeing 2020–2030*. [pdf] Available at https://moneyandpensionsservice.org.uk/wp-content/uploads/2020/01/UK-Strategy-for-Financial-Wellbeing-2020-2030-Money-and-Pensions-Service.pdf [Accessed 2 September 2020].

NESTA, 2020. *Affordable Credit Challenge*. [online] Available at https://challenges.org/affordable-credit-challenge/#:~:text=What%20was%20the%20Affordable%20Credit, and%20delivered%20by%20Nesta%20Challenges [Accessed 25 June 2020].

Ofcom, 2019. *Access and Inclusion in 2018. Consumers' Experiences in Communications Markets*. [pdf] Available at https://www.ofcom.org.uk/__data/assets/pdf_file/0018/132912/Access-and-Inclusion-report-2018.pdf [Accessed 17 June 2020].

Prahalad, C. K. and Ramaswamy, V., 2000. Co-Opting Customer Competence. *Harvard Business Review*, 78(1), pp. 79–90.

Reynolds, F., 2017. *Open Banking: A Consumer Perspective*. [pdf] Available at https://home.barclays/content/dam/home-barclays/documents/citizenship/access-to-financial-and-digital-empowerment/Open-Banking-A-Consumer-Perspective-Faith-Reynolds.pdf [Accessed 24 June 2020].

Reynolds, F. and Chidley, M., 2019. *Consumer Priorities for Open Banking*. [pdf] Available at https://www.openbanking.org.uk/wp-content/uploads/Consumer-Priorities-for-Open-Banking-report-June-2019.pdf [Accessed 22 June 2020].

Scottish Government, 2019a. *Fairer Scotland Action Plan, Shifting the Curve and the Life Chances of Young People in Scotland. Progress Report 2019*. [pdf] Available at https://www.gov.scot/publications/fairer-scotland-action-plan-shifting-curve-life-chances-young-people-scotland-progress-report-2019/pages/12/ [Accessed 1 September 2020].

Scottish Government, 2019b. *Increasing Access to Affordable Credit*. [pdf] Available at https://www.gov.scot/news/increasing-access-to-affordable-credit/ [Accessed 1 September 2020].

Student Borrower Protection Center, 2020. *Educational Redlining*. [pdf] Available at https://assets.documentcloud.org/documents/6768401/Education-Redlining-February-2020.pdf [Accessed 3 September 2020].

Welsh Government, 2016a. *Financial Inclusion Strategy for Wales 2016*. [pdf] Available at https://gov.wales/sites/default/files/publications/2018-11/money-and-financial-inclusion-strategy_0.pdf [Accessed 2 September 2020].

Welsh Government, 2016b. *Financial Inclusion Delivery Plan*. [pdf] Available at https://gov.wales/sites/default/files/publications/2018-11/money-and-financial-inclusion-delivery-plan_0.pdf [Accessed 2 September 2020].

World Bank & OECD, 2013. *Women and Finance Progress Report to the G20*. [pdf] Available at https://financialallianceforwomen.org/download/g20-women-finance-report/ [Accessed 16 June 2020].

Ylirisku, S., Jylhä, A., Lehtiö, A., Ahmed, I., Stewart, C., Sellen, A., Harper, R. and Giulio Jacucci, G., 2016. Designing for Active Place Presence at Home: The Hole in Space Design Experiment. *Proceedings of the 2016 ACM Conference on Designing Interactive Systems*. DOI: http://dx.doi.org/10.1145/2901790.2901884

Part 3
Regulation of cryptoassets and blockchains

6 Should we trade market stability for more financial inclusion? The case of crypto-assets regulation in EU

Ilias Kapsis

1 Introduction

Despite progress during the past decade, financial exclusion remains a problem in the European Union (EU). The World Bank estimated (Mastercard 2016) that as many as 136 million Europeans may still be financially excluded, while other reports (e.g. World Bank 2019) indicate a significant variation in performance across Member States, with some of them demonstrating high level of financial inclusion, with others lagging significantly behind (Coffinet and Jadeau 2017). The economic fallout from the Covid-19 pandemic, which has pushed the European economies deep into economic recession, is expected to have an adverse impact on financial inclusion.

Digital currencies (DCs) have been in existence in various forms on the Internet since its early days. Originally created by private issuers for online games and to facilitate economic interactions between closed online communities they had very limited function in the real economy (European Central Bank 2012, 2015). This changed with the appearance of Bitcoin in the aftermath of the last financial crisis. Bitcoin targeted the real economy, using sophisticated new technologies and market processes to offer a range of functions similar to official currencies but also additional ones (e.g. Bitcoin is treated by many as a commodity or stock). It inspired a wave of other similar private DC issues collectively known as crypto-assets.[1] Crypto-assets operate peer-to-peer and offer easy, efficient and affordable access to a range of financial instruments (e.g. payments and fund transfers) without the bureaucratic burdens and costs of the regulated sector. They operate independently of central banks and do not require intermediation of the regulated banking sector, which makes them attractive alternatives to those excluded from the regulated financial system.

Crypto-assets have faced a number of challenges, including market scalability issues, numerous incidents of use by criminals, cybersecurity issues and a hostile reception by regulations and the media, but they proved resilient and continue to grow. At the start of 2020, there were over 5,100 such assets in circulation (Houben and Snyers 2020). Their market endurance has pushed back critics and

---

1 Due to the use of cryptography as a key technical feature.

forced regulators over time to become more accommodative and seek ways to legitimise them by subjecting them to regulation. In EU, the Commission proposed in 2019 the adoption of an EU-wide legal framework for crypto-assets and initiated relevant consultation. Central banks around the world, the European Central Bank (ECB) between them, potentially foreseeing a long-term market presence for crypto-assets, have mobilised to consider issuing digital versions of official currencies (CBDCs) to compete against crypto-assets (Bank of England 2020b). Covid-19 pandemic with the lockdowns and social distancing rules in many countries raised the significance of digital economy, offering a further boost to the case of DCs.

This chapter approaches the issue of DCs from the perspective of financial inclusion. It argues that the digitalisation of finance and the advancement of digital economy in EU are permanent phenomena which make the case for the broader adoption of DCs more compelling as they can support the expansion of digital economy and improve financial inclusion (Chambers 2020). The chapter also considers the debate whether using CBDCs is the best way to support the digital economy or whether privately issued crypto-assets should also be used. This author argues that CBDCs and crypto-assets do not have to be viewed by policymakers and regulators as competitive and mutually exclusive because they can both contribute in a complementary way to achieving financial inclusion. The positive combined effect can be more significant than the effect of CBDCs operating alone. Finally, the chapter reviews the EU regulatory responses to crypto-assets. It discusses one of the main regulatory concerns that crypto-assets could undermine financial stability and makes recommendation for addressing that concern and for the main features and principles of a future legal framework for crypto-assets.

2 Financial inclusion: definition and the situation in EU

The World Bank (2014, p. 15) defines financial inclusion as "*...the proportion of individuals and firms that use financial services*". It sees in it "*...a potentially transformative power to accelerate development gains*", which can be achieved because "*...[i]nclusive financial systems provide individuals and firms with greater access to resources to meet their financial needs, such as saving for retirement, investing in education, capitalizing on business opportunities, and confronting shocks*" (World Bank 2019, p. 17). For societies, high levels of financial inclusion can reduce poverty and income inequality, improve economic growth and living standards, and promote sustainable development.

For consumers, access to the financial system means convenience and efficiency in day-to-day financial transactions and more protection from crime, such as fraud and money laundering due to screening. Refunds are easier, and the system offers records of all transactions helping to avoid errors and resolve disputes. Finally, the cost of finance for users compared to excluded customers who are forced to make occasional use of the financial system (e.g. for cashing cheques without having regular relationship) or to seek alternative options is usually lower (Ampudia and Ehrmann 2017; ECB 2017). For firms, especially micro, small and medium enterprises, access to finance in the form of access to bank accounts, credit, payments and financial infrastructures is essential for them to operate and grow (World Bank 2014).

The appearance in recent years of innovative financial technologies ('Fintech') has accelerated the digitalisation of finance, which has been linked to significant further benefits for financial inclusion. The fast-growing use of e-banking, mobile banking applications, credit and debit cards and innovative Fintech solutions can improve individual "*income-earning potential, ... help people manage their financial risks and smooth consumption*" (World Bank 2019). In addition, digital finance makes transferring money to long distances easier, faster and more economically efficient. This can be particularly useful in periods of crisis or to support poor families. The Covid-19 pandemic confirmed the use of digital finance by governments to send financial assistance quickly and securely to the most vulnerable individuals and affected businesses thus helping society and economy to cope with the economic impact (World Bank 2019).

The European Union, as part of the developed world, is deemed, overall, more financially inclusive (World Bank 2019) than other regions, but there is significant variation in performance between Member States. In 2017, the rate of bank account ownership, a critical metric of financial inclusion because it offers a main point of entry to the financial system, was 100% in Denmark, Finland and Sweden, indicating very high level of financial inclusion (World Bank 2019). Instead, in Romania, Bulgaria and Hungary, the rates were 58%, 72% and 75%, respectively, indicating that significant parts of the population did not have access to the financial system (World Bank 2019).

The absence of savings, financial illiteracy, costs, bureaucratic processes and financial crime legislation (e.g. money laundering and terrorism financing laws) (Carstens 2020; Coffinet and Jadeau 2017; World Bank 2019) are often cited as rising obstacles to the opening of bank accounts, and these, in turn, affect the use of other services, such as payments. For payments, problems get compounded in the case of cross-border transactions where multiple banks, payment systems, currencies and legal frameworks are involved (Bech and Hancock 2020). The costs of using opened accounts and existing financial infrastructures are often high. Fees can be charged to account owners for operating the accounts, using debit and credit cards, and electronic money transfer or currency exchanges while there is no peer-to-peer option. The fees are used to cover the bank and network operating costs and the costs of banks' regulatory compliance. Furthermore, account owners experience exclusion from other products and services (e.g. access to credit), delays in the processing of transactions and the need for their physical presence at branches to carry out transactions.

Continuing technological innovations have helped over time to improve customer experiences and boost financial inclusion. Electronic banking documents, replacing paper equivalents, can be submitted and exchanged with customers through the internet, reducing the need for face-to-face meetings and processing times for opening bank accounts, approving loans and clearing and settling transactions (Bech and Hancock 2020). E-banking allows payments, transfers of funds and other services 24/7, with customers being able to initiate these services from their computer or smartphone. Automated systems and robo-advisers can provide speedy advice and decisions on financial products and services (FCA 2018). Initiation of payments in stores or on the Internet through smartphones or contactless systems (contactless credit card payments, or use of overlays such as Apple Pay, Google Pay and PayPal) (Bech and Hancock 2020; World Bank 2019) have further improved efficiency and consumer convenience.

These improvements helped to raise the levels of financial inclusion, but several shortcomings still remain raising obstacles. As highlighted by the Committee on Payments and Market Infrastructures (CPMI) and World Bank (2016), financial inclusion is not only about achieving access but also about providing financial services which are valuable to users, who will thus use them frequently.

3 Crypto-assets: definition, features and the legal situation in EU

3.1 Definition and features of crypto-assets

Since the appearance of Bitcoin in the markets in 2009,[2] crypto-assets have grown to become an ecosystem with many different types of currency and features covering a wide range of financial functions. ECB Crypto-Assets Task Force (2019) refers to crypto-assets as "...*any asset recorded in digital form that is not and does not represent either a financial claim on, or a financial liability of, any natural or legal person, and which does not embody a proprietary right against an entity*". European Securities and Markets Authority (ESMA 2019) defines crypto-assets as assets "...*neither issued nor guaranteed by a central bank*". Crypto-assets have exclusive digital form and no physical counterpart with legal tender status (ECB 2012). Their distinguishing technological features include the use of cryptography to secure transactions and protect user anonymity and use of distributed ledger technology (DLT) to manage in a decentralised way, through copies of ledgers stored in multiple locations for the validation and recording of currencies and transactions (Financial Stability Board 2018). DLT could be far more efficient in processing transactions than the existing system because it could allow instantaneous clearing and settlement of transactions which can all be completed in one step (ESMA 2017) compared to multiple steps currently required, thus reducing costs, processing time and errors and delays observed under the existing system. The simplified process could potentially also allow for fewer legal issues and disputes.

Users can participate without having to reveal their real identity or other sensitive personal information (e.g. occupation, home address) using only one (or multiple) electronic ID and address. The online network supporting crypto-assets

2 Source: Bitcoin.org

is controlled by private parties (users and currency issuers). Decentralised electronic ledgers are used to verify and record transactions and offer transparency. The existence of decentralised ledgers dispersed in various parts of the world makes them hard to hack. Crypto-assets are stored in electronic e-wallets, which are operated by the crypto-assets networks or specialised parties. There are also custodial wallet providers who can hold the crypto-assets on behalf of the owners and transact for them (ESMA 2019).

A basic taxonomy of crypto-assets used by the European Banking Authority (EBA 2019) comprises three main categories: payment/exchange/currency tokens, investment tokens and utility tokens. Typically, popular crypto-assets, such as Bitcoin and Litecoin, are used as a means of exchange, for investment purposes or for the storage of value (EBA 2019). Some of the crypto-assets, especially Bitcoin which is the largest by market value and oldest crypto-asset, do not have identifiable issuers and their value is not backed by real assets. These features have resulted in significant price volatility, which make them less useful for payment (Financial Stability Board 2018), and absence of issuer liability and consumer protection. Newer types of crypto-assets, the 'stablecoins', use identifiable issuers and link the stablecoins' value to the value of assets backing them (asset-backed crypto-assets) or to algorithms (algorithmic stablecoins) (EBA 2019; Financial Stability Board 2019). The asset-backed are backed by fiat currencies (e.g. Tether pegged to the US dollar), commodities (e.g. Digix Gold Token backed by gold) or other crypto-assets (e.g. Dai).

The extent of legal protection for investors and consumers could vary (Financial Policy Committee [FPC] of the Bank of England, 2019). Libra is a global stablecoin being developed by Facebook for the purpose of being readily used for payments or as medium of exchange and which will be backed by a basket of assets. The ability of stablecoins to control their price volatility depends on the quality of assets backing them, the extent of backing and the way the assets are held (BOE 2020a). The results so far have been mixed (ECB 2019). For example, Tether is a leading existing stablecoin pegged one-to-one to the US dollar. It is deemed fully collateralised as its owner promises to hold in reserve (in bank accounts) amounts of US dollar equal to the number of Tether coins issued. While the quality of Tether's backing has not been in doubt, concerns have been raised on several occasions about whether adequate reserves actually exist, with critics pointing to inadequate independent audit (Eichengreen 2019). Absence of transparency about the backing assets of how they are held could undermine market confidence and affect prices.

For non-asset-backed currencies such as the Bitcoin price volatility remains high, and this will be hard to change. Bitcoin is treated by many in the market as a commodity, such as gold.

Crypto-assets also support other instruments such as initial coin offerings (ICOs), which concern tokens issued by companies or individuals in exchange for capital (Financial Stability Board, 2018). These tokens offer privileged access to goods, services or other financial instruments depending on the issuer's offer. They are an easy and affordable method for new companies and start-ups to raise funds from a broad base of investors, as these tokens can be sold to the broader public through crowdfunding processes.

3.2 The legal situation in EU

The ECB and the European Supervisory Authorities (ESAs[3]) have been closely monitoring crypto-assets since their market appearance. ECB has issued guidance in 2012 and 2015 where it acknowledged that these assets constituted useful innovations, which could offer additional alternatives to payments and other advantages. However, ECB also highlighted a number of risks for investors and consumers, including exposure to credit, liquidity and operational risks. The absence of regulation generated significant legal risks for parties and risks of exploitation by criminals. According to ECB, market stability risks could emerge if crypto-assets were used more broadly, with central banks facing reputational risks if incidents involving crypto-assets resulted in loss of public trust on the role of central banks. Such incidents could also undermine public trust in the available systems of electronic payments and e-money supported by the regulated financial sectors, which would impact on electronic commerce. However, the ECB did not see a cause of immediate action due to the small transaction volumes involving crypto-assets.

The EBA in 2013 issued a warning to consumers against the use of virtual currencies and in 2014 published an opinion on 'virtual currencies'. It identified "*more than 70 risks*" to users, market participants, financial integrity, payments systems and regulators and called national authorities to discourage the purchase, sale or holding of virtual currencies by regulated banks, thereby "*shielding regulated financial services from VCs*". In a further 2017 opinion, the EBA welcomed the Commission's proposals to include aspects of virtual currencies into the scope of to the revised Anti-money Laundering Directive and asked for the national authorities to be provided with adequate tools to ensure effective market supervision and compliance and consistent application of the new rules across EU.

On 12 February 2018, the three ESAs issued a joint warning to consumers on the risks of virtual currencies,[4] citing, among others, their extreme volatility and bubble risk, absence of protection, lack of price transparency and exit options, operational disruptions, misleading information and unsuitability for most purposes, including investments and retirement planning.

In 2018, EU included the crypto-asset exchange platforms and e-wallet providers into the scope of its Fifth Anti-money Laundering Directive (AMLD), while a study for the European Parliament (Houben and Snyers 2018) suggested further steps, including ban and criminalisation of certain aspects of crypto-assets.

---

3 ESAs comprise the European Securities and Markets Authority (ESMA), the European Banking Authority (EBA), and the European Insurance and Occupational Pensions Authority (EIOPA).
4 ESMA, EBA and EIOPA warn consumers on the risks of virtual currencies.

However, the Commission has been careful not to alienate crypto-assets, which are a part of the broader Fintech phenomenon and could support the Europeans Commission's digital market initiative. In this context, AMLD calls the adopted monitoring rules for crypto-assets "...*a balanced and proportional approach, safeguarding technical advances and the high degree of transparency attained in the field of alternative finance*".

The Commission's Action Plan on Fintech ('the Plan'), which was published in March 2018, also highlighted the rising market significance of crypto-assets and the benefits and risks associated with them for investors, consumers and market integrity. The Plan called for an assessment of the suitability of existing regulatory EU frameworks for crypto-assets to determine if further legislative action was needed. The Plan called for cooperation with international partners on the matter as crypto-assets are a global phenomenon.

In 2019, the ESMA and EBA ('the Authorities') issued separate advice on the suitability and applicability of existing EU frameworks on crypto-assets. The Authorities concluded that most crypto-assets fell outside of the existing regulatory perimeter. For those falling within the perimeter, which meant that they could qualify, for example, as payment instruments or securities and be subject to relevant EU regulations, the application of these regulations was not always straightforward raising concerns about their suitability for crypto-assets. The Authorities also found that there was no harmonisation in the approach of national laws introduced to deal with crypto-assets.

In September 2019, Ursula von der Leyen, the new President of the European Commission, highlighted the need for a common EU approach in crypto-assets aimed at identifying the opportunities and risks they may pose.

In November 2019, the Association for Financial Markets in Europe (AFME) published a report containing a number of recommendations for regulatory convergence in EU on crypto-assets. The recommendations included: establishment of a pan-European crypto-asset taxonomy; clearer guidance on the process of issuing crypto-assets; use of activity-based and technology-agnostic regulation; use of existing frameworks with necessary amendments where possible; and regulatory convergence with other global and regional initiatives.

In December 2019, a report by an Expert Group on Regulatory Obstacles to Financial Innovation (ROFIEG) called for accelerating the work to assess the adequacy and suitability of existing legal frameworks on crypto-assets, highlighting in particular the need to address the legal uncertainty and risks caused by the absence of a common taxonomy in respect of crypto-assets across Member States as well as the need to address various market risks link to them. The report also highlighted the need to address commercial law issues raised by crypto-assets, such as conflict-of-laws issues caused by their decentralised networks and to identify any other issues.

On 19 December 2019, the Commission announced a public consultation on an EU framework for markets in crypto-assets (Commission 2019b). The Commission was looking for "...*the best way to enable the development of a sustainable ecosystem for crypto-assets while addressing the major risks they raise*".

The Commission's consultation took place in parallel with the consultation on the digital operational resilience in the area of financial services (Commission 2019a); both are a part of the Commission's drive for the adoption of a Digital Finance Strategy for EU. The Commission is expected to publish its proposed regulation on crypto-assets within the third quarter of 2020.

3.3 Commentary on the latest EU crypto-asset initiatives

The Commission's search for a common approach is a reasonable step, given the existence of broad evidence from ESAs' reviews, national regulators' feedback and industry reports that the current legal fragmentation in EU on the matter does not serve the interests of the industry, regulators and consumers who all face significant uncertainty about the legal status of crypto-assets. The Commission's initiative will offer the required legal clarity, while allowing it to include crypto-assets into its Digital Finance Strategy. From a financial inclusion perspective, the Commission's initiative by offering to crypto-assets a path to legitimacy will contribute to improving financial inclusion in EU as consumers will be offered alternative options for financial access with the legal guarantees of EU law.

However, significant challenges for achieving these goals remain. Crypto-assets have to date proved difficult to regulate due to the novel and constantly evolving nature of the ecosystem, which is also very diverse. In addition, the market is small in size as the Financial Stability Board (2018) and European regulators (ECB 2018; ESMA 2019) have acknowledged, and, therefore, any regulatory initiative will be focusing on regulating perceived and future rather than real and current risks of a small sector. In such a context, creating a framework which will be successfully balancing benefits and risks from the operation of crypto-assets as the Commission wishes could prove a too ambitious goal. Furthermore, when drafting its new framework, the Commission will face the different national priorities of Member States some of which will favour a more supportive framework for crypto-assets compared to others (EBA 2019; ESMA 2019). Reaching a compromise as the Commission usually does to move legislation forward may have been useful on other occasions but not necessarily in the case of crypto-assets. The latter, like other novel technologies, need flexible and not-too-intrusive regulations in order to grow faster. Whether this will be possible in EU remains to be seen, given that any EU compromise in this case due to the many reservations expressed about crypto-assets is likely to be more towards a more restrictive framework rather than less. Finally, given the absence of international consensus about the taxonomy of crypto-assets and their legal treatment, legal uncertainty may remain after the adoption of the new EU framework. Legal interpretation issues may also continue to cause uncertainty as new crypto-asset typologies will continue to emerge.

Thus, while the creation of an EU-wide framework is a step in the right direction, whether this framework will meet the expectations of the industry and regulators remains to be seen.

4 The option of central bank-issued digital currencies

Central banks around the world have been exploring for some time (Barontini and Holden 2019; Boar et al. 2020) the possibility of issuing digital currencies ('CBDCs') to offer additional support to the digital economy and compete against privately issued DCs led by crypto-assets. To date, they have refrained from taking action due to the slow growth of crypto-assets markets, the absence of significant market demand for CBDCs and a number of uncertainties surrounding the technical and market features of these currencies. However, during 2020, more concrete steps in this direction were announced. Examples include the central banks of China, Canada and Sweden, while the Central Bank of Canada (2020) has made clear that it will proceed to such a move if privately issued currencies become widely used threatening the Canadian dollar. The European Central Bank, the Bank of England, the Bank of International Settlement and other central banks announced in January 2020 the creation of a group which will consider the case of issuing CBDCs in the future.

While the adoption of CBDCs can serve multiple purposes (e.g. in wholesale markets, retail), particular focus has been paid to their use in the retail economy. The CPMI and Markets Committee (MC) (2018, p. 3) define a CDBC for retail purposes as "*…a central bank liability, denominated in an existing unit of account, which serves both as a medium of exchange and a store of value*". Currently, central banks provide electronic digital money to commercial banks and some public institutions in the form of reserves or settlement account balances (Bech and Garratt 2017), but CBDCs are different. Barrdear and Kumhof (2016, p. 7) describe CBDC as "*…a central bank granting universal, electronic, 24x7, national-currency-denominated and interest-bearing access to its balance sheet*", but these features are not fixed due to the existence of a variety of proposed models (CPMI and MC 2018).

The issuing of CBDCs is driven by legal issues linked to the currently available e-money options. Under the current system, businesses and individuals hold any transaction balances from electronic commerce in deposit accounts held by commercial banks (sometimes called 'digital cash') (Barrdear and Kumhof 2016). The balances are denominated in one of the existing official currencies (dollar, euro, pound etc.), but, for these balances, the owner of the account has a claim against the commercial bank, an intermediary, where the balance is held, and not the central bank, which has issued the balance currency. Unlike central banks which are excluded from default, commercial banks are not, and, if a commercial bank defaults, the customer has only limited protection through deposit insurance/guarantee schemes, which protect primarily retail deposits up to a certain amount.[5] Compared to commercial banks, CBDCs could offer unlimited protection, which for central banks come at no cost, while for commercial banks,

---

5 Examples include the Deposit Guarantee Scheme of EU, which guarantees deposits of up to 100,000 euros and the UK Financial Services Compensation Scheme, which guarantees deposits of up to 85,000 pounds.

if they chose to match the central bank protection, the cost would be very high and they have to pay for the scheme. For vulnerable customers, though, who usually hold small amounts in commercial bank accounts, the current insurance limits are sufficient to ensure that they will suffer no losses.

Furthermore, current peer-to-peer transactions in electronic money are not possible without an intermediary. Credit and debit transfers and electronic money transfers, which are methods broadly used, involve financial intermediation. Intermediation raises transaction costs, and the intermediator will claim a fee for their service. The advantages of peer-to-peer transactions raise an argument in favour of creating an electronic equivalent to physical cash, which will have to be issued by central banks in the form of a digital version of existing currencies or as a token. Central banks will incur the relevant liabilities, and the digital currency's owners will be able to use it in peer-to-peer transactions as they do with physical cash. The creation of CBDCs will result in individuals and firms opening accounts with the central banks.

Other key issues about CBDCs concern the extent or absence of user anonymity, the existence or absence of any limits or caps in the CBDC use, and whether they should be interest-bearing or not (CPMI and PC 2018). There is also the possibility of using centralised systems of control through central bank registers or decentralised registers supported, for example, by DLT (Bech and Garratt 2017).

Central banks' mandate typically includes the responsibility for issuing currency and cash associated with it, while they deal with commercial banks and not with individuals directly. For CBDCs, central banks will have to allow individuals and companies to open accounts with them or the central banks will have to issue DCs (or 'tokens') or both. Such a change will require reconfiguring the role and mandate of central banks and new legislation in most countries.

5 Financial inclusion: crypto-assets versus CBDCs

Crypto-assets by offering alternative methods for payments, financing and investments can contribute to financial inclusion. Process simplification, which reduces the number of intermediaries and speeds up clearing and settlement, lowers the cost of financial transactions (especially payments) making them more affordable (Commission 2019b). The use of 'tokenisation', which converts rights to a property into a digital token (ESMA 2017) that can be then used as evidence of these rights and can be transferable, offers significant practical convenience and attractiveness.

The significant variability of models allows them to target different groups of users, while their unregulated status allows them to be less bureaucratic and not subject to the costs of regulatory compliance. They also offer user anonymity or pseudonymity which are viewed by some consumers as protecting from hacking, the intrusive banking system and the government.

For small and medium-sized companies (SMEs) often complaining of being excluded or underserved by the official financial sector, crypto-assets through a number of tools, such as initial coin offerings (ICOs) and security token offerings (STOs), can offer access to alternative sources of financing, more efficiently and at lower cost (Commission 2019b).

The appearance of crypto-assets also adds a new element of competition in financial services. Due to bank interconnectivity and extensive regulation, the financial sector has often demonstrated a low level of competition, a factor which undermines access to finance (World Bank 2014). Crypto-assets could help reduce this problem.

Conversely, and similarly to other financial innovations, crypto-assets have to pass the tests of reliability, resilience, stability and trust in order to attract a broader audience. In regards to reliability, the technology should be able to reliably address important issues with legal significance such as the 'double spending'[6] of crypto-assets and the validation of transactions (Athanassiou 2017; Auer 2019).

With regards to resilience and stability, the technology supporting crypto-assets faces scalability challenges and transaction processes delays, while hacking and other incidents have been reported (ESMA 2019). The technology has still a significant way to go to handle efficiently large transaction volumes, while the problem of high price volatility, which exceeds that of stocks, bonds and commodities (ECB 2018), could cause further market stability issues by exposing banks which are involved in crypto-assets markets to mark-to-market[7] losses and a series of others risks (Bank of International Settlements 2019).

Regarding trust, in the absence of public regulation and oversight, users will have to trust their peers, the private issuers and the supporting technology in order for crypto-assets to remain valuable. It is currently an open question the extent to which users are prepared to place their full trust upon a system which relies on limited transparency and broad user and issuer anonymity, innovative technology which still faces challenges and the absence of effective regulatory controls and consumer protection laws to safeguard the rights of investors and users. In light of all these uncertainties, which raise access barriers, it is not a surprise that despite market progress the overall size of crypto-asset market remains small.[8]

An additional problem for financial inclusion is that users of crypto-assets must have access to the Internet and have some knowledge of technology and DCs in order to use them. People with no access to the Internet or with limited or no knowledge of technology and little interest in DCs are effectively excluded.

---

6 This refers to the efforts in preventing the ability of owners of crypto-assets to transfer the same crypto-asset twice (or more) to different recipients, e.g. as payment.
7 Mark-to-market is an accounting tool which adjusts the value of an asset in the balance sheet in response to changes in the market valuation of the asset. A highly volatile asset, like most crypto-assets, could result in significant adjustments in the balance sheets of banks holding the asset, which could have negative effect in the financial position of the bank in periods where the value of the crypto-asset has crashed.
8 According to coinmarketcap.com the total market capitalisation of cryptocurrencies on 12 June 2020 stood at 268 billion USD, which cannot be deemed high.

The problem is compounded by the significant variety of crypto-asset types and features, which makes investor and consumer efforts to develop adequate knowledge of them even more challenging. This does not help to build market confidence in them (ESMA 2019). There are also issues of cybersecurity as well as of transparency and consumer protection about the ways crypto-assets are stored (e-wallet providers and custodial service providers).

However, over time as technology and processes improve and become more standardised, more consumers will familiarise themselves with their use. Legislators will implement legal frameworks, and the situation could change. Besides, the provision of online products and services and management of processes in the regulated financial sector are even more complex and difficult for consumers to understand. The regulated sector was able to find ways to overcome these challenges by adopting consumer-friendly technological applications, training consumers on their use, providing technical support and guidance and offering legal clarity about consumer rights and obligations. The same could happen with crypto-asset markets over time.

Governments and central banks seem to favour CBDCs as a potentially safer option for consumers than crypto-assets. CBDCs' value will be less volatile due to the extensive legal guarantees attached to them, the free-of-default status of central banks and state controls (BOE 2020b). CBDCs, like other functions of the regulated financial sector (e.g. payments, securities), are regulated as well as the institutions providing these functions (central banks and commercial banks). The regulation increases public trust on the system, but it also raises entry barriers in the industry (Barrdear and Kumhof 2016). It is these barriers that often grant significant market power to the banks which they use to exclude customers. Crypto-assets currently have an advantage because they are less regulated, but the situation would change if they became subjects to similar rules and regulations as do the official currencies and financial instruments offered by the regulated sector.

Furthermore, CBDCs should be able to satisfy a range of consumer diverse needs, including convenience, resilience, accessibility, privacy and ease of use in cross-border payments (Auer and Böhme (2020). It should be noted, though, that whether CBDCs will be able to satisfy these needs, especially accessibility, depends on their design and on whether national authorities will be willing to relax certain currency restrictions such as ownership by their citizens of accounts in foreign currencies or central banks allowing foreign citizens to have CBDC accounts with them.

CBDCs may also face a significant challenge engaging the informal economy comprising individuals and companies that have excluded themselves from the financial system (CPMI and WB 2016). These 'self-exclusions' are driven by a variety of factors such as negative experience of the financial system, involvement with informal labour market, gender, cultural and religious issues, and avoidance of paying tax and other government charges. These people and companies rely only on cash for their transactions and will hardly join CBDCs, which are controlled by central banks and regulated by the government financial sector. For the self-excluded, privately issued crypto-assets could be an attractive alternative.

Overall, this author argues that CBDCs and crypto-assets could coexist in the markets and perform complementary functions in regards to financial inclusion. A combination of both types of currency could achieve higher levels of inclusion than CBDCs alone.

6 Crypto-assets and financial stability

The Financial Stability Board (2018) has highlighted a number of risks, which would create financial stability implications if crypto-assets markets had a significant market size. Such risks include (i) market liquidity risks, due to the market being controlled by a few, with trade volumes being low (also ESMA 2019), carried out through trading platforms which are often unregistered with significant operational limitations and flaws; (ii) volatility risks due to big price swings causing a number of other issues such as difficulties with their use in payments and settlements; (iii) leverage risks associated with the fact that potentially significant part of the purchase of crypto-assets is financed through debt and the absence of transparency about the overall extent of leverage; and (iv) technological and operational risks associated with the fact that these new technologies face scalability and other limitations (ESMA 2017) and the operational model for some of these assets may not be viable in the longer term.

Any crisis in crypto-asset markets caused by the above weaknesses could result in broader loss of public confidence in the financial system and regulation (ECB 2015). There is currently a growing exposure to crypto-asset markets by the mainstream financial sector (ECB 2018), while the proliferation of ICOs and appearance of global stablecoins (GSCs) could raise rapidly the capitalisation of crypto-assets. Their use for payments and settlements is also growing (Financial Stability Board 2018).

While the regulators' evaluations of potential risks from crypto-assets seem valid, they do not necessarily undermine the case for broader use of these assets. The reason is that many of the identified risks exist because the legal status of crypto-assets in many countries and in the EU remains largely uncertain. ESMA (2019) in its advice on crypto-assets has highlighted the risks for investor protection and the sustainability of crypto-assets ecosystem in EU caused by the absence of legal clarity. The absence of enough liquidity and depth to support large transaction volumes highlighted by Financial Stability Board (2018) is in part due to that problem as suppliers and buyers hesitate to join due to the uncertainty about their future. Price volatility would have been lower in the presence of legal certainty. Such certainty combined with more frequent use of stablecoins could help reduce volatility further (Financial Stability Board 2020).

The leverage risks identified in crypto-assets exist also with financing of the purchase of securities and other financial products offered by the official financial sector. The main difference in the case of crypto-assets is that there is no legal framework, which would help to identify and regulate those risks or offer some protection. Absence of transparency on the extent of leverage and other crucial areas is partly also due to the absence of regulated processes and supervision.

Finally, the technological and operational issues identified by Financial Stability Board (FSB) are real, but this is hardly a surprise with nascent technologies and business models. Such problems can be addressed, and there are already steps in that direction, as the technology matures and the business model adjusts to the market realities and the legal environment.

It could be argued that, overall, and assuming that effective legal frameworks can be created to offer legitimacy to crypto-assets and legal clarity about the rights and protection of the parties involved, the market risks associated with them could be no higher than those emerging in the mainstream financial system.

CBDCs which are offered as safe alternatives by shifting deposits from commercial banks to central banks could reduce risks to financial stability from bank runs because central bank guarantees would prevent such a risk (Broadbent 2016). Also, the shift of deposits will limit the ability of commercial banks to use fractional reserve banking,[9] thus reducing their liquidity and solvency risks (Stevens 2017). However, CBDCs could also become a factor of instability because they will undermine the market position of commercial banks. The latter could suffer from reduced funding from deposits and rising borrowing costs. To address the problem commercial banks will be forced to switch to the more volatile and higher-cost wholesale markets for funding (Broadbent 2016), which will create their own liquidity and solvency risks. Furthermore, a shift of deposits from commercial to central banks will also include the latter providing additional services such as payments, money transfers and foreign currency exchanges which will gradually result in central banks dominating those markets too. The absence of alternatives and competition reduction will generate new systemic risks (Broadbent 2016).

7 The regulation of crypto-assets in EU

In search for regulatory solutions for crypto-assets, regulators should carefully balance the need for legal certainty and consumer protection with the need to facilitate delivery of the positive aspects of crypto-assets which support financial inclusion. If regulators end up creating a rigid, costly and complex regulatory and supervisory system along the line of that operating for mainstream finance, crypto-assets may end up with the same weaknesses as the latter. Participation of unbanked or underserved individuals and SMEs could also become problematic. This author therefore argues that some compromise will have to be made with crypto-assets being subject to less stringent regulatory rules. Some elements of the proposed compromise are presented below.

EU regulators should accept the possibility that some types of crypto-assets may not be fully regulated in the same way as the existing formal market. As technology will continue to produce new types of crypto-assets and new technologies to support them, regulators may have to accept that some crypto-assets

---

9 "Fractional reserve banking" is a bank practice to hold only a fraction of the accepted deposits in the form of reserves with central banks while using the rest to provide loans (Stevens 2017).

will always be able to escape coverage by existing frameworks. Partial applications of existing frameworks and use of bespoke regimes may have to be used. Such a solution could be acceptable as long as these cases are exceptional, and the crypto-assets covered offer a basic level of guarantees for financial stability and consumer protection.

In order to encourage participation in crypto-asset markets of self-excluded individuals and companies and users of cash economy, regulators may have to accept *increased informality and anonymity* for some transactions similar to transactions in the cash economy. In this context, requirements for user registrations with real IDs or efforts to record and monitor transactions or exchanges for regulatory purposes may have to take a backseat with regards to low-level transactions focusing instead more on preventing fraud and other crimes. Private mechanisms could be used to regulate the areas left outside of public controls.

In the same context, conditions of licensing for issuing of such currencies, exchanges and custodians could be less restrictive than for the formal sector. The applicable frameworks, though, *should be clearly identified*.

Consumer protection may be more limited at least for transactions of low value. For example, there may be no need for insurance protection similar to those available for deposits in commercial banks. Private issuers should be encouraged to set themselves the net of consumer protections with law establishing only some minimum standards. This approach would help to keep transactions costs low and reduce regulatory burdens.

Data protection laws and cybersecurity principles should fully apply as with the formal sector because these are essential tools for ensuring minimum protection of private data and the resilience of the market.

In consultation with the issuers, regulators should encourage the *standardisation* of crypto-asset features and business models by identifying and promoting the most viable technological and market features. Regulators could issue and legislate for the selected types. While standardisation could under certain conditions stifle innovation by favouring specific crypto-assets over others or by forcing the most successful innovators to share their innovations with the rest of the industry for standards creation (Acemoglu et al. 2012), it is nevertheless important for crypto-asset markets that a level of minimum standardisation is established, given that the current wide range of crypto-asset types[10] is not sustainable. Standardisation will also facilitate consumer knowledge and familiarisation with the new markets.

International regulatory cooperation will be required to address jurisdictional and regulatory issues arising from crypto-asset circulation and use through the internet. Crypto-assets are global assets, and, unlike formal currencies or other regulated instruments (e.g. securities) whose issuing is based on laws and regulation of the country where they are issued, they are not normally tied to any

---

10 There are currently thousands of different crypto-assets. Many of them share the same features (e.g. decentralisation), but there are also significant differences (e.g. 'stablecoins' versus bitcoin-type assets).

specific legal or jurisdictional framework. The absence of identifiable issuers and the concept of decentralisation (with absence of central registers) underpinning the operation of many crypto-assets make hard to apply national frameworks to them. Crypto-asset taxonomy, conflicts of laws and the rights and obligations of the parties should be legally addressed in a consistent manner though international regulatory cooperation. The Commission has already proposed steps in this direction, and international bodies such as the FSB and Bank for International Settlements (BIS) have initiated relevant work. On money laundering and terrorism-financing issues, the Financial Action Task Force issued in 2019[11] the first global standards for crypto-assets.

Furthermore, from the recommendations made by AFME (2019) two additional points can be made:

a   The establishment of a *pan-European crypto-asset taxonomy* will offer legal clarity and certainty, but it has to be accepted that an all-inclusive taxonomy may not always be possible. Some additional flexibility on a case-by-case basis may have to be applied.
b   Use of *activity-based* and *technology-agnostic* regulation. These principles apply broadly to all Fintech products and can encourage innovation and a level-playing field because regulation in those cases does not focus on the type of technology involved against which they take a neutral approach but on the type of activity. However, similar to other Fintech innovations, activity-based and agnostic regulation, if not properly monitored, sometimes may end up discriminating in favour of the status quo or specific issuers over others. By way of example, existing activity-based rules in financial markets (e.g. for payments, securities) in EU despite regular updates, remain largely modelled on legacy financial markets, and regulators have a hard time incorporating into the existing rules activities relating to crypto-assets. This has resulted in significant legal uncertainty about the legal status of crypto-assets undermining their market positions, while legacy-linked activities are regulated without issues. Similarly, technology-agnostic regulation should be sufficiently flexible to allow inclusion, without discrimination of the latest technologies. Flexibility is needed because technology generates new products faster than law updates its provisions.

The Commission's Fintech Action Plan identified problems existing in EU law for achieving the above goals, and the ESMA (2019) and EBA (2019) offered further confirmation. ROFIEG (2019) found that existing EU financial regulations were largely technology-neutral, but there were exceptions. The AP found that outdated laws requiring paper-based disclosures or physical presence were still in existence in EU. ROFIEG recommended amending existing frameworks to better deal with Fintech innovations, while for more radical technologies establishing novel business models and relationships with consumers, adoption of

---

11 For more details on the FATF standards, see Financial Action Task Force (2019) Guidance for a Risk-based Approach – Virtual Assets and Virtual Asset Service Providers, June.

new frameworks should be considered. 'One-size-fits-all' regulatory solutions will not work. In this sense, the Commission's decision to propose a new regulatory framework for the regulation of crypto-assets should be applauded.

8 Conclusion: crypto-assets, financial stability and inclusion

In the eyes of policymakers and regulators, crypto-assets remain a controversial phenomenon whose existence challenges existing established norms and regulatory philosophies. The extent of the challenge has been summarised by Financial Stability Board (2020) in its assessment of GSCs as follows: "...*the decentralised nature of GSC arrangements could pose governance challenges; stabilisation mechanisms and redemption arrangements could pose market, liquidity, and credit risks; and, the infrastructure and technology used for recording transactions, and accessing, transferring and exchanging coins could pose operational and cyber-security risks*".

From a market efficiency perspective, various economists have argued that crypto-assets markets, by being fundamentally different and separate from the main markets, could increase transaction costs, as they do not benefit from main market advantages such as network and economies-of-scale effects (CPMI and PC 2018). For the digital economy, government and regulators would prefer the use of CBDCs which could be more stable and easier to control. However, the adoption of CBDCs is not an easy choice either, for two reasons. First, their appearance would cause a foundational change of the competitive dynamics in the mainstream markets by introducing central banks as new players and competitors. This would intensify competition not only with crypto-assets but also with commercial banks for deposits with profound impact on all other areas of the main market (loans, payments, money transfers etc.) and rise of new systemic risks. Second, the existing regulatory and supervisory architecture of the financial systems in order to adapt will likely have to go through significant reforms similar to those in the aftermath of the financial crisis of the 2007–2009 period.

Promoting crypto-assets might be, by comparison, a better option. Due to their underlying technological and operational philosophy, these private sector innovators can operate more efficiently and offer better service to consumers faster without requiring major reconfiguration of the entire financial system. Their ability to operate outside of the financial system can also allow them to reach financially excluded customers more effectively than CBDCs.

Overall, this author is convinced that in the not-so-distant future, we will face a new financial ecosystem which will comprise of commercial banks, central banks and crypto-asset issuers, all competing for customers. This market will be more financially inclusive with potentially different levels of regulation. The latter does not endanger the level-playing field cherished by the Commission because, when it comes to radical innovations, building a level-playing field often requires treating markets or companies differently. What matters most is the market outcome and therefore outcome-based solutions should become the focus of regulators.

Bibliography

Acemoglu, D., Gancia, G., and Zilibotti, F., (2012). Competing Engines of Growth: Innovation and Standardization. *Journal of Economic Theory* 147: 570–601.

Ampudia, M., and Ehrmann, M., (2017). Financial Inclusion: What's It Worth? European Central Bank, *Working Paper Series*, No. 1990, January.

Association for Financial Markets in Europe, (2019). Recommendations for Delivering Supervisory Convergence on the Regulation of Crypto-assets in Europe, November, available from https://www.afme.eu/Portals/0/DispatchFeaturedImages/AFME%20Digital%20Assets%20Position%20Paper%20(FINAL).pdf Please insert date of access for all the electronic sources [Accessed 10 June 2020]

Athanassiou, P., (2017). Impact of Digital Innovation on the Processing of Electronic Payments and Contracting: An Overview of Legal Risks, European Central Bank, *Legal Working Paper Series*, No. 16 / October 2017.

Auer, B., (2019). Beyond the Doomsday Economics of "Proof-of-Work" in Cryptocurrencies. *BIS Working Papers*, No. 765, January.

Auer, R., and Böhme, R., (2020). The Technology of Retail Central Bank Digital Currency. *BIS Quarterly Review*, March, 85–100.

Bank of Canada, (2020). Contingency Planning for a Central Bank Digital Currency. 25 February, available from https://www.bankofcanada.ca/2020/02/contingency-planning-central-bank-digital-currency/ [Accessed 10 June 2020]

Bank of England, (2020a). Central Bank Digital Currency Opportunities, Challenges and Design. Discussion Paper. March 2020, available from https://www.bankofengland.co.uk/-/media/boe/files/paper/2020/central-bank-digital-currency-opportunities-challenges-and-design.pdf [Accessed 10 June 2020]

Bank of England, (2020b), Central Bank Group to Assess Potential Cases for Central Bank Digital Currencies. *Press Release*, 21 January, available from https://www.bankofengland.co.uk/-/media/boe/files/news/2020/january/central-bank-group-to-assess-potential-cases-for-central-bank-digital-currencies.pdf?la=en&hash=F0F25B3FC0CB1F7A64B08797C3D124C171C0BF27 [Accessed 10 June 2020]

Bank of International Settlements, (2019). Designing a Prudential Treatment for Crypto-assets. *Discussion Paper*, December, available from https://www.bis.org/bcbs/publ/d490.pdf [Accessed 10 June 2020]

Barontini, C., and Holden, H., (2019). Proceeding with Caution – A Survey on Central Bank Digital Currency. *BIS Papers*, No. 101, January.

Barrdear, J., and Kumhof, M., (2016). The Macroeconomics of Central Bank Issued Digital Currencies. *Bank of England Staff Working Paper*, No. 605, available from https://www.bankofengland.co.uk/-/media/boe/files/working-paper/2016/the-macroeconomics-of-central-bank-issued-digital-currencies.pdf?la=en&hash=341B602838707E5D6FC26884588C912A721B1DC1 [Accessed 10 June 2020]

Bech, M., and Garratt, R., (2017). Central Bank Cryptocurrencies. *BIS Quarterly Review*, September, 55–70.

Bech, M., and Hancock, J., (2020). Innovations in Payments. *BIS Quarterly Review*, March, 21–36.

Boar, C., Holden, H., and Wadsworth, A., (2020). Impending Arrival –A Sequel to the Survey on Central Bank Digital Currency. *BIS Papers*, No. 107, January, available from https://www.bis.org/publ/bppdf/bispap107.pdf [Accessed 10 June 2020]

Broadbent, B., (2016) Central Banks and Digital Currencies. Speech, at the London School of Economics, London, 2 March.

Carstens, C., (2020). Shaping the Future of Payments. *BIS Quarterly Review*, March, 17–20.
Chambers T., (2020). Unstable Coins: Cryptoassets, Financial Regulation and Preventing Financial Crime in the Emerging market for Digital Assets. FCA, Speech delivered at The Advancement of Digital Assets and Addressing Financial Crime Risk, New York University School of Law, 5 March, available from https://www.fca.org.uk/news/speeches/unstable-coins [accessed 26 March 2021].
Coffinet, J., and Jadeau, C., (2017). Household Financial Exclusion in the Eurozone: The Contribution of the Household Finance and Consumption Survey, IFC-National Bank of Belgium Workshop on "Data Needs and STATISTICS Compilation for Macroprudential Analysis" Brussels, Belgium, 18–19 May.
Committee on Payments and Market Infrastructures and Markets Committee, (2018). Central Bank Digital Currencies. Bank of International Settlements, March, available from https://www.bis.org/cpmi/publ/d174.pdf [Accessed 10 June 2020]
Committee on Payments and Market Infrastructures and World Bank Group (2016) Payment Aspects of Financial Inclusion, April.
Eichengreen, B., (2019). From Commodity to Fiat and Now to Crypto: What Does History Tell Us? National Bureau of Economic Research.
European Banking Authority, (2019). Report with Advice for the European Commission on Crypto-assets, January.
European Banking Authority, (2017). Opinion of the European Banking Authority on the EU Commission's Proposal to Bring Virtual Currencies into the Scope of Directive (EU) 2015/849 (4AMLD), EBA-Op-2016-07, 11 August.
European Banking Authority, (2014). Opinion on 'Virtual Currencies', EBA/Op/2014/08, 4 July.
European Banking Authority, (2013). Warning to Consumers on Virtual Currencies, EBA/WRG/2013/01, 12 December.
European Central Bank, (2012). Virtual Currency Schemes. October, available from https://www.ecb.europa.eu/pub/pdf/other/virtualcurrencyschemes201210en.pdf [Accessed 10 June 2020].
European Central Bank, (2015). Virtual Currency Schemes – A Further Analysis. February 2015, available from https://www.ecb.europa.eu/pub/pdf/other/virtualcurrencyschemesen.pdf
European Central Bank, (2018). Financial Stability Review. May 2018, available from https://www.ecb.europa.eu/pub/financial-stability/fsr/html/ecb.fsr201805.en.html [Accessed 10 April 2021].
European Central Bank, (2019). Stablecoins – No Coins, but Are They Stable? *In Focus*, Issue no. 3, available from https://www.ecb.europa.eu/paym/intro/publications/pdf/ecb.mipinfocus191128.en.pdf [Accessed 10 June 2020]
European Central Bank Crypto-assets Task Force, (2019). Crypto-assets: Implications for Financial Stability, Monetary Policy, and Payments and Market Infrastructures. *European Central Bank Occasional Papers*, No. 223, May 2019.
European Commission, (2019a). Digital Operational Resilience Framework for Financial Services: Making the EU Financial Sector More Secure. Consultation Document.
European Commission, (2019b). On an EU Framework for Markets in Crypto-assets. *Consultation Document*, 5 December, available from https://ec.europa.eu/info/sites/info/files/business_economy_euro/banking_and_finance/documents/2019-crypto-assets-consultation-document_en.pdf [Accessed 10 June 2020]

European Commission, (2018). FinTech Action Plan: For a More Competitive and Innovative European Financial Sector. Communication, Brussels, 8 March, COM (2018) 109 final.

European Securities and Markets Authority, (2019). Advice on Initial Coin Offerings and Crypto-assets, ESMA50-157-1391, 9 January.

European Securities and Markets Authority, (2017). The Distributed Ledger Technology Applied to Securities Markets. *Report*, 7 February, available from https://www.esma.europa.eu/system/files_force/library/dlt_report_-_esma50-1121423017-285.pdf [Accessed 10 June 2020]

Expert Group on Regulatory Obstacles to Financial Innovation, (2019). 30 Recommendations on Regulation, Innovation and Finance. *Final Report to the European Commission*, December, available from https://ec.europa.eu/info/sites/info/files/business_economy_euro/banking_and_finance/documents/191113-report-expert-group-regulatory-obstacles-financial-innovation_en.pdf [Accessed 10 June 2020]

Financial Conduct Authority, (2018). The Changing Shape of the Consumer Market for Advice: Interim Consumer Research to Inform the Financial Advice Market Review (FAMR), August, available from https://www.fca.org.uk/publication/research/famr-interim-consumer-research-report-2018.pdf [Accessed 10 June 2020]

Financial Policy Committee, (2019). Financial Stability Report, Bank of England, December, available from https://www.bankofengland.co.uk/-/media/boe/files/financial-stability-report/2019/december-2019.pdf [Accessed 10 June 2020]

Financial Stability Board, (2020). Addressing the Regulatory, Supervisory and Oversight Challenges Raised by "Global Stablecoin" Arrangements, Consultative Document, 14 April.

Financial Stability Board, (2019). Regulatory Issues of Stablecoins. October.

Financial Stability Board, (2018). Crypto-asset Markets, Potential Channels for Future Financial Stability Implications, 10 October, available from https://www.fsb.org/wp-content/uploads/P101018.pdf

Houben, R., and Snyers, A. (2020). Cryptocurrencies Crypto-assets- Key Developments, Regulatory Concerns and Responses. Study for the Committee on Economic and Monetary Affairs, Policy Department for Economic, Scientific and Quality of Life Policies, European Parliament, Luxembourg, PE 648.779-April.

Houben, R., and Snyers, A., (2018). Policy Department for Economic, Scientific and Quality of Life Policies, "Cryptocurrencies and Blockchain, Legal Context and Implications for Financial Crime, Money Laundering and Tax Evasion". Directorate-General for Internal Policies, Study Requested by the TAX3 Committee, European Parliament, PE 619.024-July.

Mastercard, (2016). The Road to Inclusion, 5 December.

Shevlin, R., (2020). The Coronavirus Cryptocurrency Craze: Who's Behind the Bitcoin Buying Binge? Forbes, 27 July.

Stevens, A., (2017). Digital Currencies: Threats and Opportunities for Monetary Policy. NBB Economic Review, 79–92.

Von der Leyen, U., (2019). Mission Letters Brussels, 10 September.

World Bank, (2019). Europe and Central Asia Economic Update, Spring 2019: Financial Inclusion, available from https://openknowledge.worldbank.org/handle/10986/31501 [Accessed 10 June 2020]

World Bank, (2014). Financial Inclusion. Global Financial Development Report, available from http://documents.worldbank.org/curated/en/225251468330270218/Global-financial-development-report-2014-financial-inclusion [Accessed 10 June 2020]

7 Initial coin offerings
Financial innovation or scam

Henry Hillman

1 Introduction

Initial coin offerings (ICOs) gained popularity in 2017/2018, enjoying the benefits of the hype created by Bitcoin's record values. This chapter explores the concept of a cryptocurrency and how ICOs have been used to launch countless cryptocurrencies. The advantages and disadvantages of ICOs are considered from the perspectives of the ICO issuer and of the investor, criminal threats are considered, and the regulatory response of the UK is identified. ICOs have faded from their peak in 2017/2018, and have been replaced by initial exchange offerings (IEOs), which are markedly similar to ICOs but offered by existing cryptocurrency exchanges instead. This chapter argues that ICOs have obvious advantages for ICO issuers, as they could raise funds without creating obligations to investors, but the benefits to ICO issuers is far outweighed by the risks to investors and the opportunities for scams.

2 Cryptocurrencies overview

Cryptocurrencies are a category of virtual currency. The term *virtual currencies* used alone refers to any currencies, which exist solely in electronic form, having no official physical form. A virtual currency is defined by FATF as

> a digital representation of value that can be digitally traded and functions as (1) a medium of exchange; and/or (2) a unit of account; and/or (3) a store of value, but does not have legal tender status.... It is not issued nor guaranteed by any jurisdiction, and fulfils the above functions only by agreement within the community of users of the virtual currency.
> (Financial Action Task Force, 2015)

The FATF definition focuses on the functions of money and how virtual currencies meet the requirements based on user acceptability. The European Central Bank (ECB) defines a virtual currency as a *"digital representation of value, not issued by a central bank, credit institution or e-money institution, which, in some circumstances, can be used as an alternative to money"* (European Central Bank,

	Centralised	Decentralised
Convertible	Linden Dollars (used in Second Life) are an example of a convertible virtual world currency; users may exchange their currency for US Dollars. The currency is centralised, Linden Labs (the developer of Second Life) act as administrators.	Examples of decentralised currencies include Bitcoin and Dogecoin. These are convertible for fiat currency but not controlled by a central administrator.
Non-Convertible	World of Warcraft (WoW) gold is non-convertible virtual world currency; users may not convert this into a fiat currency. WoW gold is controlled by the game developers, Blizzard	None exist.

Figure 7.1 FAFT categories of virtual currency (Financial Action Task Force, 2015).

2015). The ECB does not recognise virtual currencies as money but accepts that they can be used as an alternative to money. The FATF and ECB consider the interaction of virtual currencies with the traditional financial system as their primary areas of concern. The FATF categorises virtual currencies based on the transferability of the virtual currency into fiat currency, and the management structure of the virtual currency, which can be seen in Figure 7.1.

As Figure 7.1 illustrates, the FATF considers the structure and convertibility of a virtual currency in order to categorise it. Structures are either centralised or decentralised, and a virtual currency can be either convertible or nonconvertible. A virtual currency is centralised when it is controlled by a single administrating authority; examples of these are the currencies of virtual worlds. The degree of control exercised may vary according to the practices of the administrator and whether the currency is convertible or not. A decentralised currency has no central authority; instead, it is based on an algorithm or a code which dictates the production of the currency. The focus of this chapter is upon decentralised virtual currencies, known as cryptocurrencies. Cryptocurrencies are particularly novel due to their decentralised nature, which is also what makes them so challenging for regulators, as there is no administrator who can be subject to regulation. The operation of cryptocurrencies is best explained through the leading example of Bitcoin.

2.1 Bitcoin

Bitcoin warrants particular attention due to its high value in fiat currency (BBC News, 2017) and because it is the forerunner to the growth of cryptocurrencies.[1] Bitcoin is a virtual currency, as it has no physical form, and is also a cryptocurrency, a currency that uses cryptography to disguise or protect the users of the currency. Cryptocurrencies utilise cryptography techniques to conceal the identity of the sender and receiver of a message or transfer; Southall and Taylor (2013) trace the technique used by Bitcoin, and many other currencies, back to proposals made by Chaum (1981), who proposed sending private messages with a serial key system; messages were sent using a public key, but only the sender and recipient could access the message using a private key. Chaum (1982) subsequently suggested the technique could be used to facilitate anonymous payments.

Bitcoin is not the first digital currency; previous digital currencies existed but failed to persist. Examples of this include 'Beenz' which launched in 1998 and promised to create "a generation of e-millionaires" (BBC News, 1998), but closed in 2001 (Commerce Times, 2001), just weeks after rival currency 'Flooz' also shut down (CNet, 2002). Early digital currencies failed because they were not accepted by a large enough community.

Bitcoin is the first widely known cryptocurrency; it was created by Satoshi Nakamoto in 2008 (Nakamoto, 2008). The identity of Bitcoin's creator(s) is unknown as Satoshi Nakamoto is a pseudonym. It is not known if Satoshi Nakamoto is one person or a group of people as throughout the self-published paper proposing Bitcoins, the term 'we' is used to refer to the author, suggesting it may be more than one person. Bitcoins can be distinguished from early digital currencies by its use of cryptography, and subsequent digital currencies can be seen to have copied the characteristics of Bitcoin. Bitcoin operates using distributed ledger technology (DLT), summarised below as it appeared in the original paper by Satoshi Nakamoto:

1   *New transactions are broadcast to all nodes.*
2   *Each node collects new transactions into a block.*
3   *Each node works on finding a difficult proof-of-work for its block.*
4   *When a node finds a proof-of-work, it broadcasts the block to all nodes.*

---

1 Though widely considered the first cryptocurrency, the original paper proposing Bitcoin references a number of papers including previous proposals for web-based money such as: Dai, W. (1998) *B-Money*. Available from: http://www.weidai.com/bmoney.txt [Accessed 13 July 2020].

5 *Nodes accept the block only if all transactions in it are valid and not already spent.*
6 *Nodes express their acceptance of the block by working on creating the next block in the chain, using the hash of the accepted block as the previous hash.* (Nakamoto, 2008)

Stage three introduces the concept of proof-of-work; this part of the process is known as mining; this involves a user's computer, known as a node, providing an answer which matches the solution the system is requesting in order to produce a 'block' with a 'proof-of-work' attached; blocks are sets of data which are permanently recorded in the Bitcoin network; they are a record of Bitcoin transactions (Nakamoto, 2008) and known as the blockchain (Bitcoin.com). By finding the proof-of-work, and completing the block, the user then acquires some new Bitcoins, currently 12.5 Bitcoins (Bambrough and Forbes, 2018); each block can only be produced once, and the Bitcoin reward goes to the miner who first produces the block, and duplicates are not accepted. The alternative way to obtain Bitcoins is via exchanges (Bitcoin.com). Users send messages to each other in order to send and receive Bitcoins; this process uses a cryptography technique similar to that proposed by Chaum (1981). Each user has a Bitcoin wallet with a unique address; sending Bitcoins from one user to another user requires the Bitcoins to be sent from the sender's public address, which is their public key, to the recipient's public address, which is their public key. The public key tells the network of the transaction between the two addresses. The second key is a private key, which is a signature from the sender that prevents the amounts being transferred from being altered by anyone else in the network (Bitcoin.com). The recipient uses their private key in order to access the Bitcoins which have been sent.

The use of keys rather than names allows all transactions to be public and verifiable, to ensure that no Bitcoins are spent twice but still ensure the anonymity of those making the transactions. This anonymity will be lost if the user's key were to become public, and then all transactions may be traced. The anonymity attached to cryptocurrencies is described as pseudonymous by the US Government Accountability Office in their 2014 report.[2] This is because, although the users' names are not known, other details are published on the blockchain, such as their Bitcoin address, the time of the transaction, and the amount. Transactions of Bitcoins are authenticated by users of the network; authentication ensures the sender has sufficient funds and that there are no duplicated uses of Bitcoin. This authentication occurs when the proof-of-work is found; at this point, the computer which solved the proof-of work verifies all of the transactions which took place since the last proof-of-work was produced (Nakamoto, 2008). In order to limit the number of Bitcoins being produced, the proof-of-work problems increase to reduce the rate at which miners can complete blocks and obtain new Bitcoins.

2 US Government Accountability Office (2014) *Virtual Currencies: Emerging Regulatory, Enforcement, and Consumer Protection Challenges*. Available from http: //gao.gov/assets/670/663678.pdf [Accessed 1 August 2020] at p. 6.

Bitcoin's model of coin mining, transaction security, and transaction logging has been adopted by numerous subsequent currencies, such as Ethereum, Dogecoin, and LiteCoin. The various currencies compete amongst themselves by claiming to offer faster transaction speeds or increased security (Gibbs, 2013). A key feature of cryptocurrencies is the use of a blockchain, which is also known as distributed ledger (Financial Conduct Authority [FCA], 2017) and is publicly available.[3]

Bitcoin, and other cryptocurrencies, are exchanged globally and are referred to in similar terms as money, such as the term 'currency' within cryptocurrency, the term 'cash' in Bitcoin Cash, and the symbol used in Bitcoin's logo being akin to a monetary symbol. Cryptocurrencies are also traded for traditional currencies (fiat currencies), at times for significant sums, most notably Bitcoin, which has a record of $19,783 in December 2017 (Morris and Fortune.com, 2017). The growing popularity of Bitcoin has given rise to countless alternative cryptocurrencies being created, and the most common launch mechanism for new cryptocurrencies is an ICO. Whereas Bitcoin grew through a gradual increase in its online community, steadily increasing the total amount of Bitcoin as miners produce new blocks and obtain the block reward, such a long process is less desirable for a new cryptocurrency. A new cryptocurrency would be unable to compete with established cryptocurrencies because there would be too small a quantity in circulation, so the launching by way of an ICO is an appealing way to raise awareness of the new cryptocurrency or raise money for a blockchain-related project.

3 Initial coin offerings (ICOs)

An ICO is a mechanism to raise funds from investors, by selling newly created cryptocurrency coins. ICOs offer first access to a new cryptocurrency and are usually accompanied by a 'white paper' which sets out the goals of the project for which funding is sought. An ICO is endlessly customisable, the ICO will be offered for a limited time, and usually a limited number of coins are available to buy. The coins may be minable, like Bitcoin, or there may be a fixed number of them created. An ICO may be conducted through an intermediary, which holds the funds until the funding aim has been met, and can return the fund to investors if the ICO was unsuccessful.[4] Enyi (2017) notes that this is becoming increasingly common in an attempt to prevent fraud and give confidence to the market.

---

3 As demonstrated by Blockchain.com *Block Explorer: Bitcoin*. Available from: https://www.blockchain.com/explorer [Accessed 13 July 2020], Blockchain Blockchain.com *Block Explorer: Ethereum*. Available from: https://www.blockchain.com/explorer?currency=ETH [Accessed 13 July 2020], and Blockchain.com *Block Explorer: Bitcoin Cash*. Available from: https://www.blockchain.com/explorer?currency=BCH [Accessed 13 July 2020].

4 A variety of services are offered by intermediary companies: ICO Rating *Our Products*. Available from: https://icorating.com/products/token-sale/#our-products [Accessed 13 July 2020].

ICOs can be contrasted with crowdfunding and initial product offerings (IPOs). An ICO is similar to crowdfunding in that it is openly accessible to the public, and the white paper is used as an open pitch, much like a 'story' on Indeigogo,[5] or a 'campaign' on Kickstarter.[6] Other similarities to crowdfunding are the time limits placed on the funding call, and the money may be returned to the investors if the funding goal is not met.[7] A key difference between most crowdfunding and an ICO is the lack of a product in return for the investment; in an ICO, the benefit for the investor is the potential increase in value of cryptocurrency in order to return a profit for the investment.

Backing an ICO in the hope of selling the cryptocurrency for profit differentiates ICOs from crowdfunding campaigns but makes an ICO more akin to an IPO. An IPO allows a limited liability company to offer shares to the public in order to raise capital. Shares give investors a level of ownership of the company, which entitles them to dividends on company profits and the potential to sell the shares for a profit. An ICO is similar to an IPO in that it is typically used to gain funds for business, and runs for a limited period, but the similarities are limited as the crucial distinctions between an ICO and an IPO mean they are very different propositions. As Hari and Pasquier (2018) observe, IPOs are used by maturing companies with a record of performance the investor can review, whereas ICOs are used by fledgling businesses. Unlike an IPO, an ICO does not give the investor any ownership rights in a company, as cryptocurrency coins do not require an incorporated company to exist in order to be created. In addition, no dividends will be paid to ICO investors, which is a primary benefit of owning shares. This fundamental difference means that an ICO and an IPO are very different investments; one gives investors an ownership stake in a company and the right to a share in profits through dividends, whereas the other simply gives the investor early access to a cryptocurrency.

The eventual aim for a newly created cryptocurrency is for it to be accepted on cryptocurrency exchanges,[8] which will increase the level of awareness of the cryptocurrency and potentially increase its value while supporting the project attached to the cryptocurrency. Example of ICOs that took place in 2019 include

---

5 See, for example, Indiegogo page: Indiegogo *LEAF Mask, World's First FDA, UV-C N99, Clear Mask*. Available from: https://www.indiegogo.com/projects/leaf-mask-world-s-first-fda-uv-c-n99-clear-mask#/ [Accessed 13 July 2020].
6 See, for example, Kickstarter page: Kickstarter *W!CKED SAiNTS' Interactive Story Game: "Pathways."* Available from: https://www.kickstarter.com/projects/jessicamurrey/wcked-saints-interactive-story-game-pathways?ref=section-homepage-featured-project [Accessed 13 July 2020].
7 Kickstarter operates an 'All or Nothing' model: Kickstarter (25 June 2020) *Why Is Funding All-or-Nothing?* Available from: https://help.kickstarter.com/hc/en-us/articles/115005047893 [Accessed 13 July 2020].
8 A large number of cryptocurrency exchange platforms exist, many of which compete for market share, see Coin Market Cap *Top Cryptocurrency Spot Exchanges*. Available from: https://coinmarketcap.com/rankings/exchanges/ [Accessed 13 July 2020].

Initial coin offerings 111

LOL Token,[9] Oracol Xor,[10] and Tron.[11] Of these, LOL Token's website claims the ICO raised over $3 million for its education development business. Oracol Xor and Tron have not published their ICO results, but Tron trades at $0.0007 per coin. Oracol Xor figures are not available. In 2019, only 109 ICOs were completed – only a fraction of the 1,253 ICOs completed in 2018, which appears to be the peak year for ICO release; 875 ICOs took place in 2017 and just 29 in 2016 (ICOData.com). ICOs have fallen in their popularity, due to the high levels of risk for the investor, as will be explored at Section 5.2 below, and because of the development of initial exchange offerings (IEOs) in their place.

IEOs are very similar to ICOs. The key difference is that the funding call is launched directly by established cryptocurrency exchanges[12] rather than ICO platforms. This has advantages for both the issuers of the new cryptocurrency and for the investors. An issuer will have already been accepted onto an exchange, which provides a platform for trading their cryptocurrency once the IEO has finished. An investor gains a level of confidence in the IEO as it is being listed by a recognised exchange, so the exchange will have vetted the project and is risking its own reputation by listing it. While this is by no means an AAA rating, it provides a degree of accountability by having a recognised name in the industry attached to the new cryptocurrency.

4 Advantages of ICOs

This chapter looks at ICOs from the perspective of two key parties, the ICO issuers and the investors. The advantages of an ICO will be considered from each party's perspective.

4.1 ICO issuers

There are numerous advantages to the ICO issuer, especially when compared traditional funding such as an IPO. The cryptocurrency can be given a boost start in creating an initial circulation of coins, and the ICO is accessible to a wide range of the public. There will be no loss of equity in the ownership of the business; there is no obligation to repay as there would be with a loan either. There are no requirements to adhere to the legal formalities of offering shares; therefore, there will be no register of ICO purchasers, no shareholder rights to adhere to, and no dividends to pay.

---

9 White paper and outline of the project can be found here: LOL Token *ICO Roadmap*. Available from: https://www.loleiu.io/#roadmaptext [Accessed 13 July 2020].
10 White paper available here: Oracol *Oracol Xor Platform*. Available from: https://oracolxor.io/whitepaper/index.html [Accessed 13 July 2020].
11 White paper available here: Tron *About*. Available from: https://tron.network/about?lng=en [Accessed 13 July 2020].
12 For example, Latoken which lists IEOs as well as runs an exchange: Latoken *Crowdfunding>ongoing*. Available from: https://latoken.com/ieo [Accessed 13 July 2020].

An ICO involves the issuer selling a large amount of their cryptocurrency to investors; this provides a circulation of currency and helps avoid the potentially slow process of relying on a proof-of-work-based mining process. More coins in circulation allows more users to participate and achieves this much faster than early cryptocurrencies such as Bitcoin, which took several years to reach 50% of the planned total number of Bitcoins.

As well as boosting the initial volume of cryptocurrency in circulation, the ICO is accessible to a wider range of potential investors. This feature of ICOs is the most similar to crowdfunding as, compared to an IPO, an ICO is open to all investors, not just those who are within the financial sector. Crowdfunding has grown in popularity in the past decade, allowing for the raising of large sums of money from the cumulative contributions of small backers.[13] An ICO allows the issuers to benefit from the popularity of the funding mechanism.

Like most crowdfunding platforms, the ICO issuers will not lose equity in their business by raising funds using an ICO. As 'coins' are not shares, the investors will not gain an ownership stake in the issuers' business. This is beneficial in that the issuers retain full control of their company, so they will not need to face scrutiny from additional shareholders, and the investors will not be entitled to a share in the profits of the company in the same way as dividends are paid to shareholders. An ICO will not require the issuer to follow the formalities that come with issuing shares; hence, in the UK there would be no need to update Companies House[14] with a list of new coin holders or disclose relevant information regarding the beneficial owners of the coins.

4.2 Investors

There are also benefits for investors in ICOs, such as the liquidity of the asset they acquire and the potential for significant profits. The open access of an ICO means it is open to investors who may not have access to the financial sector, and ICOs have become popular as the number of 'altcoins' in existence has grown. In the same way as open access is beneficial to the issuers, the accessibility of ICOs is a benefit for investors. Individuals can purchase small quantities of cryptocurrency through the ICO, compared to the larger sums usually required when investing in traditional financial markets. The relevant ICO information can be viewed on ICO platforms and does not require the services of a financial advisor; therefore, an individual can invest in an ICO with very little fee or different kinds of service charges.

The investor will acquire an asset which they can choose to sell for profit. Cryptocurrencies have high liquidity as they are intended to operate in lieu of money. Countless cryptocurrency exchanges exist which enable users to sell

---

13 The most funded projects on Kickstarter have tens of thousands of backers: Kickstarter *Show Me "All Categories" Projects on "Earth" Sorted by "Most Funded."* Available from: https://www.kickstarter.com/discover/most-funded [Accessed 13 July 2020].

14 Companies Act 2006, ss112-144 cover the reporting requirements regarding shareholders.

their holdings for alternative cryptocurrencies, or for traditional fiat currencies; hence, selling a cryptocurrency can be achieved very quickly. The high liquidity of cryptocurrencies is beneficial for investors as the value of cryptocurrencies can swing wildly. The day 17 December 2017 saw Bitcoin hit a record value of $19,783 (Fortune.com, 2017), but in less than three months, by February 2018, it had dropped to $6,841 (XE.com), with daily swings in value by as much as 20% (Hankin and MarketWatch.com, 2019). Trading in cryptocurrencies is thus volatile and fast-moving. With volatile markets comes the potential to make huge profits if a cryptocurrency becomes popular on cryptocurrency exchanges, often referred to as the 'altcoin' market (Redman and Bitcoin.com, 2020). The values of altcoins are much lower than Bitcoin; in July 2020, a Bitcoin was priced at $9,200, Ethereum at $230, and Litecoin at $43 (Coindesk.com). Despite the comparatively low values of altcoins, the 'get rich quick' appeal of cryptocurrencies was found to be a big factor when the FCA commissioned a research into why consumer bought cryptocurrencies (FCA, 2019).

The notion of being able to get rich by being an early adopter of cryptocurrencies is propelled by examples of success stories. In February 2018, CoinTelegraph listed the ten ICOs with the highest return on investment (ROI), which was calculated as the difference between the prices per coin during the ICO to trading prices in February 2018 (CoinTelegraph). The tenth highest ROI was QTUM at 9,225%, and the highest was NXT at 1,265,555%. The figures are extremely high, but slightly distorted by the choice of metric; NXT tokens were sold at $0.0000168 during the ICO and traded at $0.213 when CoinTelegraph compiled their list. Regardless of the per-coin values, a small investment in NXT accompanied by a well-timed sale could have yielded astronomical profits.

4.2.1 Reasons the public invest in cryptocurrencies

The research by Revealing Reality for the FCA found three main factors that may be fuelling cryptocurrency investment, which included: a weakened trust in mainstream media, looking for the next 'shortcut', and acting on recommendations (FCA, 2019, p. 47). The FCA report found trust in the media to be a contributing factor to cryptocurrency investment, citing the findings of Edelman Trust (2018), which found only 32% of the general population trust the media, with the figure dropping to 23% in young people. Increasing reliance on alternative sources for news was noted by Ofcom (2017), with 47% of adults getting news mainly from social media posts. The figure is more profound in 16–24-year-olds, where 69% of respondents said they got their news mostly from social media posts. This reliance on non-traditional news sources could be linked to the third factor identified by the FCA report – acting on recommendations. The FCA report found that *"respondents' engagement with cryptoassets was often prompted by the advice of surprisingly few but inordinately influential recommendations"* (FCA, 2019, p. 47). Trusting in the advice of an influential source rather than traditional news sources could easily expose individuals to biased opinions that promote all the benefits of an ICO but do not mention the risks.

A worrying finding from the FCA report was that respondents *"described a desire to 'get rich quick' and 'get ahead'"* (FCA, 2019, p. 47) which will leave them susceptible to fraud, as they may be too focused on the gains and not consider the risks. The combination of distrust of mainstream media and a desire to get rich quickly is a dangerous mix, as it leaves a proportion of the population relying on the advice of unverifiable sources to make significant financial investments.

The FCA followed up the 2019 research in 2020. The findings show an increase in awareness of cryptocurrencies from the previous year, from 42% of adults being aware of cryptocurrencies in 2019, to 73% in 2020 (FCA, 2020b). Other observations from the 2020 research were that most respondents who did invest in cryptocurrencies, only invested small amounts; 75% of respondents invested less than £1,000. Just under half of the respondents who had invested in cryptocurrencies saw it as a gamble, with just 15% expecting to make money quickly. The results of the most recent survey suggest that many of those purchasing cryptocurrencies are experimenting and risking small amounts of money, which they can afford to lose; 40% of those who had invested more than £260 reported income over £50,000 per year.

5 Disadvantages of ICOs

As with advantages, disadvantages are relevant to the perspective through which they are viewed. Some of the advantages considered already for one party may be identified as disadvantages for the other party.

5.1 ICO issuers

The disadvantages of an ICO for the issuers are that the market can be overcrowded and the majority of ICOs do not meet their targets. In addition, while the ICO market is open, after the ICO has been completed issuers are reliant upon cryptocurrency exchanges opting to include the issuer's cryptocurrency on their platforms; a cryptocurrency is more difficult to trade if it is not on a widely used exchange. Even after completing an ICO, and being listed on an exchange, the trading value of an issuer's cryptocurrency can quickly fall in value from its ICO price, due to the volatility of cryptocurrency prices on exchanges.

ICO platforms are open access, but they can choose which projects to list on their site; hence, the first hurdle for an ICO issuer is to get accepted, then they will need obtain the funding, and then hope to be traded on an established exchange. For an ICO issuer, the market can be very crowded; therefore, it can be difficult to differentiate one project from another. The now-defunct CoinSchedule website published ongoing statistics of cryptocurrency launches on its platform. As of June 2019, there had been 7,908 funding projects submitted, of which 1,904 ICOs were completed. Only 327 of those completed ICOs ended up being listed on cryptocurrency exchanges, representing a 4% success rate. Due to a highly competitive market, issuers need to try to appeal to investors, which leads to extravagant claims within the 'white paper' proposals.

Once an ICO has been completed and the cryptocurrency is being traded, the price of a cryptocurrency can fall extremely quickly. As seen with the volatility of Bitcoin, a cryptocurrency can lose its value suddenly. For example, on 8 July 2020, CoinMarketCap showed Dogecoin having the highest 24-hour change in value of +36.42%, whereas the biggest loss on the same day was Verge which lost 5.65% of its value in the preceding 24 hours. Despite the volatility in value appearing disastrous, this may not affect the ICO issuer, as by this point they already have the money the investors paid during the ICO and have no obligation to repay it. The lack of a trading platform to trade the cryptocurrency on once the ICO has finished is a problem that has been addressed by the evolution of IEOs,[15] as in an IEO the issuer has already been accepted onto an exchange. This brings its own potential disadvantage as the need to be accepted and promoted by an exchange adds an additional hurdle for the issuer to overcome before they can reach investors.

5.2 Investors

As any financial advisor or the small print at the bottom of an advertisement or garbled speed talk at the end of a radio commercial will say, any investment is a risk. However, the potential risks for investors in ICOs are numerous. They gain no equity in the business they are investing in, there is little to no recourse if things go wrong, there is a lack of regulation, the prices of cryptocurrencies are highly volatile, and there is a huge potential for fraudulent schemes. An ICO is not like an IPO, the investor does not obtain shares in a company, and therefore they do not acquire any of the legal protections that they will benefit from if they were to purchase shares. This disadvantage for investors very much mirrors the way in which it is an advantage to the issuer. While a shareholder's level of control is minimal, it means they cannot hold the issuers to account and the investors will not be entitled to a share in the profits of the company in the same way as dividends are paid to shareholders. The lack of formalities may appeal to some investors who are seeking investments that do not require their details to be registered with Companies House or its equivalents in jurisdictions other than the UK. The lack of legal formalities mean that ICO offerings will not take the forms that established investments may take. There is a general lack of regulation and with it protection for investors. The coins purchased will not be redeemable in the way the preference share may be (Kelleher, 2006), and they cannot be insured easily.[16]

One of the biggest risks faced by investors in ICOs is the volatility in cryptocurrency values, with coins purchased being highly likely to quickly fall in value

---

15 As defined in Section 3.
16 The first insurance products have been offered for cryptocurrency products in 2020: Gangcuangco, T. and Insurance Business.com (2 March 2020) *New Cryptocurrency Coverage Rolled Out at Lloyd's.* Available from: https://www.insurancebusinessmag.com/uk/news/breaking-news/new-cryptocurrency-coverage-rolled-out-at-lloyds-215443.aspx [Accessed 13 July 2020].

relative to the price paid in the ICO. In contrast to the huge successes highlighted as an advantage for investors at Section 4.2 above, the highest funded ICOs demonstrate the potential losses investors can suffer. The ten most funded ICOs of 2018 raised approximately $8.588 billion,[17] but by May 2019, only one of the ten ICOs was trading higher than the ICO price. Of the nine non-profitable coins, two had failed to start trading; Telegram's ill-fated cryptocurrency had been blocked by US courts (Rapoza, 2020), and the Petro Dollar, which was launched by Venezuela, attracted controversy due to accusations of it being designed to avoid US sanctions (Pons *et al.*, 2018). Of the remaining seven ICOs not returning profit for ICO investors, six were trading at less than half their price at the ICO, of which three have lost over 90% of their value. This chapter cannot assess every price difference in detail, but the snapshot of the market shown by the ten most funded projects suggests the majority of ICO investors make a loss on the majority of ICOs.

5.2.1 Crime threats

It is very easy to lie on the internet, even more so than face to face with innate communicative nuances lacking and technology enhancing the armoury of the criminal. The big increase in the value of Bitcoin in 2017 helped fuel huge interest in cryptocurrencies, which remains a largely unregulated market, and thus makes an ICO appealing to the unscrupulous. More ICO scams exist than can be covered in this chapter; some high-profile examples include: OneCoin, Bitconnect, PlusToken, and PlexCoin. While OneCoin was not a cryptocurrency, it was simply an investment fraud promoting itself as a cryptocurrency (BBC News, 2019), and it never launched via an IPO; it is synonymous with cryptocurrency scams. It is not known how much money the scheme made – $4 billion is a widely suggested figure (Redman, 2019) – but it could be as high as $15 billion (BBC News, 2019). Bitconnect promised huge returns on Bitcoin investments, which were akin to a pyramid scheme, as early investors would benefit from chains of referrals (Sedgwick, 2017). In a response to how many scam ICOs existed, spoof ICOs started to appear and state clearly their nefarious aims (Solon, 2018). Ponzicoin made no effort to hide its 'scam' status. It claims never to have actually taken any money but instead highlights the issue of scams.[18] The same cannot be said for Useless Ethereum Token, which stated that users would be giving "some random person on the internet money," (Useless Ethereum Token) who will then *"go buy stuff with it."*[19] Useless Ethereum Token raised

---

17 Compiled from Grundy, C. and Coinoffering.com (30 April 2019) *The 10 Biggest ICOs and Where They Are Today*. Available from: https://thecoinoffering.com/learn/the-10-biggest-icos/ [Accessed 13 July 2020].
18 See Ponzicoin *Our Incredible Journey*. Available from: https://ponzicoin.co/home.html [Accessed 13 July 2020].
19 See Useless Ethereum Token *The World's First 100% Honest Ethereum ICO*. Available from: https://uetoken.com/ [Accessed 13 July 2020].

$83,354.[20] Even the US Securities and Exchange Commission launched their own fictitious ICO in an effort to educate consumers on the risks.[21]

High-profile examples will take the headlines, but fraud and missing information is rife within ICOs and associated documents. In 2018, the *Wall Street Journal* reviewed 1,450 ICOs and identified 'red flags' in 271 (Shifflett and Jones, 2018). The red flags included 111 ICOs pasting word for word sections from other white papers, 121 ICOs not disclosing the name of any employees, and 5 ICOs with board of executives made up of stock images. The issue of scams has been lessened by a move to IEOs instead of ICOs as the projects are vetted by a cryptocurrency exchange, which risks its reputation on the project. Investors may feel able to trust the cryptocurrency exchange and, in turn, trust the IEO more than an ICO.

There are clear links to be drawn between ICOs and Ponzi schemes, with investors putting money into 'products' that promise unrealistic returns, only for the organisers of the scheme to disappear; in cryptocurrency circles, this is known as 'exit scamming' (Jagati and CoinTelegraph, 2019). Some cryptocurrency offerings, such as Bitconnect, appear as pyramid schemes, where those who get involved early make money from referring the scheme to others. These types of ICO frauds will appear obvious to many, and well-informed consumers should not be fooled, but well-informed consumers are not the target for fraudsters. Greedy and naïve individuals are much easier victims for financial frauds, akin to the individuals identified as common cryptocurrency investor by the 2018 FCA report.[22]

6 UK regulation

The UK regulation of cryptocurrencies, and of ICOs, is limited. Regulation of ICOs, and with it consumer protection, is decided on a case-by-case basis. The Cryptoassets Taskforce published its final report in 2018, categorising cryptocurrencies and advising on their regulatory treatment, which has been adopted by the FCA. The UK refers to cryptocurrencies as cryptoassets; the reasons for this choice of terminology is unclear as it is not a term the cryptocurrency industry uses, meaning that the term 'cryptoassets' always requires clarifying with reference to cryptocurrencies.[23]

---

20 Stated on its website but now taken down.
21 See Securities and Exchange Commission (16 May 2018) *The SEC Has an Opportunity You Won't Want to Miss: Act Now!* Available from: https://www.sec.gov/news/press-release/2018-88 [Accessed 13 July 2020].
22 See Financial Conduct Authority *How and Why Consumers Buy Cryptocurrencies.* Available from: www.fca.org.uk/publication/research/how-and-why-consumers-buy-cryptoassets.pdf [Accessed 13 July 2020].
23 For example, the Bank of England pays lip service to the term 'Cryptoassets' but then refers to cryptocurrencies throughout its definitions: Bank of England *What Are Cryptoassets (Cryptocurrencies)?* Available from: https://www.bankofengland.co.uk/knowledgebank/what-are-cryptocurrencies [Accessed 13 July 2020].

6.1 Cryptoassets Taskforce

The Cryptoassets Taskforce was established in March 2018 to consider the risks and the potential benefits of cryptocurrencies and DLT and propose regulation (HM Treasury, 2018). The taskforce identified three categories of cryptocurrencies: exchange tokens, security tokens, and utility tokens (Cryptoassets Taskforce, 2018, p. 11). The coins sold through an ICO will fall under exchange tokens due to the more specified nature of the other categories. A security token must be a 'specified investment' for the purposes of the Financial Services and Markets Act 2000,[24] which requires the token to provide rights such as ownership or entitlement to a share in future profits. ICOs do not provide any rights to the purchaser that would equate to a specified investment and as such cannot fall under security tokens. A utility token is defined as a token that can be *"redeemed for access to a specific product or service"* (Cryptoassets Taskforce, 2018, p. 11), which again is not a benefit afforded to a purchaser of an ICO token.

ICOs offer investors cryptocurrencies which *"utilise a DLT platform and are not issued or backed by a central bank or other central body"* (Cryptoassets Taskforce, 2018, p. 11) and as such will be defined as exchange tokens by the Cryptoassets Taskforce and, in turn, by the FCA. Holding exchange tokens leaves investors with no protection from regulators.

6.2 FCA

The FCA last updated its guidance on ICOs in February 2019. Broadly ICOs remain unregulated, and the FCA states that it can only determine whether an ICO falls inside its regulatory perimeter on a case-by-case basis (FCA, 2019). Most ICOs will not be regulated as they issue exchange tokens, as defined by the Cryptoasset Taskforce, and are usually based outside of the UK. The FCA will only regulate if it the structure of the ICO is such that it is considered a security token. The position of the FCA in relation to cryptocurrencies in general is to caution the public against investing, stating: *"If you invest in unregulated cryptoassets, you may not have access to the Financial Ombudsman Service or the Financial Services Compensation Scheme if something goes wrong"* (FCA, 2020). Given the position of the FCA, and its wider regulatory responsibilities, it is not likely that it is monitoring the ICOs. Instead, it will react to reports from the public, as per its case-by-case approach.

While the FCA does not provide consumer protection in relation to ICOs, and it does not view cryptocurrencies to be within its regulatory perimeter, this position has been amended in relation to anti-money laundering and counterterrorist financing (AML/CTF) regulation. For AML/CTF purposes, cryptocurrency service providers must comply with the Money Laundering and Terrorist Financing (Amendment) Regulations 2019, which are enforced by the FCA. While

---

24 The Financial Services and Markets Act 2000 (Regulated Activities) Order 2001, SI 2001/544.

there are no examples of an ICO being used for money laundering purposes, if an ICO is deemed to be fraudulent, then dealing with the proceeds from that ICO would meet the criteria of the money laundering offences contained in the Proceeds of Crime Act (POCA) 2002.[25] Cryptocurrencies are capable of being criminal property for the purposes of POCA 2002, as demonstrated by the prosecutions of *Teresko*,[26] *White*,[27] and *West*.[28] Until now prosecutions have only concerned Bitcoin, but there is no reason why other cryptocurrencies would be treated differently. Sinclair and Taylor (2018) note that investors could have recourse through the Unfair Contract Terms Act 1977 and the Consumer Rights Act 2015, but as they concede, this is dependent upon the investors tracking down a party to sue, which is unlikely to be possible in the case of an ICO.

7 Conclusions

Cryptocurrencies have come from relative obscurity to headline news in a short space of time, and it is clear that, as with all novel phenomena, problems will incur and opportunities exist for both innovation and exploitation. ICOs have developed in response to the popularity of cryptocurrencies, and while they are a new concept, they clearly take characteristics from existing practices, most notably IPOs and crowdfunding. The advantages of ICOs outweigh the risks for ICO issuers; despite entering a crowded market, competition is a small price to pay for the potential to generate attention for their project and attract funding with no ongoing obligations to investors. While the ICO party appears to be over, from an ICO issuer's perspective, it was great while it lasted and generated vast sums of money. However, the opposite is true for investors. Investing in an ICO provides the purchaser with an unregulated asset that provides them with no legal rights against the issuer, in a market which favours opportunistic fraudsters. The high-profile frauds, which have led to openly fake ICOs from market participants, and even regulators, designed to warn of the risks, means that the ICO trend has been short-lived, with IEOs now being a more common mechanism for new cryptocurrency launches. IEOs provide a level of security as the exchange puts it reputation on the line by promoting the project, but the area remains unregulated. The fraudulent possibilities for cryptocurrencies and ICOs are only limited by the fraudsters' imaginations. Given that their target audience are less likely to be familiar with well-known fraudulent schemes, they have been

---

25 Sections 327–329.
26 Crown Prosecution Service (2018) *More than £1.2 Million of Bitcoin Seized from Drug Dealer*. Available from: https://www.cps.gov.uk/south-east/news/more-ps12-million-bitcoin-seized-drug-dealer [Accessed 01 August 2020].
27 National Crime Agency (2019) *Student behind $100m Dark Web Site Jailed for 5 Years 4 Months*. Available from: https://www.nationalcrimeagency.gov.uk/news/student-behind-100m-dark-web-site-jailed-for-5-years-4-months?highlight=WyJiaXRjb2luIiwiYml0Y29pbnMiXQ== [Accessed 11 September 2019].
28 BBC News (2019) *Prolific Sheerness Hacker Ordered to Pay Back £922k*. Available from: https://www.bbc.co.uk/news/uk-england-kent-49450676 [Accessed 24 September 2019].

able to succeed by recycling thinly veiled Ponzi frauds and pyramid schemes. As their audience becomes more experienced, there will still be opportunities for increasingly complex cryptocurrency products to dupe consumers into investing in a market that remains largely unregulated. Regulators are playing catch up to the development of cryptocurrencies, the first regulatory steps have been focused on AML/CFT regulation, and consumer protection is still lacking. Cryptocurrencies and ICOs remain outside of the FCA's regulatory perimeter except for AML/CTF, and it warns the public against investing as they will have no recourse for compensation. DLT remains at a nascent stage in terms of wider application in the financial system and society, and ICOs could present a novel mechanism for funding interesting and worthy projects. However, no genuinely ground-breaking projects appear to exist at present, and the technology appears to be a solution seeking a problem to solve; rather, it actually appears to be creating more problems by exploiting the uninformed public

References

Bambrough, B. and Forbes (2018) *A Bitcoin Halvening Is Two Years Away – Here's What'll Happen to the Bitcoin Price*. Available from: https://www.forbes.com/sites/billybambrough/2018/05/29/a-bitcoin-halvening-is-two-years-away-heres-whatll-happen-to-the-bitcoin-price/#4bffecd05286 [Accessed 13 July 2020].

Bank of England *What Are Cryptoassets* (Cryptocurrencies)? Available from: https://www.bankofengland.co.uk/knowledgebank/what-are-cryptocurrencies [Accessed 13 July 2020].

BBC News (1998) *Business: The Company File: Beenz Means Business*. Available from: http://news.bbc.co.uk/1/hi/business/297133.stm [Accessed 13 July 2020].

BBC News (27 November 2017) *Bitcoin Currency Hits New Record High*. Available from: https://www.bbc.co.uk/news/business-42135963 [Accessed 13 July 2020].

BBC News (24 November 2019) *Cryptoqueen: How This Woman Scammed the World, Then Vanished*. Available from: https://www.bbc.co.uk/news/stories-50435014 [Accessed 13 July 2020].

Bitcoin Charts *Markets*. Available from: http://bitcoincharts.com/markets/ [Accessed 13 July 2020].

Blockchain.com *Block Explorer: Bitcoin*. Available from: https://www.blockchain.com/explorer [Accessed 13 July 2020].

Blockchain.com *Block Explorer: Bitcoin Cash*. Available from: https://www.blockchain.com/explorer?currency=BCH [Accessed 13 July 2020].

Blockchain.com *Block Explorer: Ethereum*. Available from: https://www.blockchain.com/explorer?currency=ETH [Accessed 13 July 2020].

Chaum, D. (1981) Untraceable Electronic Mail, Return Addresses and Digital Pseudonyms. *Communications of the ACM*. 24 (2), p. 84.

Chaum, D. (1982) Blind Signatures for Untraceable Payments. In: Chaum, D., Rivest, R.L. and Sherman, A.T., eds. *Advances in Cryptology*. New York: Springer, p. 119.

CNet (2002) *E-Currency Site Flooz Goes Offline*. Available from: http://news.cnet.com/2100-1017-271385.html [Accessed 13 July 2020].

Coin Market *Cap Top Cryptocurrency Spot Exchanges*. Available from: https://coinmarketcap.com/rankings/exchanges/ [Accessed 13 July 2020].

Coin Market Cap *Tron (TRX)*. Available from: https://coinmarketcap.com/currencies/tron/ [Accessed 13 July 2020].

Coindesk *Bitcoin*. Available from: https://www.coindesk.com/price/bitcoin [Accessed 13 July 2020].

Coindesk *Ethereum*. Available from: https://www.coindesk.com/price/ethereum [Accessed 13 July 2020].

Coindesk *Litecoin*. Available from: https://www.coindesk.com/price/litecoin [Accessed 13 July 2020].

CoinSchedule (2019) *Stats*. Available from: www.coinschedule.com/stats-funnel/ALL?dates=Apr%2001,%202019%20to%20Jun%2014,%202019 [Accessed 21 June 2019].

CoinTelegraph (2018) *Top 10 ICOs with the Biggest ROI*. Available from: https://cointelegraph.com/ico-101/top-10-icos-with-the-biggest-roi [Accessed 13 July 2020].

Commerce Times (2001) *Beenz.Com Closes Internet Currency Business*. Available from: http://www.ecommercetimes.com/story/12892.html [Accessed 13 July 2020].

Companies Act 2006.

Consumer Rights Act 2015.

Cryptoassets Taskforce (29 October 2018) *Final Report*. Available from: https://assets.publishing.service.gov.uk/government/uploads/system/uploads/attachment_data/file/752070/cryptoassets_taskforce_final_report_final_web.pdf [Accessed 13 July 2020].

Dai, W. (1998) *B-Money*. Available from: http://www.weidai.com/bmoney.txt [Accessed 13 July 2020].

Dogecoin *Dogecoin*. Available from: https://dogecoin.com/ [Accessed 13 July 2020].

Edelman (2018) *Edelman Trust Barometer 2018 UK Findings*. Available from: https://www.edelman.co.uk/research/edelman-trust-barometer-218-uk-findings [Accessed 13 July 2020].

Enyi, J. (2017) Regulating Initial Coin Offerings ("Crypto-Crowdfunding"). *Journal of International Banking and Financial*. 8, p. 495.

Ethereum *Learn about Ethereum*. Available from: https://www.ethereum.org/learn/ [Accessed 13 July 2020].

European Central Bank (2015) *Virtual Currency Schemes – A Further Analysis*. Available from: https://www.ecb.europa.eu/pub/pdf/other/virtualcurrencyschemesen.pdf [Accessed 29 July 2020].

Financial Action Task Force (2015) *Virtual Currencies – Key Definitions and Potential AML/CFT Risks*. Available from: http://www.fatf-gafi.org/media/fatf/documents/reports/Virtual-currency-key-definitions-and-potential-aml-cft-risks.pdf [Accessed 13 July 2020].

Financial Conduct Authority (15 December 2017) *FCA Publishes Feedback Statement on Distributed Ledger Technology*. Available from: https://www.fca.org.uk/news/press-releases/fca-publishes-feedback-statement-distributed-ledger-technology [Accessed 13 July 2020].

Financial Conduct Authority (27 February 2019) *Initial Coin Offerings*. Available from: https://www.fca.org.uk/news/statements/initial-coin-offerings [Accessed 13 July 2020].

Financial Conduct Authority (17 March 2020a) *Cryptoassets*. Available from: https://www.fca.org.uk/consumers/cryptoassets [Accessed 13 July 2020].

Financial Conduct Authority (30 June 2020b) *Research Note: Cryptoasset Consumer Research 2020*. Available from: https://www.fca.org.uk/publication/research/research-note-cryptoasset-consumer-research-2020.pdf [Accessed 13 July 2020].

Financial Conduct Authority *How and Why Consumers Buy Cryptocurrencies.* Available from: www.fca.org.uk/publication/research/how-and-why-consumers-buy-cryptoassets.pdf [Accessed 13 July 2020].

The Financial Services and Markets Act 2000 (Regulated Activities) Order 2001, SI 2001/544.SI 2001/544. (2001).

Gangcuangco, T. and Insurance Business.com (02 March 2020) *New Cryptocurrency Coverage Rolled Out at Lloyd's.* Available from: https://www.insurancebusinessmag.com/uk/news/breaking-news/new-cryptocurrency-coverage-rolled-out-at-lloyds-215443.aspx [Accessed 13 July 2020].

Gibbs, S. (2013) Nine Bitcoin Alternatives for Future Currency Investments. *The Guardian.*

Grundy, C. and Coinoffering.com (30 April 2019) *The 10 Biggest ICOs and Where They Are Today.* Available from: https://thecoinoffering.com/learn/the-10-biggest-icos/ [Accessed 13 July 2020].

Hankin, A. and Market Warch.com (02 April 2019) *Bitcoin's One-Day Price Rally on Verge of Carving Out a Place in the History Books, in One Chart.* Available from: https://www.marketwatch.com/story/bitcoins-one-day-price-rally-on-verge-of-carving-out-a-place-in-the-history-books-in-one-chart-2019-04-02 [Accessed 13 July 2020].

Hari, O. and Pasquier, U. (2018) Blockchain and Distributed Ledger Technology (DLT): Academic Overview of the Technical and Legal Framework and Challenges for Lawyers. *International Business Law Journal.* 5, p. 423.

HM Treasury (22 March 2018) *Fintech Sector Strategy: Securing the Future of UK Fintech.* Available from: https://assets.publishing.service.gov.uk/government/uploads/system/uploads/attachment_data/file/692880/Fintech_Sector_Strategy_web.pdf [Accessed 13 July 2020].

ICO Data *Funds Raised in 2016.* Available from: https://www.icodata.io/stats/2018 [Accessed 13 July 2020].

ICO Data *Funds Raised in 2017.* Available from: https://www.icodata.io/stats/2018 [Accessed 13 July 2020].

ICO Data *Funds Raised in 2018.* Available from: https://www.icodata.io/stats/2018 [Accessed 13 July 2020].

ICO Data *Funds Raised in 2019.* Available from: https://www.icodata.io/stats/2019 [Accessed 13 July 2020].

ICO Rating *Our Products.* Available from: https://icorating.com/products/token-sale/#our-products [Accessed 13 July 2020].

Indiegogo *LEAF Mask, World's First FDA, UV-C N99, Clear Mask.* Available from: https://www.indiegogo.com/projects/leaf-mask-world-s-first-fda-uv-c-n99-clear-mask#/ [Accessed 13 July 2020].

Jagati, S. and CoinTelegraph (09 September 2019) *Crypto Exit Scams —How to Avoid Falling Victim.* Available from: https://cointelegraph.com/news/crypto-exit-scams-how-to-avoid-falling-victim [Accessed 13 July 2020].

Kelleher, E. (2006) Preference Shares: The Appeal of Certainty. *The Financial Times.*

Kickstarter (25 June 2020) *Why Is Funding All-Or-Nothing?* Available from: https://help.kickstarter.com/hc/en-us/articles/115005047893 [Accessed 13 July 2020].

Kickstarter *Show Me 'All Categories' Projects on 'Earth' Sorted by 'Most Funded.* Available from: https://www.kickstarter.com/discover/most-funded [Accessed 13 July 2020].

Kickstarter *W!CKED SAiNTS' Interactive Story Game: "Pathways."* Available from: https://www.kickstarter.com/projects/jessicamurrey/wcked-saints-interactive-story-game-pathways?ref=section-homepage-featured-project [Accessed 13 July 2020].
Latoken *Crowdfunding>ongoing*. Available from: https://latoken.com/ieo [Accessed 13 July 2020].
LiteCoin *Litecoin*. Available from: https://litecoin.org/ [Accessed 13 July 2020].
LOL Token *ICO Roadmap*. Available from: https://www.loleiu.io/#roadmaptext [Accessed 13 July 2020].
LOL Token *Loltoken Offering by Eiu.Ac*. Available from: https://www.loleiu.io/#aboutusteam [Accessed 13 July 2020].
The Money Laundering and Terrorist Financing (Amendment) Regulations 2019 SI 2019/1511. (2019).
Morris, D. and Fortune.com (2017) *Bitcoin Hits a New Record High, but Stops Short of $20,000*. [Accessed 13 July 2020].
Nakamoto, S. (2008) *Bitcoin Wiki Research*. Available from: http://bitcoin.org/bitcoin.pdf [Accessed 13 July 2020].
Ofcom (2017) *News Consumption in the UK: 2016*. Available from: https://www.ofcom.org.uk/__data/assets/pdf_file/0016/103570/news-consumption-uk-2016.pdf [Accessed 13 July 2017].
Oracol *Oracol Xor Platform*. Available from: https://oracolxor.io/whitepaper/index.html [Accessed 13 July 2020].
Pons, C., Gupta, G., Mazzilli, M. and Shumaker, L. (2018) Venezuela Says Launch of 'Petro' Cryptocurrency Raised $735 Million. *Reuters*.
Ponzicoin *Our Incredible Journey*. Available from: https://ponzicoin.co/home.html [Accessed 13 July 2020].
Proceeds of Crime Act 2002.
Rapoza, K. (2020) Telegram Gives up on Its Blockchain, Crypto Project. *Forbes*.
Redman, J. and Bitcoin.com (04 December 2019) *Onecoin Websites Suspended as the $4 Billion Ponzi Crumbles*. Available from: https://news.bitcoin.com/multiple-onecoin-websites-suspended-as-the-4-billion-dollar-ponzi-crumbles/ [Accessed 13 July 2020].
Redman, J. and Bitcoin.com (10 February 2020) *What Are Altcoins and Why Are There over 5,000 of Them?* Available from: https://news.bitcoin.com/altcoins-why-over-5000/ [Accessed 13 July 2020].
Securities and Exchange Commission (16 May 2018) *The SEC Has an Opportunity You Won't Want to Miss: Act Now!* Available from: https://www.sec.gov/news/press-release/2018-88 [Accessed 13 July 2020].
Sedgwick, K. and Bitcoin.com (09 November 2017) *Cracks Appear as Critics Label Bitconnect a Ponzi Scheme*. Available from: https://news.bitcoin.com/cracks-appear-critics-label-bitconnect-ponzi-scheme/ [Accessed 13 July 2020].
Shifflett, S. and Jones, C. (2018) Buyer Beware: Hundreds of Bitcoin Wannabes Show Hallmarks of Fraud. *Wall Street Journal*.
Sinclair, P. and Taylor, A. (2018) The English Law Rights of Investors in Initial Coin Offerings. *Journal of International Banking and Financial*. 4, p. 214.
Solon, O. (2018) Bitcoin, Titcoin, Ponzicoin: Jokes and Scams Fuel a Cryptocurrency Gold Rush. *The Guardian*.
Southall, E. and Taylor, M. (2013) Bitcoin. *Computer and Telecommunications Law Review*. 19 (6), p. 177.

Tron *About*. Available from: https://tron.network/about?lng=en [Accessed 13 July 2020].

Unfair Contract Terms Act 1977.

United States Government Accountability Office (May 2014) *Virtual Currencies: Emerging Regulatory, Enforcement, and Consumer Protection Challenges*. Available from: http://gao.gov/assets/670/663678.pdf [Accessed 13 July 2020].

Useless Ethereum Token *The World's First 100% Honest Ethereum ICO*. Available from: https://uetoken.com/ [Accessed 13 July 2020].

XE.com *USD per 1 XBT*. Available from: https://www.xe.com/currencycharts/?from=XBT&to=USD&view=2Y [Accessed 13 July 2020].

8 Cryptocurrency and crime
Sherena Huang

1 Introduction

On 15 July 2020, a covey of high-profile figures in the US was targeted by a Bitcoin scam on Twitter. The Twitter accounts of Barack Obama, Bill Gates and Kim Kardashian were hijacked spreading 'double your Bitcoin' scams (BBC News, 2020a). The scam tweets claimed a double return within 30 minutes on amount sends to a Bitcoin address. Over 30 people made transactions and the involved amount reached $100,000 in a short time. The scam was solved quite quickly within two weeks, and three teenagers were charged, two from the US and one from the UK (BBC News, 2020b). Bitcoin was also used as an international payment channel by ransomware, WannaCry, in May 2017. The hacker seized data on over 300,000 Windows system computers worldwide as hostages and demanded $300 or $600 worth of bitcoins per computer within three or six days (Millar and Marshall, 2017). The ransomware, originally called 'EternalBlue' (MS-ISAC, 2019),[1] was developed by the National Security Agency (NSA) of the US that was stolen and leaked on the internet by a hacker group called Shadow Brokers (The Express Tribune, 2017). Thousands of organisations that did not update their Windows system on time were infected, including the National Health Service (NHS) (Smart, 2018). Approximately 330 victims paid the ransom to three bitcoin addresses by early August 2017, and the amount involved was over $140,000. The Federal Bureau of Investigation (FBI) deemed that Park Jin Hyok from North Korea was responsible for the WannaCry ransom (*United States v Park Jin Hyok*, 2018, Cal.Rptr, pp. 4 and 117).

Cryptocurrencies are more than just means of transferring illicit earnings; they have been targeted by online criminals. As early as in 2013, two former Federal agents, Bridges and Force, were charged with 'Theft of Government Property, Wire Fraud, Money Laundering and Stealing Digital Currency' during their investigation of a dark web – Silk Road (*United States v Bridges and Force*,

---

[1] 'EternalBlue is an exploit that allows cyber threat actors to remotely execute arbitrary code and gain access to a network by sending specially crafted packets.... Due to EternalBlue's ability to compromise networks, if one device is infected by malware via EternalBlue, every device connected to the network is at risk' (accessed 23 August 2020).

2015, Cal.Rptr). The stolen cryptocurrencies were worth over $1.5 million and laundered on various cryptocurrency exchanges internationally.

Despite the increasing use of cryptocurrency in financial crime, relevant legal proceedings are complicated and ridden with flaws. For example, BTC-e, a cryptocurrency trading platform formed in July 2011, was involved in various ransomware and cybercriminal activities and ordered to shut down in July 2017. Its owner, Alexander Vinnik, was arrested in Greece on 26 July 2017 and was charged with a 21-count indictment, including operation of an unlicensed money service business and money laundering (Department of Justice, 2017). This case has exposed a flaw in confronting cryptocurrency crime. Vinnik was operating the BTC-e across countries including Russia, US and EU (NDC – Department of Justice, 2019), and all the authorities demanded to prosecute him on behalf of their national victims. Therefore, judicial decisions have been bounced from court to court in the past two years (Magnuson, 2020, p. 95). As of December 2019, Alexander Vinnik still remained in jail in Greece (BBC News, 2019), although the US has asserted its jurisdiction again on 25 July 2019 (*United States v BTC-e and Alexander Vinnik, Defendant*, 2019, Cal.Rptr, p. 1).

Cryptocurrency and the Distributed Ledger Technology (DLT) and Blockchain that underpin it (Dryall, 2018, pp. 158–161) have been seen a secure (BitFury Group and Garzik, 2015, p. 6)[2] and efficient tool for value transactions through their anonymous and permission-less networks (BitFury Group and Garzik, 2015, p. 9; Walch, 2015, p. 7).[3] This technology creates a channel allowing nonfinancial firms to participate in financial markets,[4] and the extensive use of the internet is blurring the boundary between the financial industry and others, which is challenging the regulatory capability (Treleaven, 2015, p. 1).[5] The possibility of misusing new technology and gaming with regulatory systems is higher when regulations are loose (Murray, 2019, Part III), cryptocurrencies being no exception (Forgang, 2019, pp. 6–9).

The DLT offers a new transaction method with enhanced privacy and efficiency that challenges the intermediary role of banks and financial institutions

---

2 '[T]he key design element of blockchains – embedded security – makes them different from ordinary horizontally scalable distributed databases such as MySQL Cluster, MongoDB and Apache HBase. Blockchain security makes it practically impossible to modify or delete entries from the database'.
3 'Permission-less blockchains are systems with an open membership allowing every node to create blocks, utilize more complex algorithms out of necessity'; 'Because there are no permissions required to join the network of computers that run the Bitcoin software and help to maintain the blockchain, the Bitcoin blockchain is said to be public, or "permissionless," distinguishing it from private, or "permissioned," blockchains that are being developed by financial and technology companies'.
4 For instance, the payment platform PayPal has been providing transaction services to their users through registered and verified email addresses or phone numbers (*PayPal User Agreement*, 2019).
5 The current regulatory pressures are: 'a) an open-source platform for FinTech regulation, b) a regulatory XML to help standardize reporting and c) an overarching international standards body'.

(The World Bank, 2017, pp. VII-X). Cryptocurrency transactions are anonymous or semi-anonymous and processed in peer-to-peer networks using encrypted keys that are generated randomly and held by transaction parties only (Murray, 2019, pp. 438–452). However, the anonymity of cryptocurrency makes financial misconduct harder to monitor. With the anonymity and permission-less networks, cryptoassets allow user information and transaction details off-the-record and eliminate the involvement of third parties – usually banks and financial institutions who carry out compliance measures for abnormal activities. The two features of cryptocurrency provide a pathway for financial criminals (Magnuson, 2020, pp. 97–98).

What are the roles of cryptocurrency in financial crimes? And what are the relevant laws and regulations to determine and prosecute such crimes? Are there flaws or weaknesses in the existing legal systems? This chapter intends to answer these questions using UK laws and international cases as examples. This chapter first discusses the role of cryptocurrency in financial crime and then classifies cryptocurrency illicit activities into two categories – direct and indirect unlawful activities. By doing so, the chapter discovers three flaws in financial regulation: micropayments, individual activities and jurisdictions. The three issues exist in the current compliance measures and international cooperation. The lack of international cooperation has caused a delay in some legal proceedings of cryptocurrency crime, whereas the micropayments and individual activities may create a grey area for criminals gaming with the system.

2 Definitions of cryptocurrency

Cryptocurrency is a digital or virtual currency representative (unofficially) or digital assets/tokens (officially in the UK) (FCA, 2019b) that operates as a medium of exchange at a person-to-person level enabling direct payments between individuals. Cryptocurrency is based on cryptography and process transactions anonymously or semi-anonymously without third parties. Such encryption technology is known as Blockchain, one type of DLT (Badev and Chen, 2014, p. 5; Dryall, 2018, p. 15; Houben and Snyers, 2018, p. 15; The World Bank, 2017, p. IV; Walch, 2015, p. 6). Cryptocurrencies have been alleged of offering alternative intermediation of exchange that is more secure and efficient through user-encrypted keys (Buocz et al., 2019; Dryall, 2018; Vandezande and KU Leuven Centre for IT & IP Law, 2018; The World Bank, 2017). As of June 2020, there are over 5,537 cryptocurrencies[6] and 265 popular cryptocurrency exchanges[7] available online. The number of cryptocurrencies doubled from July 2019.[8] Bitcoin, launched in January 2008, holds the majority of the market

---

6 According to CoinMarketCap <https://coinmarketcap.com> (accessed 3 June 2020).
7 According to Coin.market <https://coin.market/exchanges> (accessed 3 June 2020).
8 There were about 2,300 cryptoassets in July 2019 <https://coinmarketcap.com> (accessed 2 July 2019).

shares (CoinMarketCap, 2020), and it is commonly used as a representative of cryptocurrencies.

Bitcoin was conceptualised by Nakamoto aiming to provide an efficient solution for digital transactions and cybersecurity (Nakamoto, 2008, p. 1).[9] It inherits the idea and the technology of peer-to-peer sharing used by the music platform, 'Napster', which provided a music-swapping service on its peer-to-peer network for users to exchange MP3[10] files (Stern, 2000, p. 4).[11] Although Napster did not directly breach copyright since the peer-to-peer network did not hold or store the music, Napster was charged with infringement of copyright for indirectly distributing music files without authorisation and was ordered to shut down in 2001 (*A&M Records, Inc. v. Napster, Inc.*, 2001). This case brought the copyright of digital properties into intense debates. Shih and Ku (2002, p. 263) and Landes and Lichtman (2003, p. 119) state that Napster created a new approach to encourage private/individual musicians and promote creativity and new talents. A few years after the shutdown of Napster, the ideas of free sharing without central controls made a comeback and were given a boost by the use of DLT and Blockchain in the financial sector.

The definition of cryptocurrency is not yet unified internationally and even nationally. In the US, the Federal Reserve refers to cryptocurrency as 'digital currency' (Brainard, 2018) and uses the terms of 'digital assets', 'virtual currency' and 'crypto assets' interchangeably (U.S. Commodity Futures Trading Commission, 2018). In the EU, policymakers have also refrained from defining the term of cryptocurrency altogether across the EU member countries. Officially, the EU refers to cryptocurrency as 'virtual currency' under the Fifth Anti-Money Laundering Directive (5MLD) (Council Directive (EU) 2018/843, art.1, para.(2)(d)(18), p. 54).[12] Cryptocurrency is neither issued nor guaranteed by any authorities in the EU and is not fully attached to fiat money; therefore, cryptocurrency is not liable to official regulations of money businesses in the EU. However, EU member-states are permitted to have their own policies to set up their regulatory schemes. In the case of the UK, the Bank of England refers to cryptocurrency as digital currency (Bank of England, n.d.).[13] The FCA

---

9 'The network timestamps transactions by hashing them into an ongoing chain of hash-based proof-of-work, forming a record that cannot be changed without redoing the proof-of-work. The longest chain not only serves as proof of the sequence of events witnessed, but proof that it came from the largest pool of CPU power'.
10 A format of compressed digital representations of musical recordings.
11 The index/software permits one user to access another user's HDD directly to request music file swapping without maintaining copies of the music neither permanently nor temporarily.
12 '[V]irtual currency means a digital representation of value that is not issued or guaranteed by a central bank or a public authority, is not necessarily attached to a legally established currency and does not possess a legal status of currency or money, but is accepted by natural or legal persons as a means of exchange and which can be transferred, stored and traded electronically'.
13 'A digital currency is an asset that only exists electronically. Digital currencies such as Bitcoin were designed to be used to make payments, but today many digital currencies are held as speculative assets by investors who hope their value will rise'.

defines the DLT-related cryptocoins as tokens and classifies them into four categories: exchange tokens, e-money tokens, security tokens and utility tokens (FCA, 2019b). Bitcoin-like cryptocurrencies are categorised as exchange tokens (FCA, 2019a).[14] Nonetheless, with these disparate definitions, these terms reflect the main properties of cryptocurrency – digital, investable, transferable and convertible – but they are not proposed to serve as alternatives of fiat money.

The disparate definitions and classifications of cryptocurrency raise concerns over the judicial proceedings and jurisdictions (Dean Armstrong QC, Dan Hyde and Sam Thomas, 2019, p. 33).[15] For instance, the UK's 'e-money token' is detached from the EU classifications (FCA, 2019b, pp. 13–14). This means e-money-like businesses may be able to obtain a licence in the UK and operate in other EU countries under the single market system, whereas Bitcoin-like cryptocurrency regulated in some EU countries, such as Germany, as a financial instrument, falls outside the regulatory parameters of the FCA (FCA, 2019b, p. 7). Therefore, criminals may be able to game with the system as regulatory frameworks differ from one jurisdiction to another.

Irwin and Dawson (2019, p. 1)[16] address the importance of a unified legal definition and a clarified justice system for Bitcoins. The Organisation for Economic Co-operation and Development (OECD) has highlighted the potential issues of cryptocurrencies in consumer protection and financial crimes in 2014 and suggested that the policy for consumer protection shall be set to include actions against online stealing, value volatilities and business shutdown and the policy for financial crimes prevention shall focus on tax evasion and money laundering (Blundell-Wignall, 2014, p. 7). The International Monetary Fund (IMF) also has discussed the risks of cryptocurrency and peripheral applications at the Law and Financial Stability Seminar in September 2018 in the US. The seminar emphasised the rising issues in anti-money laundering (AML) and market manipulation using cryptocurrency and urged authorities to put relevant regulations on their agenda (IMF, 2018). Other studies include: the Norton Rose Fulbright (a global law firm) (2015) provided an introduction of the regulatory framework of cryptocurrency in 2015; the Law Library of Congress studied the regulation of cryptocurrency around the world in 2018; the Cambridge Centre for Alternative Finance provided an overview of the global regulatory status of

14 'The most popular forms of cryptoassets include tokens like "Bitcoin" and "Litecoin." We call these "exchange tokens" but they are sometimes referred to as "cryptocurrencies," "cryptocoins," or "payment tokens." Exchange tokens use a distributed ledger technology (DLT) platform and are not issued or backed by a central bank or other central authority so are not considered to be a currency or money'.
15 'Public blockchains have nodes which are often located in various jurisdictions across the world. This feature, once again a badge of decentralisation, causes issues with recent data regulation GDPR applies to the processing of personal data affecting EU citizens wherever the processing is taking place, as well as other EU-related jurisdictional provisions'.
16 'These challenges appear to grow exponentially when it comes to prosecuting criminals for Bitcoin-related offences, due to the enormous lack of agreement within the justice system of most countries as to the appropriate legal definition for Bitcoin'.

cryptocurrency in 2019 (Blandin *et al.*, 2019); Dean Armstrong QC, Dan Hyde and Sam Thomas (2019) list some issues that cryptocurrency may bring to the financial system. However, these studies only offer a general overview of the regulatory status in selected countries but have not provided an in-depth analysis of the laws and provisions for cryptocurrency crimes.

3 The role of cryptocurrencies in financial crime

Cryptocurrencies may be involved in financial crime directly and indirectly; offenders may treat cryptocurrencies as criminal targets or use cryptocurrency as a transaction channel for their illicit earnings. No matter the types of wrongdoings, the final step that offenders have to deal with is to realise illicit earnings into financial systems through money laundering (Alhosani, 2016, p. 12).

The first court case relating to cryptocurrency took place in 2013 in the US. The arrest of Matthew Jones, a user of a marketplace called Silk Road, in 2013 for distribution of a controlled substance in violation of 'Prohibited acts A', 21 U.S. Code §841 (a) (1) and (b) (1) (C).[17] The second case involved two former Federal agents, Bridges and Force, who were charged with Theft of Government Property (18 U.S. Code §641), Wire Fraud (18 U.S. Code §1343), Money Laundering (18 U.S. Code §1956 (h)) and Stealing Digital Currency (18 U.S. Code §208) during their investigation of the Silk Road (*United States v Bridges and Force*, 2015, Cal.Rptr.) The stolen cryptocurrency was worth over $1.5 million, and the illicit earnings were laundered on various international cryptocurrency exchanges. Bridge learned to access user accounts from a Silk Road's administrator, Curtis Green, during his investigation and seized around $800,000-worth bitcoins using Green's account. The owner of the Silk Road suspected Green and ordered Force to torture him. In return, Force received $80,000 as payment and had started extorting money from the Silk Road owner since then. Some of the bitcoins robbed by Bridge and Force were sent to and laundered at BTC-e, a cryptocurrency platform, which was also suspected for financing Trump's election in 2016 (Magnuson, 2020, pp. 95–97).

Other than those crimes investigated by the US, there are considerable amounts of cryptocurrency stolen in the EU between 2014 and 2017. According to the European Union Agency for Law Enforcement Cooperation (Europol), a cross-border and large-scale money laundering group was shut down in 2017, and 23 members of the gang were arrested. The amount involved was around €2.5 million, and the members of the group were mainly from Spain, Colombia and Venezuela (Europol, 2019b). In earlier 2019, the Europol, Canada and the US joined forces to target some users of controlled products on dark web

---

17 Code §841 (a) (1): '(a) **Unlawful acts** Except as authorized by this subchapter, it shall be unlawful for any person knowingly or intentionally – (1) to manufacture, distribute, or dispense, or possess with intent to manufacture, distribute, or dispense, a controlled substance'; 21 U.S. Code §841 (b) (1) (C) is the sentencing standards, accordingly (*United States v Matthew Jones*, 2014, M.D. Fla.).

marketplaces, 61 people were arrested, and 50 illicit dark web accounts were closed. The involved amount was over €6.2 million. The case judgements haven't been made public at the time of writing. There are possibilities that the arrests may not go to court, or perhaps the prosecution is still ongoing (Europol, 2019c). These cases unravel the uses of cryptocurrency in financial crimes: as a direct target of online stealing and as a channel of illicit transactions and assisting in money laundering. Money laundering is the key step that allows cryptocurrency to be used in real life. Therefore, many authorities have introduced AML measures for cryptocurrency businesses, including some US states, the EU and the UK.

3.1 Direct unlawful activities

Giving the UK as an example, the Crown Prosecution Service has clarified cryptocurrency-related unlawful activities similar to virtual property. Virtual properties are protected under the Theft Act 1968 (*c.60*), Theft Act 1978 (*c.31*), Computer Misuse Act 1990 (*c.18*), Forgery and Counterfeiting Act 1981(*c.45*) and Proceeds of Crime Act 2002 (*c.29*). The Theft Act 1968 defines theft as an act of a person who 'dishonestly appropriates property belonging to another with the intention of permanently depriving the other of it', regardless of the person's intention (*Theft Act 1968 c.60*, s.1). Under the act, property 'includes money and all other property, real or personal, including things in action and other intangible property' (*Theft Act 1968 c.60*, s.4(1)). The definition covers both tangible and intangible items belonging to a person or persons, and the cryptocurrency fits within this definition. The Theft Act 1968 also states that an offence is committed if a person agrees to be involved in online stealing, such as unreported suspicious activities or leaving out unauthorised access. Also, the Serious Crime Act 2007 stipulates that '[e]ncouraging or assisting offences believing one or more will be committed' (*Serious Crime Act 2007 c.27*, s.46).

The Computer Misuse Act 1990 identifies accessing unauthorised computers and data and with intent to commit or facilitate the commission of further offences (*Computer Misuse Act 1990 c.18*, ss.1 and 2). Misusing computer may accompany the intention of stealing data or intangible properties stored on a computer or make changes of access permissions, such as cryptocurrency custody wallets. Unauthorised use of computers also includes (a) authorised person/persons accessing unauthorised computers, for instance, a person from another department of an organisation, and (b) authorised person accessing authorised computers for unauthorised purposes; for instance, a police officer accesses a database of a police station for personal use. Accessing unauthorised computers with the aim of stealing or facilitating commissions of further accessing unauthorised data, information or intangible properties can be considered by the Theft Act 1968 (*c. 60,* s.4(1)). Computers misuse undertaken by a person or persons of authorised organisations is also covered by the Police and Justice Act 2006 (*c.48*, s.37). This is important as authorities hold more sensitive information and officials can easily access relevant databases. Such convenience may motivate wrongdoings. Section 37 (4) of the Police and Justice Act 2006 identifies leaking information (called "article" in the section) as any program or data held in electronic form. This includes programs that run or access data, but it does not include indicative information for unauthorised use of programs or data, for example, giving instructions on how to access unauthorised information. Authorities may need to consider improving the definition of "article" since some computer programs may be downloadable elsewhere and data can be accessed externally using internal indicative information.

In addition, section 5 of the Forgery and Counterfeiting Act 1981 refers to 'offences relating to money orders, share certificates, passports, etc.'. Specifically, section 5(5) of the act refers to misconduct in custody and money orders. Forgery and counterfeiting documentations consist of share certificates, passports and credit cards, which are prohibited goods under the Criminal Law Act 1977 and the Serious Crime Act 2007. Forging authorised documentation, custody or control of the machine, implement, paper or material for making counterfeiting documents are also illegal under the Forgery and Counterfeiting Act 1981 (*c.45*, s.5). In addition, persons who know or should know such illicit activities are also guilty under the Act (*Forgery and Counterfeiting Act 1981 c.45. s.5(1)*). Regarding cryptocurrency activities, this shall refer to false-authorised investment prospectuses and supporting documents, cloned transaction orders or exchange platforms, and counterfeited certificates for cryptocurrency businesses, which may happen to cryptocurrency issuers, exchanges and custodian wallet providers.

Illicit activities of cryptoassets may also breach the Data Protection Act 2018 (*c.12*) and the Privacy and Electronic Communications (EC Directive) Regulations 2003 (*SI 2003/2426*). The Data Protection Act 2018 defines a personal data breach as 'a breach of security leading to the accidental or unlawful destruction, loss, alteration, unauthorised disclosure of, or access to, personal data transmitted, stored or otherwise processed' (*Data Protection Act 2018 c.12*, s.33). This protects personal information, such as usernames and digital keys stored or safeguarded on a third party. The EC Directive 2003 is a parallel regulation to the Data Protection Act 2018 (*The Privacy and Electronic Communications (EC Directive) Regulations 2003, SI 2003/2426*, reg.4). Regulation 6 of the EC Directive identifies misconduct of storing information or accessing stored information. It specifies that firms shall inform users about the purposes of storing or accessing information and allow users to deny storing or accessing their information (*The Privacy and Electronic Communications (EC Directive) Regulations 2003, SI 2003/2426*, regs.6(1) and (2)). These stipulations may be difficult to cryptocurrency service providers, as data on the DLT are immutable and unremovable (Nakamoto, 2008, p. 1). These laws are applicable to direct cryptocurrency crimes but not yet exhaustive as new criminal methods may come out alongside the technology developments.

3.2 *Indirect cryptocurrency crimes*

Indirect wrongdoings refer to using cryptocurrency as a means of transactions or as a tool for concealing user identities. The role of cryptocurrency is similar to other payment methods, such as cash, in this type of illegal activities. The Twitter scam in 2020 (BBC News, 2020a) and WannaCry ransomware in 2017 (Millar and Marshall, 2017) are the typical examples of indirect unlawful activities using cryptocurrencies.

Based on the guide of Crown Prosecution Service (The Crown Prosecution Service, n.d.), indirect cryptocurrency violations, such as selling controlled goods, can be prosecuted under the Criminal Law Act 1977 and the Serious Crime Act 2007. According to the Criminal Law Act 1977, parties carrying out agreed offences in accordance with their intentions are guilty of conspiracy (*Criminal Law Act 1977 c.45*, s.1).[18] Therefore, both buyers and sellers are treated as guilty of conspiracy regardless of the original owner of prohibited goods and transaction methods. Prohibited goods include but not limited to offensive weapons, explosive substances, illegal drugs and indecent and obscene materials (*Criminal Law Act 1977 c.45*, ss.8, 16, 52 and 53). In addition, the Serious Crime Act 2007 defines activities that encourage and assist offences as serious violations. The assistance of unlawful activities also refers to information sharing and data matching for fraud or intentions relating to proceeding crimes. To decide the intention relating to proceeding serious offence, the court must ignore the reasons that offenders provide in the circumstances and offenders' mental state (*Serious Crime Act 2007 c.27*. ss.4 (2), 6, and 44). Therefore, either intentional or unintentional activities that aid and abet an offence are treated as guilty of serious crime. Moreover, indirectly encouraging and assisting offences, such as approving or allowing unauthorised accessing, is also a violation of the Law (*Serious Crime Act 2007 c.27*. s.66).

Using cryptocurrencies for illicit purposes either directly or indirectly, money laundering is the last step for offenders to depart their illicit earnings from the origins. Therefore, monitoring cryptocurrency-related money laundering can be an efficient way to prevent financial and other crimes or at least to reduce such intentions.

3.3 Money laundering

Money laundering is a process that transits illicit proceeds into the financial system for legitimate use (Alhosani, 2016, pp. 3–4; Ryder, 2011, p. 12). Laundering illicit earnings consists of three stages: placement, layering and integration. The placement stage describes the introduction of illegal money obtained from predicate offences (such as drug dealing) into the financial system. The layering stage aims to distance the money from the predicate offences. The final stage is to reintegrate the laundered money back into financial systems (Alhosani, 2016, pp. 3–4; Forgang, 2019). The anonymity of cryptocurrencies weakens the identifiability and traceability of transactions, while the encrypted and unrecorded/

---

[18] '[I]f a person agrees with any other person or persons that a course of conduct shall be pursued which will necessarily amount to or involve the commission of any offence or offences by one or more of the parties to the agreement if the agreement is carried out in accordance with their intentions, he is guilty of conspiracy to commit the offence or offences in question'.

unreported transactions through peer-to-peer networks create new obstacles to AML investigations (Alhosani, 2016; Forgang, 2019). Both direct and indirect cryptocurrency crimes discussed above are considered in the stage of 'placement' (Murray, 2019, Part III).

Cryptocurrency can play an important role in the stages of layering and re-integration. The anonymous and permission-less networks of cryptocurrency transactions collectively create an ideal shield for secluding illicit earnings from transaction parties. It is perhaps a preferable approach for money launderers. For instance, instead of offering commissions to individuals, launderers can transfer small amounts of money that are below the reporting thresholds of regulatory requirements through a large number of pseudonymous accounts to segregate illicit money (Ryder, 2011, p. 12); launderers can set up automatic transaction orders using software that works 24/7.

Although digital crimes involve less in-person contact, criminals have to realise illicit earnings and spend them in real life. An arrest that had taken place in 2019 in the UK can be another example to see how the three stages of money laundering are connected and what acts and regulations may apply to cryptocurrency crimes. In January 2019, the UK's South East Regional Organised Crime Unit (SEROCU) arrested an individual in Oxford on suspicion of cryptocurrency theft and money laundering. This arrest was in cooperation with the Hessen State Police (Germany), the UK's National Crime Agency (NCA) and Europol. The offender illegally accessed the digital keys[19] of cryptocurrency holders without authorisation on IOTA – a DLT firm that provides cryptocurrency services registered in Berlin, Germany.[20] The offender stole €10-million-worth cryptocurrency from over 85 victims worldwide and laundered the illicit earnings into financial channels between January 2018 and January 2019 (Europol, 2019a). There have been no formal decisions made public; thus, it is yet to be known whether the offender was prosecuted in the UK or in Germany. If the prosecution takes place in the UK, the offender may be charged on suspicion of online stealing and money laundering under the Theft Act 1968/1978 for stealing digital properties, Computer Misuse Act 1990 for accessing unauthorised computers, and Proceeds of Crime Act 2002 for money laundering (The Crown Prosecution Service, n.d.). Whereas the IOTA may face prosecution on suspicion of breach of the Data Protection Act 2018 (*c.12*, s.45) and the Privacy and Electronic Communications (EC Directive) Regulations 2003 (*SI 2003/2426*, reg.6) by allowing access to personal data, such as the user account info and transaction keys.

In all the three stages, the anonymity and permission-less features of cryptocurrency are the main reason for money launderers to choose cryptocurrencies; thus, recordkeeping and reporting have become essential to AML. In June 2015, the Financial Action Task Force (FATF) published a guidance paper on the global AML and counter-terrorist financing (CFT) to national authorities

---

19 81 keys stored in the background of the server.
20 <https://www.iota.org/> (accessed 11 November 2019).

worldwide (Financial Action Task Force, 2015, p. 1).[21] The guidance paper prospectively identified the associated risks of cryptocurrency to the AML measures and clarified the relevant FATF recommendations to cryptocurrency exchanges. The FATF guidance focuses on convertible cryptocurrencies – 'the virtual currency can be exchanged for fiat currency' – and classifies them as centralised and decentralised: centralised means a cryptocurrency that has a single administer, and decentralised means there is no administrator at all. The single administrator can be a third party who controls the system, such as issuing and maintaining a central payment ledger and holding the authority to redeem the cryptocurrency; decentralised cryptocurrency means 'distributed, open-source, math-based peer-to-peer virtual currencies that have no central administrating authority, and no central monitoring or oversight' (Financial Action Task Force, 2015, pp. 23 and 27). Under this classification, Bitcoin is a convertible and decentralised cryptocurrency.

The recommendations for national authorities combating cryptocurrency AML/CFT embodies: (a) identifying, clarifying and assessing the types of cryptocurrency (convertible/unconvertible, centralised/decentralised) and associated risks; (b) cooperation and coordination, business registration for legal or natural persons; (c) monitoring new financial technology developments; (d) monitoring cross-border wire transfers; (e) adequate regulation and supervision of convertible cryptocurrency; (f) establishing sanctions to deal with natural or legal persons who fail to comply with the AML requirements; and (g) efficient and effective international cooperation (FATF, 2012, Recommendations 1, 2, 14, 15, 16, 26, 35 and 40). Additional recommendations to convertible cryptocurrency businesses include undertaking customer due diligence measures for recordkeeping, reporting suspicious transactions and a one-off transaction greater than US$/EUR 15,000 (FATF, 2012, Recommendations 1, 10, 11, 15, 20 and 22).

The FATF recommendations are the guidelines of the EU 5MLD (Council Directive (EU) 2018/843, recitals (4) and (18), pp. 44 and 46) and the UK Sanctions and Anti-Money Laundering Act 2018 (*c.13*, Introductory Text). The FATF recommendations were updated in June 2019 (FATF, 2019b), and the AML guidance on cryptocurrency businesses has been amended accordingly (FATF, 2019a). The updated FATF recommendations in terms of cryptocurrency were minor and mainly placed in Recommendation 15, which revised the definition of 'virtual asset' and 'virtual asset service provider' (FATF, 2019b, pp. 126–127 and 132) and inserted a new interpretive note to set out the application of the FATF standards to cryptocurrency activities and service providers (FATF, 2019b, pp. 70–71 and 132). The revised recommendations define a virtual asset as 'a digital representation of value that can be digitally traded,

---

21 'FATF is an independent inter-governmental body that develops and promotes policies to protect the global financial system against money laundering, terrorist financing and the financing of proliferation of weapons of mass destruction. The FATF Recommendations are recognised as the global anti-money laundering (AML) and counter-terrorist financing (CFT) standards'.

or transferred, and can be used for payment or investment purposes. Virtual assets do not include digital representations of fiat currencies, securities and other financial assets that are already covered elsewhere in the FATF Recommendations' (FATF, 2019b, p. 126). Under this definition, 'new virtual assets' underpinned by the DLT are distinguished from existing catalogues of payment methods and financial instruments. This also means cryptocurrencies shall be treated separately from traditional financial products regardless of their functions or applications. The new recommendations define 'the virtual asset service provider' as 'any natural or legal person who is not covered elsewhere under the Recommendations, and as a business conducts one or more of the following activities or operations for or on behalf of another natural or legal person' (FATF, 2019b, p. 127).[22] A threshold of occasional transactions of US$/EUR 1,000 is added to the FATF Recommendation 10 (FATF, 2019a, pp. 46–54). However, the 5MLD of the EU (Council Directive (EU) 2018/843) and the Money Laundering Regulation (MLR) 2019 of the UK (*The Money Laundering and Terrorist Financing (Amendment) Regulations 2019, SI 2019/1511*) have not yet revamped their regulatory requirements in accordance with the updated FATF recommendations 2019.[23]

4 Possible flaws

Although cryptocurrency crimes can be identified and prosecuted like any conventional illicit activities, some of their unique features may not have been covered under existing laws on financial crimes, for example, micropayments, individual activities and jurisdictions. Since cryptocurrency has been active on the internet, related financial crimes are likely transnational, including individuals and organised criminal groups. Therefore, international coordination and cooperation, as well as data sharing, have become essential for combating cryptocurrency crimes. Moreover, the jurisdictions of prosecutions and law applications, as well as the sentencing standards also vary across countries (Ryder, 2011, pp. 10, 17 and 50). This situation makes the proceeding of such crimes more complicated. The micropayments refer to transactions less than the smallest unit of currency; individual cryptocurrency activities are somehow not covered by regulatory rules in many countries, such as in the UK and the US; a standardised scheme for determining jurisdictions is anticipated to facilitate the prosecution processes of international financial crimes.

---

22 The FATF defines that 'virtual asset service providers include i. exchange between virtual assets and fiat currencies; ii. exchange between one or more forms of virtual assets; iii. transfer of virtual assets; iv. safekeeping and/or administration of virtual assets or instruments enabling control over virtual assets; and v. participation in and provision of financial services related to an issuer's offer and/or sale of a virtual asset'.
23 The 'Guidance' was published in June 2019 after the EU Fifth AML Directive was released in May 2018.

4.1 Micropayments

Micropayments in the UK refer to transactions below a penny. The Bank of England deems that enabling micropayments, cryptocurrency could create a new business model: instead of paying monthly subscriptions for digital media, consumers can choose an individual news article to read (Bank of England, 2020, pp. 18 and 29). With its digital feature, cryptocurrencies can be converted to decimals rather than integer units like normal currencies. However, making small payments that fall below thresholds of reporting requirement has been a method for money laundering (Ryder, 2011, p. 12). Since using a number of gophers to launder illicit earnings can be costly and risky, small payments may only relate to small illicit earnings. With the aid of cryptocurrencies, offenders can create many pseudonymous accounts online and 24/7 process micropayments. Although processing such payments may come with fees and expenses, it should be cheaper and less risky than hiring a human.

Existing AML regulations have already lowered the thresholds of suspicious transaction reports. For instance, the FATF Recommendation 10 of 2012 specifically requires convertible cryptocurrency exchanges to undertake customer due diligence measures for a one-off transaction greater than US$/EUR 15,000 (FATF, 2012, p. 12); a threshold of occasional transactions of US$/EUR 1,000 is added to the FATF Recommendation 10 of 2019 (FATF, 2019a, pp. 46–54). The EU 5MLD also requests compliance measures for transactions above EUR10,000 (Council Directive (EU) 2018/843, art.1(1)(b), p. 53), while the UK has implemented the requirement, accordingly, in MLR 2019 (*The Money Laundering and Terrorist Financing (Amendment) Regulations 2019, SI 2019/1511*). Although high-value money laundering is more harmful to the financial system, the cumulative damage of small transactions should not be ignored. The current thresholds of AML compliance measures are still way higher than cryptocurrencies can process. Authorities may have to consider a more efficient approach to monitor micropayments of cryptocurrencies.

4.2 Individual activities

In February 2016, The FBI processed a motion (*United States v Apple Inc.*, 2016a, Cal.Rptr, No.CM16-10(SP)) under the All Writs Act[24] compelling Apple Inc.[25] to assist in an investigation of the 2015 San Bernardino attack that killed 14 and injured 21 (BBC News, 2015). Apple resisted providing technical assistance on the ground of user confidentiality as the FBI requested Apple to create a backdoor on their operating system of iPhone (Apple Inc., 2016). In the end, the FBI vacated the motion and found a third party to decode the iPhone owned

---

24 '(a)The Supreme Court and all courts established by Act of Congress may issue all writs necessary or appropriate in aid of their respective jurisdictions and agreeable to the usages and principles of law'. 28 U.S. Code § 1651.Writs.
25 A technology company that produces smartphones.

by the suspect (*United States v Apple Inc.,* 2016b, Cal.Rptr, ED No.CM 16-10(SP)). Cryptocurrency service providers may face the same dilemma as Apple had: whether they should release user information for financial crime investigation or comply with the data protection regulation. Cryptocurrency service providers hold transaction information permanently as transaction nodes/records generated on the DLT are irreversible and unremovable (Nakamoto, 2008, pp. 1–2), although users are supposed to have the right to remove their data (*Data Protection Act 2018 c.12,* s.59(6)(d)). While this technical structure may benefit financial crime investigation, it can also lead to disputes over possible breaches or violations of user confidentiality of the clients that the DLT holder serves.

In addition, authorities seem not to consider individual activities of cryptocurrency as important as commercial activities. For example, individuals (excluding self-employed or freelancers) and non-profit institutions that conduct irregular commercial activities of cryptocurrency are not recognised as Carrying on Regulated Activities by Way of Business in the UK and therefore do not require authorisation (FCA, 2019c, section 2.3), whereas individual mining and transactions between individuals do not require authorisation in Germany (BaFin, 2017). Under this situation, identifying the regulatory status of transactions carried out on both private and public chain and requiring compliance measure can be difficult (Dean Armstrong QC, Dan Hyde and Sam Thomas, 2019, p. 33); for instance, suspicious activities may be conducted on a private chain and then passed on to a public chain. The former does not require authorisation, and the latter cannot monitor previous private activities.

The conflict between user confidentiality and firm compliance measures and the absence of regulation of private activities create a grey area in cryptocurrency regulation. The grey area may further induce difficulties in prosecution and court judgement.

4.3 Jurisdictions

The EU member states and the US states have established intelligence agencies to monitor and trace cryptocurrency-related crimes. The Financial Intelligence Units (FIUs) in the EU and the Financial Crimes Enforcement Network (FinCEN) in the US have successfully combated several organised criminal groups that engage in cryptocurrency money laundering. However, the different laws and regulations across jurisdictions have caused obstacles and delay in the prosecution. Irwin and Dawson point out that 'lack of agreement within the justice system of most countries' challenges prosecuting criminals for Bitcoin-related offences (Irwin and Dawson, 2019, p. 1). The FATF recommendations of 2019 suggests member-countries devise and apply 'mechanisms for determining the best venue for prosecution of defendants in the interests of justice in cases that are subject to prosecution in more than one country to avoid conflicts of jurisdiction'(FATF, 2019b, p. 25) and to 'constructively and effectively execute extradition requests' (FATF, 2019b, p. 27).

However, the pending case of Alexander Vinnik, owner of the BTC-e, since 2017 has manifested that the mechanisms for deciding the best jurisdictions haven't been either established or functioning well: France claimed its authorisation on behalf of European victims; the US claimed its jurisdiction as '[d]efendants transact business in this District' (*United States v BTC-e and Alexander Vinnik*, 2019, Cal.Rptr, p. 1); Russia wanted the offender to be prosecuted in his home country (Magnuson, 2020, p. 95). In addition, a knocking-down of an international criminal organisation in Spain in 2017 for cryptocurrency money laundering has also not yet released a decision of the prosecution process and jurisdiction at the time of writing (Europol, 2019b). Conflicts of jurisdictions in money laundering and related offences have existed for a while despite the FATF recommendations (FATF, 2019b, p. 25). Nadelmann (1986) deems that foreign governments are not unitary actors of the US in combating international money laundering crimes. Nadelmann (1986, p. 43) believes that foreign governments are affected by various factors, such as the overall relationship with the US, the susceptibility to American pressure, concern for their reputation, attitude towards financial crimes, the power and influence over their national financial sector and the economic impact of such crimes. This suggests that standardising a mechanism for deciding jurisdictions are more than just combating financial crimes; it also depends on multiple aspects, including political relations. Such unharmonised jurisdictions, in turn, may encourage international cryptocurrency wrongdoings.

5 Conclusion

This chapter classifies illicit activities in relation to cryptocurrencies and locates relevant laws and regulations applicable to such crimes using the UK laws as examples. Criminals can use cryptocurrencies to carry out illicit activities directly and indirectly. Either can be identified under existing laws and acts. Authorities, such as the FATF, have introduced relevant compliance measures for AML to prevent/reduce illicit earnings that occur through fraudulent use of cryptocurrencies by manipulating and/or breaching the financial system's digital networks. However, the chapter identifies three issues in the current legal framework for cryptocurrency crimes: micropayments, individual activities and jurisdictions. The three issues are affected by firm business models, regulatory requirements and international cooperation. The first two issues can be solved by updating regulatory policies: micropayments are technical issues that may be solved by introducing compliance measures to transaction frequency rather than quantity; individual wrongdoings probably play a minor part in cryptocurrency transactions when most of the cryptocurrency service providers are regulated. The unharmonised mechanism for jurisdictions has caused delays in some cryptocurrency prosecutions, which requires urgent improvement.

Bibliography

Alhosani, W. (2016) *Anti-Money Laundering: A Comparative and Critical Analysis of the UK and UAE's Financial Intelligence Units.* Palgrave Macmillan.

A&M Records, Inc. v. Napster, Inc., (2001) 239 F.3d 1004 [9th Cir.].

Apple Inc. (2016) *Customer Letter*. Available at: https://www.apple.com/customer-letter/ (Accessed 4 September 2020).

Badev, A. and Chen, M. (2014) *Bitcoin: Technical Background and Data Analysis*. No.2014-104. Available at: https://www.federalreserve.gov/econresdata/feds/2014/files/2014104pap.pdf.

BaFin (2017) *Virtual Currency*. Available at: https://www.bafin.de/EN/Aufsicht/FinTech/VirtualCurrency/virtual_currency_node_en.html (Accessed 16 July 2019).

Bank of England (2020) *Central Bank Digital Currency, Opportunities, Challenges and Design*. Available at: https://www.bankofengland.co.uk/-/media/boe/files/paper/2020/central-bank-digital-currency-opportunities-challenges-and-design.pdf (Accessed 13 March 2020).

BBC News (2015) *San Bernardino Shooting: What We Know so Far*. Available at: https://www.bbc.co.uk/news/world-us-canada-34993344 (Accessed 4 September 2020).

BBC News (2019) *Hunting the Missing Millions from Collapsed Cryptocurrency*. Available at: https://www.bbc.co.uk/news/world-europe-50821547 (Accessed 23 August 2020).

BBC News (2020a) *Major US Twitter Accounts Hacked in Bitcoin Scam*. Available at: https://www.bbc.co.uk/news/technology-53425822 (Accessed 21 August 2020).

BBC News (2020b) *Twitter Hack: Bognor Regis Man One of Three Charged*. Available at: https://www.bbc.co.uk/news/business-53617198 (Accessed 21 August 2020).

BitFury Group and Garzik, J. (2015) *Public versus Private Blockchains Part 1: Permissioned Blockchains White Paper*. Available at: https://bitfury.com/content/downloads/public-vs-private-pt1-1.pdf (Accessed 26 March 2020).

Blandin, A. *et al.* (2019) 'Global cryptoasset regulatory landscape study', *Cambridge Centre for Alternative Finance*. Available at: https://www.jbs.cam.ac.uk/fileadmin/user _upload/research/centres/alternative-finance/downloads/2019-04-ccaf-global-cryptoasset-regulatory-landscape-study.pdf (Accessed 2 January 2020).

Blundell-Wignall, A. (2014) *The Bitcoin Question: Currency versus Trust-less Transfer Technology, OECD Working Papers on Finance, Insurance and Private Pensions*. doi:10.1787/5jz2pwjd9t20-en.

Brainard, L. (2018) 'Cryptocurrencies, Digital Currencies, and Distributed Ledger Technologies: What Are We Learning?', *Decoding Digital Currency Conference Sponsored by the Federal Reserve Bank of San Francisco*. Available at: https://www.federalreserve.gov/newsevents/speech/files/brainard20180515a.pdf (Accessed 17 June 2019).

Buocz, T. *et al.* (2019) 'Bitcoin and the GDPR: Allocating Responsibility in Distributed Networks', *Computer Law and Security Review*, 35(2), 182–198. Elsevier Ltd.

CoinMarketCap (2020) *Today's Top 100 Crypto Coins Prices and Data, CoinMarketCap*. Available at: https://coinmarketcap.com/coins/ (Accessed 24 August 2020).

Computer Misuse Act 1990 c.18.

Criminal Law Act 1977 c.45.

Data Protection Act 2018 c.12.

Dean Armstrong QC, Dan Hyde and Sam Thomas (2019) *Blockchain and Cryptocurrency: International Legal and Regulatory Challenges*. Bloomsbury Professional.

Dryall, S. (2018) 'Cryptocurrencies and Blockchain', in Chishti, S. (ed.) *The WealthTech Book*. John Wiley & Sons, pp. 158–161.

Europol (2019a) *Cryptocurrency IOTA: International Police Cooperation Arrests Suspect Behind10 Million EUR Theft*. Available at: https://www.europol.europa.eu/newsroom/news/cryptocurrency-iota-international-police-cooperation-arrests-suspect-behind-10-million-eur-theft (Accessed 15 October 2019).

Europol (2019b) *Cryptocurrency Laundering as a Service: Members of a Criminal Organisation Arrested in Spain*. Available at: https://www.europol.europa.eu/newsroom/news/cryptocurrency-laundering-service-members-of-criminal-organisation-arrested-in-spain (Accessed 15 June 2019).

Europol (2019c) *Global Law Enforcement Action against Vendors and Buyers on the Dark Web*. Available at: https://www.europol.europa.eu/newsroom/news/global-law-enforcement-action-against-vendors-and-buyers-dark-web (Accessed 10 November 2019).

FATF (2012) *International Standards on Combating Money Laundering and the Financing of Terrorism & Proliferation – The FATF Recommendations*.

FATF (2015) *Guidance for a Risk-Based Approach, Virtual Currencies*.

FATF (2019a) *Guidance for a Risk-Based Approach to Virtual Assets and Virtual Asset Service Providers*.

FATF (2019b) *International Standards on Combating Money Laundering and the Financing of Terrorism & Proliferation – The FATF Recommendations Updated June 2019*.

FCA (2019a) *Cryptoassets*. Available at: https://www.fca.org.uk/consumers/cryptoassets (Accessed 13 May 2019).

FCA (2019b) 'Guidance on Cryptoassets Feedback and Final Guidance to CP 19/3', PS19/22. Available at: https://www.fca.org.uk/publication/policy/ps19-22.pdf.

FCA (2019c) *The Perimeter Guidance Manual*.

Forgang, G. (2019) 'Money Laundering through Cryptocurrencies', *Economic Crime Forensics Capstones*.

Forgery and Counterfeiting Act 1981 c.45.

Houben, R. and Snyers, A. (2018) *Cryptocurrencies and Blockchain Legal Context and Implications for Financial Crime, Money Laundering and Tax Evasion*.

IMF (2018) *Private Crypto Assets & Central Bank Digital Currencies*.

Irwin, A. S. M. and Dawson, C. (2019) 'Following the Cyber Money Trail: Global Challenges When Investigating Ransomware Attacks and How Regulation Can Help', *Journal of Money Laundering Control*, 22(1), 110–131

Landes, W. and Lichtman, D. (2003) 'Indirect Liability for Copyright Infringement: Napster and Beyond', *Journal of Economic Perspectives*, 17(2), pp. 113–124.

Magnuson, W. (2020) 'Crypto-Criminals', in *Blockchain Democracy*. Cambridge University Press, pp. 93–121.

Millar, S. A. and Marshall, T. P. (2017) *WannaCry: Are Your Security Tools Up to Date? The National Law Review*.

MS-ISAC (2019) *EternalBlue*. Available at: https://www.cisecurity.org/wp-content/uploads/2019/01/Security-Primer-EternalBlue.pdf.

Murray, A. (2019) *Information Technology Law: The Law and Society*. 4th edn. Oxford University Press.

Nadelmann, E. A. (1986) 'Unlaundering Dirty Money Abroad: U.S. Foreign Policy and Financial Secrecy Jurisdiction', *The University of Miami Inter-American Law Review*, 18(1), pp. 33–81.

Nakamoto, S. (2008) *Bitcoin: A Peer-to-Peer Electronic Cash System*.

NDC-Department of Justice (2017) *Russian National and Bitcoin Exchange Charged in 21-Count Indictment for Operating Alleged International Money Laundering Scheme and Allegedly Laundering Funds from Hack of Mt. Gox, Northern District of California Department of Justice*. Available at: https://www.justice.gov/usao-ndca/pr/russian-national-and-bitcoin-exchange-charged-21-count-indictment-operating-alleged (Accessed 23 August 2020).

NDC-Department of Justice (2019) *United States Files $100 Million Civil Complaint against Digital Currency Exchange BTC-e and Chief Owner-Operator Alexander Vinnik, Northern District of California Department of Justice*. Available at: https://www.justice.gov/usao-ndca/pr/united-states-files-100-million-civil-complaint-against-digital-currency-exchange-btc-e (Accessed 23 August 2020).

Norton Rose Fulbright (2015) 'Deciphering Cryptocurrencies: A Global Legal and Regulatory Guide', p. 20.

PayPal User Agreement (2019). Available at: https://www.paypal.com/uk/webapps/mpp/ua/useragreement-full (Accessed 9 April 2020).

Police and Justice Act 2006 c.48.

Proceeds of Crime Act 2002 c.29.

Ryder, N. (2011) *Financial Crime in the 21st Century: Law and Policy*. 6th edn. Edward Elgar.

Sanctions and Anti-Money Laundering Act 2018 c.13.

Serious Crime Act 2007 c.27.

Shih, R. and Ku, R. (2002) 'The Creative Destruction of Copyright: Napster and the New Economics of Digital', *The University of Chicago Law Review*, 69(1), pp. 263–324.

Smart, W. (2018) *Lessons Learned review of the WannaCry Ransomware Cyber Attack*. Available at: www.nationalarchives.gov.uk/doc/open-government-licence/ (Accessed 21 August 2020).

Stern, R. (2000) 'Napster: A Walking Copyright Infringement?', *Micro Law*, 95, pp. 3–6.

The Crown Prosecution Service (no date) *Cybercrime – Prosecution Guidance*. Available at: https://www.cps.gov.uk/legal-guidance/cybercrime-prosecution-guidance (Accessed 23 April 2019).

The Express Tribune (2017) *Shadow Brokers Threaten to Release Windows 10 Hacking Tools*. Available at: https://tribune.com.pk/story/1423609/shadow-brokers-threaten-release-windows-10-hacking-tools (Accessed 22 August 2020).

The Law Library of Congress (2018) *Regulation of Cryptocurrency Around the World*. Available at: https://www.loc.gov/law/help/cryptocurrency/cryptocurrency-world-survey.pdf.

The Money Laundering and Terrorist Financing (Amendment) Regulations 2019, SI 2019/1511.

The Privacy and Electronic Communications (EC Directive) Regulations 2003, SI 2003/2426.

The World Bank (2017) *Distributed Ledger Technology (DLT) and Blockchain: FinTech Note 1*. doi:10.1596/29053.

Theft Act 1968 c.60.

Theft Act 1978 c.31.

Treleaven, P. (2015) 'Financial Regulation of Fintech', *Journal of Financial Perspectives*, 3(3), 114–121

United States v Apple Inc., (2016a) No.CM 16-10(SP) Cal.Rptr.1. Available at: https://epic.org/amicus/crypto/apple/In-re-Apple-FBI-Motion-to-Compel.pdf (Accessed 4 September 2020).

United States v Apple Inc., (2016b) ED No.CM 16-10(SP) Cal.Rptr.1. Available at: https://epic.org/amicus/crypto/apple/191-FBI-Motion-to-Vacate-Hearing.pdf (Accessed 4 September 2020).

United States v BTC-e and Alexander Vinnik, Defendant (2019) Available at: https://www.justice.gov/usao-ndca/press-release/file/1187756/download (Accessed 23 August 2020).

United States v Matthew Jones (2014) No.6:14-mj-1233, So.1 (M.D.Fla.). Available at: https://www.justice.gov/sites/default/files/usao-mdfl/legacy/2014/05/30/20140530_Jones_Complaint.pdf (Accessed 10 October 2019).

United States v Park Jin Hyok (2018) Available at: https://www.justice.gov/opa/press-release/file/1092091/download (Accessed 22 August 2020).

United States v Shaun W. Bridges and Carl Mark Force IV, Defendants (2015) No.3-15-70370, Cal.Rptr. 1 (N.D.Cal.). Available at: https://www.justice.gov/usao-ndca/file/765686/download (Accessed 10 November 2019).

U.S. Commodity Futures Trading Commission (2018) *Keynote Address of Commissioner Brian Quintenz before the DC Blockchain Summit*. Available at: https://www.cftc.gov/PressRoom/SpeechesTestimony/opaquintenz8 (Accessed 2 July 2019).

Vandezande, N. and KU Leuven Centre for IT & IP Law (2018) *Virtual Currencies: A Legal Framework*. Intersentia.

Walch, A. (2015) 'The Bitcoin Blockchain as Financial Market Infrastructure: A Consideration of Operational Risk', *New York University Journal of Legislation & Public Policy*, 18, 837.

9 Technology and tax evasion in the world of finance

An indispensable helping hand or a façade for crime facilitation?

Viksha Ramgulam and Sam Bourton[1]

1 Introduction

Ever since the imposition of the first income tax, individuals have attempted to evade their tax liabilities. Tax evasion involves the non-payment of a tax liability that a taxpayer was legally obligated to pay, usually because relevant information, income, and/or assets have been hidden, concealed or misrepresented to tax authorities (HMRC, 2020a; OECD, 2020). The motivation to evade taxation appears to be unaffected by the amount of income earned by each individual (Pickhardt, Prinz, 2012) although the very wealthy and the self-employed may be better able to realise this ambition (Alstadsaeter, Johannesen, Zucman, 2019). This is partly because these individuals are better placed to take advantage of the benefits of globalisation, including advances in technology and the increasing mobility of capital (McCracken, 2002). Tax evasion causes substantial losses to government revenues, posing a serious risk to public infrastructure, public services, and/or honest taxpayers through their increased burden. Indeed, the European Union (EU) estimates that Member States' revenue losses attributable to international tax evasion amounted to €46 billion in 2016 (European Commission, 2019). Domestically, the UK's tax authority, Her Majesty's Revenue and Customs (HMRC), estimates that the revenue losses attributable to tax evasion amounted to £4.6 billion in the UK in 2018–2019 (HMRC, 2020a). In recent times, international organisations and national revenue authorities have intensified their efforts to combat this financial crime. These efforts have been made in response to an increased public appetite to combat tax evasion, particularly offshore tax evasion, itself prompted by prominent tax evasion scandals involving the concealment of wealth offshore. For instance, in February 2015, it was revealed that HSBC Private Bank (Suisse) had assisted many wealthy clients in evading millions of pounds in tax, including over 1,000 of its UK clients (ICIJ, 2015). Furthermore, in April 2016, a leak of documents from the Panamanian law firm Mossack Fonseca revealed how clients of the firm utilised legal structures and banking secrecy in offshore jurisdictions, to launder money, avoid sanctions, and engage in tax-minimising activities, including tax evasion (ICIJ, 2016).

---

1 Bristol Law School, University of the West of England.

Technological innovation has played a pivotal role in the global response to this problem, with systems providing for the automatic exchange of information, such as the Organisation for Economic Co-operation and Development's (OECD) Common Reporting Standard (CRS), revolutionising attempts to combat offshore tax evasion (Pross *et al.*, 2017). Moreover, national tax authorities are making increasing use of technology, particularly data mining and analysis tools and methods, vastly improving their ability to detect and investigate tax evasion (Pijnenburg, Kowalczyk, van der Hel-van Dijk, 2017). In this respect, technology is becoming an indispensable helping hand in efforts to combat tax evasion. Indeed, in the UK, since implementing the CRS, HMRC has received 5.67 million records, relating to 3 million UK resident individuals, or entities they control, and since 2010 has raised over £2.9 billion through combatting offshore tax evasion (HMRC, HM Treasury, 2019). Moreover, HMRC's data analysis tool, Connect, plays a pivotal role in instigating 90% of HMRC enquiries (Sanghrajka, 2020) and was estimated to have raised over £4 billion by 2019 (HMRC, 2016).

On the other hand, there are fears that these efforts could be thwarted by criminals making increased use of technological innovation. For instance, Marian (2013) posits that cryptocurrencies may 'replace tax havens as the weapon-of-choice for tax-evaders', owing to their anonymity and ability to escape taxation, as well as their independence from financial institutions. In addition, technological innovation has spawned new sectors of the economy, such as the sharing economy, which encompasses businesses that provide online marketplaces, such as Airbnb, Uber, and eBay (OECD, 2017). These online marketplaces have enabled sellers to engage in income tax evasion and VAT fraud, with over £1 billion lost to VAT fraud and error via these platforms each year (Parliament, 2017c). In this respect, technology may also be an increasingly dangerous façade for crime facilitation, providing assistance to those who seek to illegally escape their tax liabilities.

Accordingly, this chapter seeks to investigate the role of technological innovation in the development of methods used to commit tax evasion, as well as the methods used to detect and respond to this financial crime. In this respect, the chapter will determine whether technological innovation ultimately helps or hinders efforts to combat tax evasion. In furtherance of this aim, the first section investigates the role of technological innovation in assisting tax evaders to conceal information, income, and assets from tax authorities to evade their tax liabilities. In particular, this section will focus on the dangers posed by cryptocurrencies in facilitating tax evasion, as well as the difficulties posed by online marketplaces in detecting and addressing tax fraud. The second section will examine the criminal offences used to address these financial crimes in the UK, while the penultimate section will consider the role of technology in combatting this financial crime. The chapter will conclude by arguing that technological innovation has assisted both those who evade their tax liabilities and those charged with the enforcement of those liabilities. However, greater use of technology could enable tax authorities to stay one step ahead of tax evaders, thwarting their attempts to remain beyond the reach of the law through technological advancement. In particular, the chapter discusses the possibilities offered by increased use of blockchain technology.

2 Technology – a façade for crime facilitation?

The legal world which could formerly merely be described as a dilettante in the subject of technology is now having to adapt itself to concepts such as Bitcoin in order to keep up with the financial industry (Srivastava *et al.*, 2018). These new concepts are creating what can only be described as 'justifiable and qualified concerns' over a potential rise in tax evasion (Weber, Baisch, 2018). New innovations such as PayPal, Revolut, Monzo, and Bitcoin therefore call for an adaptation of the rules and regulations with regards to tax evasion. Brummer and Gorfine (2014), notably, make an interesting case for further regulation, citing Fintech's disruptive characteristics as requiring an equally innovative regulatory model and rulemaking process to tackle its adverse effects. Indeed, they support the view that FinTech disrupts fundamental principles of existing regulatory approaches and thereby 'requires fresh thinking' to maximise the effectiveness of its regulation. This section aims to discuss the impact of globalisation on efforts to combat tax evasion, with a focus on technology as a complex modern component to effective law enforcement, as well as an accessory to tax evaders. In particular, the following section will discuss the challenges posed by e-commerce and cryptocurrencies.

2.1 E-commerce and VAT evasion

The demographic of the economy is moving towards gig and sharing economies (Economist, 2013; Volkin, 2020), defined as states of affairs with considerable legal persons providing resources on flexible terms on a global scale. Indeed, gig economies relate to the increase in flexitime work (Bennett, 2020), whilst the sharing economies refer to asset-sharing, for instance, letting property or crowdfunding (Asquith, 2020). With commercial exploitation on the rise, niche items such as 'Vintage designer' are being sold by small businesses on million-dollar platforms such as Etsy, Depop, and Poshmark (Indvik, Abboud, 2020; O'Flaherty, 2019). Worryingly, such items are acquiring the same uniqueness and subjectivity as art (Hufnagel, King, 2020), becoming headaches for authorities to trace concealed, misrepresented, and omitted accounts of money (Hyde, Greene, 2020). Indeed, as the Fifth Money Laundering Directive (5MLD)[2] is catering to art intermediaries and other high-value dealers, more risks are now emerging from these small enterprises. Such niche retail businesses, takeaways,

---

2 Directive (EU) 2018/843 of the European Parliament and of the Council of 30 May 2018 Amending Directive (EU) 2015/849 on the Prevention of the Use of the Financial System for the Purposes of Money Laundering or Terrorist Financing, and Amending Directives 2009/138/EC and 2013/36/EU [2018] OJ L 156/43.

and hospitality have in fact been identified as high-risk industries for tax evasion (HMRC, 2020c). Indeed, despite HMRC's far-reaching powers, such as those contained in Schedule 23 of the Finance Act 2011, it cannot identify and therefore investigate these unregistered businesses, consequently losing £1.5 billion in VAT revenue in 2016 (Parliament, 2017c).

In fact, eBay and Amazon have been accused of 'profiting from VAT evaders' with Haines (2017) explaining how their commission received from transactions is encouraging them to condone illicit activities. In such situations, making corporations fiscally responsible could be a remedy, especially virtual marketplaces. Taxes of independent retailers are now deducted through virtual marketplaces, demonstrating the UK's efforts to fight tax evasion and third-party facilitation, by tackling hidden economies (Beetham, Cape, 2018; Parliament, 2017b). Since then, Amazon has demonstrated compliance by implementing a built-in VAT returns service to its Seller Central account (Amazon, 2019; Asquith, 2020). This reinforces the endless capabilities of technology and how better knowledge surrounding it would lead to its effective use, ultimately leading to tax evasion prevention. In fact, such initiatives could benefit corporation by allowing them to undertake responsibility vis-à-vis independent retailers in their desired cost-efficient way, without the rigid instructions that often accompany compliance regulations (Highfield, Evans, Walpole, 2019).

Moreover, organisations such as RAVAS (Retailers Against Vat Abuse Schemes) and VATFraud are uncovering tax fraud before HMRC (Haines, 2017; Parliament, 2017a), denoting HMRC's lack of specialisation in technology. More importantly, it highlights technological innovation as a beneficial, but also, destructive tool to tax evasion prevention, as well as the subsequent need for authorities to recognise the role of technology and take responsibility to make regulations capable of responding to both technological and traditional methods of tax fraud and evasion. Offences involving VAT evasion, excise duties, and e-commerce, albeit not evolving in substance, are becoming more prevalent with technology and, thus, to be identified and prevented effectively, monitoring technology as well as reforming legislation is required.

2.2 Cryptocurrency creating new realms for TE

There will be no information to exchange and regulate by financial institutions for the purposes of tax returns if it is stored as a blockchain, as cryptocurrency usually is, making it harder to maintain effective tax evasion prevention. 5MLD defined cryptocurrencies broadly as 'a digital representation of value that is not issued or guaranteed by a central bank or a public authority, is not necessarily attached to a legally established currency and does not possess a legal status of currency or money, but is accepted by natural or legal persons as a means of exchange and which can be transferred stored and traded electronically'. Such an attempt was crucial considering cryptocurrency shares mutual characteristics with lower-tax jurisdictions, namely, the ability to enable individuals to anonymously conceal income from tax authorities (Marian, 2013). However, cryptocurrencies are 'super tax havens' as they add an additional layer of anonymity by operating independently from regulated financial institutions (Böhme et al., 2015). Therefore, cryptocurrencies have become more attractive for tax evasion purposes than tax havens, demonstrating the role of technological innovation in creating new virtual realms for tax evasion offences (Brown, 2016).

This concept therefore strongly defies recent initiatives to combat financial crime, such as the exchange of information to implement and promote transparency through beneficial ownership and the EU's Fourth Money Laundering Directive (4MLD).[3] The 5MLD has sought to remedy this situation, together with the UK's Money Laundering and Terrorist Financing (Amendment) Regulations (MLR) 2019, SI 2019/1511. Article 1(2)(d) of 5MLD has attempted to combat the illicit use of virtual assets by labelling virtual currency exchanges (legal persons providing the trade between fiat and virtual currencies) and custodian wallet providers (legal persons supplying services relating to the safeguard of private cryptographic keys) as 'obliged entities.' This makes them subject to identical combatting the financing of terrorism (CFT)/anti-money laundering (AML) regulations as financial institutions per 4AMLD.

The UK has implemented the EU's anti-money laundering directives post-Brexit with The Money Laundering, Terrorist Financing and Transfer of Funds (Information on the Payer) Regulations 2017, SI 2017/692 (MLR) 2017 implementing the 4MLD, and the MLR 2019 implementing the 5MLD. Considering Brexit, this denotes the UK's intrinsic efforts to combat tax evasion notwithstanding its lack of continued participation in the EU (Turner, Bainbridge, 2018). However, despite the regulations increasing the scope of the regulated sector for the purposes of anti-money laundering requirements to encompass cryptoasset exchange providers and custodian wallet providers, the UK's efforts remain lacklustre considering the fast pace of technology and the inadequate constructive advancements regarding the regulation of cryptoassets. In light of the growing use of technology by tax evaders to conceal income or assets from tax authorities, it is imperative that the legal framework is able to withstand the challenges presented by technological innovation. Accordingly, the following section examines the offences pertaining to tax evasion in the UK, considering whether the UK's tax legislation remains fit for purpose in light of technological innovation.

3 Tax evasion offences

Tax evasion offences will form the focus of this section, followed by an analysis of selected areas that have been impacted by technological innovation. Statutory and common law offences will be evaluated, and the shared key legal requirements of these offences will be discussed concomitantly.

---

3 Directive 2015/849 of 20 May 2015 On the Prevention of the Use of the Financial System for the Purposes of Money Laundering or Terrorist Financing [2015] OJ L141/73.

3.1 Income tax evasion

The offence contained in s. 106A of Taxes Management Act 1970, relating to income tax, refers to the 'fraudulent evasion' of money levied on wealth (money, property or services) resulting from earnings from employment, dividends, royalties, interest or self-employment. There are specific sections, s.106B, s.106C, and s.106D, of Taxes Management Act 1970 that contain strict liability offences such as the failure to provide notice of liability to income and capital gains tax and failure to deliver and to make accurate returns regarding offshore income, assets, or activities, respectively. Whilst it has been perceived as being too harsh and limited in scope, this offence being strict liability, it could in fact remediate the unwarranted loopholes caused by technological innovation when combined with the problematic test of dishonesty in English Law, discussed further below. It irrefutably eases convictions because it removes the *mens rea* and its drawbacks immediately from the equation and as such is deemed very effective (Bourton, 2018). However, the offence is limited in scope, applying only to income, assets, or activities in excess of the threshold amount, which is currently £25,000 of potential lost tax revenue per year, and which are not reportable under the CRS (Taxes Management Act 1970 [Specified Threshold Amount] Regulations 2017, SI 2017/988).

3.2 The IR35 and RegTech

Notable reform regarding income tax includes the IR35 rules to off-payroll workers taking effect in April 2021, as per s.38 of the Finance Act 2018 (HMRC, 2019c; Groom, 2020). This has been implemented following individuals evading taxes through self-assessment by claiming to be independent contractors to large companies. The reform thus prescribes that personal service companies be taxed equivalently to the Pay as You Earn (PAYE) scheme in instances where but for the title of 'personal service company', the individual would be an employee of the company rather than a contractor (Hyde, Greene, 2020). This reform aims at shaping the law to put the onus of these individuals on their large corporate employers as opposed to the HMRC. A failure to determine a genuine contractor from an employee through the 'but for' test mentioned could lead to such companies being liable for unpaid taxes. This option, as opposed to simply prosecuting corporates through 'failure to prevent' offence (explained below), thereby bypasses any escaped liability which could have occurred with the 'Too Big to Jail'(TBTJ) policy. Instead, no resources are wasted from aiming to prosecute large corporates, and the HMRC obtains its tax revenue owed, thereby creating an effective tax evasion prevention structure.

The IR35 rules demonstrate the role of technological innovation in improving tax collection, as RegTech will be a prerequisite for most medium and large enterprises to be equipped to do this task (Barberis, Arner, Buckley, 2019; Deloitte, 2020). This leads to the encouragement of rigid tax risk assessment and compliance and even engages companies' inclinations towards corporate social responsibility, paving the way to reinforcing the latter. Furthermore, it reduces the risk of falsification of documents through technology as the documents are filed through the large corporates. With time, this may transition into a more 'intrinsic motivation to pay taxes', also known as tax morale, which is deemed to be essential for effective tax administration (Luttmer, Singhal, 2014; OECD, 2019b).

3.3 Evasion of VAT and customs and excise duties

VAT evasion relates to the act of deliberately not paying VAT on the supply of goods and services, having taken possession of goods from the EU and outside the EU. This form of evasion is criminalised under the Value Added Tax Act (VATA) 1994, s.72(1).

Another form of tax evasion on goods relates to the evasion of Customs and Excise duties under the Customs & Excise Management Act (CEMA) 1979. s.170(1) provides for offences related to knowingly acquiring or being knowingly concerned in a transaction involving a commodity under the act, with intent to defraud the public of such duties. As per *R v Neal* [1983] 77 Cr App R 283 at 287, s.170(1) CEMA has an exceptionally wide ambit so that it is a 'catch all provision', as it relates to any 'fraudulent evasion' or 'attempt', and also implicates anyone 'knowingly concerned' in the evasion, thus also serving as a coercing mechanism to prevent individuals from even attempting or facilitating such an offence.

3.4 Providing false documents and information to HMRC

These offences, contained in CEMA 1979, s.167(1), concern making false declarations to HMRC and counterfeiting documents. Technology has inarguably enabled the falsification of documents with hacking, facial 'deep fakes' recognition technology (Hendrikse, 2019). The simple falsification of documents is becoming more widespread, making this offence particularly useful in the fight against tax evasion. For both offences, the prosecution must prove that the documents were not authentic in a 'material particular'. As per *R v Cross* [1987] Crim LR 43, this is up to the judge to establish rather than the jury. This is particularly effective to tax evasion prevention in situations where establishing the factual context of the offence is complex. Technological innovation complicates situational facts, thereby requiring the determination of the law and the capacity to innovate which the judge can more effectively provide (Dari-Mattiaccia, Deffains, Lovat, 2011). Knowledge or recklessness as to whether the information is true is essential for this offence; see *R v G and another* [2003] UKHL 50. As per *Page* [1996] Crim LR 821, a high level of negligence could suffice. This is particularly relevant to cases of technological innovation, since individuals cannot necessarily be acquitted for wilful blindness but, instead, must have taken appropriate measures for this to occur.

3.5 The corporate offences of failure to prevent tax evasion

Part 3 of the Criminal Finances Act 2017 prescribes a partnership or company guilty of a criminal offence if a person employed or otherwise having acted for, and on behalf of, the company is knowingly concerned in a tax offence committed in the UK, s.45, or abroad, s.46. The company is criminally liable if they cannot provide the defence of having taken proportionate measures in cases of suspicious activity. Again, 'Nelsonian dishonesty', the act of turning a 'blind eye' to behaviour such as tax evasion, is not tolerated (Hyde, Greene, 2020). This offence has set the tone for tax evasion prevention by bypassing the identification doctrine, which is used to attribute liability to corporations for criminal offences. As per *Tesco Supermarkets Ltd v Nattrass* [1972] AC 153, the identification doctrine is described as the process of identifying the natural person(s) acting as the directing will and mind of a company, for whose actions liability can be attributed to the company itself. The strict liability offences remedy the problems associated with the doctrine, specifically, an inability to establish the relevant *mens rea* on the part of individuals identified as 'directing minds', often because these individuals will obscure their involvement in the offence by delegating actions to junior employees and failing to record information (HMRC, 2017; Ministry of Justice, 2017). As such, the new offences prevent such discrepancies by only requiring the fact that an individual working for or on behalf of a company facilitated this offence and that the company did not have the reasonable procedures in place to cater to such occurrences. Therefore, this puts the onus on companies to adopt reasonable procedures to prevent the facilitation of tax evasion and thereby act more responsibly. This in turn should increase tax morale, thereby increasing tax compliance. In this way, reforming criminal legislation seems fair and proportional to the ever-evolving risks posed by tax evasion and prima facie seems not only highly effective but also socially and economically desirable.

3.6 Common law offence: cheating the public revenue

After cheating was abolished by the Theft Act 1968, it survived partly through 'cheating the public revenue' (Ormerod, Laird, 2015), referred to in *R v Less, The Times*, 30 March 1993, as 'conduct intended to dishonestly and deliberately deprive HMRC of tax that would otherwise be due'. As per *R v Hudson* [1956] 2 QB 252, an individual may be convicted of tax evasion if the prosecution can show that the defendant has made a false statement with the intent to defraud the HMRC. This can take the form of a positive act or failure to act. A requirement, however, is dishonest intent to evade tax or Nelsonian blindness to someone else stealing from the HMRC; recklessness is not sufficient for conviction. Nonetheless, as Ormerod (1998, p. 630) states, the scope of this offence is so broad that dishonesty is often the 'only live issue' at trial. Indeed, the argument in *Mavji* [1987] 1 WLR 1388 over the requirement of deception was rejected. Ormerod notes that the broad scope of the offence has led to concerns over the potential criminalisation of failed tax avoidance schemes, as in *R v Charlton and Ors* [1996] STC 1418. As Yorke (2017, p. 16) explains, 'what turns tax planning into tax evasion is merely the added ingredient of dishonesty'.

With regards to technological innovation, it can be argued that the wide ambit of this offence, requiring mere dishonesty, caters to innovations unforeseen by the law, especially in the case of complex case facts encompassing technology, as it removes complex subjective elements from the equation enabling the jury to identify causality and dishonesty more easily. Indeed, this is especially the case considering the new methods of tax arbitrage in light of technology (Yeoh, 2018). Tax arbitrage often involves profiting on the thin line between tax avoidance and tax evasion (Marjit, Seidel, Thum, 2017), explained further below. It is noteworthy to point out that the blurred line between these two activities could, however, also be problematic considering that the rule of law requires the law to be certain, proportionate, and reasonable. It sparks the question of whether if someone thought they were avoiding tax and acting lawfully, should they be prosecuted at all. This could cause a snowball effect in terms of uncertainty for the rule of law. Nonetheless, technological innovation has advanced to previously unthinkable extents, and, in this way, this offence is highly effective, acting as a buffer to any prospective technology that could be used to facilitate tax evasion.

3.7 Key elements of the offences

3.7.1 Knowingly concerned

A common denominator of several tax offences is the requirement of being 'knowingly concerned'. This refers to having dishonest knowledge as per *R v Montila* [2004] UKHL 50 – exceeding mere suspicion – and actual involvement in their own or someone else's fraudulent evasion (Harrison, Ryder, 2017). In this instance, the *knowingly concerned* element intends to capture enablers as well as evaders and thus serves as strong deterrent to tax evasion. Considering the 14,000 enablers uncovered by the Panama Papers, many of whom were based in the UK, this could be a useful tool in the fight against tax evasion (European Parliament, 2017). Indeed, these institutions are often hidden in plain sight, as exemplified by the HSBC case, whereby the bank was a regulated financial institution yet acted as an enabler of tax evasion (ICIJ, 2015).

Moreover, this requirement results in a significantly reduced extent of illegal tax arbitrage, such as the recent German Cum/Ex scandal (Segal, 2020). This method involves multiple counterparties (in this instance in the finance and banking industry) with differing degrees of knowledge over transactions which aim at exploiting one singular loophole regarding dividend payments, which allow them to claim the same tax rebate (Seddon *et al.*, 2020). Subsequently, paying greater attention to enablers could lead to enforcement uncovering individuals who could actually be tax evaders. In this way, benefits to this aspect are twofold, as it catches both enablers and potentially evaders. Moreover, there is a significant likelihood of detection in this area owing to its imperfect concealment technology (Marjit, Seidel, Thum, 2017). In this way, more individuals are caught causing a stronger deterrent effect. Accordingly, the 'knowingly concerned' doctrine establishes an increased scope for liability and is thus inarguably a competent measure to combat tax evasion fuelled by technological innovation.

3.7.2 Dishonesty

Most tax evasion offences require *mens rea*, and this usually encompasses an assessment of whether the offender acted dishonestly. The term *dishonesty* lacks statutory definition, thereby requiring interpretation. However, as Yorke (2017, p. 16) explains, the judiciary hold the view that they 'must not attempt to define dishonesty', as 'the act of dishonesty should be for the jury to single-handedly deliberate according to the present-day standards of the ordinary reasonable and honest man or woman'. Indeed, with the exception of the strict liability offence, it is a crucial common element of both the nature and definition of many tax evasion offences (Bourton, 2018). However, the identification of dishonesty in the assessment of criminal behaviour for the purposes of distinguishing illicit and licit noncompliance remains difficult. Salter (2002) found that 'was this dishonest?' was easier for a jury to answer than 'was this fraudulent?' However, as a general rule, juries are unlikely to have shared perceptions of dishonesty, leading to inconsistency in the criminal law, and may find it difficult to determine whether a defendant has been dishonest when dealing with unfamiliar contexts, of which tax evasion cases may be a prime example (Ormerod, 1998).

In *R v Barton and Booth* [2020] EWCA Crim 575, the judge directed the jury based on the test in *Ivey v Genting Casinos (UK) Ltd t/a Crockfords* [2017] UKSC 67 of dishonesty as opposed to the test in *R v Ghosh* [1982] 2 All ER 689. The line of thought of the Supreme Court in *Ivey* regarding the adequate standard of dishonesty was until then *obiter dicta* and therefore not legally binding. In Ivey, Lord Hughes previously cited concerns with *Ghosh*'s subjective limb potentially excusing a defendant's liability owing to their 'warped' sense of dishonesty. With the *Barton case* asserting *Ivey* as the correct test for dishonesty in criminal cases mirroring the test for civil matters in *Barlow Clowes International Ltd v Eurotrust International Ltd* [2005] UKPC 37, the issue of excessive subjective contextual variables is somewhat redeemed. Indeed, this test now means that for dishonesty to be found by a jury, as part of their fact-finding duty, they need to be aware of the defendant's knowledge of the situation and then apply the objective test of whether an ordinary reasonable person would believe that what he did was dishonest (Ormerod, Laird, 2020).

Nonetheless, issues in the context of adding advanced technology such as blockchain technology to highly technical offences requiring evidence of causality between the knowingly concerned and subsequent omission, concealment, or misrepresentation of funds could dilute the application of dishonesty. Indeed, with no constants such as specific definitions or structure to go by, the added subjective ingredient of dishonesty does not facilitate trial proceedings.

Moreover, technology in the form of non-traceable and non-identifiable forms of communication such as the dark web makes it extremely hard to prove the causal link in distinguishing intent from a failed attempt at tax avoidance, or worse, a mere accident. However, this could also make the process easier in the unlikely event that there is proof for the jury of such modes of communication, to thereby assume dishonesty. Considering the dangers of the dark web, this would only serve to be effective in the fight against tax evasion. However, if juries assume that the use of cryptocurrency means that the individual is guilty, this could be a limitation to the effectiveness against tax evasion prevention as an incorrect assumption would render the prosecution disproportional and unfair. Concerns have been raised over lay jurors not only having to consider modern commercial transactions and technical business regulations with all the relevant circumstantial evidence but also requiring knowledge of advanced technology mirroring that of the evaders (Jordanoska, 2017). Thus, technology can adversely affect dishonesty in substance. It could cause a clouded judgement, thereby negatively affecting the rule of law and simultaneously effective tax evasion prevention.

3.8 Conclusion

Whilst technological innovation does not appear to cause new problems for tax legislation, it exacerbates existing ones. Now that it has made the boundaries across countries virtually inexistent, governments and regulators need to make sure laws are able to adapt so that tax evaders cannot escape liability. It has been observed that issues seem to stem from a lack of transparency, leading to the conclusion that cooperation and communication amongst individuals, financial and legal institutions, and nations has never been so essential. Nevertheless, technological innovation may also present new opportunities for tax authorities to investigate and enforce these offences in a manner previously unthinkable. The next section provides a selected overview of the use of technological innovation in combatting tax evasion in the UK, highlighting the benefits to be derived by tax authorities.

4 Technology – an indispensable helping hand?

The digital revolution has opened unprecedented modes of commercial exploitation with wealth never travelling so far, so fast, and so much (Asquith, 2020). With tax crimes incrementally increasing, Bentley suggests that enforcement is instrumental, perhaps even more so than legislation (Bentley, 2020). He adds that its soft power and ability to lead disruptive tendencies, such as dynamic changes in an economic landscape, allow for an effective and rapid recovery from a situation caused by technological innovation. Indeed, legislation and reform notoriously have political, economic, and socially motivated time lags which are sufficiently long to cause lasting damage in these situations (Gentle, Spinks, Omer, 2019). Contrastingly, enforcement has a paternalistic nature, meaning that it refers to imposing concrete on-demand positive or negative actions on the population. This can remedy loopholes facilitated by technological innovation swiftly, which legislation can reinforce more permanently in due time where required. It is noteworthy that critics such as de la Feria (2020) believe that current taxation collection and regulation methods are more curative than preventive with the government opting for revenue maximisation from honest businesses to compensate for the tax gap rather than combatting the fraud directly. Indeed, this can be exemplified particularly by the TBTJ mentality which will be discussed further in this section.

Tax evasion is generally investigated by HMRC or by the National Crime Agency (NCA) in England and Wales subject to the safeguards, in the Police and Criminal Evidence Act (PACE) 1984 and prosecuted by the Specialist Fraud Division of the Crown Prosecution Service (CPS). Northern Ireland and Scotland also have legislation mirroring PACE. Where offences occur elsewhere as offshore tax evasion offences, they will be investigated by the HMRC, Serious Fraud Office (SFO), or NCA, and prosecuted by the SFO or CPS. In fact, the powers of the HMRC are derived from PACE 1984 whilst that of the NCA are from the Crime and Courts Act 2013 and the Proceeds of Crime Act 2002. This section seeks to assess the current tax evasion prevention regime by identifying and critically analysing the stages of enforcement: routine detection of tax evasion, targeted investigations, and prosecutions. Ultimately, this chapter will make the case for the standardisation of technology both in its use and understanding, considering how a lack thereof can be detrimental to the fight against tax evasion.

4.1 Detection, investigation, and technology

4.1.1 The connect database

Technology plays a crucial role in the stages of routine detection. The Connect database is a notable example of big data technology and works as a data-mining tool sifting through vast quantities of unrelated data, including online Suspicious Activity Reports (SAR) and records held by the Land Registry and Driver and Vehicle Licensing Agency (DVLA). This automated fraud detection tool enables the tracking down of a suspect's digital footprint, made to appear legitimate on paper, and extrapolates and identifies relationships between individuals, companies, and property (Leighton-Daly, 2019). This enables HMRC to detect discrepancies between an individual's reported and actual income, assets, and activities. In fact, the HMRC is in search of a similar tool which could uphold intelligence-gathering techniques to identify, assemble, and link crypto transactions back to cryptoasset service providers (HMRC, 2020b).

Despite HMRC having practical limitations such as mandatory full disclosure to the courts, *R (Hart and others) v The Crown Court at Blackfriars and HMRC* [2017] EWCA 3091, it has a wide array of powers, including information-gathering powers, the ability to search and arrest persons, and recover illicit assets (HMRC, 2019a). HMRC uses it data-gathering powers in

Schedule 23 to the Finance Act 2011 to extract information from third parties, such as online platforms like eBay, detecting VAT evasion and other undeclared revenue and capital gains (Palmer, 2015). It even extracts information from airline companies to identify red flags designating the true representation of individuals' or legal persons' actual lifestyles and situations (Parker, 2019). Accordingly, the Connect database's intrusive surveillance powers delve deeper into tax evasion prevention, bypassing any potential clandestine communication such as untraceable telecommunication via the dark web (Leighton-Daly, 2019). Moreover, it creates smooth transitions between the stages of detection, investigation, and prosecution owing to it providing centralised exchange of information, thus creating cost and time efficiency for more effective tax evasion prevention. In fact, the Connect database has proved to surpass itself as a return on investment, costing £80 million and providing a return of at least £3 billion in government revenue (HMRC, 2016; Rigney, 2016).

4.1.2 The common reporting standard and beneficial ownership registers

Nonetheless, there is room for improvement. As always, technological innovation and globalisation cause limitations (Zucman, 2014). Connect can easily investigate multiple people, relationships, and transactions in the UK owing to the copious amounts of information HMRC is able to obtain onshore. However, HMRC is often unable to access information relating to income or assets held by individuals in offshore jurisdictions. Accordingly, the UK has implemented the OECD's CRS, which provides for the automatic exchange of information for tax purposes between participating jurisdictions (OECD, 2014). Following the release of the CRS, 49 jurisdictions, including the UK, committed to undertaking the automatic exchange of information in 2017, and 51 jurisdictions committed to undertaking the first exchanges in 2018 (OECD, 2019a). The UK implemented the CRS via the International Tax Compliance Regulations 2015, SI 2015/878. The information HMRC receives via the CRS is fed into the Connect database (Rigney, 2016). In the UK, since implementing the CRS, HMRC has received 5.67 million records, relating to 3 million UK resident individuals, or entities they control, and since 2010 has raised over £2.9 billion through combatting offshore tax evasion (HMRC, HM Treasury, 2019). It is clear that the implementation of the CRS in the UK has led to the collection of substantial amounts of revenue, likely in excess of initial predictions of £75 million to £270 million annually (HMRC, 2015).

The UK has also implemented beneficial ownership registers, as required by 4MLD and 5MLD. It introduced the Persons with Significant Control Register, via the Small Business, Enterprise and Employment Act 2015, s.81, Schedule 3, amending the Companies Act 2006, to identify the natural persons who own or control companies. In addition, the UK introduced a register of the beneficial owners of trusts in the MLR 2017, Part 5 and is currently consulting on the introduction of a beneficial ownership register of overseas entities that own

Technology and tax evasion 157

land or real property in the UK (Department for BEIS, 2018). These registers will provide authorities with previously inaccessible information on the ultimate owners of legal entities and structures, which, due to their potentially opaque nature, may be used to evade taxation, hence the need for transparency (Meads, Jarvis, 2014). Accordingly, the registers are considered to be highly valuable in identifying those responsible for financial crimes, including tax evasion.[4] However, the UK's registers currently suffer from deficiencies, in terms of the lack of adequate mechanisms for verification of information submitted for inclusion in the register, as well as the lack of effective enforcement of these requirements (Virgo, 2019).

The automatic exchange of tax information, as well as the centralised collection of beneficial ownership information, has been made possible by technological innovation. This is because technology is essential to ensure the fast and standardised transmission of information by financial institutions and responsible authorities, as well as the safe storage of vast amounts of personal data. However, the use of technology to collect vast amounts of personal data has been persistently questioned by commentators, such as Noseda, who questions the compatibility of such measures with rights to privacy and data protection and raises the issue of harm being caused to individuals owing to data breaches through hacking and other cybercrimes (Noseda, 2017). As will be discussed below, further use could be made of technology to address these risks.

4.2 An evaluation of investigation-centric instruments

Concerning the investigation process, there remains the question of whether legislative devices have become too obsolete owing to technological innovation. Search warrants are mainly issued under s.8 of PACE 1984. The Law Commission (2018) released a report containing reform proposals listing the latter as convoluted, lacking in consistency, too expensive but, more importantly, obsolete to the point where there was complete disregard to modern-day criminal activity being largely digital and globalised. The court has tried to take heed of this in *Royal College of Nursing v Department of Health and Social Security* [1981] AC 800, stating that statutory interpretation may and should account for technological innovation. However, considering not all statutory language provides such a flexible and permissive ambit, this solution can only be transitory. Indeed, with evidence now becoming virtual (electronic data), this raises abstract questions regarding seizing material as per *R (Business Energy Solutions Ltd) v Preston Crown Court* [2018] EWHC 1534. As a matter of transition, the court can step in efficiently to fulfil its discretion, but with regards to sustainability, as technology develops further, it will become increasingly difficult for the courts to deliberate on such abstract issues. Indeed, such problems with the law

---

4 Most UK LEAs believe the Persons with Significant Control Register has had a positive impact in combatting financial crime; see Department for BEIS (2019), at p. 34.

of evidence are not conducive to tax evasion law enforcement: they would cause not only time lags in deliberations and uncertainty, opening the floodgates, but also acquittals solely based on technical deliberations.

4.3 Prosecution and technology

Owing to resource limitations, HMRC only refers cases for prosecution where 'the conduct involved is such that only a criminal sanction is appropriate' to their discretion (HMRC, 2019b). Other sanctions include civil penalties. However, following the HSBC (Suisse) scandal, HMRC were tasked with 'increasing prosecutions of serious and complex tax crime, focusing particularly on wealthy individuals and corporates' (Parliament, 2016, p. 43). Since 2013, HMRC has largely achieved its annual goals, with 1,007 prosecutions being brought forward in 2018 (*Tax Journal*, 2019). The *Tax Journal* credits compliance from 'online platforms' and Connect to this success, as well as contemporary data-mining methods by innovative technology.

Technological innovation inarguably has had a part to play in HMRC's success. The ubiquity of digitalisation itself has led to all-round cost and time efficiency. However, assessing the extent to which the prosecutions were a success owing to technology is difficult, considering the variable factors possibly involved. Irrespective of its current and past successes, one should not underestimate its efficacy to prove its worth in the foreseeable future. As a recognised pillar of the rapidly evolving economic landscape, it is irrefutably bringing an increased 'appetite and stamina' in the fight against tax evasion (*Tax Journal*, 2019).

4.4 The influence of technology on deferred prosecution agreements (DPAs)

Entrenched by Schedule 17 of the CCA 2013, DPAs are a solution found by the courts in response to criminal offences relating to fraud and dishonesty committed by corporations. They are used in the enforcement of the corporate failure to prevent offence whereby a company thinks that it may have committed tax evasion under s.45 or s.46 of the Criminal Finances Act 2017, but it is not considered to be in the public interest to prosecute (Srivastava *et al.*, 2018). The inception of DPAs has been based upon the reluctance of authorities to impose criminal sanctions on 'systematically important' institutions such as banks, which are pillars of the economy (Werle, 2018), fearing negative impacts on the latter as well as 'innocent employees, suppliers and local community' (Milford, 2017). This ideology has been named 'Too Big to Jail' (TBTJ) (Hardouin, 2017). A DPA is an agreement whereby corporate bodies pledge to help the prosecution satisfactorily in return for not giving effect to a formal prosecution later. The satisfactory aspect here relates to benefitting from 'openness' from the offender and transparency to uncover more circumstantial evidence as well as a pledge not to reoffend; hence, self-reporting as a preliminary step to a DPA is preferred. Indeed, this shows a willingness for genuine cooperation, although is not essential, as demonstrated by *Serious Fraud Office v Rolls-Royce Plc and Another* [2017] Lloyd's Rep. FC 249.

Technology can however corrode the aim and process of DPAs. Tech giants such as Amazon, Facebook, Google, and Apple are known for their inventive tax avoidance methods (European Parliament, 2016). At the outset, one loophole to DPAs could be a replica of profit-shifting in theory: tech firms could easily alter or send evidence to subsidiaries or colluders in different jurisdictions, especially digital evidence such as intellectual property, to escape liability. Worse, it could be saved virtually or deleted instead of being handed to the authorities. Companies could then mislead authorities by for instance sending them in the wrong direction of investigation, falsely implanting innocent errors in transaction, or even just burying regulatory bodies in mounds of paperwork. Self-reporting in this way, just like self-assessment, can be a defeatist modus operandi in the fight against tax evasion and give regulators and lawmakers a false sense of accomplishment. Fortunately, monitoring technology can not only counter any wrongdoing but can also uphold authorities as watchdogs regarding any subsidiaries (Srivastava *et al.*, 2019). Moreover, it can assert transparency required for some firms to prove their innocence and authenticity. In fact, technology has been found to be compatible with DPAs and law enforcement in general.

Interestingly, the use of technological innovation in a domestic criminal case was pioneered by the SFO in *Serious Fraud Office v Rolls-Royce Plc and Another* [2017] Lloyd's Rep. FC 249. Reviewing hundreds of thousands of documents daily, the technology used aimed to remove any Legally Professional Privileged documents, reducing two years' worth of work for Independent Counsel into a few months' worth (de Silva, 2018). Such technology could thus promote efficiency as well as counter misleading information or other attempted shams. Technology in this instance was praised for saving considerable time and cost. In fact, the SFO has since then acquired OpenText Axcelerate, a technology allowing them to operate more efficiently (OpenText, 2018). This resonates with the argument made throughout this chapter that technological innovation is not a solution but it will assist in ensuring compliance and maximising the collection of revenue.

4.5 Conclusion

This section demonstrated how technology's understanding and usage are a prerequisite to modern law enforcement. A lack thereof would only serve to exacerbate the repercussions that result from the use of obsolete laws and methods. Indeed, unfair and disproportionate acquittals would inevitably corrupt the whole process leading up to trial, making all efforts at tax evasion prevention futile. The rectification of the enforcement identified inarguably requires extensive efforts and resources. They are, however, key to the fight against tax evasion. Better use of technology on the part of evaders would be nefarious to tax revenue in the long run, not only in terms of escaping liability but also because this would disrupt the deterrent effect of enforcement action, which could lead to an exponential increase in this financial crime.

5 Technological innovation – an indispensable helping hand or a façade for crime facilitation?

Despite a seemingly robust system in place for TE prevention, a subsequent complacent stance would be ineffective at best and nefarious at worst. Indeed, de la Feria (2020) has observed a rising preference for current tax fraud management approach rather than tax fraud suppression, the former being defined as an enforcement regime overseeing revenue costs of tax frauds efficiently as opposed to the latter which imposes stricter anti-fraud sanctions as an aim to combat tax evasion. In fact, this tax fraud management approach puts undue strain on companies; in a bid to compensate for evaders, these companies incur increased corporate compliance costs and taxes. The recurring theme perceived throughout this study is that technology is what we make of it: it aids tax evasion prevention if used efficiently and, if not, it aids the abettor. Whilst technological innovation's function is to assist rather than be a global independent solution, it is indispensable to effective tax evasion prevention. Moreover, it can assist in supressing rather than managing tax evasion and fraud.

This section seeks to recommend the approach the law should take towards individuals and corporates who evade taxation in light of technological innovation. Ultimately, this chapter will call for reform. Precisely, it will make the case for big data technology merged with blockchain technology as an effective tool and the need for authorities to retain their paternalistic leverage over profit-maximising firms to combat tax evasion.

5.1 An assessment of the prevention of tax evasion in light of technological innovation

Technological innovation is more problematic to the procedural rather than substantial aspect of tax evasion legislation. Indeed, the definition of tax evasion does not seem to have been altered by technology; rather, technological innovation has simplified the modus operandi of tax evasion in certain instances. Nonetheless, constant legislative appraisals and reforms are required regarding cryptocurrency, the law of evidence, the attribution of liability to corporations for economic crimes, as well as the *mens rea* element of tax evasion offences. In terms of enforcement, it can be deduced that authorities are a step in the right direction by aiming at countering technology with its strongest opponent, technology itself. As has been identified, a competent tool for enforcement to use would be better education and awareness of technology. This chapter has thus made a cogent case for the need to consider technological innovation as an aid to effective tax evasion prevention. Thus, recommendations will be offered including a big data and blockchain technology proposal, and a case will be made for why governments should apply their leverage over firms to tackle tax evasion prevention.

5.2 Big data and blockchain technology: the perfect pair?

Throughout this chapter, emerging themes have included the need to counter falsification (omissions, concealment, and misrepresentation), the privacy/

information exchange dichotomy, and issues with VAT and e-commerce, inter alia. In fact, one particular tool discerned by Karafiloski (2017) could tackle these challenges. This tool can be referred to as a big data and blockchain technology hybrid (Karafiloski, 2017). Like Connect, information gathered from institutions will be stored as big data. However, it will contain the added benefits of blockchain technology: a transaction is recorded every time a document is added to the big data system. This section seeks to identify and critically analyse its characteristics in order to make a case for why it should be implemented.

5.2.1 Decentralised data

First, this tool works to take on the decentralised characteristic of blockchain technology, countering privacy issues associated with centralised 'generalised' systems identified previously (Noseda, 2017). Moreover, technology called blockchain nodes enabling the moderation of access on the server will provide a secure and private way for HMRC to have bilateral and multilateral communication with taxpayers and cross-check data with third parties (Karafiloski, 2017). In fact, in the US, a white paper including the use of 'supervisory node' for on-chain regulatory surveillance was recently proposed (Adeyanju, 2020). In addition, blockchain data are easily updated, making this tool precise and up-to-date, and thereby efficient.

Blockchain data cannot be written off and will only be accessed by concerned parties when the data are mined upon suspicion of illicit activity. To be falsified, evaders would have the virtually impossible task of deleting the whole ledger to rewrite it in their chosen way. Moreover, blockchain ledger data substantially reduce the possibility of hacking and data breaches (Rabah, 2018), which have recently occurred in the case of the cloning of the Financial Conduct Authority (FCA) register and website (Austin, Mortimer, 2020). Exploiting blockchain's non-repudiation and non-tampering properties as such would reduce the risk of identity theft enabling tax evasion, as is often the case when parties to a transaction own separate documents of the same transaction, which can easily be falsified (Xu *et al.*, 2019). As a decentralised database, this method could be more applicable in an international context to counter these innumerable complex issues to combat offshore tax evasion, making it an even more effective tool in the fight against tax evasion.

5.2.2 A breakthrough for e-commerce

In the same way, using the blockchain ledger to record e-commerce transactions could enable better control of VAT evasion. Common methods of VAT evasion include underreporting revenue via electronic sales suppression tools and over-reporting of deductions via false invoicing to underreport income (Amazon, 2019). However, transacting through blockchain ledgers or at least having information stored on the blockchain ledger from online platforms could counter this form of falsification. In fact, fintech tools currently being reviewed, such as mandatory HMRC-approved software and/or Electronic Point of Sale systems and fiscal tills, would enable highly effective tax evasion prevention in the event that they are compatible with the big data/blockchain hybrid (HMRC, 2018). Defined as structures enabling HMRC access to transaction-level data, this would remove the whole aspect of self-assessment, thereby reducing the dependence on taxpayers to be bona fide.

5.2.3 Accompanying effects

Such a tool could also have the effect of providing more knowledge and development to the field of cryptocurrency, potentially aiding the inception of legislation surrounding it in its midst. Moreover, it would potentially provide more insight into the shadow economy and its ghosts and moonlighters. These refer to unregistered people or people are known to the HMRC but undeclared as workers, respectively (HMRC, 2020a). In fact, more extensive use of big data on both public and private ledgers would improve transparency as well as create more trust in public administration owing to its complexity to defraud and its efficacy at detection. In turn, this would lead to greater tax morale, thereby extending its effectiveness as a tool for tax evasion prevention.

5.3 *An introduction to a pre-emptive strategy*

A concurring solution provided by Devanny et al. (2018, p. 89) includes the notion of regulators' investing more into next-generation intelligence analysts, as a pre-emptive strategy before the economy experiences issues with a sudden 'future crisis of perceived intelligence failure'. In doing so, this would ensure detections with regards to algorithmic and human errors such as non-transparent reasoning and any cognitive bias which often precedes detection and leads to ineffective tax evasion prevention (Moses, de Koker, 2017). In its midst, this would begin to instil a more suppressive approach to tax evasion management, deemed to be most effective to prevention.

5.4 *Feasibility*

Limits to the feasibility of this proposal could include the costs involved to implement such technology. Information being decentralised, however, would make system failures avoidable and regular backups inessential, implying increased effectiveness in the fight against tax evasion.

6 Conclusion

Whilst technology is somewhat out of the legal sector's comfort zone, this study has demonstrated that now is the ideal time to take a leap of faith and implement innovative measures with the aim towards a future with less tax evasion.

References

Adeyanju, O. (2020) *Why Bitcoin Exchanges Are Building Their Own Blockchain.* Available from: https://www.forbes.com/sites/oluwaseunadeyanju/2020/04/28/why-bitcoin-exchanges-are-building-their-own-blockchain/#312611a554dd [Accessed 14 October 2020]

Alstadsaeter, A., Johannesen, N., Zucman, G. (2019) Tax Evasion and Inequality. *American Economic Review.* 109(6), pp. 2073–2103.

Amazon Seller Central (2019) *EU VAT Calculation Services Methodology.* Available from: https://sellercentral.amazon.co.uk/gp/help/external/help.html?itemID=202084570&ref=efph_202084570_cont_home [Accessed 14 October 2020]

Asquith, R. (2020) The Gig and Sharing Economies: Millions of New Entrepreneurs; Billions in Lost VAT. *British Tax Review.* 1, pp. 5–22.

Austin, A., Mortimer, R. (2020) *Fraudsters Clone FCA Register and Website.* Available from: https://www.ftadviser.com/regulation/2020/07/22/fraudsters-clone-fca-register-and-website/ [Accessed 14 October 2020]

Barberis, J., Arner, D.W., Buckley, R.P., eds. (2019) *The REGTECH Book: The Financial Technology Handbook for Investors, Entrepreneurs and Visionaries in Regulation.* West Sussex: Wiley.

Beetham, F., Cape, J. (2018) Finance Act 2018 Notes: Section 38: Online Marketplaces. *British Tax Review.* 3, pp. 311–323.

Bennett, N. (2020) *When Flextime Makes for a Bad Time.* Available from: https://www.forbes.com/sites/natebennett/2020/01/09/when-flextime-makes-for-a-bad-time/#6368fce03691 [Accessed 14 October 2020]

Bentley, D. (2020) Timeless Principles of Taxpayer Protection: How They Adapt to Digital Disruption. *eJournal of Tax Research.* 16(3), pp. 679–713.

Böhme, R., Christin, N., Edelman, B., Moore, T. (2015) Bitcoin: Economics, Technology, and Governance. *Journal of Economic Perspectives.* 29(2), pp. 213–238.

Bourton, S. (2018) Revisiting Dishonesty – The New Strict Liability Offence for Offshore Tax Evaders. In: Monaghan, C., Monaghan, N. eds., *Financial Crime and Corporate Misconduct: A Critical Evaluation of Fraud Legislation.* London: Routledge, pp. 103–117.

Brown, S.D. (2016) Cryptocurrency and Criminality: The Bitcoin Opportunity. *The Police Journal.* 89(4), pp. 327–339.

Brummer, C., Gorfine, D. (2014) *FinTech: Building a 21st-Century Regulator's Toolkit.* Available from: https://assets1c.milkeninstitute.org/assets/Publication/Viewpoint/PDF/3.14-FinTech-Reg-Toolkit-NEW.pdf [Accessed 14 October 2020]

Dari-Mattiaccia, G., Deffains, B., Lovat, B. (2011) The Dynamics of the Legal System. *Journal of Economic Behavior & Organization.* 79(1), pp. 95–107.

de la Feria, R. (2020) Tax Fraud and Selective Law Enforcement. *Journal of Law and Society.* 47(2), pp. 240–270.

Deloitte (2020) *RegTech Universe 2020: Take a Closer Look at Who Is Orbiting in the RegTech Space.* Available from: https://www2.deloitte.com/lu/en/pages/technology/articles/regtech-companies-compliance.html [Accessed 14 October 2020]

Department for Business, Energy & Industrial Strategy (2019) *Review of the Implementation of the PSC Register.* Available from: https://assets.publishing.service.gov.uk/government/uploads/system/uploads/attachment_data/file/822823/review-implementation-psc-register.pdf [Accessed 4 July 2020]

Department for Business, Energy & Industrial Strategy (2018) *Draft Registration of Overseas Entities Bill*. London: The Stationery Office. (Cm 9635)

de Silva, C. (2018) *SFO Corporate Criminal Liability, AI and DPAs*. Available from: https://www.sfo.gov.uk/2018/06/21/corporate-criminal-liability-ai-and-dpas/ [Accessed 14 October 2020]

Devanny, J., Dover, R., Goodman, M.S., Omand, D. (2018) Why the British Government Must Invest in the Next Generation of Intelligence Analysts. *The RUSI Journal*. 163(6), pp. 78–89.

European Commission (2019) *Estimating International Tax Evasion by Individuals*. Available from: https://ec.europa.eu/taxation_customs/sites/taxation/files/2019-taxation-papers-76.pdf [Accessed 30 September 2020]

European Parliament (2017) *Role of Advisors and Intermediaries in the Schemes Revealed in the Panama Papers*. Available from: https://www.europarl.europa.eu/cmsdata/117285/Item_3_Study_Intermediaries_en.pdf [Accessed 14 October 2020]

European Parliament (2016) *Tax Challenges in the Digital Economy*. Available from: https://www.europarl.europa.eu/RegData/etudes/STUD/2016/579002/IPOL_STU(2016)579002_EN.pdf [Accessed 14 October 2020]

Gentle, S., Spinks, C., Omer, M. (2019) Proceeds of Crime Act 2002: Update 1. *Compliance Officer Bulletin*. 170, pp. 1–42.

Groom, M. (2020) IR35: Far from a Fallow Year. *Tax Journal*. 1485, pp. 11–13.

Haines, A. (2017) Amazon and eBay Profiting from VAT Evaders. *International Tax Review*. November, pp. 12–13.

Hardouin, P. (2017) Too Big to Fail, Too Big to Jail: Restoring Liability a Lesson from HSBC Case. *Journal of Financial Crime*. 24(4), pp. 513–519.

Harrison, K., Ryder, N. (2016) *The Law Relating to Financial Crime in the United Kingdom*. 2nd ed. London: Routledge.

Hendrikse, R. (2019) *How Deepfakes Could Become a Threat to Your Identity*. Available from: https://www.forbes.com/sites/renehendrikse/2019/12/20/how-deepfakes-could-become-a-threat-to-your-identity/#4b67320b1063 [Accessed 14 October 2020]

Highfield, R., Evans, C., Walpole, M. (2019) The Development and Testing of a Diagnostic Tool for Assessing VAT Compliance Costs: Pilot Study Findings. *eJournal of Tax Research* [online]. 16(3), pp. 620–654.

HM Revenue & Customs (2020a) *Measuring Tax Gaps 2020 Edition: Measuring Tax Gap Estimates from 2018 to 2019*. Available from: https://assets.publishing.service.gov.uk/government/uploads/system/uploads/attachment_data/file/907122/Measuring_tax_gaps_2020_edition.pdf [Accessed 30 September 2020]

HM Revenue & Customs (2020b) *Cryptoasset Blockchain Analysis Tools*. Available from: https://www.contractsfinder.service.gov.uk/Notice/ec88ae4b-4f4c-4926-982a-723636cf2f82?p=1 [Accessed 14 October 2020]

HM Revenue & Customs (2020c) *Electronic Sales Suppression: Summary of Responses*. Available from: https://assets.publishing.service.gov.uk/government/uploads/system/uploads/attachment_data/file/894194/Electronic_sales_suppression_Summary_of_responses.pdf [Accessed 14 October 2020]

HM Revenue & Customs (2019a) *Guidance: HMRC's Criminal Investigation Powers and Safeguards*. Available from: https://www.gov.uk/government/publications/criminal-investigation/criminal-investigation [Accessed 14 October 2020]

HM Revenue & Customs (2019b) *Guidance: HMRC's Criminal Investigation Policy*. Available from: https://www.gov.uk/government/publications/criminal-investigation/hmrc-criminal-investigation-policy [Accessed 14 October 2020]

HM Revenue & Customs (2019c) *Policy Paper: Rules for Off-Payroll Working from April 2020*. Available from: https://www.gov.uk/government/publications/rules-for-off-payroll-working-from-april-2020/rules-for-off-payroll-working-from-april-2020 [Accessed 14 October 2020]

HM Revenue & Customs (2018) *Electronic Sales Suppression: Call for Evidence*. Available from: https://assets.publishing.service.gov.uk/government/uploads/system/uploads/attachment_data/file/765247/Electronic_sales_suppression_-_call_for_evidence.pdf [Accessed 14 October 2020]

HM Revenue & Customs (2017) *Tackling Tax Evasion: Government Guidance for the Corporate Offences of Failure to Prevent the Criminal Facilitation of Tax Evasion*. Available from: https://assets.publishing.service.gov.uk/government/uploads/system/uploads/attachment_data/file/672231/Tackling-tax-evasion-corporate-offences.pdf [Accessed 14 October 2020]

HM Revenue & Customs (2016) *Making Connections*. Available from: https://www.tax.org.uk/system/files_force/file_uploads/151218%20Connect%20Briefing_Public%20v1.0.pdf?do [Accessed 1 October 2020]

HM Revenue & Customs (2015) *Tax Administration: Regulations to Implement the UK's Automatic Exchange of Information Agreements*. Available from: https://assets.publishing.service.gov.uk/government/uploads/system/uploads/attachment_data/file/413976/TIIN_8148_tax_admin_automatic_exchange.pdf [Accessed 10 August 2019]

HM Revenue & Customs, HM Treasury (2019) *No Safe Havens 2019: HMRC's Strategy for Offshore Tax Compliance*. Available from: https://assets.publishing.service.gov.uk/government/uploads/system/uploads/attachment_data/file/802253/No_safe_havens_report_2019.pdf [Accessed 10 August 2019]

Hufnagel, S., King, C. (2020) Anti-Money Laundering Regulation and the Art Market. *Legal Studies*. 40(1), pp. 131–150.

Hyde, I., Greene, M. (2020) Tax Risks in the Gig Economy: Large Business as HMRC's Policeman. *Compliance & Risk*. 9(1), pp. 2–5.

Indvik, L., Abboud, L. (2020) *Dressing Up Again? Fashion Tries to Recover from "Brutal" Crisis*. Available from: https://www.ft.com/content/89e9de1c-0213-49b8-82ba-edca04e1e910 [Accessed 1 October 2020]

International Consortium for Investigative Journalists (2016) *Giant Leak of Offshore Financial Records Exposes Global Array of Crime and Corruption*. Available from: https://panamapapers.icij.org/20160403-panama-papers-global-overview.html [Accessed 30 September 2020]

International Consortium for Investigative Journalists (2015) *Banking Giant HSBC Sheltered Murky Cash Linked to Dictators and Arms Dealers*. Available from: http://www.icij.org/project/swiss-leaks/banking-giant-hsbc-sheltered-murky-cash-linked-dictators-and-arms-dealers [Accessed 30 September 2020]

Jordanoska, A. (2017) Case Management in Complex Fraud Trials: Actors and Strategies in Achieving Procedural Efficiency. *International Journal of Law in Context*. 13(3), pp. 336–355.

Karafiloski, E. (2017) *Blockchain Solutions for Big Data Challenges: A Literature Review*. Available from: https://ieeexplore.ieee.org/document/8011213 [Accessed 14 October 2020]

Law Commission (2018) *Search Warrants: Consultation Paper No. 235*. Available from: https://s3-eu-west-2.amazonaws.com/lawcom-prod-storage-11jsxou24uy7q/uploads/2018/06/Search-Warrants-final-consultation-paper-12062018.pdf [Accessed 14 October 2020]

Leighton-Daly, M. (2019) Identity Theft and Tax Crime: Has Technology Made It Easier to Defraud the Revenue? *eJournal of Tax Research.* 16(3), pp. 578–593.

Luttmer, E.F.P., Singhal, M. (2014) Tax Morale. *The Journal of Economic Perspectives.* 28(4), pp. 149–168.

Marian, O. (2013) Are Cryptocurrencies Super Tax Havens? *Michigan Law Review First Impressions.* 112(38), pp. 38–48.

Marjit, S., Seidel, A., Thum, M. (2017) Tax Evasion, Corruption and Tax Loopholes. *German Economic Review.* 18(3), pp. 283–301.

McCracken, MSK. (2002) Going, Going, Gone… Global: A Canadian Perspective on International Tax Administration Issues in the 'Exchange-of-Information Age'. *Canadian Tax Journal.* 50(6), pp. 1869–1912.

Meads, R., Jarvis, E. (2014) In Practice: Practice Points: Rules Governing Trusts. *Law Society Gazette.* 111(25), p. 36.

Milford, A. (2017) *Speech: Deferred Prosecution Agreements.* Available from: https://www.sfo.gov.uk/2017/09/05/alun-milford-on-deferred-prosecution-agreements/ [Accessed 14 October 2020]

Ministry of Justice (2017) *Corporate Liability for Economic Crime: Call for Evidence.* London: The Stationery Office. (Cm 9370)

Moses, L.B., de Koker, L. (2017) Open Secrets: Balancing Operational Secrecy and Transparency in the Collection and Use of Data by National Security and Law Enforcement Agencies. *Melbourne University Law Review.* 41(2), pp. 530–570.

Noseda, F. (2017) Common Reporting Standard and EU Beneficial Ownership Registers: Inadequate Protection of Privacy and Data Protection. *Trusts & Trustees.* 23(4), pp. 404–409.

OECD (2020) *Glossary of Tax Terms.* Available from: https://www.oecd.org/ctp/glossaryoftaxterms.htm [Accessed 30 September 2020]

OECD (2019a) *AEOI: Status of Commitments.* Available from: https://www.oecd.org/tax/transparency/AEOI-commitments.pdf [Accessed 14 October 2020]

OECD (2019b) *Tax Morale What Drives People and Businesses to Pay Tax.* Paris: OECD Publishing.

OECD (2017) *Technology Tools to Tackle Tax Evasion and Tax Fraud.* Paris: OECD Publishing.

OECD (2014) *Standard for Automatic Exchange of Financial Account Information in Tax Matters.* Paris: OECD Publishing.

O'Flaherty, M.C. (2019) The Rise and Rise of the Designer Resale Market. Available from: https://www.ft.com/content/a7e5d5f8-7c91-11e9-8b5c-33d0560f039c [Accessed 14 October 2020]

OpenText (2018) *UK Serious Fraud Office Selects OpenText to Expedite Data Discovery and Investigations.* Available from: https://www.opentext.com/about/pressreleases?id=27DE2D13774A4B8E82776CBEBFF19D40 [Accessed 14 October 2020]

Ormerod, D. (1998) Cheating the Public Revenue. *Criminal Law Review.* September, pp. 627–645.

Ormerod, D., Laird, K. (2020) The Future of Dishonesty - Some Practical Considerations. *Archbold Review.* 6, pp. 8–10.

Ormerod, D., Laird, K. (2015) *Smith and Hogan's Criminal Law.* 14th ed. Oxford: Oxford University Press.

Palmer, K. (2015) *HMRC Targets Etsy, eBay and Gumtree Sellers – But When Is Your Hobby Taxable?* Available from: https://www.telegraph.co.uk/finance/personalfinance/

household-bills/11632478/HMRC-targets-Etsy-eBay-and-Gumtree-sellers-but-when-is-your-hobby-taxable.html [Accessed 14 October 2020]

Parker, J. (2019) *U.K. Tax Authority and Tax Fraud Investigations*. Available from: https://news.bloombergtax.com/daily-tax-report-international/insight-u-k-tax-authority-and-tax-fraud-investigations [Accessed 14 October 2020]

Parliament. House of Commons, Committee of Public Accounts (2017a) *Tackling Online VAT Fraud and Error, Session 2017–19*. London: The Stationery Office. (HC 2017-19 312)

Parliament. House of Commons, HM Treasury (2017b) *Autumn Budget 2017, Session 2017–19*. London: The Stationery Office. (HC 2017-19 587)

Parliament. House of Commons, National Audit Office (2017c) *HM Revenue & Customs Investigation into Overseas Sellers Failing to Charge VAT on Online Sales, Session 2016–17*. London: The Stationery Office. (HC 2016-17 1129).

Parliament. House of Commons, HM Treasury (2016). *Summer Budget 2015, Session 2015–16*. London: The Stationery Office (HC 2015-16 264)

Pickhardt, M., Prinz, A. (2012) The Nature of Tax Evasion and the Shadow Economy. In Pickhardt, M., Prinz, A. eds., *Tax Evasion and the Shadow Economy*. Cheltenham: Edward Elgar, pp. 3–12.

Pijnenburg, M., Kowalczyk, W., van der Hel-van Dijk, L. (2017) A Roadmap for Analytics in Taxpayer Supervision. *The Electronic Journal of e-Government*. 15(1), pp. 19–32.

Pross, A., Kerfs, P., Hondius, P., Housden, R. (2017) Turning Tax Policy into Reality – Global Tax Transparency Goes Live. *International Tax Review*. 27(10), pp. 16–21.

Rabah, K. (2018) Convergence of AI, IoT, Big Data and Blockchain: A Review. *The Lake Institute Journal*. 1(1), pp. 1–18.

Rigney, P. (2016) *The All Seeing Eye – An HMRC Success Story?* Available from: https://www.ifa.org.uk/media/653935/Tax-HMRC-Connect-system.pdf [Accessed 14 October 2020]

Salter, D. (2002) Some Thoughts on Fraudulent Evasion of Income Tax. *British Tax Review*. 6, pp. 489–505.

Sanghrajka, J. (2020) Degrees of Connection. *Taxation*. 186(4752), pp. 8–10.

Seddon, J., Berges, P., Stott, C., Howard, A., Paul, R., Saunders Gregor, K. (2020) *Cum/Ex Convictions- Implications for Financial Institutions in the UK*. Available from: https://www.ropesgray.com/en/newsroom/alerts/2020/03/Cum-ex-convictions-implications-for-financial-institutions-in-the-UK [Accessed 14 October 2020]

Segal, D. (2020) *It May Be the Biggest Tax Heist Ever. And Europe Wants Justice*. Available from: https://www.nytimes.com/2020/01/23/business/cum-ex.html [Accessed 14 October 2020]

Srivastava, A., Moffatt, N., Burkova, K., Best, T., Dayanim, B., Flickr, S. (2019) Money Laundering Update. *Compliance Officer Bulletin*. 167, pp. 1–23.

Srivastava, A., Simpson, M., Thomson, C., Tomas, J., Dennien, P.M., Garfield, H., Powell, R. (2018) Financial Crime Update. *Compliance Officer Bulletin*. 157, pp. 1–30.

Tax Journal (2019) *HMRC Prosecutions against Individuals Reach 1,000s*. Available from: https://www.taxjournal.com/articles/hmrc-prosecutions-against-individuals-reach-1-000 [Accessed 14 October 2020]

The Economist (2013) *The Rise of the Sharing Economy*. Available from: https://www.economist.com/leaders/2013/03/09/the-rise-of-the-sharing-economy [Accessed 14 October 2020]

Turner, S., Bainbridge, J. (2018) An Anti-Money Laundering Timeline and the Relentless Regulatory Response. *Journal of Criminal Law.* 82(3), pp. 215–231.

Virgo, E. (2019) Trust Registers and Transparency: A Step Too Far? *Trust Law International.* 33(3), pp. 95–112.

Volkin, M. (2020) *Why the Gig Economy Will Drive the Future of Employment.* Available from: https://www.forbes.com/sites/forbescoachescouncil/2020/03/27/why-the-gig-economy-will-drive-the-future-of-employment/#419d87a74f52 [Accessed 14 October 2020]

Weber, R.H., Baisch, R. (2018) FinTech - Eligible Safeguards to Foster the Regulatory Framework. *Journal of International Banking Law and Regulation.* 33(10), pp. 335–350.

Werle, N. (2018) Prosecuting Corporate Crime When Firms Are Too Big to Jail: Investigation, Deterrence, and Judicial Review. *The Yale Law Journal.* 128, pp. 1366–1438.

Xu, C., Wang, K., Li, P., Guo, S., Luo, J., Ye, B., Guo, M. (2019) Making Big Data Open in Edges: A Resource-Efficient Blockchain-Based Approach. *IEEE Transactions on Parallel and Distributed Systems.* 30(4), pp. 870–882.

Yeoh, P. (2018) Financial Secrecy Business Offshore and Onshore. *Company Lawyer.* 39(9), pp. 279–285.

Yorke, C. (2017) Dishonesty and the Failure to Prevent Evasion. *Tax Journal.* 1377, p. 16.

Zucman, G. (2014) Taxing Across Borders: Tracking Personal Wealth and Corporate Profits. *The Journal of Economic Perspectives.* 28(4), pp. 121–148.

10 The Bank of England's approach to central bank digital currencies – considerations regarding a native digital pound and the regulatory aspects

Monica Laura Vessio

1 Introduction

Virtual currencies, digital currencies, cryptoassets, and similar virtual concepts are becoming part of common vernacular. Governments the world over have been trying to formulate ways to regulate the trades associated with such digital resources.[1] All the while, however, a new matter has arisen and that is whether governments should be looking at these phenomena in a different light altogether by taking these virtual assets one step closer to being recognised as state-backed currency in the form of central bank digital currencies (CBDCs).[2]

---

1 In the UK, the Financial Conduct Authority issued Guidance on Cryptoassets: Feedback and Final Guidance to CP 19/3 in July 2019. Following a public consultation conducted in March 2020, the European Union Commission has published a proposal for a Regulation of Markets in Crypto-Assets. The objective is to harmonise the European framework for the issuance and trading of various types of crypto tokens as part of Europe's Digital Finance Strategy (European Union Commission, 2020). There is no current federal legal approach to cryptocurrency regulation in the United States regulating cryptocurrencies, and laws governing exchanges vary by state. A cryptocurrency bill of 2020 has been proposed but not yet enacted.
2 What makes the discussion more pertinent is that in many countries (notable examples include Sweden, Canada, Russia, and China) the use of cash for payment has been declining. That is not to say that the demand for cash has been declining (Sweden appears an exception here). In Canada, for example, the overall demand for cash continues to grow at a rate similar to that of their nominal GDP, so the cash-to-GDP ratio remains stable at around 3%–4%. This is a ratio that has persisted for more than three decades (Engert et al., 2018). This type of steady demand for cash (relative to GDP) can be observed in a number of other advanced economies. Since 2000, cash in circulation is, on average, up from 7% to 9% of GDP. Generally, a majority of countries have seen higher cash in circulation with the largest increases occurring in Hong Kong and Japan (by 9% and 7% of GDP, respectively) since the global financial crisis of 2008. In contrast, demand for cash in China declined by 5%. In effect, cash demand varies considerably across countries. Cash in circulation is below 2% of GDP in Sweden, but ten times larger in Japan at 20%. Demand differs, however, even among countries that are otherwise similar in terms of economic and social characteristics. The Nordic region is a prime example. In the early 2000s, Iceland's cash-to-GDP ratio was at 1.2%, while Denmark, Norway, and Sweden were at around 3%–4%. Since then, demand for cash has shown a material decline in Sweden and Norway, while in Denmark it has

As of January 2019, some 80% of central banks around the world are engaging in research and/or experimenting with CBDC (Boar et al., 2020).[3] In 2018 Mark Carney, the then Governor of the Bank of England (BoE), gave a speech entitled *The Future of Money* (Speech, Edinburgh, 2018). During this speech he canvassed the viability of having a (native) CBDC and concluded that due to certain technological shortcomings in distributed ledger technologies (DLT) and the risks with offering central bank accounts for all, a true, widely available reliable CBDC did not appear to be a near-term prospect (ibid). During the same year, the BoE issued a staff working paper where it claimed that although it had no imminent plans to issue CBDC, it had published an extensive research agenda on the topic. In 2020, the BoE issued a discussion paper on CBDC (2020). While the BoE appears to be the first central bank to publish research on DLT in 2014,[4] it is no longer the leader of the sovereign digital coin pack. Other nation-states, including but not limited to, China and the European Union, are making progress with the design, development, and implementation of

---

remained stable at around 3.5%. However, in Iceland, demand has more than doubled since its banking crisis and now exceeds that of Norway and Sweden (Bech et al., 2018). In the UK, the use of cash accounted for the largest number of payments (by number not value) (UK Finance, 2020). However, the use of cash in transactions was declining before the Covid pandemic. With the impact of Covid and the UK lockdown, cash withdrawal volumes have dropped further. At their lowest during the UK lockdown, cash withdrawals were 60% lower in April 2020 than in April 2019. Even as the UK lockdown has eased, cash withdrawal volumes have remained low. In July, they were around 40% lower than the year before (Link Report, 2020). At the start of 2004, the value of notes in circulation was £34 billion; in March 2011, it was £49 billion, whilst presently it stands at £77 billion. It took 310 years to get to £34 billion and then just over 16 years to move on to £77 billion, and this figure has not fallen. Paradoxically, whilst the use in payments is declining, the value of the stock in issue is not (Bailey, 2020).

3 '[C]entral banks are undertaking extensive work on central bank digital currencies. Globally, emerging market economies are moving from conceptual research to intensive practical development, driven by stronger motivations than those of advanced economy central banks. Central banks representing a fifth of the world's population say they are likely to issue the first CBDCs in the next few years'.

4 On a more contemporary note, the Association of Banks in Italy (ABI) has piloted a blockchain-DLT-based application for interbank reconciliations called the Spunta Project. They have completed the technical testing phase, which was conducted on 200 million data points across 35 nodes. Spunta involves a blockchain proof-of-concept for straight-through processing of interbank reconciliations. Eighteen Italian banks participated, which makes up 78% of the banking sector in terms of employee numbers. The application matches corresponding accounts that involve different banks. Traditionally, the interbank reconciliation procedure is carried out by the back office based on bilateral registers with low levels of standardisation and operating processes. The Spunta implementation makes it possible to automatically detect nonmatching transactions using a shared algorithm, standardising both the process and the single communication channel, and gives the interested parties the possibility of being able to view transactions. The new system, when implemented, is envisioned to provide banks with complete visibility of own and counterparty movements, daily reconciliations, and improved communication *inter se* (Attanasio et al., 2019). In South Africa in 2017, the South African Reserve Bank initiated Project Khokha, with the project team consisting of seven banking industry participants, a technical service provider, and consulting practice. The scope of Project Khokha was to trial interbank wholesale settlement using DLT (2018).

state-issued digital coins. Despite the six-year lapse, many of the technological challenges are still prevalent, as are the issues relating to monetary and fiscal policy that a national digital coin could bring with it (Boar et al., 2020, 1).[5] This chapter looks to provide an understanding and analysis of what a CBDC is or has the potential to be. This is an important aspect to canvass, given that a CDBC has not yet come into existence and thus its potential capabilities are vast and have the scope to affect economic policy and banking regulation. The chapter also looks at the direction the BoE appears to be taking, in terms of technological modelling. While the bank states in its 2020 discussion paper that it has not yet made a decision on whether to introduce a CBDC (and rather intends to engage on the benefits, risks, and practicalities of so doing) it is surprisingly specific about some features that a native digital currency would adopt. While the BoE's assumptions are canvassed here, the aim of this chapter is to foster an understanding as to what CBDCs are, in order to cultivate a discourse on what type of regulatory concerns might ensue with the introduction of a digital pound.

2 What is CBDC?

> [I]n the evolution of money, after primitive money, coins and notes, electronic money and digital money, we are now on the verge of creating digital money 2.0, the form and characteristics of which are as yet unknown.
>
> (Bech, 2018, 11)

A CBDC can take several forms depending on the coding architecture (Vessio, n/d). Different designs – 'that is, different bundles of attributes – would generate different trade-offs along several dimensions' (Engert et al., 2018, 64). The BoE has the parliamentary imperative to maintain monetary and financial stability and therefore springboards off this objective when considering the design of a CBDC (2020).[6] Thus, the BoE is concerned with a CBDC that would be an electronic form of central bank money that could be more widely used by households and businesses to make payments and store value (ibid).

---

5 'Most central banks are still working to understand the implications for their jurisdiction and a significant minority representing a fifth of the world's population look likely to issue a CBDC very soon'.
6 Engert and Fung (2018) propose that to the extent that individuals and firms were to rely on CBDC as a means of payment and a store of value, overall risk and financial stability could benefit because CBDC is essentially risk-free. They go on to point out, however, that a shift from bank deposits to CBDC could have an impact on bank funding and credit provision, which could affect financial stability and efficiency. They conclude that the overall impact of CBDC would depend on the specific attributes of the CBDC and on the behaviour of economic agents over time. As will be seen later in this discussion, presently, the design posited by the BoE for a digital pound does not consider disintermediation of private stakeholders, for example, banks. Rather, the bank has taken an inclusive approach in what appears to be an attempt to stimulate private sector involvement.

While initially it may be thought of as a 'digital bank note', practically it may have other features that will depend on its final design (ibid). From a high-level view, there are two potentialities for a CBDC, namely, the *wholesale* CBDC and the *retail* CBDC.[7] Whereas a *retail* CBDC (Bech and Garratt, 2017) is one that would be issued for the general public, that is, a widely available, consumer-facing payment instrument targeted at retail transactions (WEF, 2019), a *wholesale* CBDC would be a central bank-issued digital currency that would be operated and settled in a peer-to-peer and decentralised manner (no intermediary), available only for commercial banks and clearing houses for use in the wholesale interbank market (ibid).[8] The distinction between *retail* and *wholesale* comes from the banking custom of differentiating between 'retail' and 'wholesale' payments.[9] 'Retail' in a payments context refers to all payments that involve households and/or small or mediumsized businesses, while wholesale payments are those made between financial institutions (e.g. banks, pension funds, insurance companies) and/or large (often multinational) corporations. It can also be that financial institutions make 'retail' payments to households and businesses, for example, when collecting insurance premiums or paying staff (Bank of England, 2020). However, while the distinction is common in payment economic parlance, there is no legal distinction between wholesale and retail payments just as presently there is no legal distinction between retail and wholesale CBDCs (Bank of International Settlements,

---

7   In fact, the variability in the design of CBDC with a multiplicity of potential characteristics is superabundant. Fernandez De Lis gives four scenarios, with more combinations conceivable, of CBDC. He discusses a non-yield-bearing CBDC with restricted access and full identification which might be conceived for interbank settlement (this is the wholesale CBDC referred to above). Fernandez De Lis posits that this kind of CBDC would improve wholesale money market efficiency, and the reduction of barriers to entry would open participation of third-party providers. The second type is a non-yield-bearing CBDC with universal access and anonymity that might replace physical cash, at lower cost and with higher efficiency. In his view, this would improve retail payments efficiency. Having an account with the central bank might need to be made obligatory. It must be noted, however, that this is not the design favoured by the BoE. Fernandez De Lis posits that with this second type, bank deposits and credit might fall, however, overall; it would be convenient for end-users; and, with anonymity, the informal economy might be encouraged to use it. Finally, he discusses a yield-bearing CBDC with universal access and anonymity which in his view may help central banks overcome the zero-lower bound on interest rates (2018, 13). Again, the design capabilities are vast, and the exact format the BoE decides to take are not yet clear.
8   Much like the Italians have done in the Spunta Project initiative, the BoE in its 2020 discussion paper does not focus on wholesale payments. In a different paper, the writer questioned the rationale for creating two CBDCs – retail and wholesale. Once created it seems, at least initially, redundant as to why the wholesale CBDC would have to have a different technology to retail CBDC. Practical differences would be in technological design, functionality, and store of value. If the intention is to differentiate the value between retail and wholesale CBDC, then this appears a complication of the monetary and payments system. Again, because the concept is still in its novice stages, plausibility of a two-tiered system may become patent.
9   Another common differentiation is domestic and crossborder payments.

2020).[10] The BoE in its 2020 discussion paper focuses on retail CBDCs, as does this chapter.[11]

In 2018, the Bank of International Settlements (BIS) stated that the concept of CBDCs is so obscure that it is probably easier to define what a CBDC is not[12]:

> CBDC is not a well-defined term. It is used to refer to a number of concepts. However, it is envisioned by most to be a new form of central bank money. That is, a central bank liability, denominated in an existing unit of account, which serves both as a medium of exchange and a store of value. This would be an innovation for general purpose users but not for wholesale entities. Central banks already provide digital money in the form of reserves or settlement account balances held by commercial banks and certain other financial institutions at the central bank. This mix of new and already existing forms of central bank money makes it challenging to precisely define what a CBDC is.
>
> (2018)

Economists and jurists have been attempting to define what CBDC's are. Unfortunately, because these discussions are preceding the creation of CBDCs, each has approached the definition from different definitional angles (Shukla, 2020, 1).[13] The fact that commentators in different jurisdictions are coming up with various classifications may in and of itself be a problem, which will only manifest once the internal CBDCs, in say England, are wanting to be used in say Italy. Thus, either the technological platforms will have to be the same, or there will be programmes that will have to be developed to integrate the exchange -.[14]

---

10 The distinction is becoming more patent as CBDC's become more plausible as a form of money. The Bank for International Settlements has indicated that a general purpose or retail variant can be based on tokens or accounts. A key difference between tokens and accounts is in how they are verified. When a person receives a token they will verify that the token is genuine, whereas an intermediary verifies the identity of an account holder.

11 However, the wholesale potentiality of CBDC should not be discounted. In effect 50% of the 80% of banks engaging in CBDC research and experimentation are looking at wholesale CBDC (Boar et al., 2020).

12 However, it has to be noted that in a January 2020 publication the authors quite simply stated that '[a] CBDC is, by definition a digital, a central bank-issued digital money'.

13 The following quote is pertinent: '[a]s an emerging technology, the innovative technical and operational frameworks are often bespoke. The terminology used to describe forms of digital money tokens is also inconsistent across these frameworks' (Shukla, 2020). Both (terminology and technical variances) are not insurmountable issues. A rose by any other name ... and as far as the technological functional differences, see footnote 26 below for suggestions on 'surmountability'.

14 A SAP-like integration system for CBDCs to 'talk to each other', which would need to incorporate current exchange rate functionality if all other CBDCs are based on their own currency rate. The matter gets even more complicated if CBDCs were to take on stablecoin-like properties and backed by a basket of assets, taking on different values to the country's currency. Already

This will be a relatively fluid exercise if each CBDC value is pegged to its currency. This is indeed one of the conventions the BoE has stipulated – that is, if a CBDC were to be introduced in England it would be denominated in pounds sterling, so £10 of CBDC would always be worth £10 banknote (ibid).[15] One of the main issues when deliberating CBDCs is in fact a generally accepted terminology or taxonomy, as absence of agreed terminology has the potential to inhibit in-depth dialogue and analysis (Didenko and Buckley, 2019).

In 2017 the BIS, in an attempt to answer this 'deceptively simple question', started by looking at the taxonomy of money based on four key properties: issuer (central bank or other); form (electronic or physical); accessibility (universal or limited); and transfer mechanism (centralised or decentralised) (Bech and Garratt, 2017, 55). The BIS then came up with their definition of CBDCs: 'an electronic form of central bank money that can be exchanged in a decentralised manner known as *peer-to-peer*, meaning that transactions occur directly between the payer and the payee without the need for a central intermediary' (ibid).[16] This definitional concept is derived from the acceptance of the concept that there are three types of money in existence today: central bank-issued reserves, bank account money (bank deposits), and cash (Bjerg, 2017, 1). Each of these forms lacks an important characteristic held by the other two. Bank account money is universally accessible and electronic but not issued by the central bank. Cash is issued by the central bank and universally accessible, but it is not electronic, and central bank money is not universally accessible but electronic and obviously central bank-issued. We can see how a CBDC would have all the three qualities described. The following Venn diagram, incorporating CBDC, probably provides the clearest (visual) understanding of where a CBDC falls in relation to other types of money (ibid):

Andrew Bailey has made the very pertinent observation that '[s]tablecoins and CBDC are not necessarily mutually exclusive. Depending on design choices, they could sit alongside each other, either as distinct payment options, or with elements of the stablecoin ecosystem, such as wallets, providing consumers with access to a CBDC. So there will likely be a role for the private and public sector working together in the future of payments'.

15 This is where the reliability and trust factor would play a vital role. A CBDC would presumably elicit more confidence than other digital coins (assets) as these are volatile in value. For example, Tether, a controversial cryptocurrency (tokens issued by Tether Limited), initially claimed that each token was backed by one US dollar, but in March 2019 the company changed the backing to include loans to affiliate companies. It is submitted, however, that appropriate regulation could have prevented this election and again one must defer to the comments by the governor that standards must be set 'early on so that innovation can take place with confidence on what will be required. This gives certainty not only to regulators and users but also to innovators'; he goes onto warn, however, that 'given the novel form, existing standards do not necessarily easily apply. There need to be minimum international standards for stablecoins. In addition, any stablecoin with potential for widescale use in the UK must meet our domestic expectations'.

16 A cash transaction is the traditional form of a peer-to-peer exchange; whereas, on a computer network, the peer-to-peer concept means that transactions can be processed without the need for a central server.

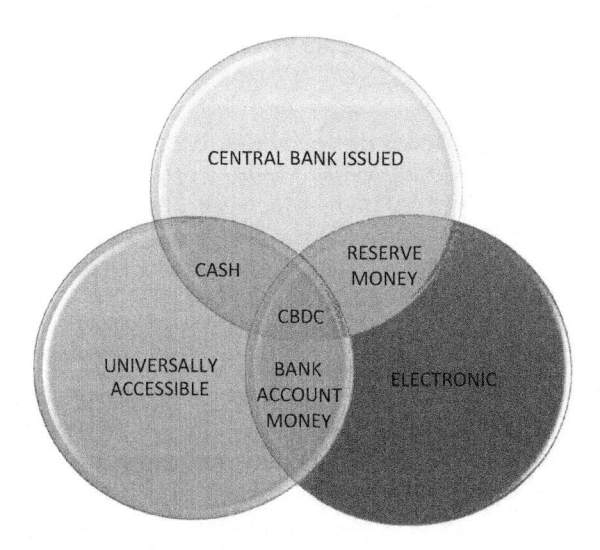

[Venn diagram with three overlapping circles labeled CENTRAL BANK ISSUED, UNIVERSALLY ACCESSIBLE, and ELECTRONIC. Intersections are labeled CASH, RESERVE MONEY, BANK ACCOUNT MONEY, and CBDC at the centre.]

The World Economic Forum has described CBDCs as a potential application of blockchain and DLT where the central bank issues new money equivalent to – and redeemable for – its domestic currency (2019, 8). It can also alternatively operate on traditional centralised technologies (ibid). Ideally, simultaneously removing the equivalent amount of currency from the money supply (ibid). The BoE looks to a potential CBDC to provide both a new form of money and a new payment infrastructure (2020). The public would be able to hold central bank money, that is, money issued by the BoE, in the form of banknotes and CBDC, to be used by households and businesses to make payments and store value (ibid). Broader access to central bank money could create new opportunities for payments and the way the BoE could maintain monetary and financial stability (ibid). This section examines some of the favoured capabilities the BoE desires in a native digital coin.

3 Design principles set out by the Bank of England

In its discussion paper, the BoE outlines its 'wish list' in terms of objectives that a CBDC could achieve. The BoE acknowledges that in a real-world implementation there will be tradeoffs between different principles, making it impossible to achieve the best outcome for every principle; consequently, careful choices about which principles to prioritise and the optimal tradeoffs between them would have to be made (2020). In a BoE Staff working paper, Koomhof and Noone defined CBDC as:

> electronic central bank money that (i) can be accessed more broadly than reserves, (ii) potentially has much greater functionality for retail transactions than cash, (iii) has a separate operational structure to other forms of central bank money, allowing it to potentially serve a different core purpose, and

(iv) can be interest bearing, under realistic assumptions paying a rate that would be different to the rate on reserves.

(2018, 4)

This is a slightly more nuanced description of the characteristics that a native central bank digital coin could carry. Much of these characteristics have not been referred to in the BoE's 2020 discussion paper. Some of the above features have been assumed however, such as the fact that a CBDC would be introduced alongside – rather than replacing – cash and commercial deposits (Bank of England, 2020). The BoE's objective would be to create a fast, secure, and resilient technology infrastructure to support a CBDC that would sit alongside the banks' real-time gross settlement (RTGS) system (ibid). The Koomhof and Noone model would allow scope for exploring whether CBDC can be used as a second monetary policy tool, either having a price rule – this is where the central bank sets the interest rate on CBDC and allows the quantity to vary – or a quantity rule, where the central bank sets the quantity of CBDC supplied and allows the interest rate to vary (Bank of England, 2018).

Any CBDC payment system would need to be reliable and resilient, especially by having the capacity to recover from operational disruption, for example, hardware or software failures (Bank of England, 2020). CBDC access should provide 24/7 transactions with no 'planned' downtime (ibid). The concept of unplanned downtime is of concern and raises alarms in terms of accessibility to personal funds and ability to conduct transactions. Lack of continued and guaranteed access to their money would be disruptive for consumers and have a deterrent effect in CBDC investment. This is problematic, and any potential unplanned downtime should be a CBDC implementation deal-breaker or at least delay to entry. Reliability, security, and availability are the core of any monetary system. Without one of which a trust issue would surely arise. The BoE will have to implement critical disaster recovery plans that incorporate failover systems, data recovery systems, and data redundancy systems. This is where we see the attractiveness of a private blockchain system, which has inherent built-in security (and disaster recovery) – it is for all intents and purposes a so-called self-healing system. The nature of this discussion is not meant to be technical in nature, but the characteristics of the blockchain technology reveal that it is a system that is difficult to hack. The nodes would be natural parts of disaster recovery on a private blockchain system. A native digital currency could have its own nodes (in whichever global cities it deems necessary), and these could be the nodes (much like in the Bitcoin blockchain system, except they would be privately as opposed to publicly accessible) that would back up all and at any time the CBDC system, making it as stated, self-healing, secure, and resilient. Another option to gain and retain trust in a sovereign digital coin would be to make it a hybrid coin – that is a coin that could have private and public qualities; for example, anyone who downloads the software could be a node, but only the bank would be able to issue more coins into the system.

CBDC would need to guard against or ensure minimisation of credit and liquidity risk arising in the wider CBDC ecosystem (Bank of England, 2020). It would have to follow the highest standards of cybersecurity, with clear policies around who is responsible for redress in the case of fraudulent payments (ibid), and be compliant with the antimoney laundering (AML), countering the financing of terrorism regulations (CFT), and the sanctions regime (Ryder, 2020). The technology powering CBDC payments should be scalable, which means the system would need to be able to handle increased volumes when demand for CBDC payments increases significantly (Bank of England, 2020). In general, cryptocurrencies have been modelled on DLT, the most commonly known of which is blockchain.[17] Much of the studies and discussions on CBDC's assume that their underlying structure would indeed be DLT (Fernández de Lis, 2018, 56). In such instances, however, scalability remains a challenge in blockchain-based payment systems compared to traditional central bank-based payment systems (Real-Time Gross Settlement Systems), which shows that the latter are commonly more efficient than blockchain-based payment systems (ibid). However, DLTs are in their infancy and dramatic improvements in efficiency is imminent, which would inevitably solve the scalability problem (ibid).[18] The BoE does not presume that an English CBDC would be built on DLT and state that while the distribution and decentralisation as used in DLT would enhance resilience and availability, it could impact aspects such as performance, privacy, and security negatively (Bank of England, 2020). Bringing it to the conclusion that there is no inherent reason why the CBDC should not be built on centralised technology stacks with the potentiality to adopt certain features of the DLT (ibid).

Qualities such as speed, user-friendliness, efficiency, and transparency are all ideal characteristics for a new digital coin. The payment process should be guaranteed and should conclude as quickly as possible. The solution should be intuitive, with payment being completed in the minimum number of steps and with minimum levels of technical literacy (Bank of England, 2020). Canada, for example, is considering a universal access device; that is a device that would store and transfer CBDC without consumers having to have a mobile smartphone. This would look something like a prepaid card but would be available to everyone and at a low cost (Lane, 2020).

Payments should happen in an efficient and safe manner that would ensure that the cost of CBDC payments would be as low as possible while ensuring resiliency and security. The costs of making payments in CBDC should be transparent (Bank of England, 2020). CBDC payment systems should be designed to be inclusive and thus minimise barriers to use from technical literacy, disabilities, and access to hardware (for example avoiding reliance on latest smartphones) or

17 The DLT upon which bitcoin is built.
18 With the same argument extended in terms of their including energy consumption. The same author goes on to argue that although presently DLTs are less efficient than RTGS, the distance between both is not huge, with the implication that a little improvement in DLTs would offer a suitable alternative to RTGS.

access to mobile data networks (for example in rural areas) (ibid). Canada has also factored in that a universal access device for CBDC would have to be designed to accommodate the needs of people with motor, sensory, and cognitive impairments (Lane, 2020).

The BoE also envisions a CBDC structured to facilitate a competitive market for providers of CBDCrelated payment services. This requires an appropriate regulatory regime to protect consumers while minimising barriers to entry.[19] The design would have to ensure that there are no structural elements that would lead to 'a winner take all' market dynamic in so far as provision of CBDCrelated services are concerned (Bank of England, 2020). Interoperability of CBDC is also important as the design should avoid a closedloop payment system. That is where payments can only be made between users of the same payment provider. Rather, CBDC payments should allow payments between users of different providers and between users of CBDC and users of deposit accounts. Furthermore, the bank anticipates that a UK CBDC should also be designed to interoperate with other countries' CBDC payment systems (to support future crossborder payments in CBDC) (ibid).

4 What genre of CBDC is the Bank of England projecting?

The BoE distinguishes two main elements to a potential CBDC: (1) the CBDC itself (that is – private access to a new form of central bank money) and (2) the CBDC infrastructure that would allow CBDC to be transferred and used for payments (Bank of England, 2020). In terms of infrastructure, the bank's report presents a hypothetical model of CBDC as a publicprivate payment platform (ibid). The illustrative model proposed is 'built' around certain design principles (ibid).[20] The BoE has developed a so-called *platform model*, to develop further discussion (ibid). The bank envisions building a fast, highly secure, and resilient technology platform that would provide the minimum necessary functionality for CBDC payments. This would be the 'core ledger', which would serve as the platform on which private sector firms could connect to provide customerfacing CBDC payment services. These firms, called Payment Interface Providers or PIPs, could also develop additional functionality that would not form part of the bank's core ledger, but which could be provided as a valueadded service for some, or all, of the PIP users. These additional privately supplied services would be known as 'overlay services'. The bank would oversee the overlay services by imposing standards and regulations, to ensure their security, resiliency, and interoperability.

---

19 See the discussion on regulatory requirements below.
20 The discussion paper does point out that the design principles for infrastructure are intended as a basis for further discussion and research rather than a proposal for a CBDC.

4.1 What is the core ledger?

The core ledger, a database, would form the centre of the CBDC payment system (Bank of England, 2020). It would have records of the CBDC value and would process transactions made using CBDC (ibid). The functionality of the core ledger is envisioned to be limited to the essential features required to enable CBDC payments, for example, providing push payments[21] and the ability to query latest balances or transaction history (ibid). The idea behind providing a limit on the range of functionality to essential features is to build a system that is simple, fast, and resilient and which could then allow most of the innovation in CBDC payment functionality to happen in the private sector through overlay services (ibid). The possible downside of this type of system is that while it would provide good private sector stimulus, it would likely push the costs onto consumers. It would no longer be a direct access to central bank currency, but it would simply be a hybrid form of cash. The upshot is the prevention of disintermediation, often viewed as a contributor to possible financial instability (Huber, 1999; Niepelt, 2018; Pollack, 2018).[22]

The core ledger would be accompanied by an Application Programming Interface (API) to allow PIPs to securely send payment instructions and ask for updates from the ledger (Bank of England, 2020). According to the BoE, with the adoption of the correct technology, security issues could be thwarted. The BoE acknowledges that it could operate the core ledger itself, there is also the possibility of distributing or decentralising aspects of the maintenance of the ledger and processing of transactions (ibid).[23] However, the bank is adamant that whatever technology approach is used, it is essential that only it will be able to 'create' or 'destroy' CBDC (ibid).

4.2 What is a Payment Interface Provider (PIP)?

In the platform model, PIPs are envisioned to be private sector firms that would manage the interaction with users of CBDC and provide overlay services that would extend the functionality of CBDC (Bank of England, 2020, 27).[24]

---

21 Payments initiated by the payer.
22 The discussion on the pros and cons of a CBDC and the potential impact on fiscal and monetary policy are beyond the scope of this chapter. Suffice to say that there are strong proponents both for and against the disintermediation model, as both models will impact financial stability.
23 Chapter 6 of the 2020 discussion paper considers the technology benefits, costs, and tradeoffs involved in adding degrees of distribution and decentralisation to a CBDC payment system.
24 Whether this functionality will be fulfilled by small-to-medium private sector firms or swallowed by big techs remains to be seen. Big techs are defined by the Financial Stability Board as 'large companies with established technology platforms and extensive established customer networks' (FSB, 2019). However, in a joint report, the International Banking Federation and Oliver Wyman extended this and classified the big techs' business model as 'one that aims to create (and concentrate) an ecosystem covering as many areas of customers' lives as possible'. It is likely that big techs with their amplified buying power, global scale, large customer bases, and cutting-edge technology will gain most of the ground. Big techs' focus on customers' needs and experiences

There are two methods in which the PIPs could interact with the BoE: they could hold individual accounts of each customer on behalf of that customer, and payments between users would still be processed through the core ledger even if both users have the same PIP (ibid). Alternatively, each PIP could maintain a single 'pooled' account in the ledger, which holds all of their customers' CBDC (ibid). The PIP would record how the funds in the pooled account are divided between its users and payments between two users of the same PIP could then be processed within the PIP's own systems, rather than each transaction being run through the core ledger (ibid). Where transactions occur between a user of a PIP and any other PIP, these would still need to go through the core ledger (ibid). Depending on the technology adopted, however, PIPs could record transactions *inter se* and only run a final balance of their transaction through the core ledger; this would probably be a daily exercise.

The following description demonstrates how digital pound exchanges could occur. Suppose we have PIP A and PIP B and Customer A, Customer B, and Retailer. Customer A sells her vehicle to Customer B for D£10,000 (10,000 digital pounds). Both customers use PIP A as their service provider. At the close of business on the day of the sale, PIP A does not record a change in its core ledger account (in so far as the sale of the vehicle transaction is concerned). On the same day, Customer B purchases new tyres from the Retailer for D£250. Customer A uses its usual service provider, PIP A; however, Retailer uses PIP B. At the close of the day, PIP A decreases its pooled account with the central bank by D£250, and PIP B increases its pooled account with the bank by D£250. Here is a diagram showing these transactions.

---

allows them to monetise core businesses easily and thus create ecosystems to serve customers in all aspects of life, including finance, increasing their 'stickiness' to their core platforms. Their entry in financial services is largely in the retail and small- and medium-sized enterprise segments (while limited in corporate and investment banking). Much of what they offer pioneers new territory untapped by traditional banks, either with novel services or by addressing underserved or unbanked customer sectors. In some areas, this increases the size of the market. Big techs in such markets operate mostly in customer-facing functions, analytics, and in providing infrastructure and digital capabilities such as cloud computing and artificial intelligence, with limited interest in more regulated activities such as deposit-taking. Nonetheless, many of these services are overlays on existing bank infrastructures and can, over time, substitute for traditional financial products and services. It is submitted that big techs are forever looking to find new market share and that services that are envisioned by the BoE to be provided by PIPs will likely be dominated by big techs. Development costs are a barrier to entry (or at least to continuity) with most start-ups. This is where big techs have the upper hand, as they have the buying power to reach coding goals at more efficient rates, facilitating entry to new service markets faster, capturing customer's attention first and establishing trust, with capacities to handle security and downtime issues with relative ease.

Central bank digital currencies 181

RESERVE BANK
CORE LEDGER

+ D£10000

⬇⬆⬇ PIP A's REPORTING   ⬇⬆ PIP B's REPORTING

- D£10000   - D£250   - D£250   + D£250

PIP A   **PIP B**

⬇   ⬇

TRANSACTION **A** IN D£   TRANSACTION **B** IN D£

CUSTOMER A ⬅➡ CUSTOMER B ⬅➡ RETAILER A

In the event that the platform model of a sovereign digital coin is not by virtue of pooled accounts but where every transaction (despite the PIPs) is recorded in the core ledge, our diagram (based on the same set of transactions as described above) would look like this.

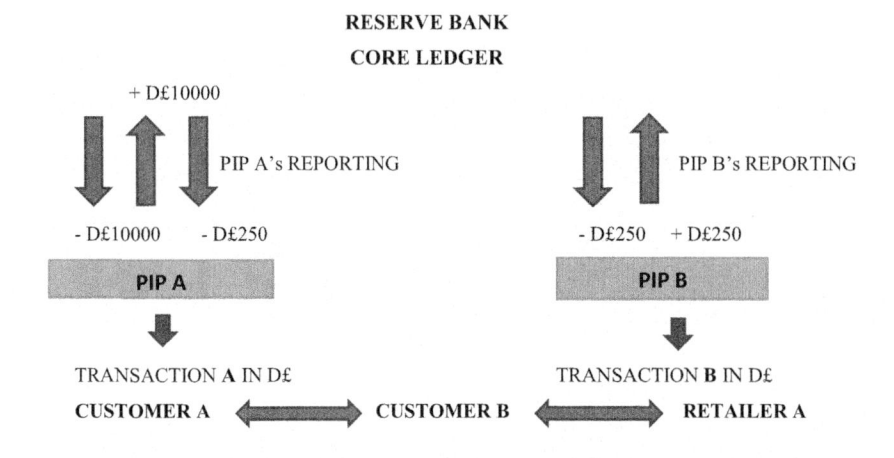

RESERVE BANK
CORE LEDGER

+ D£10000

⬇⬆⬇ PIP A's REPORTING   ⬇⬆ PIP B's REPORTING

- D£10000   - D£250   - D£250   + D£250

PIP A   **PIP B**

⬇   ⬇

TRANSACTION **A** IN D£   TRANSACTION **B** IN D£

CUSTOMER A ⬅➡ CUSTOMER B ⬅➡ RETAILER A

In the first diagram, there is less activity in the core ledger, and the details of the transactions are recorded at PIP level; in the second diagram, each transaction is 'run' through the core ledger. PIPs are envisaged to provide several services, such as:

- Userfriendly interface, such as a mobile application or website, to allow the user to initiate payments and manage their CBDC;
- Apply Know-Your-Customer checks to verify the identity of users (or commission a thirdparty service to do this);

- Register one or more accounts for the user in the core ledger. This account could be what the discussion paper refers to as 'pseudonymous' on the core ledger, meaning that the core ledger would not need to record identity information. However, the PIP would record the identity of the user on its own systems and would know which pseudonymous account(s) the user holds at the bank;
- Authenticate the user when they initiate payments, to protect them against fraud (for example where the user's phone is stolen), protect their personal data, and ensure cyberresilience;
- Apply antimoney laundering and sanctions checks to relevant payments (or commission a thirdparty service to do this);
- Develop overlay services to provide additional functionality;
- PIPs may also provide 'merchant services' to enable retailers and businesses to take CBDC payments from consumers.

(Bank of England, 2020)

It is plausible to expect some PIPS to be exclusively payment-focused, while others may also provide CBDCrelated services (ibid). The bank will incur costs in building and running the core ledger, and they foresee recovering these by charging transaction fees to PIPs (ibid). PIPs would incur costs in getting established and building and maintaining their own systems. The bank appears to be taking a hands-off approach in so far as the PIP's revenue models are concerned (provided charges or other methods of revenue generation are transparent) (ibid). The bank emerges of the notion that a demand-and-supply smoothing out of fees will occur naturally. It is submitted that this is an alarming stance, as private sector consumer fees have been notorious for becoming disproportional,[25] and while the potential offerings are wide and the economic stimulus would be welcome in a post-Covid economy, the focus of concern would be to a 'download' of costs onto consumers.

5 Regulatory considerations

The BoE has the responsibility to regulate and supervise systemically important payment systems[26] and designated critical providers (Bank of England, 2020, 29). To ensure consumer protection and resilience, payment service providers are subject to regulation by the Financial Conduct Authority, with the Payment Systems Regulator being the economic regulator for the payment systems and their participants (ibid). The BoE's Financial Policy Committee recently announced that the current regulatory framework requires adjustment to accommodate innovation in the payments sector; stablecoin was used as one example (Bank of England, 2019). By extension, any PIPs offering sovereign digital coin-related

---

25 Credit and mobile-phone industries are recent cases in point in the UK.
26 The core infrastructure that undertakes the activities of authorisation, clearing, and settlement.

services would have to be subjected to the same regulatory regimes. The Financial Policy Committee outlined three principles that payments regulation should aim to achieve:

i   Reflect the financial stability risk, rather than the legal form, of payment activities;
ii Ensure endtoend operational and financial resilience across payment chains that are critical for the smooth functioning of the economy; and
iii Ensure that sufficient information is available to monitor payment activities so that emerging risks to financial stability can be identified and addressed appropriately.

(Bank of England, 2020, 30)

PIPs and any other role-players in the CBDC ecosystem would need these criteria and any other standards that may be set by the bank and relevant regulators when offering overlay services (ibid). PIPs would have to have the appropriate authorisations or licenses and would be supervised on an ongoing basis (ibid). This includes considerations of how CBDC-related regulation would function within or alongside the current regulatory regime (ibid). The new measures would have to ensure that PIPs and any other role-players maintain the relevant standards of operational and financial resilience to ensure that any risk posed to the end-to-end payments chain is mitigated in the event of their operational or financial failure, more especially in the case of systemically important firms (ibid). Conformity to conduct and other standards that is set by the FCA or other relevant regulators will also be required (ibid).

The standards set by the BoE and other relevant regulators to ensure that the CBDC payments system is resilient, reliable, open, and interoperable will not regulate how CBDCrelated services should be developed or what technology PIPs or overlay services should use (ibid). These standards and requirements will make up the payment scheme that would apply to CBDC and would regulate issues such as standards for interoperability between different PIPs, including how transactions will take place between different customers of different PIPs and how a customer would be able to transfer to another PIP (ibid).

The regulatory deliberations posited in the 2020 discussion paper are still very high level and have not yet concretised the discussion into finer elements. However, and indeed because of the novel technology being dealt with and the as-yet-not-finalised payment instrument, it is indeed imperative to consider high-level discussions before entering statutory-level discourse.

In a joint research paper, the International Banking Federation and Oliver Wyman made important suggestions regarding the regulation of the next evolution in the financial market (2020). These considerations are critical in light of the BoE's discussion paper and Andrew Bailey's most recent comments on the issue of a digital pound (2020). The regulatory considerations are divided into three broad themes. First, the suggested revision of already existing local financial regulatory measures (International Banking Federation, 2020). More particularly that relevant authorities update or expand legislation to incorporate new products and services that need inclusion (ibid). Furthermore, choices on regulatory formats should be considered, such as whether new rules should be legislated or whether recommended guidelines would suffice (ibid).[27] Revision would also be required to be able to facilitate the identification and isolation of activities and their risks, including systemic risks. Regulators need to enhance consumer awareness in so far as protection is concerned (across products and services). For example, by increasing responsibilities on customer-facing platforms and imbedding in-product notices such as in-app alerts (ibid).

The second suggestion is to strengthen policy response on themes that cut across industries (ibid). This would require a re-examination of legislation in both the finance and other key economic sectors and the relevant technology sectors (ibid). A closer look needs to be taken at matters such as competition, especially how 'market dominance' is defined; guarantee fair access to infrastructures and improvement of regulation of monopolistic practices (ibid). Financial stability issues, such as what (new) threats and systemic activities should be encompassed and what critical infrastructure provision should be put forward by banks and non-banks, including matters related to data protection and exchange, would have to be canvassed. The latter could include methods that would foster universal principles and standards across industries and perhaps even defining bespoke regulation around financial data, taxation, cybersecurity, and AML and CFT, especially to ensure clear mandates, minimum requirements, and regulations in nonfinancial sectors (Ryder, 2020).

Finally, where inconsistencies in regulation and enforcement have arisen these need to be addressed through the extension of finance-specific regulations (International Banking Federation, 2020). This would include areas such as consumer protection and corporate governance, for example, by expanding good practices from financial conduct regulations to commerce, advertising, and other technology-based services (ibid). Minimum requirements for firm resilience and business continuity should be re-examined and, where necessary, extended, for example, for non-bank deposit-takers and availability of internet or cloud services (ibid). Despite the financial sector legal overhaul which came into effect after the 2008 global financial crisis, there may still be asymmetries in regulatory standards given the technological advancements since 2012 and the rising need to enforce these on non-banks performing specific banking activities. This requirement will become especially relevant when technology companies enter the market as service providers (PIPs) in the supply of the overlay services. The regulatory authorities will have to reflect on disruption of the structure of financial markets and their functioning, caused by technological advancements, and will have to take a forward-looking stance.

Standards for PIPs and overlay payment services provided will have to cover a myriad of issues, as do the standards and expectations set by the bank and

---

27 ibid.

other regulators for role-players in the current payment system (Bank of England, 2020, 30). The regulatory regime will need to cover (expected issues) such as minimum standards for ensuring security; appropriate levels of consumer protection; guidelines and principles for CBDC user interfaces, that is, applications; messaging standards used in CBDC payments (such as adoption of the ISO 20022 data standard); mandating the use of identifiers like the Legal Entity Identifier and rules about who would bear responsibility when CBDC payments do not go according to plan, including in cases of fraud, failed transactions, cyberrisks, and privacy (ibid, 31).

As a starting point, the identity of CBDC users would need to be known to an authority or institution in the wider CBDC network who can validate the legitimacy of their transaction (ibid). In the platform model suggested, they foresee that the core ledger would only store pseudonymous accounts and balances (ibid), with each account in the core ledger linked to a PIP. The PIPs would know the identity of each user, having the responsibility for applying AML checks to users, and for reporting suspicious transactions to the authorities (ibid). This arrangement would mean that the bank would not hold personal data on any user, in the hopes that this would reduce any privacy concerns that could arise in connection with holding personal user data, while AML requirements would still be met by the CBDC system (ibid).

Privacy and data protection are issues that are of concern to policymakers in government and other authorities, such as the Department for Digital, Culture, Media and Sport and the Information Commissioners' Office, and should be considered at the design stage of CBDC (ibid). The CBDC system would need to be compatible with privacy regulations, such as the 2018 General Data Protection Regulation, which would be applicable to all role-players in the CBDC payment system, that is, the BoE, PIPs, and any other firms providing CBDCrelated services (ibid).

The discussion regarding anonymity is a socio-political question that needs to be answered before the design and build are initiated and which can then be regulated according to the elected imperative (Bank of England, 2020, 32).[28] Because any CBDC would need to be compliant with AML regulations, truly anonymous payments are not plausible. In the discussion paper, it is stated that the bank does not have a specific mandate to provide untraceable or anonymous payment methods (ibid).

This dispels any ideas that a sovereign digital coin may have the same qualities as cash. It is digital, and it has the potential to store information and thus will never be anonymous. However, CBDC could be designed to provide some privacy and to give users control over with whom they share data (ibid). An example is where a user may wish to make a payment to a supermarket without sharing

---

28 The value attached to privacy of the individual versus state power is one of the central distinguishing features between advocates and adversaries of CBDC.
   Fernández de Lis (2018, 46).

her identity with the supermarket, in order to avoid the supermarket building a picture of their shopping habits (ibid). The idea is that in such cases the payer would be able to pay without revealing their identity to the payee (ibid). This would have the effect of providing the desired anonymity with regards to other users, without identity concealment with regards to law enforcement (ibid).

New products, new strategies, new business models, and new participants are testing the boundaries of existing regulatory frameworks and regulators' speed of response (International Banking Federation, 2020). In addition, supervisory needs are increasingly cross-sectoral (ibid). As such, regulatory measures require collaboration across countries' authorities and at the international level (ibid). The traditional firm-based regulatory model is placed under pressure due to value chains being unbundled across multiple players, as it is not always clear who should be accountable for which risk or activity (ibid). An issue that is amplified by big techs' cross-country and cross-sector reach, in both regulated and unregulated activities as well as their propensity to partner with multiple parties (ibid).

Regulatory authorities in England, but worldwide really, face the challenge of ensuring that regulation and supervision safeguard consumers and systemic stability while also sustaining the advantages of innovation and competition (ibid). Regulation is notorious for bringing up the rear, rather than the vanguard. However, it must be speculated that in this arena, with so many variables (design, technology, accessibility, etc.) it is only possible to speculate on the conceivable regulatory themes that will ensue. A forward-looking mind-set needs be adopted to ensure new and complex risks are quickly identified and understood and that clearly defined criteria are established in order to determine which activities need inclusion in the financial regulation remit (ibid).

6 Conclusion

The BoE has been studying for some time now, and quite cautiously, the potential benefits and risks of introducing a native digital coin. Under consideration are the impact that a sovereign digital coin would have on monetary and fiscal policy, the effects on financial stability, and what technological infrastructure would best suit the economy. The BoE has kept its eye on the potential regulatory remit that would have to accompany a CBDC, especially given that global standards are important in a world where there will be a need for interoperability and friction-free movement between CBDC, private stablecoins, and other payment mechanisms. The issue really is then – is the BoE's progress too slow? With cryptocurrencies celebrating (*circa*) their 12th year in the market and private investors bringing up the rear rather furiously with stablecoin issuances backed by fiat currencies or asset-baskets, it seems that the BoE will face fierce competition from global corporate players. It will be difficult to win back the market once the accepted legal tender is assumed by the population to be something 'other' than the digital pound. Money is a social convention and although it has historically been accepted to fulfil certain requirements (store value, medium of exchange, and unit of account), a CBDC without acceptance and confidence will not find fluidity. The chapter echoes the question posed by the Deputy Governor of the Bank of Italy, Fabio Panetta, already in 2018:

> In a world where securities and contracts are dematerialized and traded electronically, where payments are made with smartphones and investment advice is provided by computers, why should cash be only physical? Is the central bank missing out on the benefits of innovation by not issuing a CBDC?
>
> (Bocconi University and Baffi Carefin 2018)

The Governor of the BoE pointed out that we have reached the point in the cycle of innovation in payments where it is essential that standards are set and thus the expectations for how innovation will take effect. He posits that it should not happen the other way round, with the standard-setting playing catch-up. While the answer is not to strangle innovation and dialogue between stakeholders, it is indeed required. It seems, however, that the regulatory aspect of this digital forge will indeed be compelled to play catch-up, simply because the potentiality of the technology has not yet been completely exploited. The alternative, to belated regulatory tactics, would be to adopt an agile approach in this area and facilitate fluid rulemaking. The down-shot of this approach would be the satiation of industry in absorbing a shifting rulebook. However, this may be the only option in a period of transition until technology innovations stop spiking at dramatic rates and reach a plateau or, at least, a less precipitous incline.

References

Attanasio, S., Romani, N. and Spadafora, F. (2019) Spunta project: Il punto D'incontro Fra La DLT e Il Settore Bancario Italiano. Available at: https://docplayer.it/115533946-Spunta-project-il-punto-d-incontro-fra-la-dlt-e-il-settore-bancario-italiano.html [Accessed 18 November 2020].

Bailey, A. (2020) Reinventing the wheel (with more automation). Speech given at Brookings Institution. Virtual Event, 3 September. Available at: https://www.bankofengland.co.uk/speech/2020/andrew-bailey-speech-on-the-future-of-cryptocurrencies-and-stablecoins [Accessed 18 November 2020].

Bank for International Settlements, Committee on Payments and Market Infrastructure and Markets Committee (2018). Central bank digital currencies. Available at: https://www.bis.org/cpmi/publ/d174.htm [Accessed 18 November 2020].

Bank of England (2020). Central bank digital currency opportunities, challenges and design. Discussion Paper. Bank of England, Financial Payments Committee. Financial Stability Report. Available at: https://www.bankofengland.co.uk/paper/2020/central-bank-digital-currency-opportunities-challenges-and-design-discussion-paper [Accessed 18 November 2020].

Bank of England (2019). Financial Policy Summary and Record of the Financial Policy Committee Meeting on 13 December 2019. Available at: https://www.bankofengland.co.uk/-/media/boe/files/financial-policy-summary-and-record/2019/december-2019.pdf [Accessed 18 November 2020].

Bech, M., Faruqui, U., Ougaard, F. and Picillo, C. (2018) Payments are a-Changin' but cash still rules. Bank for International Settlements Quarterly Review. Available at: https://www.bis.org/publ/qtrpdf/r_qt1803g.htm [Accessed 18 November 2020].

Bech, M. and Garratt R. (2017) Central bank cryptocurrencies. Bank for International Settlements Quarterly Review. Available at: https://www.bis.org/publ/qtrpdf/r_qt1709f.htm [Accessed 18 November 2020].Bjerg, O. (2017) Designing new money – The policy trilemma of central bank digital currency. CBS Working paper 1.

Boar, C., Holden, H. and Wadsworth, A. (2020) Impending arrival – A sequel to the survey on central bank digital currency. Bank of International Settlements: Monetary and Economic Department Paper No 107. Available at: https://econpapers.repec.org/bookchap/bisbisbps/107.htm [Accessed 18 November 2020].

Carney, M (2018) The Future of Money Speech given at the Inaugural Scottish Ecnomics Conference, 2 March. Available at: https://www.bankofengland.co.uk/-/media/boe/files/speech/2018/the-future-of-money-speech-by-mark-carney.pdf?la=en&hash=A51E1C8E90BDD3D071A8D6B4F8C1566E7AC91418 [Accessed 18 November 2020].

Didenko, R.P. and Buckley, A.N. (2019) The evolution of currency: Cash to cryptos to sovereign digital currencies. *Fordham International Law Journal* 42(4), 1041.

Engert, W. and Fung, B.S.C. (2018) Motivations and implications of a central bank digital currency. In: E. Gnan and D. Masciandaro (eds), *Do We Need Central Bank Digital Currency? Economics, Technology and Institutions.* Vienna: Suerf Conference Proceedings, p. 56.

Engert, W., Fung, B.S.C. and Hendry, S. (2018) Is a cashless society problematic? Bank of Canada Staff Discussion Paper 2018-12. Available at: https://www.bankofcanada.ca/wp-content/uploads/2018/10/sdp2018-12.pdf [Accessed 26 May 2020].

European Commission (2019) Proposal for a Regulation of the European Parliament and of the Council on Markets in Crypto-assets, and amending Directive (EU) 2019/1937COM/2020/593 final. Available at: https://eur-lex.europa.eu/legal-content/EN/TXT/?uri=CELEX%3A52020PC0593 [Accessed 18 November 2020].

Fernández de Lis, S. (2018) Central bank digital currencies: Features, options, pros and con. In: E. Gnan and D. Masciandaro (eds), *Do We Need Central Bank Digital Currency? Economics, Technology and Institutions.* Vienna: Suerf Conference Proceedings, p. 46.

Financial Stability Board (2019). Big Tech in finance — Market developments and potential financial stability implications. Available at: https://www.fsb.org/2019/12/bigtech-in-finance-market-developments-and-potential-financial-stability-implications/ [Accessed 11 November 2020].

Huber, J. (1999) A proposal for supplying the nations with the necessary means in a modern monetary system. Der Hallesche Graureiher 99 – 3, Revised version.

International Banking Federation and Oliver Wyman (2020) Big Banks, Bigger Techs? How policy-makers could respond to a probable discontinuity. Available at: https://www.oliverwyman.com/our-expertise/insights/2020/jul/big-banks-bigger-techs.html [Accessed 18 November 2020].

Niepelt, D. (2018) Central bank digital currencies – What difference does it make? In: E. Gnan and D. Masciandaro (eds), *Do We Need Central Bank Digital Currency? Economics, Technology and Institutions.* Vienna: Suerf Conference Proceedings, p. 99.

Pollock, A.J. (2018) Testimony to the Subcommittee on Monetary Policy and Trade of the Committee on Financial Services, United States House of Representatives, Hearing on 'The future of money: Digital currency' July 2018. Available at: https://

republicans-financialservices.house.gov/uploadedfiles/hhrg-115-ba19-wstate-apollock-20180718.pdf [Accessed 18 November 2020].

Project Khokha (2018). Increasing transaction volume and network resistance while maintaining confidentiality requirements for real-time gross settlement on enterprise ethereum. Available at: https://consensys.net/blockchain-use-cases/finance/project-khokha/ [Accessed 11 November 2020].

Proposal for a Regulation of the European Parliament and of the Council on Markets in Crypto-Assets, and Amending Directive (EU), COM (2020) 593 final (24 Sept.)

Kumhof, M. and Noone, C. (2018) Central bank digital currencies — Design principles and balance sheet implications. Bank of England Staff Working Paper No. 725 May 4, 2018. Available at: https://www.bankofengland.co.uk/-/media/boe/files/working-paper/2018/central-bank-digital-currencies-design-principles-and-balance-sheet-implications [Accessed 18 November 2020].

Lane, T. (2020) On CBDCs and why the private sector is no competition for central banks. Central Banking Available at: https://www.centralbanking.com/fintech/cbdc/7659466/timothy-lane-on-cbdcs-and-why-the-private-sector-is-no-competition-for-central-banks [Accessed 18 November 2020].

Link Report (2020) Link Report July 2020. Available at: https://www.link.co.uk/media/1634/monthly-report-july-2020-final.pdf [Accessed 4 September 2020].

Ryder, N. (2020) Cryptoassets, social media platforms and defence against terrorism financing suspicious activity reports: A step into the regulatory unknown. *Journal of Business Law*, 8, 668.

Shukla, S. (2020) Historical context and key features of digital money tokens. Barclays. Available at: https://www.researchgate.net/publication/343877303_Historical_Context_and_Key_Features_of_Digital_Money_Tokens [Accessed 18 November 2020].

UK Finance (2020) UK payment markets. Summary, June. Available at: https://www.ukfonance.org.uk/system/files/UK-Payment-Markets-Reports-2020-SUMMARY.pdf [Accessed 18 November 2020].

Vessio, M.L. (2020) To CBDC or not to CBDC? In: C Hugo and S du Toit (eds), *Recent Legal Developments of Interest to Banks, Annual Banking Law Update, Centre for Banking Law*, p. 63

World Economic Forum (2019) Central banks and distributed ledger technology: How are central banks exploring blockchain today? White Paper March. Available at: https://www.weforum.org/whitepapers/central-banks-and-distributed-ledger-technology-how-are-central-banks-exploring-blockchain-today [Accessed 18 November 2020].

Part 4
Artificial intelligence and the law

11 AI, big data, quantum computing, and financial exclusion

Tempering enthusiasm and offering a human-centric approach to policy

Clare Chambers-Jones

1 Introduction

"Some have said that in the future we will not live in a democracy, where the citizens decided how we are governed, not in a bureaucracy, where officials like me decide, but in an alogcracy, where algorithms decide" (Randall, 2018).

Within this chapter a critical review of the position of financial exclusion and a possible solution of artificial intelligence (AI) and other innovative technologies will be considered. The chapter states that there has been much written about the different aspects of financial exclusion, and this chapter aims to add new thinking to existing literature. The wealth of information provides an excellent basis on which to take stock and review why there are still millions of people who are unbanked within society. The chapter argues that past and present regulations have been and are inefficient. Regulations and policy have focused on trying to solve the whole umbrella term of *financial exclusion* without seeing the individual elements and trying to solve those. The chapter considers the legal and ethical impacts of AI as a possible solution to financial exclusion and argues that AI is an innovative and exciting technology which has the potential to help some of those who are financially excluded, while tempering enthusiasm by detailing legal, social, and ethical issues which must be addressed in any regulation or policy. The chapter concludes that AI and other technologies could only be a solution for some people who are financially excluded if the regulation and policy were drafted to ensure they are safeguarded and have at their heart the good of the people they are being drafted to serve. This chapter offers the start of the new conversation surrounding effective, realistic, and meaningful policy approach to financial exclusion. The chapter is divided into four parts. The first part considers financial exclusion; the second the use of AI, big and open data, and quantum computing as a solution to some forms of financial exclusion; and the third part provides a critical review of the legal and policy agenda within the UK. In the fourth and final part, the chapter provides concluding remarks tempering enthusiasm and offering caution to financial exclusion and the benefits of AI and technology.

2 Financial exclusion

Financial exclusion is part of wider socioeconomic issues, these being social exclusion and poverty (Devlin 2005, p. 75). Kempson and Whyley (1999a, b) describe financial exclusion as a multidimensional construct and state that providing a single definition for the term is problematic. Financial inclusion "enables people to fully participate in the economy and empowers them to achieve their goals in life, whilst offering them protection in the face of adversity" (HM Treasury, 2019b, p. 2). From the early 1990s to the mid-2000s, the focus from government and academia was centred upon financial exclusion.[1] After an acquiescent period, financial exclusion/inclusion is gaining traction again. Devlin's (2005) comprehensive analysis of financial exclusion provides an excellent basis and discussion as to what constitutes financial exclusion. Devlin focuses on the issues with the pool of research and investigations into financial exclusion, stating that the policy review approach has been piecemeal, with no defined or agreed remit of focus (Devlin 2005, p. 76). This chapter agrees with this summation and goes further to argue that since Devlin's research in 2005, financial exclusion, although remaining a current and distinct issue, has lost stringent and meaningful government and academic focus.

A House of Lords Report in 2017 demonstrates the lack of innovation and progressive research that has been undertaken in the intervening years (HL 132, 2017). The report examines the nature and extent of financial exclusion and uses reports such as those by Friends Provident (2016), Charitable foundations such as Joseph Rowntree Foundation (2008), and one European Commission report (2008) as their grounding literature. The reports knowledge base is limited and demonstrates that further academic investigation is required. The report states that the term *financial inclusion* has replaced *financial exclusion* in much of the literature on this topic (HL 132, 2017). The optics around *financial inclusion*, a term first used in UK public policy in 1997 (HL 132, 2017), is argued to be very different from that of financial exclusion. The report (HL 132, 2017) agrees stating that financial exclusion should be viewed as "the problem" and financial inclusion as "the solution". This should not be the case because the two though interlinked are actually very separate issues. Financial exclusion is the process of where people, individuals or groups, lack basic financial services for a variety of reasons. These reasons give way to a number of different issues, which cannot be dealt with together. Each individual strand of financial exclusion should be investigated and dealt with separately.

This chapter argues that financial exclusion deals with the people at the bottom of the financial marketplace. Financial inclusion is different; although the term refers to access to financial services in general, the connotations of the term, positive and negative, get heavier and complex when applied to those people who can still access some financial services but may be on the margins of the financial

---

1 For more, see FSA, 2000a, b, c; 2001, 2003a, b; Hogarth & O'Donnell, 2000; Kempson & Whyley, 1999a, b; Lee, 2002; Leyshorn & Thrift, 1993; Morrison & O'Brien, 2001.

marketplace. In essence, it is a line between those who have and those who have not. The line is blurred and greyed, but it is there. Both are worthy of investigation and need to have public policy directed at them to ensure people have access to basic financial products and that people who are on the margin of financial exclusion are given help and guidance to prevent them slipping backwards.

Terming financial inclusion as the solution suggests that once within the financial marketplace a person has succeeded, their journey ends there. This chapter argues that it is just as important to ensure that those who are on the precipice of financial exclusion be given as much focus as those in financial exclusion. It is a continuum of financial problems, which cannot be seen as final or as joint or standalone issues. It is for this reason financial exclusion and inclusion are seen as multidimensional and multifaceted and lack a robust and clear definition. This chapter states that this is an important distinction to make when finding solutions to the issues.

The Financial Inclusion committee (2020) defined financial inclusion as the means by which people can make their money work well for them, enabling them to maximise opportunities, move into employment, become more self-reliant, and enhance physical and mental well-being. Financial inclusion contributes to greater social mobility and levelling up, a more effective welfare system, and greater national resilience from economic shock (Financial Inclusion committee, 2020). This more positive and outward-looking definition does not talk about people who are poor or who have no access to credit or those who cannot pay the utility bills. This stance on financial inclusions assumes that the people have money but need to be wiser, more educated, and more resilient. It assumes people are within the financial marketplace. Therefore, a solution which looks at financial exclusion would not work for financial inclusion.

This definition is very different from the more negative definitions offered by academics to outline what constitutes financial exclusion. For example, Panigyrakis et al. suggests that financial exclusion is where people are "unable to access financial services in an appropriate form" (2002, p. 55). Even this could be argued to be a vague definition. Early research looked at the geographical nature of financial exclusion, looking at bank closures and post office closures as a means of excluding communities from financial services (Leyshorn and Thrift, 1993). The research emphasis moved on to examine the nuances of financial exclusion in terms of who was being excluded and from what aspects of financial services (FSA 2000a, b, c; 2001, 2003a, b; Kempson & Whyley 1999a, b).[2]

The Financial Services Authority (the Financial Conduct Authority [FCA]) was very keen to discuss the figures surrounding financial exclusion. In 2000, the FSA suggested that 1.5 million households or 7% of households in the UK had no financial services and a further 4.4 million or 20% were on the margins of

---

2 Other academics keen to define financial exclusion were Anderloni, 2003; Anderloni & Carluccio, 2006; Carbo et al., 2005, 2007; Gloukoviezoff, 2004; Sinclair, 2001; and policymakers – Treasury Committee, 2006a, 2006b; HM Treasury, 2004 (European Commission 2008).

financial services (FSA 2000a, p. 21). In 2015, the FCA commissioned an independent report, which explored the barriers people faced with access to financial services (Rowe et al., 2015). The report divided the findings into three issues which affect people's access to financial services and thus lead to their financial exclusion. Like the previous research, this report, too, found financial exclusion to be multidimensional. The classifications are as follows: the maze – process, requirements, and eligibility; the fog – market navigation and comprehension; and the voice – digital and physical barriers (Rowe et al., 2015).

Exploring these classifications affirms research in the early 2000s in relation to financial exclusion. Under the maze classification, it was found that often barriers to financial services arose because of the requirement of forms of identification such as ID documentation or an address or issues with health or income levels. Similarly, it was found that consumers were often not given information about why they had been turned down for a financial service product and that if a product was available not enough clear information was given to the consumer as to how to use the product (Rowe et al., 2015).

Rowe's et al.'s (2015) next classification was the fog, where market navigation and comprehension were found to be key barriers to financial services. Within this classification it was found that financial services were often too complex and written in such a way that consumer struggled to understand the financial product, its cost, its benefits, its detriments, or even the consumer's ability to search for the right financial product (Rowe et al., 2015).

The final classification is the void, where it was identified that there are digital and physical barriers to accessing financial services. It was reported that those with disabilities, those who are older, and those who live in rural areas struggle with accessing financial services. The report also notes that it is the same group, along with low-income groups, that struggles with the digital nature of accessing financial services (Rowe et al., 2015). Digital literacy and access to technology cause many issues for people wanting to access financial services.

The report highlighted that "the research identified a diverse range of challenges, barriers and problems effecting a huge variety of consumers" (Rowe et al., 2015). The issue of financial exclusion is therefore still multidimensional and fraught with complex and intertwined problems. The inability to form a single definition as to what encompasses financial exclusion allows therefore for governments and policy makers to address different needs and aspects of financial exclusion. By recognising this, it allows regulations to be drafted in a unique way to see the problem broken down.

The FCA notes the problems associated with people who are vulnerable and their ability to access financial services is another element to financial exclusion and one which should be regulated separately. The research found that financial services providers were not treating vulnerable consumers fairly, and this in turn limited the vulnerable customers' ability to access financial services (FCA, 2015). The research stated that consumer protection legislation was designed with the ordinary customer in mind and not with thought for the vulnerable consumer. This means that products and services would be out of reach for those vulnerable consumers. Legislation is therefore a considerable hurdle for those consumers who are vulnerable and/or financially excluded. Blame is also attributable to the financial service providers who are using ill-equipped and poorly drafted legislation to aid their own profit margin and not assessing whether it is fair and just or in the interest of social justice to interpret rules more fairly. The report provides examples where vulnerable people are having to fight for justice and peace in difficult periods of their life when there is already a huge amount of stress placed upon them. In such situations, a single common rule for financial access may not work for the ordinary consumer, give their unique shortcomings and life challenges, and may not appear to be just, fair, or reasonable.

The FCA moved on from just thinking about the vulnerable (FCA, 2015) to exploring problems associated with access to financial services, which as they righty surmise is not just an issue for the vulnerable. The research explores whose responsibility it is for people to get access to financial services. They question whether it is financial service providers who are socially obligated to provide access or whether government should legislate access to services. Logically they concluded that a joined-up and systematic approach among government, financial service providers, and consumer organisation needs to foster (FCA, 2016, p. 132). Until this happens, consumers will continue to remain excluded from the financial marketplace and products.

This joined-up approach is still being considered by the government, and in the House of Lords (2017) the government was keen to highlight who was at risk of financial exclusion yet used many outdated sources as key statistics.[3] An issue with reflective pieces of research is that they concentrate on identifying the dimensions within financial exclusion. What is needed is to explore individual responses in a strategic manner to each dimension of financial exclusion.

The government, therefore, assesses financial exclusion using a top-down approach. It explores who are at risk of financial exclusion (House of Lords, 2017, Chapter 2:21). It opines that people who are in the low-income group or living in poverty, young people, older people, people with difficulty to access banks, and those who lack digital access are at risk of being financially excluded. These classifications are similar to those identified by Rowe et al. (2015). They both look at the identifying factors of people in financial exclusion and their characteristics. It is clear that those who are young, old, vulnerable, without access to financial services, or are digitally excluded face financial exclusion. The government here draws from a number of resources that also affirm these classifications (Joseph Rowntree Foundation 2016). There is clearly academic and government agreement as to what constitutes financial exclusion and its characteristics and its issues. This has not to have changed or evolved from the work in the early 2000s. What has changed is the deepening gap between those who have access

---

3 See Joseph Rowntree Foundation, "Monitoring Poverty and Social Exclusion 2016" (7 December 2016): https://www.jrf.org.uk/report/monitoring-poverty-and-social-exclusion-2016 (accessed 10 September 2020).

to financial services and those who do not, and a driving factor in this is the development of technology and its business effects on the financial services sector, despite academic and government conversations. This chapter suggests a new approach which is holistic but individualised when considering financial exclusion and based on a clear understanding that a one-size-fits-all approach will not and cannot solve the issues of financial exclusion.

A proposed solution to financial exclusion has been the advancement of technology. Technology has also been considered as an integral part in causing or promoting financial exclusion with the movement towards electronic banking, leading to bank closure. However, this chapter goes on to discuss whether technology, in the forms of AI, big data, or open data, could possibly offer opportunities to bank the unbanked. Caution is therefore offered here. Technology and the next new big development are not always necessarily the solution to problems, and, in some cases, they cause more issues than they resolve.

3 The power of technology

Technology is seen as a possible solution to the issues associated with financial exclusion. If we put aside the issues it has been seen to create with the increase of electronic banking and therefore reactive bank closures and the digitally excluded being kept out of the financial market place, technology offers some possible solutions to some of the multidimensional issues of financial exclusion. Technology will not stop bank closures; it will not help those who cannot or do not want to use technology. As iterated above, there are many issues associated with financial exclusion. What technology is being suggested as being able to achieve financial inclusion, it is to provide a platform for inclusion in the financial marketplace and therefore looking at just one aspect of financial exclusion and trying to solve it through technology won't suffice. In this next section of the chapter, there will be a discussion focused on how novel technologies could offer solutions to financial exclusion.

'AI, Big data, and Open data' are technologies which are considered as the next big thing in technology and finance. Our lives are run already by algorithms and various forms of AI. Decisions are being made for us each time we use the computer, internet, or bank cards. AI, big data, and open data are terms that cover a spectrum of different technologies. "No one quite agrees" (Deloitte, 2018) as to the definition of AI; "every definition has its variation" (Deloitte, 2018). The UK Government defines AI as "the use of digital technology to create systems capable of performing tasks commonly thought to require intelligence" (GOV.UK, 2019). AI involves the use of machines to make decisions through its ability to perform repetitive tasks to reach an answer. AI therefore handles a lot of data, and it is with the advancements in the way machines can handle data that AI has once again begun to be feasible.

Large data sets are called big data (GOV.UK, 2014). Big data is defined as large volumes of data with high levels of complexity (GOV.UK, 2014); these big data sets are needed to be analysed and processed by means of complex technology. Alongside 'big data' is the idea of 'open data' whereby data are freely and openly available for people to use. The UK government has an Open Standards Principles (2018) which allows users "permission to copy, distribute and use technology freely or at low cost". The financial industry is viewing the emergence of AI through the use and implementation of 'big data' as positive. APIS' White Paper (2019) states that "financial services industry is likely to lead … AI … due to its inherent advantages of having large data sets" (APIS, 2019, p. 6).

Financial service firms, alongside using AI for high-end banking, have begun to think about the possibilities of using AI as a means to bank the unbanked and to provide access to financial services to those who are unable to access them through the traditional means. Johnson et al. (2019) have called FinTech firms who are using AI as a means of providing access to financial services to those who are excluded as neo-banks (Johnson et al., 2019, p. 504). Johnson et al. (2019) further expound that the technology could transform us into a "more equitable and just society" (Johnson et al., 2019, p. 502). The reason for this is because AI could offer financial services such as credit based on different criteria than a normal financial service firm would have access to. Johnson et al. state it is "extremely expensive to be poor" (Johnson et al., 2019, p. 503). Firms could use big data as a means of making a more holistic overview of a person's financial well-being. It can have different grades attributed to different aspects. For example, if a person manages to pay rent each month, in time and in full, but then that leaves them short to pay their phone bill. Yet the payment for the phone bill is a criterion which needs to be met in order to get a good credit score, which then allows the person credit, it is the smaller amount associated with the phone bill and not the larger amount for the rent which stops them from obtaining credit. The parameters are therefore moved to take into account the amounts of debt owed and paid to show the financial responsibility of the person.[4] Large and complex computations are used in order to provide a more realistic and often more suitable financial outlook, especially if it is skewed to look for financial exclusion issues. "Learning algorithms may [therefore] help regulators and lender fulfil an altruistic promise of inclusion, compensation for decades of discrimination and exclusion in financial market" (Johnson et al., 2919, p. 505).

It is not only AI, open data, and big data that have been highlighted as possible avenues to help the unbanked. Alternative digital currencies and distributed ledger technologies (DLTs) have been linked to possibly finding solutions (ITU, 2017). DLTs have been described as "a new type of secure database or ledger for keeping track of who owns a financial, physical, or electronic asset, but without

---

4 For more information, see the Governments Rent Recognition Challenge. https://www.gov.uk/government/publications/rent-recognition-challenge-using-fintech-to-help-renters (accessed 24 September 2020) and The Credit Worthiness Assessment Bill https://services.parliament.uk/Bills/2017-19/creditworthinessassessment.html (accessed 24 September 2020). The bill failed to complete its passage through parliament before the end of the session. It will make not further progress on Open Banking.

the need for a centralised controller of this data" (ITU, 2017). The data are shared peer-to-peer across locations and people. An example of a DLT is a blockchain, which is also the technology which underpins bitcoins. It is outside the scope of this chapter to discuss the technical working of a blockchain; rather, attention is focused on the idea of the technology aiding financial inclusion because of its ability to manipulate large sets of data without the central control of an authorising state.

The usefulness of DLTs is still to be established. Many questions are apparent in terms of creating an environment for DLTs to work, and, if such an environment created, then by the very virtue of creating the environment, does it go against what DLTs are for (their ability to act free of state control or fiat currencies or regular banking systems)? For example, for DLTs to be a viable option to help the unbanked enter the financial marketplace, a robust infrastructure needs to be in place in countries. Countries need to have regulatory systems such as anti-money laundering (AML) controls, as DLTs cannot become a haven for financial crime. For this to happen, regulatory oversight by a centrally recognised authority needs to be established. This in turn takes away the benefit of the DLTs not being centrally controlled and governed by a state. This chapter argues that although the theory is there, the practicalities are holding the technology back, for DLTs do not operate in a financial vacuum.

The benefits of DLTs are many; for example, they can offer swift and inexpensive transfer of payments between people due to their ability to minimise costly operational complexities at present (ITU, 2017). DLTs also can provide unique biometric identifiers for people who cannot prove their identity and thus cannot access the financial marketplace due to the AML regulations requirement to provide ID (ITU, 2917).

Quantum computing is another form of technology which could reengineer financial service business processes (IBM, 2019). Quantum computing "will begin significantly transforming the financial service landscape over the next five years" (IBM, 2019). Quantum computing may offer some of the solutions to the issues raised above regarding AML regulations. Quantum computing can handle very large sets of data by converting data into QuBits. These are then run through complex algorithms enabling efficient and quick decision to be made on a wide range of data. Quantum computing is said to be able to assist front-end bank office decision-making on client management for "know your customer", credit origination, and onboarding (IBM, 2019). The UK Government is investing in the first commercially available to business quantum computing in 2020 (GOV.UK, 2020). Given how innovative and new this technology is, there is little guidance from government on the regulatory landscape for quantum technologies (HC 820, 2018).

4 Legal and policy

The UK has one of the most comprehensively regulated financial marketplace in the world, but it also has a huge number of unbanked or financially excluded among its population (HM Treasury, 2019b). The government's legal and policy approach to regulating the financial marketplace has been piecemeal over successive governments. Political will has ebbed and flowed depending on which financial crisis has spurred on reactive regulation. We can see that with the banking scandals of BCCI, Baring Bank, LIBOR, PPI mis-selling, Money Laundering, Lehman Brother's Collapse, the Financial Crisis, 2007–2009, each spurred a flurry of financial regulation, yet financial crises continue to occur despite the new regulations. Financial exclusion regulation is no different from these financial scandals listed above. Policy is put forward, yet little comprehensive oversight is provided in any form which is meaningful. Any long-term initiatives often fall from favour depending on the political party in charge. This can be linked to the issue mentioned above, regarding the multidimensional issues of financial exclusion, and how hard it is to find a solution that covers more than one aspect. The present discussion on AI and financial exclusion is peaking industry's and governments' interest.

However, "AI will raise questions that challenge government and society, promoting the need for a new set of norms to protect humans, regulate machines, and remake the financial infrastructure" (Deloitte, 2018, p. 7). The European Commission (2018) has stated that "[f]inding a policy response to what is undoubtedly 'the next big thing' is both urgent and challenging". A policy response is therefore needed which is considered and measured. This author fears that time will be spent on the regulation of the technology rather than tackling the inherent issues of financial exclusion, only to realise that the technology promulgates financial exclusion rather than eradicating it.

Policy makers are trying to consider the ramifications of using AI in this novel way and the new thinking that AI "will take public policy into unchartered territory" (Deloitte, 2018). Charles Randall highlighted the importance of ensuring that whatever benefits the use of big data and algorithms may bring, we must be mindful that they do not impede upon our freedoms and rights. Randall opines that we must be seen "as people, [and] not just numbers" (Randall, 2018). Randall is therefore exploring the notion of rights and freedoms of individuals within the discussion of technology rather than against the need to ensure financial exclusion is tackled. The small nuances in his speech demonstrate that using technology as a means of diminishing financial exclusion is difficult, as there are other legal and policy issues that must be addressed before the technology can be used as a means of creating a benefit. The political will and the governance of power wielded by government demonstrate the very precarious position and emotive substance financial exclusion exudes.

This chapter argues that new policy must hold the position of the consumer at the very heart of these discussions. The law and policy surrounding the technology must align with the rights and freedoms of citizens in the UK, but attention must also be paid to those consumers who are vulnerable, excluded, or in a position of exclusion. Firms and government are already working on possible avenues of using technology as an aid to obviate financial exclusion.

This chapter questions whether consumers and especially vulnerable consumers are aware or fully understand the implications big data, algorithms and, in turn, AI have in making financial decision for them. The law and policy surrounding financial services are not written in a way in which it is easily accessible or understandable for the ordinary or vulnerable consumers. This, it is argued, demonstrates the inability of government to tackle financial exclusion head on. If law and policy are not presented in a manner that is comprehensible to consumers and thus it is not easy for consumers to understand their rights, then no matter what agendas or solutions are put in place, consumers will be disadvantaged.

The UK's financial markets have a liberal approach, whereby it is assumed that if consumers are given fair disclosure they can and will make good financial decisions; this view of course is disputed. As Randall points out, "financial education is … important but it will never be a sufficient protection against firms selling bad financial products" (Randall, 2018). He further argued that policy makers need to investigate further to ensure that FinTech firms are "innovating ethically" to ensure that the most vulnerable and those socially and financially excluded are not put in a position which worsens their situation and limits further their access to financial services (Randall, 2018). There is still this assumption that regulation and policy are created with the best interest of those excluded and vulnerable consumers in mind. It is this chapter's argument that they are not.

The FCA's policy has stated that to innovate ethically, three elements must be present, and these are found within purpose, people, and trust (Randall, 2018). In the first instance, the firm must have a clear purpose, and this must be disseminated throughout the organisation. The purpose of the organisation could be solely to maximise profit, or it could be to open up the financial marketplace to those who have not had previous access to it, providing long-term benefit to individuals and society as a whole. The Treasury's Rent Recognition Challenge (2017) demonstrates this positive purpose that creates inclusive opportunity rather than creating a prepare-to-fail environment. The challenge recognised that renters' largest outgoings were their rent and this was not considered in credit scores which then limited the ability of renters to gain credit. If rent payments were considered on credit scores, then it can provide a more accurate view of the person's ability to manage their finances and pay bills and allow greater opportunities to access credit. This can help vulnerable consumers and those who were often financially excluded from mainstream financial services.

The second element is that it is essential to ensure the ethical development of technology in financial decision-making. The FCA argues strongly that people must be at the heart of decision-making and that technology cannot take the place of the human mind and rationality or erode or undermine their ability to ascertain truths and demonstrate compassion and common sense. It could be all too easy to hide behind a computer's decision, while lacking ethical underpinning and morality in our own judgements (Randall, 2018).

The final element that must not be forgotten in innovation is trust. Over the past decade or two, the trust in our financial services industry has been eroded, if not lost. What is needed is for people to trust that the financial services industry is acting in their best interests and not with erroneous intentions. It is argued that firms need to share common values with the communities that they serve. In 2017, the City of London launched its 'Business of Trust Campaign', which when researching in 2020 appeared to be no longer viable. What is suggested to improve trust in the financial service providers is to ensure effective communication with the consumers that they serve. Randall argued that regulations, contracts, guidance, all need to be "short and clear" outlining clearly the position of the consumer and the firm (Randall, 2018). Without these three elements then it is argued within this chapter that using AI to make financial decisions, especially for vulnerable consumers, would be a dangerous place.

The UK Government in 2018 protected the rights of consumers to share their financial data with third parties, allowing them more control over their finances and financial decision-making. The Competition and Markets Authority (CMA) called for these reforms. The reforms came in the form of 'Open Banking' and runs together with the second Payment Service Directive of EU (PSD2; 2015/2366). The FCA's scope of regulation was increased by the implementation of PSD2 (FCA, 2017). The scope of the directive aims to "help consumers manage their finances by bringing all of their bank account details in one place" (FCA, 2017). Technology is then used to manipulate the data to find the best financial product for the consumer. AI is therefore already present in the financial marketplace demonstrating its ability.

The FCA outlined five key themes within their research agenda. Three of these, household finance and consumer behaviour; technology – big data and AI; and regulatory efficiency and effectiveness, demonstrate the regulatory support for finding solutions to financial exclusion (FCA, 2019). In relation to the first two, the FCA is wanting to learn more about the issues. A policy review is required to understand the interplay between technology, its governance, its potential, and financial exclusion. The FCA's approach to research on regulatory efficiency and effectiveness warrants a holistic analysis of how regulation is written to ensure compliance from the start, rather than being reactive (FCA, 2019). This is a welcome call for a policy review, and this chapter is offered as the start of a much larger conversation on the interplay of financial exclusion and technology.

The House of Lords considered the economic, ethical, and social implication in advances in AI (HL 100, 2018, p. 12). One of the key elements from the paper demonstrates that social understanding of new technology needs to be considered for it to be effective and for regulation to be commensurate (HL 100, 2018, para 243). If not approached carefully, AI regulation may hinder not only the essence of the technology but also contribute to excluding further members of society. The Lords recommended that digital understanding and data literacy need to be improved as a foundation base on which regulation can grow. The government has created an Office for Artificial Intelligence within its Department for Digital, Culture, Media and Sports and Department for Business, Energy and Industrial Strategy. This chapter has found that financial exclusion and AI are not a policy issue mentioned within these parameters.

The Europeans Commission High Level Expert Group on Artificial Intelligence also explores the social side of the technological development and puts forward a human-centric approach and lists seven key requirements that AI systems should meet in order to be trustworthy (COM 2019168 and EC Ethics Guidelines). A pan-European approach is being taken with the European AI Alliance promoting the beneficial impacts on society and the economy through the use of AI. Again, within all these communications, financial exclusion or inclusion and AI were not discussed. The use of AI for consumers, including those who are excluded or vulnerable, poses privacy and data protection legal issues. By the UK Government extending the reach of financial firms in relation to gaining access to people's financial data though Open Banking, issues arise of people's privacy via the European Parliament and Council of Europe Union (2016) Regulation (Regulation (EU) 2016/697; General Data Protection Regulation (GDPR in)).

The UK is subject to European privacy laws through the adoption of the GDPR, which came into effect on the 25 May 2018 via the Data Protection Act 2018, c. 12. The GDPR replaced the Data Protection Directive 95/46/EU. The introduction of the GDPR means that for all companies and organisations operating within the EU, they must comply to one set of harmonised rules. In turn, people have more control over their data, and businesses are put on a level-playing field. The European Commission is clear that at the heart of regulation of AI must be the protection of human and ethical rights relating to AI. The Commission has launched two consultations: A European strategy for data, and its white paper on artificial intelligence – A European approach to excellence and trust. Both are based on developing AI in line with European privacy laws with the impact on humans. They recognise that people must be able to trust systems and that there is a "cohesive approach throughout the union" (Wiewiorowski, 2020). This ideological thinking corroborates the thinking that AI could be used to benefit the unbanked, if and only if, there is adequate data protection. The UK's Information Commission's Office (IOC) has in 2020 published guidance for businesses on the application of AI and its protection of data. The IOC has developed a framework for auditing AI. The guidance provides several chapters which guide business, compliance experts, and technology designers to ensure compliance with UK and EU laws. It is a good basis on which AI compliance should be structured in light of legal principles.

The government acknowledges that "the lack of central Government coordination on financial exclusion can lead to gaps in provisions of appropriate financial services" (HL132, 2017, para. 66).

The government states that they are putting financial inclusion as a priority (HM Treasury 2019a). Yet issues lay with the regulatory approach. The House of Lords outlined issues with the FCA oversight stating that "existing legislation did not give … a clear enough mandate to take decisive action in encouraging the sectors to develop services to meet the needs" of vulnerable consumers (HL 132, para. 81). The House of Lords said a reaffirmation should be made by the government to financial exclusion by "giving the FCA a specific and clear direction to promote financial inclusion" (HL, 132, para. 88). The House of Lords went as far as making a recommendation that the government should expand the statutory remit of the FCA to include a statutory duty to promote financial inclusion (HC 132, para. 84).

This chapter states that the regulatory approach towards financial exclusion is inadequate and does not enable financial inclusion. The chapter argued that a review of policy needs to be undertaken should technology play a part in promoting financial inclusion.

5 Conclusion

Financial exclusion is still a problem for many and for society as a whole, not only economically but also socially and ethically. It is an issue which is both collective and individual. There are many different shades of financial exclusion. To say someone is financially excluded does not paint the whole financial or social picture of the person and why they are excluded from the financial marketplace. As such, financial exclusion will never be eradicated. It is a problem that needs to be continually reviewed, and different solutions need to be moulded around the ever-changing problems inherent to financial exclusion. This is not an easy regulatory or policy task. Government's cannot lose interest in financial exclusion or get disheartened that huge numbers are not now within the system. What we have seen is that government policy along with FCA oversight has been poor. There have not been enough resources directed at breaking down financial exclusion into different categories and tackling each of them with different solutions. Academics and policy makers have written prolifically on the subject. They focus on different elements of financial exclusion, and different solutions have been offered. They try to solve financial exclusion with one policy reform. This will never work. There are so many different approaches, all looking at the broad issue of financial exclusion. Acceptance that this will not work needs to be achieved. Policy makers need to start again and divide the issues up, looking for solutions for each of the issues identified after categorisation.

This chapter has considered a new strategy that AI and technology could be a possible solution to financial exclusion. This chapter states that this is not a single solution to financial exclusion. It could possibly help some. The chapter adds to the existing literature on financial exclusion and brings forward the debate on using AI and technology as a means of helping financial exclusion. The use of AI, although exciting and innovative, brings about other issues such as data protection, contractual, ethical, and moral issues. The chapter demonstrates that governments and policy makers need to ensure that any firms using AI as a mechanism to offer financial solutions to the unbanked are cleverly regulated to meet legal standards but allow innovation. More so, any form of AI needs to be accessible and be able to be understood by people. This is a new way of thinking about policy and financial exclusion.

The chapter's novel approach suggests that in order to achieve this, there needs to be more than an acknowledgement that there is a problem with current regulations and policies. Regulations and policies need to be drafted keeping in mind the end-user, the society, and the good of people. We are in a novel situation that there are relatively little policy and laws which touch on AI and other forms of technology. Those in power need to use this to their and societies' advantage. Any regulations and policies need to be able to be adaptable due to changes in technology but ensure financially excluded people are not taken advantage of. It is not an easy balance to achieve when some of the technologies have emerged purely because of the lack of central authority oversight.

Once regulations and policies are in place that safeguard people, then there needs to be consumer buy-in that specifically accommodates financially excluded peoples' buy-in so that they can access appropriate technology that in turn helps them to become banked.

Therefore, this chapter argues that there can be no one-solution-fits-all approach to resolving the issue of financial exclusion and a combination of strategies, including facilitating the use of appropriate technology such as AI under central banks' oversight, are required to deal with financial exclusion. Financial exclusion is multidimensional and as such both the government and the policy makers need to find smaller-scale, customised solutions targeting specific needs of different groups among the financially excluded population. In this context, AI may provide a solution to those who struggle to get access to credit and need a wider range of credit scoring attributes or a wider range of choices in the line-up of financial products from which to choose according to their needs. Furthermore, another issue with technology in relation to its use is that it will not work for those who cannot or do not want to integrate into the digital age or those who cannot or do not have access to the internet or technology. It will not help those who are homeless or have other attributable social issues. Caution needs to be paid as to the way regulation is drafted and disseminated. At the heart of any regulation or policy must exist the rationale and consideration of the impact a regulation or policy may have on the targeted person or persons among those seeking to avail financial services, especially those who are financially excluded. Regulators and policy makers are in a unique position to create laws which are socially focused and user-friendly. The future is unclear, but promises to unveil exciting technological solutions; nevertheless, regulators and policy makers must tread cautiously and put human interest first while drafting policies and regulations aimed at incorporating advanced technology, such as AI, to facilitate wider utilisation of technology-driven financial services across different population groups, especially those who are financially excluded.

References

Anderloni, L., & Carluccio, E. (2006) "Access to bank accounts and payment services", in L. Anderloni, E. Carluccio & M. Braga (eds.), *New Frontiers in Banking Services: Emerging Needs and Tailored Products for Untapped Markets*. Berlin: Springer Verlag, pp. 5–105.

APIS. (2019) Artificial Intelligence & Financial Services. Cutting through the noise. https://apis.pe/insight/artificial-intelligence-financial-services-cutting-through-the-noise/ (accessed 8 August 2020).
Carbo, S., Gardner, E., & Molyneux, P. (2005) *Financial Exclusion*. Basingstoke: Palgrave Macmillan.
Carbo, S., Gardner, E., & Molyneux, P. (2007, February) Financial exclusion in Europe. *Public Money & Management* 27(1): 21–27.
Clifford Chance. (2018) Emerging technologies. AI and risk for financial institutions. https://talkingtech.cliffordchance.com/en/emerging-technologies/artificial-intelligence/ai-and-risk-for-financial-institutions.html (accessed 8 August 2020).
Communication from the Commission to the European Parliament, the Council, the European Economic and Social Committee and the Committee of the Regions – Building Trust in Human Centric Artificial Intelligence (COM(2019)168).
Communication from the Commission to the European Parliament, the European Council, the Council, the European Economic and Social Committee and the Committee of the Regions on Artificial Intelligence for Europe, Brussels, 25.4.2018 COM(2018) 237 final.
Deloitte. (2018) The new physics of financial services. How artificial intelligence is transforming the financial ecosystem. https://www2.deloitte.com/global/en/pages/financial-services/articles/artificial-intelligence-transforming-financial-ecosystem-deloitte-fsi.html (accessed 12 August 2020).
Devlin, J. (2005) A detailed study of financial exclusion in the UK. *Journal of Consumer Policy* 28: 75–108.
European Commission. (2008, March) *Financial Services Provision and Prevention of Financial Exclusion*, p. 9. http://www.bristol.ac.uk/media-library/sites/geography/migrated/documents/pfrc0807.pdf (accessed 10 September 2020).
European Commission. (2015) Payment Services (SD 2) – Directive (EU) 2015/2366. https://ec.europa.eu/info/law/payment-services-psd-2-directive-eu-2015-2366_en (accessed 24 September 2020).
European Commission. (2018) EPSC strategic notes. The age of Artificial Intelligence. Towards a European strategy for human-centric machines. Issues 29. 27 March 2018. https://op.europa.eu/en/publication-detail/-/publication/f22f6811-1007-11ea-8c1f-01aa75ed71a1 (accessed 21 September 2020).
European Commission. (2019) High level expert group on Artificial Intelligence. A definition of AI: Main capabilities and disciplines. file:///C:/Users/cj6343/Work%20Folders/Downloads/AIDefinitionpdf%20(1).pdf (accessed 10 August 2020).
European Commission. (2019) High level expert group of Artificial Intelligence. Ethics guidelines for trustworthy AI. file:///C:/Users/cj6343/Work%20Folders/Downloads/AIHLEG_EthicsGuidelinesforTrustworthyAI-ENpdf.pdf (accessed 24 September 2020).
FCA. (2015) Occasional paper No. 8. Consumer vulnerability. February 2015. https://www.fca.org.uk/publication/occasional-papers/occasional-paper-8.pdf (accessed 21 September 2020).
FCA. (2016) Occasional Paper 17. Access to Financial Services in the UK. May 2016. https://www.fca.org.uk/publication/occasional-papers/occasional-paper-17.pdf (accessed 23 September 2020).
FCA. (2017). FCA finalises revised Payment Services Directive (PSD2) requirements. https://www.fca.org.uk/news/press-releases/fca-finalises-revised-psd2-requirements (accessed 24 September 2020).

FCA. (2019) Policy FCA Research Agenda FCA. April 2019. FCA Research Agenda. https://www.fca.org.uk/publication/corporate/fca-research-agenda.pdf (accessed 24 September 2020).

FCA. (2017) PERG 15: Chapter 15. Guidance on the scope of the Payment Services Regulation 2017. https://www.handbook.fca.org.uk/handbook/PERG/15.pdf (accessed 24 September 2020).

Financial Inclusion Committee. (2020). Financial Inclusion Committee Strategy 2020. https://financialinclusioncommission.org.uk/wp-content/uploads/2020/09/Financial-Inclusion-Commission-Strategy-website.pdf (accessed 9 September 2020).

Friends Provident Foundation, University of Birmingham. (2016). *Financial Inclusion Annual Monitoring Report 2016*, p. 8. http://www.birmingham.ac.uk/Documents/college-social-sciences/social-policy/CHASM/annual-reports/financial-inclusion-monitoring-report-2016.pdf (accessed 10 September 2020).

FSA. (2000a) In or out? Financial exclusion: A literature and research review. London. http://www.bristol.ac.uk/geography/research/pfrc/themes/finexc/in-or-out.html (accessed 25 September 2020).

FSA. (2000b) FSA publishes research on the causes and issues of financial exclusion. London: Financial Services Authority. http://www.fsa.gov.uk/pubs/ press/2000/093.htm; downloaded 06/02/2003 (accessed 25 September 2020).

FSA. (2001) Women and personal finance: The reality of the gender gap. London: Financial Services Authority. Consumer Research Paper 7.

FSA (2003a). Consumer education. London: Financial Services Authority. http:// www.fsa.gov.uk/consumer-education (accessed 25 September 2020).

Gloukoviezoff, G. (2004) "De la bancarisation de masse a l'exclusion bancaire puis sociale" in *Revue Française des Affaire Sociales n3–2004*. Paris: La Documentation Francaise, pp. 11–38.

GOV.UK. (2014) Horizon scanning programme. Emerging technologies: Big data. 18 December 2014. https://assets.publishing.service.gov.uk/government/uploads/system/uploads/attachment_data/file/389095/Horizon_Scanning_-_Emerging_Technologies_Big_Data_report_1.pdf (accessed 23 September 2020).

GOV.UK. (2019) A guide to using artificial intelligence in the public sector. 10 June 2019. https://www.gov.uk/government/publications/understanding-artificial-intelligence/a-guide-to-using-artificial-intelligence-in-the-public-sector (accessed 23 September 2020).

GOV.UK. (2020) Government backs UK's first quantum computer. 2 September 2020. https://www.gov.uk/government/news/government-backs-uks-first-quantum-computer#:~:text=Centre%20in%20OxfordshireThe%20UK's%20first%20quantum%20computer%20to%20be%20commercially%20available%20to,today%20(2%20September%202020 (accessed 24 September 2020).

HM Treasury. (2019a) Financial Inclusion Report. March 2019. https://assets.publishing.service.gov.uk/government/uploads/system/uploads/attachment_data/file/789070/financial_inclusion_report_2018-19_web.pdf (accessed 24 September 2020).

HM Treasury. (2019b) Consumers access to financial services: Government response to the Committee's Twenty-Ninth Report. 5 July 2019. https://publications.parliament.uk/pa/cm201719/cmselect/cmtreasy/2530/253002.htm (accessed 24 September 2020).

AI and financial exclusion   209

HM Treasury. (2019c) Consumers access to financial services: Twenty-Ninth report of Session 2017–19. (HC1642) 8 May 2019. https://publications.parliament.uk/pa/cm201719/cmselect/cmtreasy/1642/1642.pdf (accessed 24 September 2020).

Hogarth, J.M., & O'Donnell, K.H. (2000). If you build it, will they come? A simulation of financial product holdings among low-to-moderate income households. *Journal of Consumer Policy* 23: 419–44.

House of Commons. (2018) Science and Technology Committee. Quantum technologies. Twelfth Report of Session 2017–19. 27 November 2018. HC 820. https://publications.parliament.uk/pa/cm201719/cmselect/cmsctech/820/820.pdf (accessed 24 September 2020).

House of Lords. (2017) Select Committee on Artificial Intelligence. Report of Session 2017–19. AI in the UK: ready, willing and able? HL Paper 100. https://publications.parliament.uk/pa/ld201719/ldselect/ldai/100/100.pdf (accessed 24 September 2020).

House of Lords. (2017) Select Committee on Financial Exclusion: Tackling financial exclusion: A country that works for everyone? Report of Sessions 2016–17. 25 March 2017. HL Paper 132. https://publications.parliament.uk/pa/ld201617/ldselect/ldfinexcl/132/13202.htm (accessed 10 September 2020).

IBM. (2019) Exploring quantum computing use cases or financial services. https://www.ibm.com/downloads/cas/2YPRZPB3 (accessed 21 September 2020).

ITU. (2017) Distributed Ledger Technologies and Financial Inclusion. https://www.itu.int/en/ITU-T/focusgroups/dfs/Documents/201703/ITU_FGDFS_Report-on-DLT-and-Financial-Inclusion.pdf (accessed 14 April 2021).

Johnson, K., Pasquale, F., & Chapman, J. (2019) Artificial intelligence, machine learning, and bias in finance: Towards responsible Innovation. *Fordham Law Review* 88(2): 499–529 (Article 5).

Joseph Rowntree Foundation. (2008) Financial Inclusion in the UK: Review of policy and practice. 16 July 2008. https://www.jrf.org.uk/report/financial-inclusion-uk-review-policy-and-practice (accessed 10 September 2020).

Joseph Rowntree Foundation. (2016) Monitoring poverty and social exclusion 2016. 7 December 2016. https://www.jrf.org.uk/report/monitoring-poverty-and-social-exclusion-2016 (accessed 10 September 2020).

Kempson, E., & Whyley, C. (1999a) *Kept in or opted out? Understanding and combating financial exclusion*. Bristol: Policy Press.

Kempson, E., & Whyley, C. (1999b). Understanding and combating financial exclusion. *Insurance Trends (The Association of British Insurers)* 21: 18–22.

Leyshorn, A., & Thrift, N. (1993). The restructuring of the UK financial services in the 1990s. *Journal of Rural Studies* 9: 223–41.

Open Banking. (2020) Open Banking adoption surpasses one million customer mark. https://www.openbanking.org.uk/about-us/latest-news/open-banking-adoption-surpasses-one-million-customer-mark/ (accessed 24 September 2020).

Panigyrakis, G. G., Theodoridis, P. K., & Veloutsou, C. A. (2002). All customers are not treated equally: Financial exclusion in isolated Greek islands. *Journal of Financial Services Marketing* 7: 54–66.

Randall, C. (2018) How can we ensure that Big Data does not makes us prisoners of technology? Financial Conduct Authority. 11 July 2018. https://www.fca.org.uk/news/speeches/how-can-we-ensure-big-data-does-not-make-us-prisoners-technology (accessed 10 August 2020).

Rowe, B., De Ionna, D., Peters, D., & Wright, H. (2015) Mind the Gap. Consumer Research exploring experiences of financial exclusion across the UK. FCA. ESRO. November 2015. https://www.fca.org.uk/publication/research/mind-the-gap.pdf (accessed 21 September 2020).

Sinclair, S. (2001) *Financial Exclusion: An Introductory Survey.* Edinburgh: Heriot Watt University Centre for Research into Socially Inclusive Services.

Wiewiorowski, W. (2020) CPDP 2020: Data protection and Artificial Intelligence. 24 January 2020. https://edps.europa.eu/sites/edp/files/publication/20-01-24_cpdp_ww_concluding_remarks_en_0.pdf (accessed 25 September 2020).

12 Risk of discrimination in AI systems

Evaluating the effectiveness of current legal safeguards in tackling algorithmic discrimination

Jennifer Graham

1 Introduction

The use of artificial intelligence (AI) is widespread. Most 'stakeholders of global society' see the infinite potential that modern technology holds for their organisations (Schwab, 2017). Ultimately, this is thanks to the growing availability of data, which has become an invaluable commodity in today's society. The ability to access and use the information made available via these large data sets is a skill that is now critical to the success of an organisation (Janssen et al., 2016). Therefore, it has become common practice to use artificially intelligent systems to process this data; as a result, we are able to identify indicators and predictors present within the data that can be used within automated decision-making processes.

The use of such intelligent technology has meant that interpreting data and using the outputs to make informed decisions can now be done autonomously, typically by a decision-making algorithm as opposed to a human. By algorithm, we are referring to a set of rules or instructions that are to be followed, typically by a computer, in order to complete a problem-solving task (Puntambekar, 2010). This technological advancement has benefits that are far-reaching; for example, time-consuming and time-sensitive tasks can be undertaken within a fraction of the time it would have previously taken to complete. The popularity of using algorithmic decision-making systems is neither a new nor an unfamiliar concept, and we are subject to the outcomes of automated decision-making processes every single day. These systems are used to assess credit card applications, sift CVs within recruitment processes, to aid in judicial decision-making, and in medical settings to confirm diagnoses, to name just a few instances.

As with any significant technical development, there are always ramifications, and in this instance both legal and ethical questions arise. Use of AI, particularly within automated decision-making, has a recognisable history of discrimination and bias (Whittaker et al., 2019), and those who are subjected to these automated decisions are at risk of falling victims to a largely unfair and inequitable process.

This chapter addresses the risk of discrimination in AI systems and is structured as follows. The first part of this chapter considers what bias within AI systems actually looks like, various examples of such bias, and why this bias leads to discrimination. Here the question of transparency is also briefly evaluated; in particular, how a lack of transparency often exacerbates the issue of algorithmic discrimination. The second part of this chapter features the central focus of this work: an evaluation of current legal safeguards and their effectiveness in tackling AI-based discrimination.

The analysis of these safeguards is essential, as these legal measures are the first line of defence in dealing with algorithmic bias and discrimination. This chapter focuses part of its analysis on the legal protections awarded by the General Data Protection Regulations (GDPR), in particular Article 22 of the GDPR, and also the effectiveness of current anti-discrimination law, including The European Convention of Human Rights (ECHR) and the Equality Act 2010. Therefore, this work considers both EU-centric and law domestic to the UK in its analysis.

The chapter then moves on to consider these legal safeguards in line with the action brought by the Joint Council for the Welfare of Immigrants and Foxglove against the Home Office. This case is the first known legal challenge to the use of algorithms in the UK; therefore, this work evaluates the effectiveness of current legal safeguards such as GDPR and relevant anti-discrimination laws and how they were applied in this case. Following this, the chapter ends in summary by considering a number of the ways in which we can deal with the bias and discrimination problems present within AI, as highlighted throughout the work.

2 What does bias within AI systems look like?

Before delving into the intricacies of bias within AI systems, it is important to generate a common understanding of what is meant by the term 'artificial intelligence'. A precise definition of AI is often hard to come by, and it is usually held that one distinct definition does not exist; however, for the purpose of this chapter the following definition as provided by the House of Lords is deemed appropriate in providing a concise overview as to what is typically understood by the term 'AI':

> AI ... applies to a broad range of concepts and systems, but it can be regarded as a group of algorithms that can modify and create new algorithms in response to learned inputs and data, as opposed to relying solely on the inputs it was designed to recognise. This ability to change, adapt and grow based on new data is described as 'intelligence'.
> (House of Lords Library, 2020, p. 1)

Thanks to the immense capability shown by these intelligent systems, it is often presumed that when AI is deployed within a decision-making context, human input is no longer required or present due to the devices' ability to "change, adapt and grow" (House of Lords Library, 2020, p. 1). This is partly because we expect that decisions that are made by computers will be based purely on fact and nothing else (Tolan, 2019). Yet the opposite is actually true; bias that is present within decision-making algorithms is often there due to human bias existing within the data already, and the algorithm then continues to bolster this existing bias. Therefore, the assumption that AI-powered automated decision-making "takes the place of human discretion" is not entirely true (Doleac and Stevenson, 2019, p. 1). Thus, in order to begin to rid these systems of bias, it is important to consider the bias present within algorithmic decision-making processes in further detail and to examine why this bias is present and why its presence ultimately leads to discrimination.

2.1 What is bias?

As with the term 'artificial intelligence', the term 'bias' also has a number of meanings depending upon the context in which it is considered. The term bias has the capacity to be applied in a neutral context or alternatively with a "significant moral meaning" (Friedman and Nissenbaum, 1996, p. 332). This is because in its most simple form, 'bias' means an inclination to choose one thing over another, and, given this, the term can be applied in a neutral context. An example of this provided by Friedman and Nissenbaum (1996, p. 332) is that of a person purchasing ripe fruit over damaged fruit. The person is 'biased' because they chose the ripe fruit over the damaged fruit. However, compare this to a person refusing to hire somebody based upon their ethnicity; the person is still 'biased', but here there is a significant moral meaning behind the term. Therefore, for the purpose of this work, it is worthwhile considering the term bias within a moral and ethical context. As such when we consider bias, we are considering it in relation to its AI counterpart, typically known as algorithmic bias (which results in unfair and often discriminatory outputs).

Discrimination resulting from the use of automated decision-making is typically the consequence of biases already embedded in the data used to train an algorithm. As put by Shrestha and Yang (2019), this means that historic prejudices and stereotypes are perpetuated by the new, automated system. Unfortunately, the groups of people most affected by this are those from minority backgrounds, who are discriminated against based upon characteristics such as gender, race, and even socioeconomic factors such as place of residence and where they attended school. This of course makes for unfair decision-making processes that are making life-altering judgements based upon factors and indicators that are unnecessary and are to some extent unlawful to take into account. As a result, there are many instances in which individuals have been discriminated against based upon these various protected characteristics; a few recent examples of this will be examined in the next part of this chapter.

The scholarship on the topic of algorithmic bias is abundant, and it is widely acknowledged that there is a bias and discrimination problem when it comes to algorithmic decision-making. There appears to be what some describe as a growing suspicion on behalf of both the public and those within academia as to the fairness of algorithms used to make important decisions (Shrestha and Yang, 2019). To a certain extent, it can be argued that this mistrust is encouraging as it means that there is growing awareness and possibly less tolerance of AI-based systems that are less than transparent in the way they operate.

This inherent problem acts as an obstacle to real progress in using algorithmic decision-making on an even wider scale. This is because deep-seated and well-established prejudices are merely echoed back at us via this modern technology, leaving these biases to remain (Rovatsos et al., 2019). Therefore, it is essential that policymakers and regulators are aware of the risk posed by the bias that is present within automated systems.

2.2 Examples of discrimination caused by algorithmic decision-making

There is a plethora of cases of algorithmic decision-making gone wrong, and these span across a wide range of sectors. Examples can be found within education as seen at St Georges Medical School (Lowry and Macpherson, 1988), within recruitment as found with Amazon's discriminatory CV sifting tool (Maedche et al., 2019), and within the criminal justice system as evident via the COMPAS recidivism tool (Angwin et al., 2016). These are well-known examples of algorithms discriminating against individuals and most of which have been discussed repeatedly throughout the literature already. This chapter, however, discusses three less familiar occurrences of AI-based discrimination; the calculation of A-level results in the UK during 2020, applications for the Apple credit card, and facial recognition software used by Microsoft, IBM, and Face ++. The impacts of these case studies are broad in scope, ranging anywhere from being given a lower credit limit, to missing out on the opportunity to attend university. It is therefore clear to see just how far-reaching and extensive the impact of using biased data to power an automated decision-making process can be.

2.2.1 UK A-level results 2020

In a year of disarray, the release of A-level results in the UK during 2020 caused controversy. Due to the Covid-19 pandemic, students were unable to sit the exams that would usually determine their A-level results. Instead, an algorithm was used in order to assist in the calculation of student grades. This model took into account a number of factors, including historical data regarding past attainment of students at the same school, attainment of this year's students, and the results of past students at the same school in the same subjects (*The Telegraph*, 2020). These data were used alongside predicted grades that teachers were asked to formulate for their students and the order in which a teacher ranked their students from highest achievers to lowest achievers (*The Telegraph*, 2020). The results of this algorithmic decision-making process led to 31.9% of students being downgraded from their predicted grade in England (*The Guardian*, 2020). Of course, the knock-on effect of this is that many students lost their conditional offers to attend university after being considerably downgraded.

Bias was demonstrated after it was discovered that private school students seemed to have fared much better than their comprehensive school counterparts; with 48.6% of private school students scoring A grades and above, whilst only 21.8% of comprehensive students scored the same (*The Guardian*, 2020). This was because more weight was given to teacher-predicted grades when students were in smaller classes (Goodier, 2020). Consequently, private schools benefited from the decision made by Ofqual due to their small cohort sizes, whilst state schools with larger cohorts were disadvantaged. As a result, it was made evident that students attending school in less affluent areas were being wrongfully discriminated against. Further transparency regarding the weighting of predicted grades with regard to class size in the final decision-making process would have perhaps provided further necessary insight at the outset.

In a country where access to higher education is already a contentious topic for debate, this outcome provides clear evidence that when using a predictive decision-making, attention must be paid to the data powering the algorithm, and the potential impact of using such. Teachers' assessments and predictions made for students based upon actual classwork and previous observed performance seemed to have less weighting compared to the judgements made by the algorithm using school-wide historic data, which of course appears to be unjust and unfair.

Following this incident, the government responded by acknowledging the error made. As a result, teacher-predicted grades would again take precedent over the controversial downgraded algorithm-predicted results. This response is an interesting one; the algorithm was specifically designed with its primary goal being to prevent grade inflation (Jones and Safak, 2020). Therefore, the motive behind utilising such an algorithm is sound and reasonable; however, the issue is that the algorithm was designed specifically to meet the goal of producing exam results that were free of grade inflation. This meant that the algorithm paid less consideration to other factors and resulted in the bias exhibited here (Jones and Safak, 2020). Despite this U-turn, the fact remains that in this particular case an algorithmic decision-making tool was relied upon with seemingly minimal testing and scrutiny.

2.2.2 *Apple credit card*

Gender-based discrimination is hardly a new phenomenon when it comes to risks related to using AI-based systems, and a recent reminder of this is the reported sexist algorithm used to calculate credit limits for the new Apple credit card (BBC, 2019). This concern was raised by both David Heinemeier, a prominent tech developer, and Steve Wozniak, one of Apple's co-founders (*The New York Times*, 2019). In this instance it was found that despite having a better credit rating, Heinemeier's partner was denied a request to increase her credit limit, but her husband's credit limit was able to remain 20 times higher. In response to this, the New York State Department of Financial Services stated that they would investigate the workings of the card application system in order to determine whether or not the algorithm violated any financial regulations (*The New York Times*, 2019).

Yet the question has still not been answered as to how the algorithm had formulated these sexist outcomes. Issuing bank Goldman Sachs released a statement affirming that the algorithm did not actually recognise gender as a factor in its decision-making process (Knight, 2019). Algorithmic discrimination can still occur even if the algorithm in question doesn't recognise a particular variable as a factor for consideration, for example, gender. Despite an algorithm not recognising gender as an indicator, other available information about an individual such as purchases they've made or the job title that they hold can still be used to infer that a person is potentially of a certain gender and thus cause indirect discrimination (Berg et al., 2018).

Indirect discrimination, or structural discrimination, is just as impactful as direct discrimination as it still puts an individual at a disadvantage even though a neutral practice or provision might be in place (Žliobaitė, 2015). A good example of this, as provided by Žliobaitė (2015), is that of a person being required to show a driver's license as a form of ID; whilst this might be a neutral requirement, this indirectly discriminates against those with visual impairments who cannot obtain a driver's license. The same principle applies to indirect discrimination based upon gender. The inclusion of so-called proxy information within a data set means that information such as a person's height, which can correlate with gender, might mean that they are still discriminated against based upon their sex (European Union Agency for Fundamental Rights, 2018).

Further evidence of indirect discrimination based upon gender can be observed within an experiment conducted by Nikhil Sonnad. In this particular experiment, Sonnad used Google translate to translate words from Turkish into English with the Turkish text being in a neutral third-person form (Sonnad, 2017). Good Translate assigned the words with a gender, such as 'hard-working' with 'he' and 'lazy' with 'she'. Therefore, the algorithm revealed its apparent gender bias (Wellner and Rothman, 2020, p. 192). Whilst the gendering of words is common within many languages, the introduction of AI in this context has actually demonstrated the pre-existing bias existing within these algorithms.

It is arguably just as harmful to 'turn a blind eye' to an important identifier such as gender, as it is to ignore it. If an algorithm is taught to recognise a factor such as gender, and this algorithm creates sexist outputs, it will be easier to identify bias within the system and to stop this from occurring again in the future, than if the system didn't recognise gender at all.

2.2.3 Facial recognition—Microsoft and IBM

Facial analysis software aims to recognise an individual based upon their appearance. This type of software can make predictions regarding a person's gender or race, but the possibilities are seemingly endless. As discussed by Buolamwini and Gebru (2018), variations of this software have claimed to be able to identify emotions and even an individuals' sexuality based on images of the subject.

Research carried out by the Gender Shades project identified that Microsoft, IBM, and Face ++, all of whom offer 'gender classification products', had difficulties in identifying subjects accurately (Gender Shades, 2018).

This project grouped subjects by gender and skin type. As a result, "bias in this context is defined as having practical differences in gender classification error rates between groups" (Gender Shades, 2018). In this particular instance, it was found that Microsoft had difficulties in correctly identifying the gender of darker-skinned subjects, IBM struggled with identifying darker-skinned females, and Face ++ frequently 'misgendered' female subjects (Gender Shades, 2018). Interestingly, both IBM and Microsoft responded to these findings by stating that their gender classification software would undergo investigation, whereas Face ++ did not respond (Gender Shades, 2018). The lack of transparency provided in instances such as this, particularly with regard to Face ++, is yet another reason for the growing distrust of artificially intelligent systems.

This project highlights the lack of neutrality in AI systems that we often falsely assume exists (Buolamwini and Gebru, 2018). If we are to use facial analysis software far and wide, it needs to be accurate and regulated so as not to fall into the hands of those who will abuse it. It is made clear here that using this type of software of course has its benefits, but when past biases and preconceptions of those who create these AI-based systems are present, the risk of discrimination based on protected characteristics is high.

2.3 Lack of transparency

It would therefore appear that many of the issues relating to discrimination within AI-based systems are the result of, or are exacerbated by, a lack of transparency, i.e. lack of information regarding the data and how the system is using the data. As we become increasingly subject to the automated decision-making process, it is expected that there will be further questioning regarding the use of algorithms and the processes undertaken to reach such decisions. To answer these questions, we need more transparency in AI-based systems.

In fact, during the summer of 2020, two UK drivers have commenced legal action against their employer Uber, requesting access to their personal data and requesting transparency regarding the use of automated decision-making within their employment (Hayes and Wall, 2020). They allege that these automated decisions have an impact upon the jobs that drivers are allocated and the pay that they receive (Hayes and Wall, 2020). This case is clear evidence that transparency is a growing concern with regard to automated decision-making, and to ensure trust in the process we need to ensure transparency first.

Finck (2020) discusses that as automated decision-making begins to take the place of human decision-making, administrative law principles, such as transparency, are likely to be challenged. Transparency is a key public law principle that has arguably already been jeopardised, alongside other fundamental rights such as the right to a fair trial. The well-known case of Loomis v Wisconsin (2017) highlights this issue. Here it was argued that an algorithm that could calculate the likelihood of recidivism used in the sentencing of Loomis was shrouded in secrecy and violated Loomis' right to due process (Smith, 2017).

This means that with regard to algorithmic decision-making, transparency is now a key concern (Burrell, 2016), and a lack of transparency usually aids occurrence of algorithmic bias. If the system is not transparent and the outputs are discriminatory, it is going to be more difficult to find the source of the bias. As a result, it would appear that the primary focus in creating more responsible AI should be on creating more transparent systems. According to Felzmann et al. (2019), this transparency can take two forms: either prospective or retrospective. The former provides information about how the system operates from the start, whereas the latter describes how a decision was reached after the process is complete, providing a retrospective explanation for the process (Felzmann et al., 2019). Arguably, both of these approaches could be used in order to help uncover the bias that exists within many algorithmic decision-making processes.

Despite this wish for opacity often by those affected, here are also concerns that the desire to achieve such a high standard of transparency within intelligent systems is unrealistic (Zerilli et al., 2019). This is primarily because automated decision-making is often compared to human decision-making; with regard to the latter, a logical explanation is typically achievable, whereas for the former this is not always the case. The aim of many contemporary pieces of legislation and recent amendments to such is to increase transparency in AI-based systems. As a result, it is interesting to consider how effective these current legal frameworks are in safeguarding against and preventing discrimination within AI-based systems.

It is acknowledged that the topic of transparency, particularly with regard to eliminating bias in artificially intelligent systems, is one in need of a chapter of its own. Therefore, this chapter now moves on to consider relevant legal safeguards and the role that they play in preventing AI-based discrimination.

3 Which legal safeguards might help to tackle AI-based discrimination?

With the exponential growth of AI and the evolution of an 'algorithmic society' (The Community Research Development Information Service [CORDIS], 2020), it is integral that current legislation and regulatory frameworks have either adapted to or are able to adapt to accommodate these technological advancements. As discussed previously, it is now widely acknowledged that there is a bias and discrimination problem within AI. It is also now evident that there is a universal understanding that we must have legal safeguards in place that adequately protect us from these risks.

Therefore, it is important to examine the current legal frameworks already in place in order to assess their success in dealing with AI-based discrimination and to identify any potential areas for improvement. This section considers the effectiveness of GDPR, in particular the rules on automated decision-making included within Article 22 in tackling AI-based discrimination. This section also considers relevant anti-discrimination regulations such as the ECHR and other supplementary legislations like the Equality Act 2010, which functions as the primary source of anti-discrimination law in the UK. Much of the literature on the effectiveness of current legal safeguards in dealing with the issues presented by AI, although there is little, does so from a distinctly EU perspective (Borgesius, 2020). This work, however, assesses not only EU-based regulation but also legislation domestic to the UK.

3.1 GDPR

It is customarily acknowledged that protection of personal data is a fundamental right and as such must be upheld (GDPR2016, Art.1). From a European perspective, from around 2010, there has been acknowledgement that existing data protection laws were no longer adequate in meeting the challenges presented by new technological developments (European Data Protection Supervisor). In 2012, the European Commission expressed their position that there was a need to make privacy rights, with regard to use of data online, more robust (European Data Protection Supervisor) and reform of the existing Data Protection Directive (Directive 95/46/EC) was necessary. With the implementation of GDPR, it was intended that the use and processing of personal data, particularly when processed in an automated fashion, would be effectively dealt with under the new regulations.

Interestingly, and as highlighted by Drożdż (2020), it is important to note the difference between the old directive and the new regulations; where an EU directive leaves some discretion as to how principles are to be incorporated domestically, the creation of a regulation ensures 'homogenous' implementation of the ruling principles in each applicable state. Arguably, this ensures more stringent data protection rules that are more secure in their protection of personal data use. Therefore, from the outset it is clear that the implementation of GDPR was intended to be binding across jurisdictions and to promote trust within those whose data would be processed and used particularly in an automated setting. However, with the rapid development of intelligent technology, and the ability for devices to now make inferences about one's personal attributes with ease, it is questionable as to whether this trust can be upheld, and if it even existed in the first place.

Enshrined in UK law via the Data Protection Act 2018, the scope of the GDPR is stated as applying to the processing and use of personal data, whether by fully or semi-automated means, or where data are processed in a different manner (General Data Protection Regulations 2016, Art.2). Here, we can see efforts to break into the 'black box', with efforts being made to ensure that regulations exist to govern the use of personal data within automated decision-making processes. There are also references throughout the regulations to transparency, particularly with regard to information and communication between the controller and the data subject (General Data Protection Regulations 2016, Art.12). This mention of transparency is encouraging; it signals that there is a growing understanding of the importance of transparency within AI-based systems.

With regard to the rights of the data subject as listed under Chapter 3 of the GDPR, including Articles 12–23, data subjects have the rights to receive information about the use of their personal data, to access the data and to have this provided in an easily accessible format, to rectify incorrect personal data, to be forgotten, and to restrict use of their data. Interestingly however, with regard to the rights of the data subject as found within Chapter 3 of the Regulations (General Data Protection Regulations 2016, Ch.3), there are no specific rules governing the rights that an individual has regarding assumptions made about them via an automated system. These are the type of assumptions discussed earlier in this chapter, the type of inferences that often stem from bias and lead to discrimination. For a closer look at the rules regulating automated decision-making, it is necessary to consult Article 22 of the GDPR.

3.1.1 Article 22

From the outset, it is clear that one of the primary purposes of Article 22 is to prohibit discrimination from occurring within an automated decision-making setting. This is evident in that Article 22 clearly states that decisions made regarding an individual should not be based upon any factor included within the 'special category of personal data' (General Data Protection Regulations 2016, Art.22, Para.4), i.e. race, religion, and sexuality (General Data Protection Regulations 2016 Art.9, Para.1.). Reference to profiling is also made in Article 22, whereby it is listed that a data subject also has the right to not be subject to a decision based solely on profiling (General Data Protection Regulations 2016, Art.22, Para.1); this typically includes using personal data in order to analyse, predict, or make inferences regarding an individual's probable behaviour and abilities (Article 29 Data Protection Working Party, 2017).

Initially, it would appear that all bases are covered by GDPR with regard to the processing of personal information by automated means, and in turn the occurrence of discrimination is minimised. However, upon closer analysis, it can be seen that there are a number of issues. First, and most importantly, it would appear that in theory removing protected characteristics such as ethnicity or sexual orientation from a data set and then allowing decisions to be made based upon the remaining data would be enough to satisfy the regulations as per Article 22. The decision reached via the automated system would not be based upon a special category of personal data but on the other 'non-special' data in the data set (Baldini, 2019).

Yet we know that removing data pertaining to a protected characteristic does not mean that the algorithm is incapable of discrimination. As already discussed with regard to the Apple credit card, removing sensitive data relating to a protected characteristic such as religious beliefs or ethnicity does not mean that bias and discrimination are avoided: it can in fact exacerbate the issue.

Although a protected characteristic such as ethnicity might be deliberately excluded from a data set, inferences can still be made regarding an individual's ethnic background based upon other arguably 'non-special' data that remain, for example, their residential postcode (Baldini, 2019). Therefore, removing the offending data (relating to a protected characteristic) is not necessarily enough to prevent discrimination from occurring. It is therefore believed that these inferences, and lack of robust legal mechanisms governing them, are a good reason to reform data protection law and that this would better protect individuals from AI-based discrimination (Tene and Polonetsky, 2013; Wachter and Mittelstadt, 2019).

This gives rise to a second issue. Inferences made by an automated system through processes such as profiling are typically not classed as 'special' data and so do not fall within one of the categories as listed within Article 9 of the GDPR (Wachter and Mittelstadt, 2019). As per Wachter and Mittelstadt (2019) and the Article 29 Data Protection Working Party (2017), there is a case to be made that these inferences create a 'new' type of personal data that if rendered identifiable would fall within this 'special' category as per Article 9. With this in mind, it is evident that there are obvious gaps within the protections awarded by GDPR; although the regulations aim to decrease occurrences of discrimination and bias within automated, intelligent systems, the regulations are not completely effective.

Thus, the efforts made via GDPR to introduce a more rigid and uniform set of regulations to govern personal data use online and within automated processes were necessary and to some extent sufficient. It is one of the first wide-scale regulations to directly deal with the issues posed by automated decision-making. Yet GDPR alone does not seem to be the solution to tackle AI-based discrimination. However, as established here, there are accountability gaps with particular regard to both the approach to riding bias from an automated system and in the approach to which data are and which data should be classified as being 'special' personal data. Without more refined regulation here, there is a real risk that instances of bias and discrimination will occur and that they will fall outside the remit of GDPR due to the narrow understanding of 'special' data. There are accountability gaps within the regulations, and thus there is room for reform. It is therefore useful to consider which other legal safeguards may be of use in tackling the discrimination and bias problem within AI.

3.2 Anti-discrimination laws

When considering the effectiveness of legal safeguards in tackling discrimination within AI-based systems, it is essential to consider not only relevant data protection regulations but also existing anti-discrimination legislation. The challenges posed by algorithmic discrimination are not limited to data protection and privacy issues, but as is clear, these challenges also include bias-driven unequal treatment of those within our society. It is therefore necessary to consider relevant anti-discrimination law and its effectiveness in dealing with AI-based discrimination. Thus, it is of critical significance to consider how widely current legislation would have to be interpreted in order for it to apply to instances of algorithmic discrimination and if this wide-scale interpretation is possible.

It is believed that a rather fragmented approach to anti-discrimination law is evident across a variety of jurisdictions. This means that some states have legislation that is better equipped than others to deal with the bias and discrimination problem present within AI (Hacker, 2018). This is notably the case with regard to US anti-discrimination law, which has been described as falling short in safeguarding against AI-based discrimination when compared to anti-discrimination regimes in place such as in Europe (Barocas and Selbst, 2016).

In a similar vein to the discussion regarding data protection, it is worthwhile considering anti-discrimination safeguards present within Europe that may help in tackling AI-based discrimination. As such, a useful place to start is with both the ECHR and the Charter of Fundamental Rights of the European Union (the Charter). The former binds all of its signatories and is enshrined in UK law via the Human Rights Act 1998. The latter applies to EU member states particularly when implementing EU law. Both of these legal safeguards contain provisions that prohibit discrimination. Article 14 of the ECHR, and as a result the Human Rights Act 1998, distinctly prohibits discrimination on a series of protected characteristics similar to those listed within the GDPR; these include:

> sex, race, colour, language, religion, political or other opinion, national or social origin, association with a national minority, property, birth or other status.
>
> (European Convention on Human Rights, Art. 14)

And likewise, Title III of the Charter (specifically Article 21) forbids discrimination based upon a similar list of protected characteristics.

Within the UK, it is worthwhile considering the Equality Act 2010 in particular. This piece of legislation is slightly different in that it offers more general protection against discrimination within various aspects of daily life (Equality and Human Rights Commission, 2018). This is in comparison with that of the Human Rights Act 1998; this Act's focus is on discrimination affecting one's enjoyment of a human right (Equality and Human Rights Commission, 2018). Despite the abundance of anti-discrimination provisions in place, particularly within the UK, it is suggested that at present these provisions are equipped to tackle algorithmic bias to a certain extent, but they are not fully competent and inclusive as of now (Rovatsos et al., 2019).

Arguably, one of the primary issues with regard to the effectiveness of anti-discrimination legislation in tackling AI-based discrimination lies within the very nature of automated decision-making and profiling. Mann and Matzner (2019, p. 4) contend that the whole point of profiling, predicting, and inferring is to find pieces of information that are not directly provided by a given individual; the purpose of this process being to use this new information to find "differences among people to entail that they are treated differently". This is in contention with the entire purpose of anti-discrimination law, which is to prevent individuals from being treated differently on the basis of their differences (Mann and Matzner, 2019). Therefore, it would appear that the essence of algorithmic decision-making, and particularly predictive profiling, is at odds with anti-discrimination principles. With this theory in mind, it is highly unlikely that we would be able to find any current anti-discrimination legislation that fully safeguards against algorithmic discrimination without a specific provision included to deal with inferences and predictions made by automated systems.

This issue regarding inferences is similar to that which arises in relation to data protection laws. While the use of inferences and predictions to classify people based upon their differences is seemingly at odds with anti-discrimination principles, a combination of factors that are not strictly classed as a protected characteristic when combined can still result in discrimination and cause disadvantage. This could be the case despite the fact that these factors (again, such as online shopping habits and holidaying choices) are not classed as protected characteristics capable of causing discrimination. As a result, a number of revealing factors, such as a person's postcode, are typically not deemed to be capable of causing discrimination when in actual fact if combined they are. Therefore, it appears as if this is a commonality that exists between both data protection regulations and anti-discrimination measures.

Consequentially, it would appear that current legal safeguards as discussed in this section, including GDPR, the ECHR, and the Equality Act 2010, are to a very limited extent capable of tackling AI-based discrimination. In order for existing legislation to effectively deal with the causes of algorithmic bias and discrimination as discussed in this work, significant reform is necessary. The primary change would appear to be the need to recognise certain factors as being capable of causing discrimination despite not being strictly classed as protected 'special' characteristics. Another potential alternative would be a more innovative approach, to create a new type of legal safeguard that encompasses and combines both data protection law and anti-discrimination principles. A combination of these two types of legislation would be arguably better equipped to tackle AI-based discrimination than just one on its own; further details with regard to this will be included within the final section of this chapter.

3.3 Case analysis

Following an analysis of existing legal safeguards and their effectiveness in tackling AI-based discrimination, it is worthwhile considering these safeguards within the context of current litigation. In particular, this work considers the recent action brought by The Joint Council for the Welfare of Immigrants and 'tech-justice' group Foxglove against the Home Office regarding the use of an algorithm within the Home Office's visa application process (The Joint Council for the Welfare of Immigrants, 2020). The algorithm in question used is what can be described as a 'traffic-light system' for rating visa applicants. The issue here appeared to be that the algorithm rated and discriminated against individuals based on their nationality (The Joint Council for the Welfare of Immigrants, 2020). Individuals from 'higher risk' nations were given a lower rating than their counterparts from more 'suitable' nations, which meant that their applications were scrutinised in much more depth, prolonging the process and meaning they would likely be denied a visa.

Interestingly, the legal challenge brought by The Joint Council for the Welfare of Immigrants and Foxglove was founded on the basis that the use of this algorithm directly violated the Equality Act 2010, as it discriminated against applicants on a race. Their action was successful in that at the beginning of August 2020, Home Secretary Priti Patel agreed to cease the use of the visa application system in question and to review the process. Therefore, this gives some indication that current legal safeguards, in particular anti-discrimination laws such as the Equality Act 2010, are to some extent successful in protecting against algorithmic bias.

It is worth noting however that discrimination based upon an individual's nationality, which is a protected characteristic, is clearly recognised as being unlawful. If other 'non-special' characteristics were used in this instance to make inferences and thus a decision about a person, there is a likelihood that discrimination and unfair treatment will still occur. Unfortunately, this discrimination would likely not be recognised or protected by the Equality Act 2010 and other similar legislations. It is therefore encouraging that current legislation can and has successfully been used to tackle AI-based discrimination in this instance. However, it is evident that there is still some way to go before we have fully competent anti-discrimination safeguards that can tackle algorithmic bias and discrimination.

With regard to this action brought against the Home Office, it was contended that following incidents such as the Windrush scandal, it was obvious that the Home Office had an entrenched history of racism. As such, these historical prejudices against particular nationalities formed the basis of the visa application software in question (The Joint Council for the Welfare of Immigrants, 2020, para. 3). Interestingly however, an issue still remains with regard to transparency. We know that the algorithm in question here used a list of suspect nationalities to discriminate against applicants; however, the Home Office would not provide any further information regarding other factors that were considered by the algorithm when reaching a decision (The Joint Council for the Welfare of Immigrants, 2020). Once again, we see the potential issues posed by a lack of transparency within automated decision-making systems. We know that discrimination was established on the grounds of racism; however, we are unaware of other factors involved in the process that could have caused further discrimination on different bases.

Interestingly, the opinions held by The Joint Office for the Welfare of Immigrants regarding safeguards against algorithmic decision-making are in line with the ideas presented in this chapter. At some point, a combination of anti-discrimination and data protection principles would form the basis of adequate measures to be used in tackling algorithmic discrimination. The Joint Office for the Welfare of Immigrants states that Home Secretary Priti Patel agreed to implement their agreed legal measures which come in the form of an Equality Impact Assessment and a Data Protection Impact Assessment. However, this is only in relation to the aforementioned visa application process. Therefore, it is hypothesised that a similar approach taken to similar algorithmic decision-making processes could help tackle existing discrimination caused by algorithms and bias present within the automated process. By employing the approach adopted here, potential instances of discrimination, bias, and unfair treatment are more likely to be identified, which provides more robust grounds for tackling algorithmic discrimination on a wider scale.

This case highlights and re-enforces a number of issues discussed so far within this work. There is a clear issue with regard to historical prejudices being present within data sets used to train algorithms meaning that these biases are exacerbated, there is an inherit lack of transparency within most algorithmic decision-making processes, and reform to current legal safeguards is necessary in order to fully tackle the number of issues presented by AI-based discrimination. Unfortunately, with the inevitable continued reliance upon automated decision-making, further legal challenges are also to be expected. However, as with cases like that brought by The Joint Council for the Welfare of Immigrants against the Home Office, it is encouraging that there appears to be further recognition of this bias and discrimination problem within intelligent systems and some limited efforts being taken to tackle the issue at its core.

4 Conclusion

The issues posed by algorithmic bias and discrimination are obvious, and there is clear evidence that we are becoming increasingly aware of the potential wide-ranging impacts that these issues have. As demonstrated in this work, the first line of defence in tackling discrimination, particularly within automated decision-making systems, is via legal measures such as legislation, regulation, and policy. Resultantly, it would appear that a key focus going forward in the response to these tech-based issues would be to more closely consider the effectiveness and functionality of the legal safeguards that may be used to tackle occurrence of bias and discrimination within AI-based systems. This analysis would feature scrutiny of not only domestic law but also international law.

As is present in the evaluation provided, it is clear that there is room for improving the effectiveness of existing legal safeguards to fully protect against the risk of discrimination present within these automated decision-making systems. There are, however, a number of ways in which this could be achieved; one of which would be by establishing a set of measures that incorporate both personal data protection and anti-discrimination principles as suggested by The Joint Council for the Welfare of Immigrants in their attempt to reform the current visa application process within the UK. In addition to this and as highlighted throughout this chapter, efforts could and should be made to recognise certain pieces of 'non-special' information (such as a person's postcode) as protected and categorically 'special' data. This is primarily because of the capability available to use these data in order to make inferences about an individual that can once more reveal a protected characteristic and lead to discrimination.

As such, this work proposes that reform to the law is necessary in order to properly safeguard against the risks of discrimination posed by the increasing use of automated, for example AI-based, decision-making systems. Continuous and widespread use of AI and other intelligent systems in order to assist with everyday tasks is inevitable: any attempt to stop this is counterproductive and futile. Therefore, it is recommended that one part of a multifaceted approach in dealing with this problem is to begin by modifying the law in such a way that it is more suited to adequately protect against the risks posed by these automated systems.

Bibliography

Angwin, J. Larson, J. Mattu, S. Kirchner, L. (2016) Machine Bias: There's Software Used across the Country to Predict Future Criminals. And It's Biased against Blacks. *ProPublica* Available at: https://www.propublica.org/article/machine-bias-risk-assessments-in-criminal-sentencing (Accessed 6 October 2020)

Article 29 Data Protection Working Party (2017) *Guidelines on Automated Individual Decision-Making and Profiling for the Purposes of Regulation 2016/670 Adopted on 3 October 2017 As Last Revised and Adopted on 6 February 2018.* Available at: http://ec.europa.eu/justice/data-protection/index_en.htm (Accessed 3 August 2020)

Baldini, D. (2019) *Article 22 GDPR and Prohibition of Discrimination. An Outdated Provision?* Available at: https://www.cyberlaws.it/2019/article-22-gdpr-and-prohibition-of-discrimination-an-outdated-provision (Accessed 9 September 2020)

Barocas, S. Selbst, A.D. (2016) Big Data's Disparate Impact. *California Law Review.* 104(3), 671–732

BBC (2019) *Apple's "Sexist" Credit Card Investigated by US Regulator.* Available at: https://www.bbc.co.uk/news/business-50365609 (Accessed 20 August 2020)

Berg, T. Burg, V. Gombović, A. (2018) *On the Rise of the FinTechs — Credit Scoring Using Digital Footprints.* Available at: https://www.fdic.gov/bank/analytical/cfr/2018/wp2018/cfr-wp2018-04.pdf (Accessed 10 August 2020)

Borgesius, F.J.Z. (2020) Strengthening Legal Protection against Discrimination by Algorithms and Artificial Intelligence Algorithms and Artificial Intelligence. *The International Journal of Human Rights.* Available at: https://www.tandfonline.com/doi/full/10.1080/13642987.2020.1743976?scroll=top&needAccess=true (Accessed 5 September 2020)

Buolamwini, J. Gebru, T. (2018) Gender Shades: Intersectional Accuracy Disparities in Commercial Gender Classification. *Proceedings of Machine Learning Research.* 81, 1–15

Burrell, J. (2016) How the Machine "Thinks": Understanding Opacity in Machine Learning Algorithms. *Big Data & Society.* 1–12

Charter of Fundamental Rights of the European Union (2000/C 364/01)

The Community Research Development Information Service (CORDIS) (2020) *Safeguarding Equality in the European Algorithmic Society: Tackling Discrimination in Algorithmic Profiling through EU Equality Law.* Available at: https://cordis.europa.eu/project/id/898937 (Accessed 26 August 2020)

Davide, B. (2019) Article 22 GDPR and Prohibition of Discrimination. An Outdated Provision? *CyberLaw.* Available at: https://www.cyberlaws.it/2019/article-22-gdpr-and-prohibition-of-discrimination-an-outdated-provision/ (Accessed: 3 September 2020)

Directive 95/46/EC of the European Parliament and of the Council of 24 October 1995 on the protection of individuals with regard to the processing of personal data and on the free movement of such data. *OJ L 281, 23.11.1995* Available at: https://eur-lex.europa.eu/legal-content/EN/TXT/?uri=celex%3A31995L0046

Doleac, J. L. Stevenson. M. T. (2019) *Algorithmic Risk Assessment in the Hands of Humans.* Available at: https://ssrn.com/abstract=3489440 (Accessed 18 August 2020).

Drożdż, A. (2020) *Protection of Natural Persons with Regard to Automated Individual Decision-Making in the GDPR.* Netherlands: Kluwer Law International B.V.

Equality and Human Rights Commission (2018) *Article 14: Protection from Discrimination.* Available at: https://www.equalityhumanrights.com/en/human-rights-act/article-14-protection-discrimination (Accessed 15 September 2020)

European Data Protection Supervisor (2018) *The History of General Data Protection Regulation* Available at: https://edps.europa.eu/data-protection/data-protection/legislation/history-general-data-protection-regulation_en (Accessed 26 August 2020)

European Union Agency for Fundamental Rights (2018) *#BigData: Discrimination in Data-Supported Decision Making.* Available at: https://fra.europa.eu/sites/default/files/fra_uploads/fra-2018-focus-big-data_en.pdf (Accessed 6 October 2020)

Felzmann, H. Villaronga, E.F. Lutz, C. Tamo-Larrieux, A. (2019) Transparency You Can Trust: Transparency Requirements for Artificial Intelligence between Legal Norms and Contextual Concerns. *Big Data & Society.* 1–14

Finck, M. (2020) Automated Decision-Making and Administrative Law. *Max Planck Institute for Innovation & Competition Research Paper No. 19-10* Available at: https://ssrn.com/abstract=3433684 (Accessed 13 August 2020)

Friedman, B. Nissenbaum, H. (1996) Bias in Computer Systems. *ACM Transactions on Information Systems.* 4(13), 330–347.

Gender Shades (2018) *Overview.* Available at: http://gendershades.org/overview.html (Accessed 20 August 2020)

Goodier, M. (2020) *Top A-Level Grades Soar at Private Schools as Sixth Form Colleges Lose Out* Available at: https://www.newstatesman.com/politics/education/2020/08/top-level-grades-soar-private-schools-sixth-form-colleges-lose-out (Accessed 6 October 2020)

The Guardian (2020) *A-Level Results Day 2020 Live.* Available at: https://www.theguardian.com/education/live/2020/aug/13/a-level-results-day-2020-live-students-teachers-government-ucas-mock-exams-triple-lock-nick-gibb#:~:text=A-levels-, A-level%20results%20day%202020%20live%3A%2039.1%25%20of%20pupils, England%20downgraded%20-%20as%20it%20happened&text=That's%20all%20from%20me%2C%20Caroline%20Davies.&text=More%20than%20a%20third%20of, were%20downgraded%20by%20three%20grades (Accessed 20 August 2020)

Hacker, P. (2018) Teaching Fairness to Artificial Intelligence: Existing and Novel Strategies against Algorithmic Discrimination under EU Law. *Common Market Law Review.* 55, 1143–1186

Hayes, E., Wall, S. (2020) *The Legal Risks of Automated Decision-Making.* Available at: https://www.peoplemanagement.co.uk/experts/legal/the-legal-risks-of-automated-decision-making (Accessed 10 October 2020).

House of Lords Library (2020) *Predictive and Decision-Making Algorithms in Public Policy.* Available at: https://lordslibrary.parliament.uk/research-briefings/lln-2020-0045/ (Accessed 3 August 2020)

Human Rights Act 1998

Janssen, M. van der Voort, H. Wahyudi, A. (2017) Factors Influencing Big Data Decision-Making Quality. *Journal of Business Research* 70, 338–345. Available at: http://www.sciencedirect.com/science/article/pii/S0148296316304945) (Accessed 14 August 2020)

The Joint Council for the Welfare of Immigrants (2020) *We Won! Home Office to Stop Using Racist Visa Algorithm.* Available at: https://www.jcwi.org.uk/news/we-won-home-office-to-stop-using-racist-visa-algorithm (Accessed 15 September 2020)

Jones, E. Safak, C. (2020) *Can Algorithms Ever Make the Grade?* Available at: https://www.adalovelaceinstitute.org/can-algorithms-ever-make-the-grade/ (Accessed 6 October 2020)

Knight, W. (2019) *The Apple Card Didn't 'See' Gender—And That's the Problem* Available at: https://www.wired.com/story/the-apple-card-didnt-see-genderand-thats-the-problem/ (Accessed 20 August 2020)

Loomis v Wisconsin 881 N.W.2d 749 (Wis. 2016), cert. denied, 137 S.Ct. 2290 (2017)

Lowry, S. Macpherson, G. (1988) A Blot on the Profession. *British Medical Journal.* Available at: http://europepmc.org/backend/ptpmcrender.fcgi?accid=PMC2545288&blobtype=pdf (Accessed 6 October 2020)

Maedche, A. Legner, C. Benlian, A. Berger, B. Gimpel, H. Hess, T. Hinz, O. Morana, S. Söllner, M. (2019) AI-based Digital Assistants: Opportunities, Threats, and Research Perspectives. *Business and Information Systems Engineering.* 61(4), 535–544

Mann, M. Matzner, M. (2019) Challenging Algorithmic Profiling: The Limits of Data Protection and Anti-Discrimination in Responding to Emergent Discrimination. *Big Data & Society.* Available at: https://journals.sagepub.com/doi/10.1177/2053951719895805 (Accessed 6 September 2020)

The New York Times (2019) *Apple Card Investigated after Gender Discrimination Complaints* Available at: https://www.nytimes.com/2019/11/10/business/Apple-credit-card-investigation.html (Accessed 20 August 2020)

Puntambekar, A.A. (2010) *Design & Analysis of Algorithms* (First). Pune: Technical Publication

Regulation (EU) 2016/679 of the European Parliament and of the Council of 27 April 2016 on the protection of natural persons with regard to the processing of personal data and on the free movement of such data, and repealing Directive 95/46/EC (General data Protection Regulation) *OJ L 199/1, 4.5.2016* Available at: https://eur-lex.europa.eu/legal-content/EN/TXT/HTML/?uri=CELEX:32016R0679&from=EN

Robin, S. (2017) Opening the Lid on Criminal Sentencing Software. *Duke Today.* Available at: https://today.duke.edu/2017/07/opening-lid-criminal-sentencing-software (Accessed 18 August 2020)

Rovatsos, M. Mittelstadt, B. Koene, A. (2019) *Landscape Summary: Bias in Algorithmic Decision-Making.* Available at: https://assets.publishing.service.gov.uk/government/uploads/system/uploads/attachment_data/file/819055/Landscape_Summary_-_Bias_in_Algorithmic_Decision-Making.pdf (Accessed 3 August 2020)

Schwab, K. (2017) *The Fourth Industrial Revolution.* London: Penguin

Shrestha, Y.R. Yang, Y. (2019) Fairness in Algorithmic Decision-Making: Applications in Multi-Winner Voting Machine Learning, and Recommender Systems. *Algorithms.* 12(9), 199–227.

Sonnad, N. (2017) *Google Translate's Gender Bias Pairs "He" with "Hardworking" and "She" with Lazy, and Other Examples.* Available at: https://qz.com/1141122/google-translates-gender-bias-pairs-he-with-hardworking-and-she-with-lazy-and-other-examples/ (Accessed 6 October 2020)

Smith, R. A. (2017) *Opening the Lid on Criminal Sentencing Software*. Available at: https://today.duke.edu/2017/07/opening-lid-criminal-sentencing-software (Accessed 7 September 2020)

The Telegraph (2020) *A-Level and GCSE Results Update: How Are 2020 Grades Being Calculated without Exams?* Available at: https://www.telegraph.co.uk/education-and-careers/2020/08/18/a-level-gcse-results-grades/ (Accessed 20 August 2020)

Tene, O. Polonetsky, J. (2013) Big Data for All: Privacy and User Control in the Age of Analytics. *Northwestern Journal of Technology and Intellectual Property*. 11(5), 239–273

Tolan, S. (2019) *Fair and Unbiased Algorithmic Decision Making: Current State and Future Challenges*. Available at: https://arxiv.org/abs/1901.04730 (Accessed 7 August 2020)

Wachter, S. Mittelstadt, B. (2019) A Right to Reasonable Inferences: Re-Thinking Data Protection Law in the Age of Big Data and AI. *Columbia Business Law Review*. 2019(2), 494–620

Wellner, G. Rothman, T. (2020) Feminist AI: Can We Expect Our AI Systems to Become Feminist? *Philosophy & Technology*. 33, 191–205

Whittaker, M. Alper, M. Bennett, C.L. Hendren, S. Kaziunas, L. Mills, M. Morris, M.R. Rankin, J. Rogers, E. Salas, M. West, S.M. (2019) *Disability, Bias, and AI*. Available at: https://ainowinstitute.org/disabilitybiasai-2019.pdf?fbclid=IwAR3ldX3o_nkVf-cirQ9P-yJqRRkT1vcKU3MgcEAeWVwUgA0Ue1c-60Zd9OE (Accessed 5 October 2020)

Zerilli, J. Knott, A. Maclauri, J. Gavaghan, C. (2019) Transparency in Algorithmic and Human Decision-Making: Is There a Double Standard? *Philosophy & Technology*. 32, 661–683

Žliobaitė, I. (2015) A Survey on Measuring Indirect Discrimination in Machine Learning. Available at: https://arxiv.org/abs/1511.00148 (Accessed 6 October 2020)

13 Unprecedented times

Artificial intelligence and the implications for intellectual property

Ana Carolina Blanco Haché

1 Introduction

These are unprecedented times for the intellectual property (IP) system and for humanity. As technology and its accessibility advances, we are increasingly using tools to achieve work that are considered overwhelming, complex, or time-consuming from a human perspective. Artificial intelligence (AI) is not new.[1] However, it has been further empowered by recent computational developments and exorbitant volumes of data, which are AI's lifeblood. This technology can analyse, predict patterns, complete tasks, and thus optimise its performance generating solutions and products involving creativity and innovation – once considered human traits.

There is an understanding that by making an AI capable of autonomous decision-making it is in fact acting 'intelligently' and 'independently' (Li and Koay, 2020, 399). This belief is credited to Alan Turin's idea of 'thinking machines', where computers have to reason like human beings and complete 'reasoning puzzles' in order to think in an autonomous manner, the Turin Test (1950, 433–460). It is possible that in the future, humans will also have machine characteristics such as prosthetics or chips and policymakers "will not be able to discriminate based on biological grounds" (Noto La Diega, 2016, 402). It is also argued that AI is not intelligent but programmed to follow orders and thus automation does not equal autonomy (Mik, 2020). Even lacking of cognitive abilities they have "taken over the world" (Asay, 2020, 1193). Therefore, making the AI similar to humans is understood that someday it will become one, but the "simulation of a thing is not the thing itself" (Solum, 1992, 1262).

---

1 The term was first used in 1956 (attributed to John McCarthy) at a Dartmouth College sponsored by DARPA. See *Stanford Encyclopaedia of Philosophy*, "Artificial Intelligence" (12 July 2018) <https://plato.stanford.edu/entries/artificial-intelligence/#HistAI> (Accessed 28 September 2020).

IP principles and concepts were written and implemented when AI was not even conceived (Nard, 2008, 7).[2] Except for the UK,[3] India,[4] New Zealand,[5] Hong Kong (SAR),[6] South Africa,[7] and Ireland,[8] copyright laws did not contemplate computer-generated works when they were enacted; such works were uncommon. Nowadays our reality is different. AI's proliferation is requiring the IP system to solve the uncertainty and ambiguity surrounding AI-generated works. It is difficult to distinguish between an art created by a human being and another created by AI. Similarly, it is challenging to identify if an invention has been independently generated by AI or if it had a human contributor, knowing that under the current IP regime, independent AI-generated inventions are not patentable[9]; hence, such revelations are disincentivised. This does not seem appropriate or effective, especially if inventions involving AI are thriving (WIPO, 2019). This chapter analyses different roles that AI might have in order to see if legal personhood should be granted (Part 2). IP rights such as patents, trade secrecy, and copyrights will be examined (Part 3) in order to propose a special regime for AI-generated creations (Part 4). AI is used throughout this chapter to mean similar concepts such as robots, software and hardware, or algorithmic mechanisms such as ML, DL, and neural networks.

2 The role and status of AI

The role of AI is crucial to understand how to regulate this technology and determine AI's rights and responsibilities, if any. The first death caused by an AI occurred when an autonomous car killed a pedestrian in March 2018 (TS, 2018). It is progressively having implications into our lifestyles, and automated vehicles

---

2 First patent was issued in 1421 to architect and inventor Filippo Brunelleschi for a ship used for marble transportation; see NARD, Craig Allen, *The Law of Patents*, Aspen Publishers: New York, 2008, p. 7 in Mermer, J.E., "The Impact of Intellectual Property in Fostering Innovation" (2018) *SSRN* <https://ssrn.com/abstract=3379331>; also UK Justice Robin Jacob has been attributed of saying that the history of Intellectual Property can be traced back to 600 BCE, for a patent granted for "some kind of newfangled loaf of bread". See Kwong, M., "Six Significant Moments in Patent History", *Thomson Reuters Intellectual Property & Science Division and Reuters Brand Content Solutions* (4 November 2014) <https://www.reuters.com/article/us-moments-patent-idUSKBN0IN1Y120141104> (Accessed 28 September 2020).
3 Section 9(3) of the UK Copyright Design and Patent Act 1988 (CDPA).
4 Section 2 (d) sub-clause (vi) of India Copyrights Act 1957.
5 Section 2 and section 17 of the New Zealand Copyright Act 1994. See also section 5(2)(a) New Zealand Copyright Act 1994.
6 Section 11(3) Hong Kong (SAR) Cap. 528 Copyright Ordinance 1997 and section 17(3) Hong Kong (SAR) Cap. 528 Copyright Ordinance 1997.
7 Section 1 of the South Africa Copyright Act (1978) as amended up to Copyright Amendment Act (2002), letter h.
8 Section 2 (III) (v) Ireland Copyright and Related Rights Act, 2000 and section 30 Copyright And Related Rights Act, 2000.
9 See *Stephen L Thaler v. The Comptroller-General of Patents, Designs and Trade Marks* [2020] EWHC 2412 (Pat) (Applicant Stephen Taylor could not register his creation DABUS as the inventor of two patents GB1816909.4 and GB1818161.0.).

are but one example of an increasingly widespread technology that indicates a need for clarifications. There are inconsistent definitions of AI (McCarthy, 2007), mainly because it has evolved in many subsets. World Intellectual Property Organization (WIPO) considers it to "be a discipline of computer science that is aimed at developing machines and systems that can carry out tasks considered to require human intelligence[10] [with limited or no human intervention]" (WIPO, n/d). The UK government defines it simply as "technologies with the ability to perform tasks that would otherwise require human intelligence such as visual perception, speech recognition, and language translation" (Department for Business, Energy and Industrial Strategy, 2017, 37). Some argue it is better to define AI by its range (*Oxford Computing Dictionary*, 2008, 26) considering that the main AI development involves machine learning (ML) – a technique that concerns algorithms allowing computers to self-improve by receiving data to train itself and predict technical solutions[11] – and Deep Learning (DL), a subset of ML that uses 'virtual neurons' to learn from enormous amounts of data called neural networks (McClelland, 2017) which imitate the human brain by forming layers to enable learning, perform complex tasks, and give solutions to technical problems. All these techniques are considered weak and narrow AI (ANI) because it only deals with specific tasks as opposed to a stronger AI – still unknown – that will imitate human cognitive behaviour completely, considered Artificial General Intelligence (AGI), and, subsequently, Artificial Super Intelligence (ASI), which arguably will exceed human's intelligence also known as Technological Singularity (Silicon AI & Cybersecurity, 2020).

AI has hardware and software that comes in different forms and shapes. Some are mere objects, but others have humanoid characteristics that may have different legal implications. It is unclear if the law should treat AI as legal persons, such as corporations or 'whether a new category should be created' as implied by the EU Committee on Legal Affairs (European Parliament, 2015). Nonetheless, this was heavily criticised by robotics experts. The majority agree that AI should not be given 'moral agency' and it would be immoral to give personhood that will put machines to compete with humans (Panel for the Future of Science and Technology, 2020). Conceivably, it could follow similar considerations to animals which distinguish dangerous animals from domestic ones by assigning rights and regulations.

2.1 AI(D) as tools

AI is mainly perceived as property created to aid humanity for which corporations or individuals are responsible (Bennet and Daly, 2020, 64) and for which they have domination and control (Asimo, 1950). Experts in robotics have

---

10 WIPO, "*Artificial Intelligence and Intellectual Property*" < https://www.wipo.int/about-ip/en/artificial_intelligence/> (Accessed 28 September 2020).
11 EPO, "Request from the United States Patent and Trademark Office for Comments on Patenting Artificial Intelligence Inventions: Comments by the European Patent Office (EPO)" <https://www.uspto.gov/sites/default/files/documents/European-Patent-Office_RFC-84-FR-44889.pdf> (Accessed 10 October 2020).

determined that "it becomes obvious that robots themselves are not where responsibility lies. Robots are simply *tools* of various kinds, albeit *very special tools*, and the responsibility of making sure they behave well must always lie with human beings" (Engineering and Physical Sciences Research Council, n/d). Treating AI as property will not assign any rights but seems appropriate since it allocates responsibility of its actions to persons for any crime due to negligent supervision, as it occurs with animals and their owners.

AI is generally regarded as products (Mik, 2020, 8), and strict liability might be imposed on dangerous or defective AI such as in product liability legislations (European Parliament, 2020). The law should clarify upon commercialisation of AI, if negligent actions caused by software where end-users do not have control due to unknown programmed codes or trade secrets embedded. In such circumstances, liability should be imposed on developers. However, the EU Parliament considers the possibility that AI may become an independent subject in civil law considering compulsory schemes for insurances and limited liability for manufacturers, programmers, owners, or users if they jointly contribute to a compensation fund or issue policy for insurance for damages caused (European Parliament, 2017). Giving property treatment means no change in legislations and hence not able to hold titles of property.

2.2 Animals

Some argue that AI should have animal rights since both are capable of autonomous decision-making (to an extent) and are both considered property 'in some sense', but most importantly they are their owners' responsibility.[12] This analogy comparing AI to animals has been considered misleading (Winfield, 2007, 6). While animals cannot speak for themselves, animal rights movement have accomplished recognition and rights for animals in many jurisdictions. Comparing animals to property when the latter are inanimate seems inadequate (Kelch, 1998) as well, but courts have treated pets as personal property when allocating it in a divorce (Rook, 2014). Other courts in the US have established that "a pet is not just a thing but occupies a special place somewhere in between a person and a piece of personal property".[13] Nonetheless, there seems to be an agreement that "all animals and AI regardless of their level of autonomy, intelligence or consciousness, are property" (Patrick, 2014).

2.3 Legal person

AI robots may have human appearance such as Sophia, the first robot in the world to be recognised with a citizenship (Wootson, 2017). In Japan we have seen humans marrying robots (Miyazaki, 2020), which exemplifies the implications AI is having in our society. The decision of granting AI legal personality is not a question of physical characteristics and abilities; it can never have the

---

12 In the UK Animals Act 1976.
13 *Corso v. Crawford Dog & Cat Hosp.*, Inc., 415 N.Y.S.2d 182 (N.Y. Civ. Ct. 1979).

same prerogatives as humans. Other nonhumans have achieved legal personality; for example, in New Zealand environmentalists affirmed legal personhood for a river (Dremliuga, 2019, 109). In India sacred places have also obtained personhood.[14] Many academics consider that legal personality should be granted to AI (Solum, 1992). They are compared to corporations with possibilities of occupying board membership positions. The concept of legal personality of commercial companies is a *fictio juris* that evolved from Roman law to conveniently separate a jointly owned patrimony between partners from the assets and liabilities of each partner individually in order not to liquidate the gains or losses of each business by a creditor (Vivante, 1932, 9–10). Hence, legal personhood of corporations occurred as a convenience for humans to enable them to be autonomous organisations with economic rights and obligations. However, it has its limitations, since in some jurisdictions corporate veil could be lifted and criminal sanctions are granted to its members.[15] Therefore, policy should evaluate why personhood is necessary for AI, and, if the reason is to attenuate liability, then that strategy will not suffice. We see that corporations are still liable, and their members could also subject to criminal laws. AI will not be an exemption (Hallevy, 2015).

If personhood is wanted to be able to name AI as authors or inventors in order to transfer ownership to a human, this can be accomplished without devising such considerations of an AI. In civil law jurisdictions, corporations are never authors; that is reserved for humans only. The law however allows these entities to be rights-holders, owning a copyright title or patent in a derived ownership that most certainly has to be transferred by a human individual or by a group of people. In common law jurisdictions in some circumstances, works generated during the course of an employment can allow authorship to legal persons. So, even though the law could consider AI to be a legal person, for copyrights this does not solve the authorship issue of AI-generated creation or the transfer of such rights. Even without such legal personality in the US, the Ninth Circuit Judge William Fletcher established a precedent[16]:

> It is obvious that an animal cannot function as a plaintiff in the same manner as a juridically competent human being. But we see no reason why Article III [of the US Copyright Act] prevents Congress from authorizing a suit in the name of an animal, any more than it prevents suits brought in the name of *artificial persons* such as corporations, partnerships or trusts, and even ships, or of juridically incompetent persons such as infants, juveniles, and mental incompetents.

---

14 In *Mohammed Salim vs State of Uttarakhand* (2017).
15 In UK Tesco Supermarkets Ltd v Nattrass [1972] AC 153 ("directing mind" theory of corporate liability); in the US in Broward Marine, Inc. v. S/V Zeus, No. 05-23105CIVOSULLIVAN, 2010 WL 427496 (S.D. Fla. Feb. 1, 2010).
16 In *Naruto v. Slater*, 888 F.3d 418, 424 (9th Cir. 2018) (United States) (citing *Cetacean Cmty.*, 386 F.3d at 1175).

This precedent has opened discussion considering that AI might as well be regarded as an artificial person to have standing for lawsuits. If AI has standing, it might as well be able to hold compulsory liability insurance just as property does without any further implications to the system.

Legal personhood for AI is not straightforward. Even if we considered AI-generated works as art, other implications such as freedom of expressions or liability for defamation would have to be considered. One could speculate that even a right to maintenance and care is entailed. This is no longer science fiction; definitely, the law will have to provide answers if AI gets rights such as those of animals and legal personality such as those of corporations. AI most certainly will have to pay taxes as any natural or legal person do. Definitely it will come back to humans acting on behalf of the AI; therefore, is it really necessary? They should remain as tools regardless of its shape. Legal personhood is not necessary.

3 AI inventions in the current IP system

IP refers to creations of the mind which are susceptible to protection through copyrights and IP. The former protects original expressions of scientific, literary, and artistic works independently of registration.[17] Industrial property requires administrative approval to certify exclusive rights on trademarks and trade names and on inventions that can be protected through patents, including in some jurisdictions utility models and designs. IP has been vastly harmonised on its principles by regional directives in the EU and international treaties, most of them administered by WIPO; nonetheless, IP rights are territorial on its application, that is, within the territory for which protection is claimed.

We are experiencing the "Fourth Industrial Revolution" (Schwab and Davis, 2018), and, therefore, the IP system will also have to adapt itself to AI. There is no doubt that AI enhances human performance and capabilities and provides inventions more accurately with less cost and in less time. Difficulty arises when these machines create 'autonomously' circumventing human intervention and imposing real challenge to the IP system, which was created to reward human achievements encouraging innovation and creativity.

There are different opinions regarding protection of AI outputs by patents and copyrights. Some understand that leaving such inventions without protection will hinder innovation since computer-generated outputs result in additional invention (Abbott, 2019, 48). In the European Parliament, proponents pled for AI copyrights (European Parliament, 2020). Nonetheless, this view might impose a risk of having excessive works competing with humans and excessive patents that on the contrary will "stifle, rather than promote, the progress of the useful

---

17 Article 5(2) Berne Convention for the Protection of Literary and Artistic Works 1886 (as amended on 28 September 1979).

arts"[18]; this very approach could lead to disastrous consequences in other contexts, for example, in trade and commerce and economy in general; it has the potential to destroy markets and limit access to essential medicines (Abbott, 2019, 47). Some believe these creations should be available in the public domain (Noto La Diega, 2016). AI does not need motivation to create because it is programmed to do so and potentially its outputs are infinite.

3.1 AI cannot tell the difference: copyright and moral rights

AI systems already write journal articles (*The Guardian*, 2020), generate poems from images create musical compositions and lyrics,[19] paint with Creative Adversarial Networks (CAN), take photographs (Fang and Zhang, n/d), and fabricate images of people (Karras et al., 2020). The difference between art created by a human being and one created by AI does not stand out from one another at sight. The Next Rembrandt[20] exemplifies the latter, and since there is no requirement for registry[21] in copyrights this is an area that could easily be deceiving.

Copyright does not protect ideas, but the expression of such.[22] It is reserved for original works of authorship in literary, scientific, and artistic expressions.[23] In some jurisdictions such as the US and the UK, these expressions are required to be done in a fixable tangible medium[24]; other civil jurisdictions do not require fixation. As consequence of the Berne Convention, all member-states recognise the principle that copyright does not need formalities to exist or registration to be acknowledged. When an original work is created, it emerges with an economic right and a moral right. The former you can transfer, sell, or renounce, but the latter is an unbreakable bond between the author and its work that is perpetual and cannot be assigned. Article 6*bis* of the Berne Convention recognises moral rights and involves protection of the author's personality: the right of integrity (protecting the work from harm due to modifications, mutilations,

---

18 *KSR Int'l Co. v. Teleflex Inc.*, 550 U.S. 398, 427 (2007).
19 A neural net that generates music; see OpenAI, "*Jukebox*" Open AI <https://openai.com/blog/jukebox/> (Accessed 16 September 2020). In particular, *listen* SONY CSL Research Lab "Daddy's Car: A Song Composed by Artificial Intelligence – In the Style of the Beatles" <https://soundcloud.com/user-547260463> (Accessed 16 September 2020); see also Google DeepMind A.I., "*Composes and Performs Piano beyond the Masterpiece Level in Realtime*" <https://www.youtube.com/watch?v=TnUYcTuZJpM> (Accessed 16 September 2020).
20 ING, "The Next Rembrandt" <https://www.nextrembrandt.com> (Accessed 6 October 2020). See also The Next Rembrandt <https://www.youtube.com/watch?v=IuygOYZ1Ngo> (Accessed 6 October 2020).
21 Article 5 (2) Berne Convention.
22 See US Copyright Act 17 U.S.C. § 102 (b).
23 In the UK, literary, dramatic, musical, and artistic (LDMA) works, section 1 of the UK CDPA 1988; article 2 of the Berne Convention; see also 17 U.S.C. § 102 (a) of the US Copyright Act.
24 17 U.S.C. § 101 of the US Copyright Act and 17 U.S.C. § 102(a).

or distortions) characterised as a right to reputation or a personality right and the right of attribution (paternity of the work – being recognised as the author) even if the author has transferred the work and does not own the economic rights. Moral rights are conceived for humans to preserve author's spirits and the authenticity of how the work was conceived. Overall, the expression of the personality of the author should be respected. Vesting moral rights on machines seems absurd. The IP system should never place moral rights on the creations of an AI, just like the UK model for computer-generated works[25] which only have economic rights[26]; therefore, authors (programmers) cannot object to transformation or derivative works.

3.1.1 Originality

In the UK, originality is not defined by CDPA 1988.[27] In *Infopaq*, the ECJ harmonised the standard of originality for all works and concluded that to attract copyright protection, a work needs to be original, namely, the author's "own intellectual creation".[28] Copyright does not protect historical and factual items.[29] AI's writings are produced by the inputs of data fed into it. Arguably, AI alone cannot impregnate its essence without copying it from others, even if the outputs may appear to have some level of originality. AI is trained with others' works to imitate them. That said, the outputs are not less impressive and commercially attractive and are even capable of having some degree of creativity by such mixture of inputs. Humans just like an AI could also be inspired by the works of others. However, that is why works of authorship need to be original in order for them to be protected. Authors have to make it their own. In the EU, in *Painer*,[30] the originality of portrait photographs was discussed. The court held the author needs "to express his creative abilities in the production of the work

---

25 The UK CDPA 1988 model for computer-generated works provides in section 178 that a computer-generated work, in relation to a work, means that the work is generated by computer in circumstances such that there is no human author of the work; section 12 (7) establishes that if work is computer-generated, copyright expires "at the end of the period of 50 years from the end of the calendar year in which the work was made".
26 Moral rights of attribution and integrity do not apply to computer programs or to computer-generated works. Section 81 (2) CDPA 1988 establishes that the right to object to derogatory treatment of work does not apply to a computer program or to any computer-generated work; section 79 (2) (a) and (c) CDPA 1988 establishes that the right to be identified as author or director does not apply to a computer program and any computer-generated work.
27 Before *Infopaq* a work must have originated from the author and its creation must have entailed the expenditure of the author's own "labour, skill and judgement" (*University of London Press Ltd v University Tutorial Press Ltd* (1916)).
28 *Infopaq International A/S v Danske Dagblades Forening* (2009) (C-5/08) (EU:C:2009:465).
29 Article 10.2 TRIPS Agreement.
30 C-145/10 *Eva-Maria Painer v Standard Verlags GmbH and Others* (ECLI:EU:C:2011:798) para 89 and 93.

by making free and creative choices",[31] effectively being able to "stamp the work created with his 'personal touch'".[32] This is not the case with AI.

The US Supreme Court in *Feist*[33] established that in order for a work to be copyrightable that work has to be original and refused to award copyright protection to a telephone book because there was no creativity in the arrangement of the work. The court distinguished factual works created by a sweat-of-brow (labour) efforts which are not protected. The Court defined works are original as long as "they are independently created by the author (as opposed to copy from other works), and that it possesses at least some minimal degree of creativity.... The requisite level of creativity is extremely low; even a slight amount will suffice" as long as it is able to be attributed to an author. The court also clarified that originality does not mean novelty since a work may be original even though it resembles other works as long as the similarity is "fortuitous, not the result of copying" (ibid). Works produced solely by AI seem unable to fulfil this requirement.

International harmonisation regarding protection of AI-generated works is needed (International Association for the Protection of Intellectual Property, 2020, 5); as an example, in China different rulings occurred. An AI's financial report (Tenacent Robot Dreamwriter) was used by a technology company on its website, and the court determined that the article had 'certain originality' and required the defendant to pay a fine (Li, 2020). In another case, in the same country, the Beijing Internet Court decided that only works created by humans could be protected by copyrights and refused authorship of an AI. However, the court analysed originality in an objective perspective, dividing the text from the graphics; the latter were a consequence of data inputs and therefore not original since "different users will get same results with the same data", but the summary report prepared by a software had 'originality to some extent'. The court ruled that originality as a sole requirement does not suffice.[34] Many jurisdictions have regarded that even if the output has some level of originality, the works must have a human author.

3.1.2 Authorship

The authorship issue was discussed in a US case involving a crested macaque named Naruto, who was not able to own the copyright on selfie that he took of himself. Wildlife photographer David Slater set the scene and prepared the

---

31 *Ibid*. at para 89, p. I-12622 and 93, p. I-12623.
32 *Ibid*. at para 92, p. I-12622.
33 *Feist Publications, Inc. v. Rural Telephone Service Co.,* Inc. – 499 U.S. 340, 111 S. Ct. 1282 (1991).
34 *Beijing Feilin Law Firm v Baidu Corporation*, No 239 [2019], Civil First Instance, Beijing Internet Court, 25.
   April 2019 in Chen, M., "Beijing Internet Court Denies Copyright to Works Created Solely by Artificial Intelligence" *Journal of Intellectual Property Law & Practice*, 2019, Vol. 14, No. 8 at 594.

camera, but Naruto took the selfie by itself. Slater claimed that he arranged for it to happen and selected the photos, but this was not sufficient since the actual pictures were not taken by him. Wikimedia Foundation used the pictures and omitted Slater's takedown notices on the grounds that they belong to the public domain since works done by animals are not protected by copyrights. The People for the Ethical Treatment of Animals ('PETA') and Antje Engelhard as 'Next Friends' tried to defend Naruto and filed a complaint on behalf the monkey alleging defendants David Slater and Wildlife Personalities who included the photographs in a book published by Blurb Inc. had violated the monkey's copyrights.[35] US District Court for the Northern District of California dismissed the action, on the grounds that that "the [US] Copyright Act does not 'plainly' extend the concept of authorship or statutory standing to animals". PETA appealed to the Ninth Circuit, which affirmed the district court's ruling in a published opinion. However, Slater was not able to continue to pay legal fees and chose to settle the matter. This case is particularly important for nonhuman authors since it established the precedent. After this case, the US Copyrights Office Compendium now specifically states that it will not register works produced by nature or animals, citing the example of "A photograph taken by a monkey". Equally, the US Copyright Office suggests that protection is not available to "works produced by a machine or mere mechanical process that operates randomly or automatically without any creative input or intervention from a human author".

In the UK, the s.9(3) of the Copyright Design and Patent Act (CDPA) provides that the author of a computer-generated work is the person by whom the arrangements for the creation of the work were undertaken. The act grants the author 50 years protection but does not include moral rights. Similar approach has been taken in New Zealand, South Africa, India, Ireland, and Hong Kong. In the US, Burrow-Giles[36] photographs were perceived as a mechanical process, but the Supreme Court qualified photography as original work of authorship where the use of the camera is a mere tool to aid the photographer to impregnate his idea into a tangible form. One might argue that the creator of the camera does not own all the photographs taken by such device. The reason is, this device is a mere tool which facilitates the art of photography. The same can be said about an AI system. It will enable humans to provide creations. AI in paintings can also be helpful; it can be used to restore art, to help fix and protect the spirits of human authors, but creations done solely by AI should be left in the public domain and there should be harmonisation towards this principle internationally. Humans using AI as tools should be protected, but their contributions must be significant; it should not only be about discovering the outputs or pressing a button. Based on these judgements, we can see AI alone will not assert copyrights. The human factor has always been crucial to IP. For the majority of works, the date

---

35 *Naruto v. Slater*, Case No. 15-cv-04324-WHO (N.D.) Cal. Jan. 28, 2016.
36 *Burrow-Giles Lithographing v. Sarony*, 111 U.S. 53 (1884).

of the author's death is used to calculate the remainder term of validity of the copyrighted works before ruling it to the public domain. Nonetheless, in software, date of publication is taken into account. Therefore, AI-generated works should only assert copyrights if there is a substantial human contribution, provided such outputs are original. AI tools help authors with their creations, from drawings (Google, n/d) to creating novels; it helps authors with story lines and poems (ibid). Without humans, AI lacks passion and purpose; there is no love towards its creation. AI without human conception, direction, and supervision might as well be producing noise. Effectively, it could be said this biblical verse applies to AI: "If I speak in the tongues of men and of angels, but I do not have love, I am only a noisy gong or a clanging cymbal".[37]

The Association for the Protection of Intellectual Property has provided guidance toward substantial contribution for humans to an AI providing that there are efforts by humans for the selection of data (data trainer); however, it is argued that this would be favouring rights based on labour efforts which copyrights have expressly rejected. Then efforts involved in the creative directions and providing instructions to the AI seem more appropriate. Nonetheless in patents, a data trainer could be considered an inventor.

3.1.2.1 WHAT IS BANKSY AND AI?

The copyright system universally protects works of anonymous authors. In the US, EU, and UK anonymous or pseudonymous works are permitted on assumptions as to expiry of copyright or death of author.[38] An "anonymous work" is a work on the copies or phono records of which *no natural person* is identified as author",[39] and a "pseudonymous work" is a work on the copies or phono records whose author is identified under a fictitious name. These principles are granted based on the moral rights of attribution versed in the Berne Convention on the premise that the author does not want to be identified. However, in the context of AI, how does the copyright system should know who the author is as long as these types of works are permitted? This seems to be a total incongruence. The wording 'no natural person' seems like approving nonhuman works. If the system does not need an identity or does not care about who the author is – irrespective if a human being or not – by virtue of vesting the rights in an agent, then why is it that nonhuman creations are not permitted? Understandably, copyrights protect original works, but this might seem a way not to reveal who the real authors are.

3.2 AI as the invention

The IP system provides protection for inventions through patents, but not all inventions are patentable. It is often said that patents are a 'deal' between the

---

37 1 Corinthians 13:1 NIV.
38 Section 57 CDPA 1988.
39 17 U.S.C. § 101 of the US Copyright Act.

society and inventor, where the public agrees to grant a 'monopoly' by exclusive rights for a limited period of time in exchange of disclosure to the patent system, subsequently transferring into open, accessible public domain without costs.[40] Internationally, the grant of patents follows this principle, and, in most jurisdictions, a patent is granted for 20 years. Even if the inventor 'discovered' the invention or emanated by 'accident', it is capable of protection similar to expensive researched and developed inventions. The costs of patents are high for society since it imposes a restriction in competition. Nonetheless, they are deemed to be justified because the benefits of such innovation outweigh any restrictions. For that reason, patent offices need to interpret the requirements very strictly. The examination involves analysing the subject matter as not excluded and that such an invention is new and nonobvious. It also has to be properly disclosed. Moreover, a patent application has been declined by not having a human inventor. The alternative for protection is trade secrets which may be appropriate if security for key information regarding the invention is maintained undisclosed.

In AI, there have been more than 340,000 patent fillings since 1950 (WIPO, 2019). There is need to patent in AI that might be due to an economical factor. A patent is a title of property that sends "a positive message about the state of the firm's research and development" (Schuster, 2018, 1982–1983), which could result in effectively obtaining outside investment (ibid). Other factors include limiting rivals from similar technologies impeding competition.

3.2.1 *Patents*

3.2.1.1 PATENT ELIGIBILITY

AI patent applications have to be examined like any other invention. In the EU, patent eligibility for all inventions is established by article 52(1) of the European Patent Convention (EPC), which states that "inventions must be *new*, involve an *inventive step* and be susceptible of *industrial application*" to be patentable. The industrial applicability standard means the invention is capable of exploitation in an industry[41]; this criterion is not an issue when it comes to patenting an invention.

Patent eligibility for AI is clarified by EPO guidelines (GII 3.3.1) providing that AI and ML are "based on computational models and algorithms such as neural networks, genetic algorithms and support vector machines which are *per se* of an abstract mathematical nature irrespectively they are 'trained' based on

---

40 Failing to pay annual fees can effectively lapse a patent rendering it invalid in the public domain even before the date of expiry. In the UK, the High Court refused to restore a patent that lapsed after the proprietor's failure to pay the renewal fees due to financial difficulties in *Betson Medical (Ireland) Limited v Comptroller General of Patents* [2010] EWHC 687 (Pat).
41 EPO, "*Guidelines for Examination: Chapter II – Content of a European Patent Application (Other than Claims): 4.9 Industrial Application (G-II,4.9)*" <https://www.epo.org/law-practice/legal-texts/html/guidelines/e/f_ii_4_9.htm> (Accessed 10 October 2020).

training data".[42] Mathematical methods and computer software 'as such' are not patentable.[43] However, computer-implemented inventions may be patentable if they have a 'technical purpose' which contributes to the technical character of the invention. The invention should produce a 'technical effect' to solve a 'technical problem' with a 'technical solution'. Depending on how the AI is implemented and the field of its application, it may have a 'technical character' and thus be a patentable invention.[44] As an example, even though 'neural network' according to EPO usually refers to an abstract model lacking of technical character,[45] the use of a neural network in a heart-monitoring apparatus to identify irregular heartbeats makes technical contribution and therefore is patentable. Applying AI to one process of the invention may not suffice the technical effect desired to obtain a patent. Mere classifications of text documents in respect of written content do not provide a technical purpose.[46] Considering how rapidly AI technology is developing, policymakers will have to decide if the current patent subject matter promotes inventions that justify such benefit for society or if the subject matter should be more specific towards AI applications and techniques.

Similarly, in the US, patentable subject matter is limited to "new and useful process, machine, manufacture, or composition of matter, or any new and useful improvement thereof".[47] While each country may have different requirements for patentable subject matter, regularly mere discoveries, scientific theories, and mathematical methods are not patentable.[48] The US Supreme Court ruled that "laws of nature, physical phenomena and abstract ideas" are not patentable in the context of section 101.[49] Patentable subject matter became more rigorous for computer-related inventions in the US after the Supreme Court's decision in *Alice Corporation Pty. Ltd. v. CLS Bank International* establishing a two-part test to determine patent eligibility: (1) Whether the claims are directed

---

42 EPO, *"Guidelines for Examination: 3.3.1. Artificial Intelligence and Machine Learning"* <https://www.epo.org/law-practice/legal-texts/html/guidelines2018/e/gii331.htm> (Accessed 10 October 2020).

43 Article 52 (2) and (3) EPC excludes from patentability the following: "(a) discoveries, scientific theories and mathematical methods; (b) aesthetic creations; (c) schemes, rules and methods for performing mental acts, playing games or doing business, and programs for computers; (d) presentations of information (3) shall exclude the patentability of the subject-matter or activities referred to therein only to the extent to which a European patent application or European patent relates to such subject-matter or activities as such".

44 See EPO, G-II 3.3 *Supra*; see also EPO, *"Request from the United States Patent and Trademark Office for Comments on Patenting Artificial Intelligence Inventions. Comments by the European Patent Office (EPO)"* <https://www.uspto.gov/sites/default/files/documents/European-Patent-Office_RFC-84-FR-44889.pdf> (Accessed 10 October 2020).

45 EPO, G-II 3.3 *Id*.

46 T 1358/09 (*Classification/BDGB ENTERPRISE SOFTWARE*) ECLI:EP:BA:2014:T135809.20141121.

47 Title 35 U.S.C. § 101.

48 *Alice v CLS Bank International* (2014) 135 S. Ct 2347; *Mayo Collaborative Services v Prometheus Labs* (2012) 566 US 66.

49 Title 35 U.S.C. § 101; see also MPEP §2104.

AI and intellectual property 243

to a patent-ineligible concept (e.g. abstract idea or mathematical method) and (2) whether such claimed elements 'as an ordered combination' or individually transform 'the nature of the claim' into a patent-eligible one. In *Alice*, a method of computerised risk mitigation in financial settlements was found to be an 'abstract idea' since risk mitigation is an established "fundamental economic practice" and the claims merely required generic computer implementation.[50] Courts have enforced *Alice's* tests to exclude patent claims of patentable subject matter establishing that those claims could be performed through an "ordinary mental process",[51] "in the human mind",[52] or by "a human using a pen and paper"[53] and therefore not patentable to prevent a complete control of such "... basic tools of scientific and technological work"[54] key to innovation. The US Patent Office (USPTO) has reflected all these jurisprudential developments in its Manual of Patent Examining Procedure.

3.2.1.2 INVENTIVE STEP (NONOBVIOUS)

AI inventions that meet patentable subject matter will have to prove involvement in an inventive step, that is, considering the prior art (all knowledge available, including patent documents, or any document published until the day of patent application)[55] that such invention is "*not obvious* to a *person skilled in the art*".[56] For patents, the EPO defines 'obvious' as not going beyond normal progress of technology but merely logically following from prior art not involving any skill or ability beyond what is expected of the person trained in the art.[57]

In the US, non-obviousness is determined by what a 'hypothetical' person of ordinary skill in the art finds obvious. The skilled person represents the average worker in the scientific field of an invention.[58] If such person who, in theory, possesses all the relevant knowledge of the art at the time of the invention application and finds such invention obvious, then patent will not be granted

---

50 *Alice Corp. v. CLS Bank International*, 134 S. Ct. 2347, 2350 (2014).
51 *Synopsys, Inc. v. Mentor Graphics Corp.*, 78 F. Supp. 3d 958, 963 (N.D. Cal. 20 January 2015) (holding that a mental process is "a subcategory of unpatentable abstract ideas").
52 *Fair Warning IP, LLC v. Iatric Sys., Inc.*, 839 F.3d 1089, 1097 (Fed. Cir. 2016).
53 *Intellectual Ventures I LLC v. Erie Indem. Co.*, No. 2017-1147, 2017 U.S. App. LEXIS 22060, at 6–14.
54 *Mayo Collaborative Servs. v. Prometheus Labs, Inc.*, 132 S. Ct. 1289, 1293–94 (2012) (citing *Gottschalk v. Benson*, 409 U.S. 63, 67 (1972); see also *Alice*, 134 S. Ct. at 2354.
55 EPO, "Guidelines for Examination: 3.1 Common General Knowledge of the Skilled Person (G-VII,3.1)" <https://www.epo.org/law-practice/legal-texts/html/guidelines/e/g_vii_3_1.htm> (Accessed 6 October 2020).
56 Art. 56 EPC (emphasis added) ("involving an inventive step if, having regard to the state of the art, it is *not obvious* to a *person skilled in the art*").
57 EPO, "Guidelines for Examination: Chapter VII Inventive Step, 4. Obviousness (G-VII,4)" <https://www.epo.org/law-practice/legal-texts/html/guidelines/e/g_vii_4.htm> (Accessed 6 October 2020).
58 Title 35 U.S.C. Subpart I.D.

because it does not advance the prior art.[59] In the US Supreme Court provided a non-restrictive list of rationales to determine obviousness.[60] The skilled person standard varies according to the field; depending on the invention's complexity, the skilled person may be highly educated and sophisticated.[61] In the EU, the skilled person might also be a team.[62] Some commentators agree that the non-obviousness requirement ensures that technical achievement in the face of uncertainty – where there is no assurance of success – is more likely to merit the exclusive rights (Merges, 1992).

3.2.1.3 DISCLOSURE AND THE BLACK BOX EFFECT

The EU and the US have mandatory disclosure requirements which impose an additional challenge for AI inventions. Regarding the invention, it must be disclosed in a "manner sufficiently clear and complete for it to be carried out by a person skilled in the art".[63] Similarly in the US, inventions shall contain "a written description of the invention, and of the manner and process of making and using it, in such full, clear, concise, and exact terms as to enable any person skilled in the art to which it pertains to make and use".[64] For AI tools, making such disclosure may be particularly impossible. Often AI suffers from a black box effect, or algorithm opacity, meaning that the process of obtaining the invention is unknown to the human contributor or supervisor. Even if that person recognised the output, the process could not be explained sufficiently clearly and concisely by this person. Moreover, because ML algorithms have the ability to change and alter their own code and characteristics for specific tasks – perceived as one of the major breakthroughs of this technology – 'inner workings' are opaque or incomprehensible to humans to visualise patterns due to the layers of deep neural networks even for experts in the field (Knight, 2017). Some innovators may use several ML algorithms to obtain numerous answers to the same problem, adding even more complexity. This black box effect also presents hurdles for obviousness and patent eligibility requirements since it is impossible to distinguish relevant features of the invention to claim it thus unable to comply with clear disclosure requirements in patents (Bathaee, 2018). IP system should advocate for an explainable method – DARPA's XAI is a proposition where ML techniques would be able to maintain its performance capabilities

---

59 The "person having ordinary skill in the art" abbreviated by most US academics as "PHOSITA". See Title 35 U.S.C. § 103(a).
60 *KSR Int'l Co. v. Teleflex Inc.*, 550 U.S. (2007) at 418.
61 *Imperial Chem. Indus., PLC v. Danbury Pharmacal, Inc.*, 777 F. Supp. 330, 371 (D. Del. 1991).
62 EPO, "Guidelines for Examination: 3. Person Skilled in the Art" (G-VII, 3) ("There may be instances where it is more appropriate to think in terms of a group of persons, e.g. a research or production team, rather than a single person") <https://www.epo.org/law-practice/legal-texts/html/guidelines/e/g_vii_3.htm> (Accessed 6 October 2020).
63 Article 83 of the EPC.
64 Title 35 U.S.C. § 103 and 112(a).

and will enable humans to understand, trust, and manage AI effectively. Other proponents encourage XAI fairness and accountability without any prior bias.

In biotechnology,[65] the patent system has adapted to allow inventions in this area. It is argued that similarly patent offices can ask the inventor to employ "product-by-process"[66] disclosure focusing on the process (e.g. the methods and steps for the production of the starting material)[67] provided the resultant product is patentable subject matter; in such a case, protection extends to product as well.[68] Arguably this can also be done with ML algorithms. It has been proposed to include a deposit for algorithms, similar to the one of microorganisms, and the data used to train the algorithm should be included in the disclosure as well. This commentator also suggests that for patent renewal, which has to be done yearly, algorithm should be deposited to keep track of any changes in hopes of transparency (Noto La Diega, 2019).

Failure to disclose the true names of inventors can later render a patent invalid, and changing such information cannot be easily done.[69] However, this only applies to humans. Some argue that a new requirement should be put in place for applicants that make it mandatory to disclose when a machine contributes to the 'conception' of an invention, which is the standard to qualify as an inventor (Abbott, 2019, 6). This requirement will reveal how inventions are created in a field – if the majority of are done by people or machines – in order to develop appropriate innovation policies.

3.2.1.4 SKILLED PERSON OR MACHINE

The skilled person could also mean skilled human using a machine (Abbott, 2016, 1126) to enhance the examiners' work in prior art search results. Skilled machines are no longer an assumption. WIPO is using an AI-empowered tool for IP administration. A "state-of-the-art neural machine translation tool" enables image search for trademarks, delivering accurate, expedited results (2018). WIPO is also exploring other AI applications' development using training data

---

65 Article 53(b) EPC states that plants and animals are not patentable, but articles 4 (2) and (3) of the Directive 98/44/EC of the European Parliament and of the Council of 6 July 1998 on the legal protection of biotechnological inventions) express that: "2. Inventions which concern plants or animals shall be patentable if the technical feasibility of the invention is not confined to a particular plant or animal variety".

3. Paragraph 1(b) shall be without prejudice to the patentability of inventions which concern a microbiological or other technical process or a product obtained by means of such a process".

66 Article 64(2) of the EPC states that the protection conferred by a patent for a process shall extend to the product obtained by that process. Therefore, the patentee will still have protection to the product obtained. See also *T 0020/94 (Amorphous TPM/ Enichem)* ECLI:EP:BA:199 8:T002094.19981104.

67 *T0642/14 (Epichlorohydrin production/SOLVAY)* ECLI:EP:BA:2018:T064214.20180507.

68 EPO, "Guidelines for Examination: 4.12 Product-by-Process Claim (G-IV 4.12)".

69 *Egenera v. Cisco Systems* (Fed. Cir. (D. Mass.) (2020).

provided by member-states and patent offices to exchange such AI applications that benefit from data input of such institutions to improve systems (ibid). There are concerns over using AI-skilled machines as examiners since they will learn from innovations and will be able to predict future outcomes potentially rendering "everything obvious" (Abbott, 2019, 31). The more capable the skilled person is, the more they will find patent claims obvious. It will result in stricter patentability measures by continuously raising the bar for innovations and, thus, making patents harder to obtain (ibid). However, even though this is a possibility, inventions will still occur. Commercial motivations are a huge driver for innovation, and consumers will have their preferred choices even if patent protections are not asserted. Alternatives as trade secrets and contractual obligations will always be available.

AI is already assisting in the administrative processing of patent offices and helps applicants to do the patent application filing correctly (World Economic Forum, 2018, 6) and thus improving the filing's quality. Therefore, AI is becoming an integral part of the innovation cycle. AI is involved in the creative process; it also helps fills the patent applications and potentially will be examining the application as well (ibid). If such an AI examiner becomes a reality, it could finally digest all the volumes of data that patent applications create – remembering every possible invention, capable of reproducing them and predicting inputs of the patent application disclosure, depending on transparency and proper filing disclosure. It is from this patent office AI examiner that an AGI and subsequent ASI could be envisioned – a super intelligent AI in custody of all of our human advancements.

The skilled machines need to be up to date with the world's latest patent applications. In fact, all patent offices should give data inputs to such AI. Patents are granted territorially; however, novelty is against the world. Having the patent office nurture the AI system could make it more efficient. In a public consultation for the USPTO, commentators argued that registry offices should be transparent with their customers when they use specific AI tools in examination and this should remain the case in other official proceedings as well. A patent applicant ought to know a machine will be the examiner.

3.2.2 Trade secrets

Trade secrets can protect any useful information, regardless if it is patent-eligible or not. Trade secrets are the best option for protection when patent eligibility is not clear (Sankers, 2020, 46) especially for software considered abstract ideas. Trade secret is best for inventions that cannot be reverse-engineered or independently discovered. In the EU, trade secrets protect information that meets requirements of article 2 of the Trade Secrets Directive.[70] Such information requires taking reasonable measures to keep it secret. In the US, there is a

---

70 Article 2 of the Trade Secrets Directive (EU) 2016/943.

possibility of hybrid approach not available in other jurisdictions which seems reasonable. This approach enables applicant to issue a non-publication request; thus, patent filling can be done without risk of disclosure. If patent is allowed, owner can effectively pay the fees and obtain its patent certificate. If not allowed, then the owner can continue protecting its invention as a trade secret (ibid). An invention can effectively have both protections, meaning that patent may protect the technical features of the AI and the trade secret may protect the know-how associated with that invention.[71] Trade secrets are not subject to limited time period (e.g. Coca-Cola's formula is secret since it was created in 1886), just as long as the information remains secret. However, the protection is only against unlawful appropriation or disclosure. Like any other IP rights, trade secrets have limitations, meaning that if a mere discovery of the secret information happens or reverse engineering occurs by working 'backward' on a product legally obtained[72] then the protection ceases.

In the EU, computer software legally obtained can be reverse-engineered by doing experiments and observing its performance[73] not subject to the author's authorisation. Techniques in the software industry have enabled programmers to reverse-engineer the computer-readable code, known as 'object code', into a readable and understandable language to programmers, thus potentially recreating the so-called source code. Even if source code is kept secret, there could be a legitimate discovery through access of the object code (LaRoque, 2017, 438–439). There are limitations to the decompilations[74] (or reverse engineering) of software described in article 6 of the Directive 91/250.[75] Another limitation to trade secret is that it allows employees to leave for new employments with their general knowledge and skills; sometimes these are related to the information protected. Therefore, risks of disclosure may dissuade AI inventors from trade secrecy protection over patents or copyrights. Particularly in software where knowledgeable programmers could emigrate to other software or IT firms, relying exclusively on trade secrets is a risk. Nonetheless, AI inventions could operate with very 'highly complex doors' which potentially assert efficient protection indefinitely. Moreover, if algorithms change themselves and automation means no more employment rotation, the secrecy is even more 'robust' because it limits the knowledge that can potentially incentivise competition by lawful limitations to trade secrets. Some commentators argue this protection is disproportionate and should be limited for AI software (Fromer, 2019, 727). However, it is disputed that before limiting AI developers or owners the only protection mechanism available to them, policymakers will have to evaluate

71 Directive (EU) 2016/943 of the European Parliament and of the Council of 8 June 2016 on the protection of undisclosed know-how and business information (trade secrets) against their unlawful acquisition, use, and disclosure.
72 Unif. Trade Secrets Act § 1 cmt., 14 U.L.A. 539 (1985).
73 EU Directive 2009/24/EC, article 5, paragraph 3.
74 See section 50B of the UK Copyright, Designs and Patents Act 1988.
75 In the case C-406/10 *SAS Institute Inc. v World Programming Ltd.* (ECLI:EU:C:2012:259).

the benefits of disclosure and assert a mechanism of protection rethinking and balancing society's needs with that of the inventors.

3.3 AI as the inventor

Under the current regime, AI cannot be an inventor. The law does not recognise AI as creators and therefore not able to own and hold property.[76] For this to happen, it is necessary to recognise legal personhood to AI. The question of whether inventions created by AI should be patentable or not and if AI should be named as the inventor or author has been discussed by governments and international organisations.[77] The concept of inventorship is associated with humans. In the EU, article 81 EPC establishes that patent applications shall designate the inventor. Nonhumans are not contemplated in the designation of inventor.[78] In the UK, an inventor according to the Patent Act 1977 is required to be a person in line with section 3 of the Act – "where a *person* has been mentioned as sole or joint inventor".[79] In the US, 35 U.S.C. § 100 defines "inventor" as "the *individual* or, if a joint invention, the individuals collectively who invented or discovered the subject matter of the invention".[80] Furthermore, 35 U.S.C. § 116 provides that an invention may be made done jointly by two or more *persons* even though "(1) they did not physically work together or at the same time, (2) each did not make the same type or amount of contribution, or (3) each did not make a contribution to the subject matter of every claim of the patent". Therefore, it is clear that under the current framework only a natural person can be an inventor.[81] However, this does not mean that a legal person cannot be a patent owner, but such title vests first on the inventor who could then assign the right by a transfer of patent ownership in writing.[82] Many scholars have regarded that

---

76 *Stephen L Thaler v. The Comptroller-General of Patents, Designs And Trade Marks* [2020] EWHC 2412 (Pat) at para 3.
77 EPO, "Artificial Intelligence" <https://www.epo.org/news-events/in-focus/ict/artificial-intelligence.html>; European Commission, "Artificial Intelligence" <https://ec.europa.eu/digital-single-market/en/artificial-intelligence>; UK IPO, "Artificial Intelligence and Intellectual Property: Call for Views" <https://www.gov.uk/government/consultations/artificial-intelligence-and-intellectual-property-call-for-views>; USPTO "Artificial Intelligence" <https://www.uspto.gov/initiatives/artificial-intelligence>; WIPO, "Artificial Intelligence and Intellectual Property"<https://www.wipo.int/about-ip/en/artificial_intelligence/>; WEF, "Shaping the Future of Technology Governance: Artificial Intelligence and Machine Learning"<https://www.weforum.org/platforms/shaping-the-future-of-technology-governance-artificial-intelligence-and-machine-learning> (Accessed 12 October 2020).
78 Rule 19 Designation of the inventor EPC.
79 Section 13, UK Patent Act 1977.
80 Title 35 U.S.C. § 100 (f) and (g).
81 Title 35 USC § 100(f) and (g); *Beech Aircraft v EDO*, 990 F.2d 1237, 1248 (Fed Cir 1993) and MPEP § 2137.01.
82 See *Univ. of Utah v. Max-Planck-Gesellschaft Zur Forderung Der Wissenschaften E.V.*, 734 F.3d 1315, 1323 (Fed. Cir. 2013). See also *New Idea Farm Equip. Corp. v. Sperry Corp.*, 916 F.2d 1561, 1566 n.4 (Fed. Cir.1990).

the traditional patent system is no longer appropriate to AI (Yanisky-Ravid and Jin, 2020). Some understand that the system can subsist (Lauber-Rönsberg and Hetmank, 2019) and, historically, it has indeed adapted to other inventions; namely, photography, databases, computer programs, and biotechnology. Other scholars claim that AI-generated outputs should go to the public domain (Noto La Diega, 2016) and therefore allowed to be used without authorisation. It also has been argued that since machines need no incentives to create anything, the public should freely benefit from their creations.

3.3.1 DABUS

The Device for the Autonomous Bootstrapping of Unified Sentience (DABUS) is an example of a patent capable of making other patented inventions. DABUS is an AI creative machine[83] that generates inventions using neural networks without human intervention. Its creator, Dr Stephen Thaler, has been inventing Creative Machines (CM) since early 1994 and obtaining patents for it.[84] According to Thaler, DABUS is a 'different proposition' from the other CM; "the enormous difference between ... DABUS [and the other CM] is that ideas are not represented by the 'on-off' patterns of neuron activations, but by ... ephemeral structures or shapes formed by chains of nets that are rapidly materializing and dematerializing" (n/d). The US patent, relating to the cross-bristle design of the Oral-B CrossAction toothbrush, is the first-known patent to be issued by an AI.[85] However, Thaler listed himself as the sole inventor and did not disclose the involvement of DABUS to the USPTO in the patent application (Abbott, 2016, 1085). The Invention Machine is another example of an AI invented by John Koza based on genetic programming capable of solving complex engineering problems with virtually no human guidance. This invention is said to be the creator of US Patent No. 6,847,851 on 25 January 2005,[86] a system using

---

83 US Patent No. 7,454,388 (Device for the autonomous bootstrapping of useful information) on 18 November 2008, USPTO Patent Full Text and Image Database <http://patft.uspto.gov/netacgi/nph-Parser?Sect1=PTO2&Sect2=HITOFF&p=1&u=%2Fnetahtml%2FPTO%2Fsearch-bool.html&r=1&f=G&l=50&col=AND&d=PTXT&s1=7454388.PN.&OS=PN/7454388&RS=PN/7454388> (Accessed 4 October 2020).

84 US Patent No. 5,659,666 (filed on 13 October 1994) Device for the autonomous generation of useful information, USPTO Patent Full Text and Image Database <http://patft.uspto.gov/netacgi/nph-Parser?Sect1=PTO2&Sect2=HITOFF&p=1&u=%2Fnetahtml%2FPTO%2Fsearch-bool.html&r=1&f=G&l=50&col=AND&d=PTXT&s1=5659666.PN.&OS=PN/5659666&RS=PN/5659666> (Accessed 4 October 2020).

85 US Patent No. 5,852,815 (filed 15 May 1998) Neural network based prototyping system and method, USPTO Patent Full Text and Image Database http://patft.uspto.gov/netacgi/nph-Parser?Sect1=PTO1&Sect2=HITOFF&d=PALL&p=1&u=%2Fnetahtml%2FPTO%2Fsrchnum.htm&r=1&f=G&l=50&s1=5,852,815.PN.&OS=PN/5,852,815&RS=PN/5,852,815 (Accessed 4 October 2020).

86 See U.S. Patent No. 6,847,851 (filed 12 July 2002) Apparatus for Improved General-Purpose PID and Non-PID Controllers (circuit designed by a genetic programming algorithm), USPTO Patent Full Text and Image Database <http://patft.uspto.gov/netacgi/nph-Parser?-

genetic algorithms that optimises efficiency and minimise emissions, therefore making factories more productive, but Koza never disclosed that and listed himself, Keane, and Streeter as co-inventors.

In 2018, Dr Thaler filed on his own name two patent applications in the UK[87] but stated in the same application that he was not the inventor of either inventions. Upon request of the UK's Intellectual Property Office (UKIPO), Thaler filed the statement of inventorship and of right to grant a patent for both applications establishing that DABUS was the true inventor of both patents and that he had the right to the patents by being its successor in title, by virtue of ownership of the creative machine. Both patents were rejected by the UKIPO. On an oral hearing UKIPO decided DABUS did not comply with the definition of an inventor for the purposes of section 13 of the UK Patents Act 1977 and as a non-person could not transfer ownership either. The decision was appealed, and the High upheld UKIPO's decision[88] on the same grounds and reconsidered section 7 of the UK Patent Act 1977 – the right to apply and obtain a patent.[89] Dr Thaler's applications were also rejected by the EPO[90] and the USPTO[91] which denied on the same grounds – that an AI machine cannot be considered a natural person.

3.3.2 Inventorship and ownership

To determine inventorship, US courts pose the question of who has actual contribution to the 'conception of the invention' especially in cases where there are several persons involved.[92] The conceiver normally gives 'physical structure or operative steps'[93] to those members reducing it to practice. Members who acted

---

Sect1=PTO1&Sect2=HITOFF&d=PALL&p=1&u=%2Fnetahtml%2FPTO%2Fsrchnum.htm&r=1&f=G&l=50&s1=6,847,851.PN.&OS=PN/6,847,851&RS=PN/6,847,851>(Accessed 4 October 2020).

87 GB1816909.4 (a food container with a special-shaped lid designed for robotic gripping) and GB1818161.0 (a search and rescue beacon with a flashlight system for attracting human attention in emergencies).

88 UKIPO Decision: BL O/741/19 was upheld by Justice Marcus Smith in *Stephen L Thaler v. The Comptroller-General of Patents, Designs And Trade Marks* [2020] EWHC 2412 (Pat).

89 Justice Marcus Smith in *Stephen L Thaler v. The Comptroller-General of Patents, Designs and Trade Marks* [2020] EWHC 2412 (Pat) considered section 7 of the Patent Act 1977 at para 26.

90 EPO, "EPO Publishes Grounds for Its Decision to Refuse Two Patent Applications Naming a Machine as Inventor" <https://www.epo.org/news-events/news/2020/20200128.html>; see EP3563896 – Devices and Methods for Attracting Enhanced Attention <https://register.epo.org/application?number=EP18275174#blank> and EP3564144- Food Container <https://register.epo.org/application?number=EP18275163#blank> (Accessed 4 October 2020).

91 USPTO, "Decision on Petition: In Re Application of Application No.16/524,350 (Filed July 29, 2019) Attorney Docket Number: 50567-3-01-US for Devices and Methods for Attracting Enhanced Attention" <https://www.uspto.gov/sites/default/files/documents/16524350_22apr2020.pdf (Accessed 4 October 2020).

92 *In re Hardee*, 223 USPQ 1122, 1123 (Comm'r Pat. 1984) (a person who shares in the conception of a claimed invention is a joint inventor of that invention).

93 MPEP § 2109 Inventorship [R-10.2019].

following the direction and supervision of conceivers are not considered inventors.[94] Unless a person contributes to the conception of the invention, traditionally they cannot be recognised as an inventor.[95] Conception has been defined as the formation 'in the mind of the inventor'.[96] Similarly in the UK, Lord Hoffmann, in *Yeda*, defined the inventor as "the actual deviser of the invention"… "the natural person who 'came up with the inventive concept'".[97]

This could also be interpreted that DABUS, in the eyes of Thaler, as a conception occurred when he envisioned it for the purposes of creating more inventions. He programmed it and structured it with that chief objective in mind. In his mind, DABUS exists to reproduce creativity. Conception should follow DABUS creations because it is part of his purpose. Therefore, Thaler should be considered inventor of DABUS extensions of creativity. If you planted and nurtured a plant in your property, you are also the owner of the fruits yielded by the plant. If we interpret US common law on AI, they follow orders and commands. Even applying ML or DL, machines still depend on humans. AI technology was at its infancy when she said this, but the statement remains relevant. In *re DeBaun*, it was established that "there is no requirement that the inventor be the one to reduce the invention to practice so long as the reduction to practice *was done on his behalf*".[98] AI is creating on behalf of a human where the ownership could remain within that human or legal person. The AI invents through commanded instructions. In that sense, AI was programmed by humans to act as a tool, for which humans supervise its outputs and inputs to ensure its functionality. Justice Smith stated what could be argued should enact policy towards AI:

> In some instances of machine invention, a natural person might qualify as an inventor by virtue of having exhibited inventive skill in *developing a program* to solve a particular problem, or by *skilfully selecting data* to provide to a machine, or by *identifying the output of a machine as inventive*.[99]

The solution for AI inventions is to entrust the rights of AI's creations to the owner of the invention. DABUS invented 'on behalf of' Thaler and therefore should have remained the inventor. It is understood that Thaler is the owner of DABUS as well as its programmer, user, and its trainer. Difficulty could arise in

---

94 *Fritsch v. Lin*, 21 USPQ2d 1737, 1739 (Bd. Pat. App. & Inter. 1991).
95 *Fiers v. Revel*, 984 F.2d 1164, 1168, 25 USPQ2d 1601, 1604-05 (Fed. Cir. 1993).
96 *Burroughs Wellcome*, 40 F.3d at 1228.
97 *Yeda Research and Development Company Limited v Rhone-Poulenc Rorer International Holdings Inc and others* [2007] UKHL 43 at 20.
98 *In re DeBaun*, 687 F.2d 459, 463 (C.C.P.A. 1982).
99 *Stephen L Thaler v. The Comptroller-General of Patents, Designs and Trade Marks* [2020] EWHC 2412 (Pat) at para 5.

the commercialisation of AI or when these functions are not embodied in one person. Therefore, ownerships of AI creations are complex.

3.3.3 Candidates for ownership

Throughout this chapter, it has been established that ownership to the AI itself is not possible. It should not be possible. Giving legal personhood to an object can open discussions in other areas of the law. AI is a tool with purpose, either to create innovations on behalf of humans or to give companionship, but it is not a living being that feels and suffers or comprises of humans such as corporations. The IP system can adjust to give protection to different types of works such as *sui generis* rights to databases and computer programs – extensions that TRIPS gave to the Berne Convention[100] – however, it would not impose personhood and change long-established judicial precedents and principles. To conceive that is to think that every possible jurisdiction on earth would adapt its laws and change its constitutions. Bureaucratically and practically it is impossible. Organisations such as WIPO can promote a specialised treaty that can make extensions of the ownership concepts in patents and copyrights of AI outputs. To ask for more is to be naïve. Regarding liability to AI, it should also extend to the person in control with the duty to supervise. Any owner of such invention who tries to exempt responsibility by giving personhood to an AI is admitting that some rights will not be respected. One could argue that other humans may have assertions of AI-generated works' copyrights and industrial property rights: programmers or developers, data trainer, owners, or end-users. If the AI is not owned, trained, programmed, and used by the same person then there should be legal certainty for its commercialisation. Many scholars have regarded that policy should consider the overall social benefit and promotion of innovation to see who it would serve best.

3.3.3.1 WORK FOR HIRE

AI is comprised of computer software; therefore, the programmer is prima facie the inventor or author for being responsible for the creation of the AI since computer software is also protected by copyrights. In some jurisdictions, computer software is considered work-for-hire. Even though programmers had the conception of such work and executed it, the law presumes ownership to the institution responsible for funding the development of the AI where the programmers were ordered to carry out development throughout the course of employment. Common law is perceived more capitalist than civil law jurisdictions whose *droit the auteur* (author's rights) conceive a more romantic author whose moral rights ought to be protected perpetually. In common law, the work-for-hire doctrine

---

100 Directive 96/9/EC of the European Parliament and of the Council of 11 March 1996 on the legal protection of databases (Database Directive) gives exclusive right independently of the copyright system.

bestows ownership to the employer for the creative works of employees made under the scope of employment. In some common law jurisdictions, such as the UK and civil law jurisdictions, exceptions are made regarding ownership based on the work at issue, but the parties have the liberty to agree and assign ownership of the works.

Civil law jurisdictions such as those in France, Spain, Germany, and China are inclined to favour the author vesting the authorship and ownership of works on the person (or persons) who creates the work. The authorship never vests on the corporation since it is understood that a person does the creative work. Corporations can have a derived ownership as a result of assignment. In case there is no agreement for the transfer of ownership or an employment contract that contemplates that, then the law interprets that the author is the owner. However, in civil law jurisdictions, the law creates work-for-hire presumptions for certain types of collaborative works such as films and sound recordings and computer software vesting the rights in the owner. For audio-visual works, the law presumes in civil jurisdictions joint authorships but leaves the possibility to be regulated by contract.

In the US, programmers, as independent contractors, are also deemed eligible for made-for-hire ownership. The commissioner of the work can also be hired for a service but will also have to contemplate the ownership of such works in writing. The programmer, or in some cases joint authorship between the trainer and the programmer, seems to be the best candidate for authorship in the interests of fostering innovation. Some commentators have suggested that the term 'employee' should be reinterpreted to include AI and assign ownership through work-for-hire (Hristov, 2017, 450) and avoid such creations to fall in the public domain. However, it is not a collective principle applicable to all jurisdictions. AI cannot assign rights. First, it cannot assign something that was never vested in it. Second, it does not have legal personhood to be contracted as an employee. What is possible is to amend the laws to make a special regime for AI works, just like UK CDPA does with computer-generated works, and extend it to all IP systems. The law has to vest such rights that facilitate the AI producing the invention or original works of authorship.

3.3.3.2 PROGRAMMERS, USERS, AND DATA TRAINERS

For AI works, it should be decided if these works will remain with programmers or end-users. For instance, a camera takes automatic pictures, but the inventor of the device is not the owner of those pictures. Photographs are works of authorship that are vested in the photographer and hence the end-user. However, it can be said that automation is not the same as autonomous. Cameras do not take photos when they desire. Therefore, users operating AI should pay licenses to create. If they use the default algorithms, then works do not belong to this user. If the user develops a new, completely different algorithm and inputs data in the machine, they become a programmer. In pursuing for a patent, then, it could be argued if a utility patent is applicable because the base invention that is being improved existed previously. Otherwise end-users are just pressing buttons and hence the law should not promote this considering how detrimental it has been on slave-owning societies' institutionalisation of slavery (Gunke, 2017, 8). Imagining AI robots[101] creating for end-users for moral and ethical purposes should not be permitted since they do not have merits over such creations. The law should also consider scenarios where a joint authorship will emerge if users and programmers jointly contribute either for copyright or for patents.

Data trainers cannot have copyrights and thus do not qualify in our view as inventors because a data trainer is virtually feeding AI facts that are not copyrightable; copyrights are granted based on the sweat-of-brow efforts. Is it the same as factory workers classifying products being called artists? The IP law does not protect data; what it protects is the expression subject to originality of such data and compilations like databases with some degree of originality in the classification and organisation of the data.[102] Data as such should not be owned by anyone. Protecting data as such would be like monopolising ideas.

3.4 Liability

Opacity also presents risk for infringements. The AI system can "break data into electronic nano components and rebuild it in different ways" (Hickman, 2009, 115), diluting proof of infringement and making it difficult to establish. If policymakers remain silent about this, they are potentially enabling it to happen; considering patent infringement is a strict liability offense, the obstruction of justice opposes what a responsible patent system should promote. Commentators who argue in favour of legal personhood for AI establish that it is not fair for the human contributor to be liable for offenses that arguably they did not commit and therefore the AI itself should be held responsible (Burk, 2020, 12). However, it is also argued that AI only follows its programming; therefore, if limits can be put in place for such machine, they can obey.

Even if ML changes algorithms, humans are still responsible for feeding into AI system data biases that the AI system then takes into account. Humans have a degree of control over such tasks the machine does with the data it receives as input. This is simplifying the copyrights matter since humans can ask for authorisation to nurture the AI with licensed works. Even though this presents practical hurdles and economic difficulties for start-ups finances, it is the correct process and justified for the artists. AI training data should be available

---

101 The term "robot" in Czech language is "serf labour", which appeared in the 1920 R.U.R. (Rossumovi Univerzální Roboti [Rossum's Universal Robots]), a science fiction play by the Czech writer Karel Čapek; see Jordan, J., "The Czech Play That Gave Us the Word 'Robot'" *MIT Press Reader* <https://thereader.mitpress.mit.edu/origin-word-robot-rur/> (Accessed 10 October 2020).
102 See *Feist Publications, Inc., v. Rural Telephone Service Co.*, 499 U.S. 340, 348 (1991); see Directive 96/9/EC of the European Parliament and of the Council of 11 March 1996 on the legal protection of databases (Article 1(2)).

for reasonable prices considering that the data would be applied by a private individual to create art or innovations. Meanwhile, artists deserve to financially benefit since the AI produces results for the economic gain of their owners. Potentially, AI collective societies can be created to serve as intermediaries to facilitate the process of identifying the correct titleholders and compensation for such works. If liability in patents emerges from an AI creating an already patented invention, then it should not be considered an infringement if the AI owner does not exploit such invention commercially or use it for commercial interests without a license.

In *Bowman v. Monsanto*,[103] self-replicated GMO seeds were used to harvest crops bypassing the patent owner. Court ruled that the farmers could not use the soybean from the community grain and raise them as crops because it amounted to a replication of the patented technology.[104]

The US Supreme Court said that the "blame-the-bean defense [was] tough to credit". Bowman was not "a passive observer of his soybeans' multiplication".[105] He was responsible for planting and nurturing them; thus he was accountable for making them and using the invention in violation of Monsanto's rights. Self-replicating beans were not found guilty themselves, but their human supervisor. It is also argued with regards to AI inventions in light of this case that they seem to be autonomous and spontaneous, that they depend on a human who feeds them data, supplies the electrical power, initiates the device, and gives them regular maintenance. *Mutatis Mutandis* it could be said about an AI device that it would "not generate any kind of output without human initiation". AI creators could argue that they should receive the right to exclude others from using the second-generation knowledge to ensure the first-generation AI is created (Gabison, 2019, 5). In the UK, an analogy to non-dangerous species in section 2(2) of the Animals Act 1976 could be brought to apply to AI in order to identify liability when there is likelihood of damage done[106] if the AI had likely breached a third party's right or inflicted harm and the owner or developer had not put in systemic restraints in order not to infringe. This is especially so if such AI characteristics were already known to the owner, developer, or user (or the person in charge).

4 Conclusion: a special regime for AI within IP

The IP system has adapted to accommodate new types of technology throughout the years. Computer programs are an example of works that were not included in the Berne Convention, but now they qualify as work of authorship

---

103 *Bowman v. Monsanto Co., 569 U.S. 278* (2013); 133 S.Ct. 1761 (2013).
104 *Ibid.* 1768–69.
105 *Ibid.* at 288.
106 Section 2(2) of the UK Animals Act 1976.

protected within article 2.[107] The Berne Convention[108] itself is a result of the instigation of authors, in particular Victor Hugo, founder of the Association Littéraire et Artistique Internationale (ALAI), after Guttenberg's printing press facilitated unauthorised reproductions. Therefore, the convention emerged as a necessity for international harmonisation to exercise ownership rights across borders. Nevertheless, AI advocates continue to argue for AI's inclusion in the agenda of policymakers.

Human inventors using only their brain, skills, and bare hands cannot compete with AI capabilities to digest all the data in an expedited manner. IBM's Watson for example exceeds any standard since it analyses a patient's complete genome and prepares a clinically actionable report in 10 minutes, rather than the regular 160 hours of work of a team of experts. AstraZeneca is using AI for drug discovery to treat cancer. Therefore, this technology is definitely beneficial. However, patent system has to level the playing field between AI-aided, AI-generated, and single humans. This can be done by reducing the years of protection. Duration of patents in most jurisdictions is 20 years. AI patents should have a shorter duration. Design rights for instance in most jurisdictions are allowed for a period five years, which is renewable for two periods of equal duration. It is argued that AI patents can be protected for five years with one renewable period of equal duration for a total of ten years. Technology evolves very rapidly, which means that individuals will no longer be able to pass the threshold of novelty and obviousness without AI. However, just like 3D printers, the development of such technology had to await the expiry of the patent. Therefore, individuals will have to wait for this to use AI and compete. Therefore, the years of protection cannot be equal in unequal settings.

Patents are not being discouraged, even though AI-generated outputs are not protected. Therefore, if they are able to be protected – for a less number of years – it would continue to foster innovation. Utility patents are another category of patents that are granted to useful improvements that advances prior art of former developments patented or not. Therefore, the inventive step requirements are less rigorous and protected for less number of years. Arguably, AI emerges from data available in the prior art and, in a similar logic, as utility patents; they should be protected even if they are autonomously (or through automation) created. AI is essential to innovation, and the patent system has to rethink itself to see the possibility of granting patents for AI inventions irrespective of who is considered the inventor. It is a possibility that in the future patents will not be entirely new and nonobvious. They will emerge from prior art just like utility patents do, but they are always going to be needed to perfect our inventions.

---

107 They are also protected under the copyright laws of a number of jurisdictions as well as under the *WIPO Copyright Treaty* (WCT) (1996).
108 Article 10.1 of the TRIPS Agreement.

A special regime for AI patents as a 'new layer' of the IP system is a possibility just like *sui generis* rights for databases or plants' patents. Requirements for disclosure should be imposed in order to determine the AI involvement similar to disclosure requirements in other areas; failing to do so will also render AI patent invalid. Algorithms will have to be disclosed as well and the training data, but this information should remain secret until patent expires. In other areas, data openness is also promoted in order to determine ethical perspectives and analyse biases (ibid). A human inventor is required to disclose everything regarding the inventions to make possible the reproduction of such. With AI, training data is part of those instructions to reproduce the invention as the original prototype.

By that same logic, patent offices must know how that algorithm is trained to be able to learn. The patent system aims to promote innovation which translates into economic and social benefits for society and should be able to keep a registry of all the inventions of humanity to secure such advancements for future generations. WIPO should also promote compulsory licences for algorithms in order to keep fostering innovations since such algorithms may also be protected through copyrights with different years of duration in the private domain. Ownership should be vested in owners, and AI should not be considered a legal personhood but a sophisticated tool that is routinely used to enhance our capabilities in order to serve a purpose that we as humans conceived.

References

Abbott, R., "Everything Is Obvious" 66 *UCLA Law Review* 2 (2019).
Abbott, R., "I Think, Therefore I Invent: Creative Computers and the Future of Patent Law" 57 *Boston College Law Review* 1079 (2016) at 1126. See also Abbott (2019).
Asay, C., "Artificial Stupidity" 61 *William & Mary Law Review* 1187 (2020).
Asimov, I., *I, Robot*. New York: Gnome Press, 1950.
Bathaee, Y., "The Artificial Intelligence Black Box and the Failure of Intent and Causation" 31(2) *Harvard Journal of Law & Technology* 890 (2018).
Bennett, B. and Daly, A., "Recognising Rights for Robots: Can We? Will We? Should We?" 12(1) *Law, Innovation and Technology* 60–80 (2020).
Bertolini, A., "Robots as Products: The Case for a Realistic Analysis of Robotic Applications and Liability Rules" 5(2) *Law, Innovation & Technology* 214 (2013).
Burk, D., "AI Patents and the Self-Assembling Machine" 105 *Minnesota Law Review* 12 (2020) <denies-women-equal-rights-makes-a-robot-a-citizen/?utmterm=.775b22127547> (Accessed 10 October 2020).
Department for Business, Energy and Industrial Strategy, "*Industrial Strategy: Building a Britain Fit for the Future*" (November 2017) <https://www.gov.uk/government/uploads/system/uploads/attachment_data/file/664563/industrial-strategy-white-paper-web-ready-version.pdf>.
Dremliuga, R., "Criteria for Recognition of AI as a Legal Person" 12(3) *Journal of Politics and Law* 105–112 at 109 (2019).

European Parliament, "*Civil Law Rules on Robotics: European Parliament Resolution of 16 February 2017 with Recommendations to the Commission on Civil Law Rules on Robotics (2015/2103(INL))*", at para 59 <https://www.europarl.europa.eu/doceo/document/TA-8-2017-0051EN.pdf>.

European Parliament, "*Committee on Legal Affairs: Report with Recommendations to the Commission on Civil Law Rules on Robotics (2015/2103 (INL))*", Motion for a European Parliament Resolution at para AC, p. 7 <https://www.europarl.europa.eu/doceo/document/A-8-2017-0005EN.pdf> (Accessed 10 October 2020).

European Parliament is among the first institutions to put forward recommendations on AI regulations. See European Parliament, "*Committee on Legal Affairs: Draft Report on Intellectual Property Rights for the Development of Artificial Intelligence Technologies*" (24 April 2020) at p. 6 para 10 <https://www.europarl.europa.eu/meetdocs/2014_2019/plmrep/COMMITTEES/JURI/PR/2020/05-12/1203550EN.pdf> (Accessed 20 October 2020).

Fromer, J., "Machines as the New Oompa-Loompas: Trade Secrecy, the Cloud, Machine Learning, and Automation" 94 *New York University Law Review* 706 at 727 (2019).

Gabison, G., "Who Holds the Right to Exclude for Machine Work Products?" (2019) at p. 5 <https://ssrn.com/abstract=3498941>.

Google Creative Lab A.I. Experiment, "*AI + Writing*" <https://experiments.withgoogle.com/collection/aiwriting>. See also Artists + Machines Intelligence, "Precursors to a Digital Muse: Can Machine Learning Inspire a Writer's Process?"<https://medium.com/artists-and-machine-intelligence/precursors-to-a-digital-muse-2653a3025700> (Accessed 6 October 2020).

Google Creative Lab A.I. Experiment, "*AutoDraw*" <https://www.autodraw.com> (Accessed 10 October 2020). See also Google Creative Lab A.I. Experiment, *Quick, Draw! The Data* ("The Quick Draw Dataset Is a Collection of 50 Million Drawings across 345 Categories, Contributed by Players of the Game Quick, Draw!") <https://quickdraw.withgoogle.com> (Accessed 28 September 2020).

Gunkel, D.J., "The Other Question: Can and Should Robots Have Rights?"(2017) *Springer*, at p. 8 <https://link.springer.com/article/10.1007/s10676-017-9442-4> (Accessed 28 September 2020).

Hallevy, G., "AI v. IP - Criminal Liability for Intellectual Property IP Offenses of Artificial Intelligence AI Entities" (2015) *SSRN* <https://ssrn.com/abstract=2691923>.

Hickman, S., "Reinventing Invention: Why Changing How We Invent Will Change What We Patent and What to Do About It", 91 *Journal of the Patent & Trademark Office Society* 108, 115 (2009).

Hristov, K., "Artificial Intelligence and the Copyright Dilemma" 57(3) *IDEA: The IP Law Review* (2017) at p. 450 <https://ssrn.com/abstract=2976428> (Accessed 28 September 2020).

International Association for the Protection of Intellectual Property (AIPPI), "Resolutions 2020" No. 4 (October 2020) at p. 5 <https://aippi.org/wp-content/uploads/2020/10/AIPPI-Resolutions_2020_Final.pdf> (Accessed 20 October 2020).

Karras, T. et al., "Analyzing and Improving the Image Quality of StyleGAN" (2020) <https://arxiv.org/pdf/1912.04958.pdf>.

Kelch, T.G., "Toward a Non-Property Status for Animals" 6 *New York University Environmental Law Journal* 531 (1998) <https://fewd.univie.ac.at/fileadmin/user_upload/

inst_ethik_wiss_dialog/Kelch__Thomas_1998._Toward_a_Non-Property_Status_for_Animals._New_York_University_Environmental_Law_Journal_6.pdf>

Knight, W., "The Dark Secret at the Heart of AI" *MIT Technology Review* (11 April 2017) <https://www.technologyreview.com/2017/04/11/5113/the-dark-secret-at-the-heart-of-ai/> (Accessed 10 October 2020).

LaRoque, S. "Reverse Engineering and Trade Secrets in the Post-Alice World" 66 *Kansas Law Review* 427 (2017).

Lauber-Rönsberg, A. and Hetmank, S., "The Concept of Authorship and Inventorship under Pressure: Does Artificial Intelligence Shift Paradigms?" 14(7) *Journal of Intellectual Property Law & Practice* 570–579 (2019).

Li, N. and Koay, T., "Artificial Intelligence and Inventorship: An Australian Perspective" 15(5) *Journal of Intellectual Property Law & Practice* 399 (2020).

Li, Y., "Court Rules AI-Written Article Has Copyright" *China Daily Global (Ecns.cn)* (9 January 2020) <http://www.ecns.cn/news/2020-01-09/detail-ifzsqcrm6562963.shtml>.

McCarthy, J., "*What Is Artificial Intelligence?*" Stanford University (12 November 2007) <http://jmc.stanford.edu/artificial-intelligence/index.html> (establishing that there is still no consensus on the definition of AI). (Accessed 28 September 2020).

McClelland, C., "The Difference between Artificial Intelligence, Machine Learning, and Deep Learning" *Medium* (4 December 2017).

Merges, R., "Uncertainty and the Standard of Patentability" 7 *High Technology Law Journal* 1 (1992) in Burk, D., "AI Patents and the Self-Assembling Machine" 105 *Minnesota Law Review* (2020) at p. 7 <https://ssrn.com/abstract=3628791> (Accessed 28 September 2020).

Mik, E., "AI as a Legal Person?" in *Artificial Intelligence & Intellectual Property* edited by Hilty, R. and Liu, K.C. (Oxford University Press, 2020) <https://ssrn.com/abstract=3616732> (Accessed 20 September 2020).

Miyazaki, T., "AI Love You: Japanese Man Not Alone in 'marriage' to Virtual Character" *Mainichi Japan National Daily* (18 April 2020) <https://mainichi.jp/english/articles/20200417/p2a/00m/0na/027000c> (Accessed 2 October 2020).

Noto La Diega, G., "*Can Artificial Intelligence and the Internet of Things Be Governed to Achieve the UN Sustainable Development Goals? An Intellectual Property Law Perspective*" WTO Public Forum, AIPPI's Working Session "New Digital Technologies: The Protagonists of a Change in Perspective in the Global Supply Chain" (2019) <https://papers.ssrn.com/abstract=3505247> (Accessed 28 September 2020).

Noto La Diega, G., "Machine Rules. Of Drones, Robots, and the Info-Capitalist Society" 02(02) *The Italian Law Journal* 367–403 at 402 (2016).

Oxford Computing Dictionary (6th ed.) (2008) at p. 26 <https://www.oxfordreference.com/view/10.1093/acref/9780199234004.001.0001/acref-9780199234004-e-204> (Accessed 1 October 2020).

Panel for the Future of Science and Technology (STOA), "The Ethics of Artificial Intelligence: Issues and Initiatives" European Parliament Research Service (EPRS), Scientific Foresight Unit (STOA), University of the West of England (UWE), PE 634.452 (March 2020) at para 2.2.4 p. 20 <https://www.europarl.europa.eu/RegData/etudes/STUD/2020/634452/EPRS_STU(2020)634452_EN.pdf> (Accessed 12 October 2020).

Patrick Hubbard, F., "Sophisticated Robots: Balancing Liability, Regulation, and Innovation" 55 *Fla Law Rev* 1803 (2014).

Rook, D., "Who Gets Charlie? The Emergence of Pet Custody Disputes in Family Law: Adapting Theoretical Tools from Child Law" 28 *International Journal of Law, Policy & Family* 177 (2014).

Sankers, D., "Decision Time", Intellectual Property Magazine (June 2020) at p. 46.

Schuster, M., "Artificial Intelligence and Patent Ownership" 75 *Washington & Lee Law Review* 1945 at 1982–1983 (2018).

Schwab, K. and Davis, N., *Shaping the Future of the Fourth Industrial Revolution: A Guide to Building a Better World*. London: Penguin Random House, 2018.

See generally UK Intellectual Property Office (IPO) and Cardiff University, "*AI-assisted Patent Prior Art Searching-Feasibility Study*" (2020) <https://assets.publishing.service.gov.uk/government/uploads/system/uploads/attachment_data/file/887907/aI-assisted-patent-prior-art-searching-feasibility-study.pdf> (Accessed 10 October 2020).

Silicon AI & Cybersecurity, "*ANI, AGI, & ASI: The 3 Types of Artificial Intelligence*" (4 June 2020) <https://siliconaicybersecurity.wordpress.com/2020/06/04/ani-agi-asi-the-3-types-of-artificial-intelligence/> (Accessed 10 October 2020).

Solum, Lawrence B., "Essay, *Legal Personhood for Artificial Intelligences*" 70 *North Carolina Law Review* 1231 at 1235–1240 (1992) and Wagner, G., "Robot, Inc.: Personhood for Autonomous Systems?" 88 *Fordham Law Review* 591 at 609 (2019).

Solum B., "Lawrence Legal Personhood for Artificial Intelligences" 70(4) *North Carolina Law Review* (1992), 1231.

Stanford Encyclopaedia of Philosophy, "Artificial Intelligence" (12 July 2018) <https://plato.stanford.edu/entries/artificial-intelligence/#HistAI> (Accessed 28 September 2020).

T.S., "Why Uber's Self-Driving Car Killed a Pedestrian" *The Economist* (29 May 2018).

The Guardian, "A Robot Wrote This Entire Article. Are You Scared Yet, Human? GPT-3" (8 September 2020) <https://www.theguardian.com/commentisfree/2020/sep/08/robot-wrote-this-article-gpt-3> (Accessed 16 September 2020).

Turin, A.M., "Computing Machinery and Intelligence" 59 *Mind* 433–460 (1950) <https://www.cs.ox.ac.uk/activities/ieg/e-library/sources/t_article.pdf> (Accessed 28 September 2020).

Vivante, C., *Tratado de derecho mercantil*. Madrid: Reus, 1932 at pp. 9–10.

Winfield, A., "How Intelligent Is Your Intelligent Robot?" *Bristol Robotics Lab (University of the West of England)* (2007) at p. 6.

WIPO, "Artificial Intelligence and Intellectual Property: An Interview with Francis Gurry" *Wipo Magazine* (2018) <https://www.wipo.int/wipo_magazine/en/2018/05/article_0001.html> (Accessed 6 October 2020).

WIPO, "*Frequently Asked Questions: AI and IP Policy: Artificial Intelligence and IP*" <https://www.wipo.int/about-ip/en/artificial_intelligence/faq.html> (Accessed 28 September 2020).

WIPO, *WIPO Technology Trends 2019: Artificial Intelligence*. Geneva: World Intellectual Property Organization, 2019 at p. 14 <https://www.wipo.int/edocs/pubdocs/en/wipopub1055.pdf> (Accessed 28 September 2020).

Wootson, C., "Saudi Arabia, Which Denies Women Equal Rights, Makes a Robot a Citizen" *Washington* (2017).

World Economic Forum (WEF), "Artificial Intelligence Collides with Patent Law", Center for the Fourth Industrial Revolution (2018) at p. 6 <http://www3.weforum.org/docs/WEF_48540_WP_End_of_Innovation_Protecting_Patent_Law.pdf> (Accessed 28 September 2020).

World Intellectual Property Organization (WIPO), "What Is Intellectual Property?" About IP, <https://www.wipo.int/about-ip/en/> (Accessed 28 September 2020).

Yanisky-Ravid, S. and Jin, R., "Summoning a New Artificial Intelligence Patent Model: In the Age of Pandemic" 2021 *Michigan State Law Review* 1 (4 June 2020).

14 Towards a responsible use of artificial intelligence (AI) and fintech in modern banking

Lola Ololade Durodola

1 Introduction

Schwab commented on the advance of the next industrial revolution: "we stand on the brink of a technological revolution that will fundamentally alter the way we live, work, and relate to one another. In its scale, scope, and complexity, the transformation will be unlike anything humankind has experienced before" (Schwab, 2017). What were once imaginary threats, existing in the world of film and fiction, seem to have started evolving as actual concerns, in line with recent advancements in the field of AI (Thompson, 2017). Schwab advocated that though no one knows yet how the AI-led fourth revolution will unfold, the key to getting things right will be the levels of coherent preparation and response dedicated to it (Schwab, 2017). Stephen Hawking buttressed this point by stating, "unless we learn how to prepare for, and avoid the potential risks, AI could be the worst event in the history of our civilization" (Martin, 2017). Significant corporate investments are being made by major financial corporations to advance AI and fintech (Marous, 2017). Consequently, concerns such as responsibility and ethical issues, privacy fears, transparency and accountability concerns, as well as legal ramifications are starting to build up. Studies are now beginning to focus on these concerns in relation to the introduction and deployment of AI and fintech into banks.

AI can be defined as "technologies with the ability to perform tasks that would otherwise require human intelligence, such as visual perception, speech recognition, and language translation" (DBEIS, 2018). AI combines science and engineering to build machines capable of intelligent behaviour, adding work from the fields of brain science and philosophy (Bryson and Wyatt, 1997). However, a more diversified field of ethics is required to be involved so that the use of AI and fintech tools within banking can be better prepared for future changes and innovations in service provision. Better preparation by managers will help to ensure AI's impact and potential risks on employees, customers, and society in general can be ameliorated, particularly within banking institutions, as they are relied upon daily and are crucial for the lives and the livelihoods of humanity (Bank of England, 2018). This chapter will focus on the AI and fintech that are being trialled or deployed in modern banking, the attendant challenges, and the ethics and responsibility strategies that managers should adopt to ensure the future of the employees and customers of banks across the globe are not compromised.

2 The journey so far

AI technologies such as Bank of America's Erica being deployed in the financial services industry could affect up to 1.2 million jobs (Autonomous Research, 2018). At India's Digi Bank, for example, approximately 82% of their tools for customers support run through 'Kasisto', a chatbot. This is done at only a fifth of the costs required by a traditional high-street bank (Crosman, 2017). Global banks are choosing and actively embracing innovation, with fintech companies developing new solutions based on AI regularly (KPMG, 2017). However, there does not seem to be the necessary commensurate acknowledgement of the responsibilities of managers and boards deploying AI (Crossman, 2018). The key to AI's success and its effective operations in banking institutions may therefore be jeopardised if there is no trust. This trust will be crucial to managers. It could be determined by how managers and boards of banks respond to the challenges that are mounting, by designing and implementing effective ethical principles and responsibility strategies within their organisations. Thus, the #AIFearFactor, which can be described as the feeling of apprehension people have towards AI and usually viewed as a reason not to engage or even to overreact to AI, may not deteriorate any time soon.

To add to the current body of work within social science on AI, this chapter is important because, first, as seen from the global financial crisis of a just over ten years ago, the financial sector is the bedrock of society, and its failure has the tendency not only to weaken the financial institutions that are culpable but the entire fabric of society (Ferran and Goodhart, 2001). Second, from the legal and regulatory angles, the current focus on AI and fintech is mostly based on impressive progress being made in its technical fields (see Appendix 1 for definitions of AI terms) of machine learning (ML) and deep neural networks. These have had successes such as strong performances from HSBC's customer service robot named 'Pepper'). Also, Natural Language Processing (NLP) is exhibiting good potentials to improve the experiences of banks' customers through interpretations of their voice, email, and even unstructured requests made to the bank. Another technically beneficial example is Know Your Customer (KYC) onboarding processes being shortened significantly due to AI tools using document text extraction. There have been, however, concerns regarding the legality and ethical soundness of these AI applications and fintech tools. The advances, while innovative, suggest that potential ethical palavers have not been fully considered, nor have laws or regulations been put in place to mitigate against any unintended consequences (Bossmann, 2016). With unprecedented investments, trials, and deployments by global banks and, further, world governments encouraging AI's use as a gear for increased economic influence with more than $30 billion investments (McKinsey, 2017b), AI and fintech within banks have a more pervasive influence. It is therefore beholden on banks and their managers to go beyond recent technical successes, to do their duties and responsibilities and ensure accountability in AI, because they could be considered as AI's moral agents, as per Zlatev's semiotic hierarchy (Zlatev, 2009). Semiotics is defined as "the systematic study of meaning making" (Füller, 1997). Zlatev argued only living systems, and not artificially created machines, have the properties of self-organisation, autopoiesis, identity–ümwelt polarity, and an intrinsic value system, serving their own interests, rather than optimising some externally defined function. If an artificial system were to be created in the future with these properties, which they currently do not possess, then the term "artificial life" would become more than a metaphor. Zlatev advocated the need for a more ethical attitude to fellow living beings (Zlatev, 2009).

3 Use cases of artificial intelligence and fintech in banking today

The McKinsey Global Institute report, "A Future That Works: Automation, Employment and Productivity", details that one of the earliest adopters of AI is the financial services sector (McKinsey, 2017a). The possibilities of AI, fintech, and its subfields of ML and deep learning are innumerable, so predictions of how the future may turn out may be futile. However, banks have already started to identify, trial, and adopt some AI and fintech use-cases. These are the ten categories identified:

Algorithmic trading: AI is helping to make trading decisions and placing trade orders; it is deployed in understanding changing market conditions and altering trading strategy accordingly. Fintech tools assessing creditworthiness at Zest Finance are being developed with the capability to help advisers pick stocks at Goldman Sachs. An AI tool named Kensho is on trial to help banks in predicting how market prices could be affected by natural disasters.

Credit decision-making: In modern banking, AI and fintech applications are being used to determine the likelihood of defaults on the basis of patterns of behaviours; AI combines large datasets from different sources to determine risk. 'Document-heavy' parts of finance at JP Morgan Chase is having natural language processes (NLP) developed, coupled with voice-, visual-, and tone-analysing capabilities. The AI tool is able to review 12,000 commercial loan contracts in seconds, in comparison with over a million seconds that would have been required for loan officers and their managers to undertake the same amount of work.

Customer engagement: Chatbots help with triaging customer queries and in resolving customer requests. Fintech tool 'Email analyser' can sort up to 350,000 emails per day, including analysing and identifying those which are of the greatest urgency. AI helps in making product recommendations and assists in personal financial management tailored specifically for every bank client. 'PayMe', an AI app which combines instant payments with social-media-style interactions, is among the most downloaded free mobile banking apps in Hong Kong.

Employee surveillance: Intelligent Voice, an ML-driven speech transcription tool is under development for monitoring calls by bank traders which could reveal fraudulent moves like insider trading. Humanyze is also being trialled, which monitors employees' speech, movements, and even whether they are in optimal form.

Fraud detection: AI algorithms detect unique activities or behaviours (anomalies) and flag them to the relevant fraud teams to check; it helps to reduce the number of fraud alerts from existing systems, automating know your customer KYC, anti-money laundering (AML), and counterterrorist financing processes. A group of financial institutions, Dawn Capital, British Patient Capital (a subsidiary of British Business Bank), HSBC Bank, and Albion Capital, together invested in a UK-based software developer Quantexa, that uses AI to scrutinise datasets that are both structured and unstructured, which they use to search for suspicious activities at speed. A robotics process automation (RPA) solution called Artemis was designed by HSBC teams to help carry out KYC checks up to 70% more quickly and accurately too. It is used in conjunction with vendor partner EXL Services who are digital intelligence specialists that will further develop the product to help the banking industry tackle financial crime effectively.

Insurance: AI tools with the ability to calculate premiums based on a customer's behaviour and profile are also being tested and set up; these tools are able to complete insurance claims risk assessments. An example is Lemonade, an insurance start-up tool which autonomously determines eligibility for policies, with ability to review, approve, and pay claims in three seconds.

Legal and sentiment/news monitoring: AI within legal departments of banks are used to read thousands of legal contracts in minutes and extract useful or unusual information. In bank sentiment and news analysis, AI and financial technology tools are being used for social media monitoring to track current and emerging consumer trends. This helps in the bank's understanding of the needs and desires of its individual customers for personalised communications and tailored offers. It also highlights wordings that may have legal and regulatory connotations that need to be checked out. Fintech Company Bud received investments from ANZ, Goldman Sachs, and Investec in developing its 'Artha App', which is a marketplace solution that meets the regulatory changes of open banking. It enables bank clients to see all their bank accounts in one place, including the accounts from other banks.

Portfolio management: AI and fintech tools are used in automating/streamlining the asset management process; robo-advisers are used to create, calibrate, and manage portfolios according to the goals and risk tolerance of different clients and customers. AI applications are getting used in improving portfolio risk management. In modern ways that are becoming increasingly commonplace, legacy banks are collaborating with fintech start-ups such as Xcelerit and Kinetica, who are developing tools with the ability to constantly monitor capital requirements, with an almost real-time measurement of exposures to risk (The Economist, 2017).

Security/verification: AI is being trialled and deployed in voice recognition and face recognition in mobile banking technology. AI is used to flag up sensitive cross-border conditions and proximity risks, as well as card, cardholder, and transaction authorisations. Biometrics, Touch ID, Face ID, and voice recognition tools are used via telephony and mobile apps banking services to make life simpler without bank clients going through the hassle of trying to remember passwords. The use of biometrics in banking has to be closely monitored due to the high levels of risks involved.

Transactions: AI trials are ongoing in fractional share trading, automatic rebalancing, and smart dividend reinvestments. Applications are used for online and electronic channels for transaction management. Transaction monitoring with AI such as those developed by companies like IBM, Feedzai, and Shift Technology and banks like Monzo help to monitor unusual transactional patterns, which highlights fraud quicker. Blockchain technology are being used in commercial banking transactions and are steadily flowing through various departments in banking. AI is being advanced into every fabric within banking. AI and fintech are modernising banking and it is clear that banks provide an obvious market for the use-cases of fintech and AI detailed above. All of the categories and use-cases carry their own risks, so the use of these AI and fintech tools by banks have therefore started to raise concerns regarding customer data protection and privacy rights, employee surveillance issues, and problems of access to credit facilities. All which could potentially be more impactful on the more vulnerable in society, the entry-level/lower-paid banking employees, and less able or less technologically savvy individuals, all with lowered chances of financial inclusion. Lowered financial inclusion will consequently widen the gaps of inequality in communities.

4 Challenges for artificial intelligence and fintech in modern banking

The current use-cases of AI and fintech in banking indicate there are legitimate concerns. Some of these include challenges that are mentioned below:

#AIFearFactor: New technologies in the past have led to unintended consequences such as nuclear fission causing the Chernobyl disaster (Russell and Norvig, 2003). The full capacity of AI and fintech tools and apps being developed, trialled, and deployed are yet to be fully known and understood. The challenges for AI within modern banking is compounded by the complexity in the preparing of clients and employees for AI change, which may be due to uncertainties of what AI is being adopted. The fear includes the impact of the AI and fintech tools, the lack of transparency, impact on financial decisions, and whether boards and managers are fully aware of their responsibilities to their customers, employees, and all other stakeholders. Deloitte Consulting's report illustrate that just 17% of global leaders have AI readiness; that is, the ability to manage AI and their employees working alongside each other. They suggest these data translate to the lowest levels of readiness for any trend in five years

(Deloitte, 2017). Yet preparation for AI is crucial within banks. If bank managers are not yet ready, they will not be able to choose to act responsibly. Without managers taking ownership and leading, AI and fintech in banks may induce the #AIFearFactor. This may manifest in different forms, including, but not limited to, fear of job loss, concerns over violation of privacy rights, fear of fundamental and human rights violations, and inability to access credit on account of AI bias, for example, in the AI verification systems assessing creditworthiness or loan eligibility (Margaris, 2017). Sometimes it is the application of the technologies, rather than the technologies themselves, which requires oversight (CDEIS, 2020). If this fear is not addressed, employees may be worried and demoralised, bank customers may be confused, and the bank brand may suffer. These unwanted developments could lead to financial upheavals which may impact not just the banks themselves but societies at large. This is because banks do not exist in isolation; rather, they play a big part in determining the economic livelihoods of numerous households (Bird, 1988). In modern banking therefore, the major challenges may not be costs, computing power, or technology. The biggest concern that needs to be addressed may be the fear of AI itself.

Responsibility and knowledge fears: AI and fintech applications in financial institutions are typically designed in a central office/head office, sometimes outsourced to external partners such as software vendors, cloud providers, consultants, and financial technology firms who help to show proof of value by developing proof of concepts (POCs) for AI. These are then alpha- and beta-tested at pilot sites before deployment (HSBC, 2018). New, exciting names may be given to the projects and attendant financial products in robo-advising, AML monitoring, or voice recognition technology without clearly labelling them as AI or fintech tools. So, though it may seem that algorithms have started to have bigger roles, they are usually not labelled as "AI" (Bostrom et al., 2014). If these products being tested or deployed are clearly named as AI and fintech applications and tools, there will be a difference in how they are received by bank employees and clients. It may make them more aware and guarded, or even worried, yet it should still be paramount that they are adequately informed. AI- or fintech-enabled technologies not fully understood, or explained before its deployment in banking, are an example of the serious governance and responsibility issues facing the boards and managers of banks regarding their use (Floridi and Taddeo, 2018).

Privacy rights and data protection fears: In order to build AI and fintech tools to support the way they learn, and how they apply the learning and make decisions, a great deal of data are needed. Therefore, the possibility that large amounts of personally identifiable and sensitive data that are already held by financial institutions may be used, with more being collected, creates fears for people's privacy and worries about the potential misuse of personal data including possible discriminatory tendencies (Buolamwini, 2017). The standard data protection view is that data should only be used when vital (Big Brother Watch, 2017). That legacy banks in modernising with AI may share client data with fintech start-ups, which are usually third-party entities, is another challenge that banks need to focus on. The fears that banking corporations may increasingly use their data power arbitrarily, including to track their customers' lifestyles, health status, and spending habits or to keep watch on employees' behaviours, may be brought to the fore. With AI and fintech tools comes the potential for data to be compromised in faster ways. For instance, StatusToday, an AI cybersecurity start-up, working with financial institutions recently developed an AI platform dependent on banking employees' metadata. It analysed individual's access to files, their frequency of accessing files, and even how they moved around the building. The datasets collated were then used to build profiles of employees that could ascertain in real time any behaviours that may be perceived to be outside of the normal functioning behaviours developed. This AI tool is expected to be able to detect security risks in bank staff who then behave outside of the usual patterns established and flags them up. For example, an employee who may start to copy work files that they would not normally view will be flagged up. However, AI tools such as this will need to assess if this employee is on secondary duties on a new project or they may be stealing bank information. The implications these AI tools may have on whistleblowing policies within banks will also need to be researched. Similarly, HSBC bank launched the first facial recognition technology for its commercial customers (Hodgson, 2018), and how facial technology may impact on human and fundamental rights have not been clearly articulated. Therefore, employees and clients of banks may have reasonable cause to fear for their private lives and rights when AI and fintech tools are developed to collate their data and behaviours, monitoring their every stance through their facial contours, apps usage, voice recognition, and speech mannerisms on telephones.

Employee surveillance fears: An AI system 'OccupEye' is being piloted at Barclays Bank which is a box system used to record how often staff are stepping away from their desks while some other banks are trialling Humanyze's AI. With Humanyze, a tracker is worn around the neck, which uses Bluetooth, accelerometer, GPS, and a microphone to acquire data that monitors an employee's location, body language, and can assess their stress levels based on heart rate and through the tone of their conversations by analysing their voice. Humanyze collects data on the amount of time the employee talks, , the tone of their voice, and their activity levels. The dynamics of how often they interrupt colleagues are also able to be analysed. Though Humanyze does not collect or record identifying information such as the content of their speech from employees, analysis the mined data to get detailed information on how they communicate and whether they interrupt colleagues too frequently is done., It is able to predict how happy and productive employees are at work and can establish staff that maintain fitness by taking the stairs instead of using the lifts. It even has the capacity to uncover how much sleep an employee has had at night, and if they are at their optimum readiness levels for morning meetings. Serious questions need to asked and answered by bank managers and boards on the relevance of some AI and fintech tools and their potential for abuse. They must be held accountable to determine what the responsible use of AI and fintech tools in modern banking is. That tools like Humanyze is to be worn only by employees who have given consent is not enough justification because some employees may give consent out of fear of losing their jobs. The knowledge of the ethical and legal implications as well as governance oversight that may be lacking in the adoption of these AI and fintech applications within banks cannot be overemphasised, and how bank managers prepare and respond to these are important for trust to be established and maintained.

Governance and accountability fears: The upper echelons theory explains that the experiences, values, and personalities of executives influence, to a large extent, their interpretations of situations confronting them and, in effect, the choices they make (Hambrick, 2007). That nudge concepts (Thaler and Sunstein, 2009) can be used by corporations to gain physiological data from employees in AI is a case in point. Also, if a customer undergoes sufficient facial changes such as reconstruction due to an accident for instance, and AI autonomously determines they cannot access their bank account with facial technology as usual, then who the adjudicator will be is to be determined. Bank lending officers are not able to intervene on decisions finalised by AI and fintech tools; for instance, where a young customer's spends are considered frivolous because money has been 'wasted' on night-outs as captured by the bank's app. Therefore, this client judged by AI may not be able to access lending facilities. Courts have determined that medical expert systems play the same role as medical textbooks; that physicians are responsible for understanding the reasoning behind any decisions they make. They decide based on their medical knowledge and judgements if any system recommendations are accepted (Russell and Norvig, 2003). This does not seem to be the case for banks. Some automated decision-making systems that are in use are governed by section 12 of the current Data Protection Act and section 17 of the new Europe-wide GDPR law, but the augmented and autonomous AI now being built or trialled does not yet fall under any regulations or ethical principles at the moment. This has left various institutes, entities, and banks writing their own principles and adjusting policies internally (see Appendix 2 for a list of principles on AI – Winfield and Jirotka, 2018). Clients and employees need to have better awareness and understanding of AI and fintech tools. Responsibility lies with bank managers, and any algorithmic or automated decision-making must be subjected not only to laws and regulations but also to rigorous governance and responsibility oversight.

The challenges elucidated above are a few of the scenarios where AI and fintech tools in banks may not be used responsibly thereby raising fears in their clients, employees, and, by extension, in society. The imminent questions therefore are whether banking corporations are being responsible and whether their boards and managers will use the current lack of knowledge around AI to give an air of legitimacy to the acquisition of customer and employees' data beyond what is required for normal banking or employment services. There may also be concerns that bank managers may reduce their workforces without retraining employees or that they may even deny services such as lending to customers as AI and fintech tools decide instead of humans. If the issues raised herein are not attended to, bank managers will not be prepared for the future of work. They may rather be seen to be embracing the stakeholder theory which suggests the focus of corporations is primarily to its shareholders (Friedman, 1970). This chapter instead advocates for the concept of corporations being more responsible, which is captured by Colin Mayer in his paper, "Reinventing the corporation"". He explained that a corporation's purpose is to produce services that are beneficial to its customers and their communities and suggested that every corporation should prioritise the welfare of its employees by having their well-being at its heart (Mayer, 2016). Close attention must therefore be paid to the promulgation of AI strategy and governance, laws and regulations, as well as the clear responsibility for banks; otherwise, such fears as the #AIFearFactor may be exacerbated.

5 AI should be for good – proposed ethical, governance, and responsibility strategies for banks

AI and financial technologies aim to revolutionise how banking is done today, and financial institutions are using AI positively to prevent and detect fraud, insider trading, and money laundering. ML solutions are using advanced algorithms to reduce false alerts in transaction monitoring (Barclays, 2018). For example, PayPal's false alerts have been halved, and banks now file 20 times more suspicious activity reports in 2018 than they did in 2012. AI and fintech tools such as Vala help to reduce international remittances costs, and others like Samurai have helped boost decisions being made by employees in the options trade. A fintech tool named Remesh is said to allow individuals tap into the intelligence of a crowd, while another called Seldon enables a more efficient deployment of an enterprise's own ML initiative (Barclays, 2018). These AI and fintech applications being trialled and implemented permit financial institutions to conduct deep learning analyses at speed and at lower costs. Another case in point is the Royal Bank of Scotland (RBS) using Vocalink Analytics payments, an AI system to scan for fake invoices, saving RBS' customers over £8 million from loss prevention. Morgan Stanley bank is utilising AI to improve services and enhance communications to their customers by leveraging the data (both structured and unstructured) that they have in-house, thereby also making lives easier for their employees and reducing operational costs (Crosman, 2017).

All of this is good news for banks and fintech companies; however, as seen in some of the fears, the Fourth Industrial Revolution, in its most pessimistic, dehumanised form, may have the capacity to "robotise" humanity by depriving it of its heart and soul (Son, 2018). If necessity is the mother of invention, ethics must be the twin of AI innovation and adoption in banking. AI and fintech tools and applications can certainly improve lives and society, but it is all down to people and values in the end (Schwab, 2017). Managers and boards of bank must be responsible; hence, the following governance and responsibility strategies are proposed to be the starting point of ensuring AI dehumanisation does not occur in global financial institutions (Freeman and Hasnaoui, 2011). They are:

ACTWISE – All financial institutions to mandatorily develop and adopt a responsible AI, computer, technology, wearables, internet, sensors, email (ACTWISE) policy, guided by the EU's GDPR as the minimum standard. Institutions must ensure consent is gained for data collection and the specified data use, and their customers and employees sign off on understanding their AI and fintech usage policies. They should also be involved in initiatives to educate their customers and employees regularly so that they are familiar with all company undertakings and expectations of them. Banks must be open on exactly what AI and fintech applications are being trialled or deployed, what they are being used for, and what happens to the data generated during the use of the new technologies. In addition, knowing which third-party starts-ups or fintech firms' clients and employee data may be transferred to, as well as for what specific purposes, may help to ensure no detrimental consequences to any nonparticipants.

TEA (transparency, education, and accountability) – Banks should rewrite their values and codes of conduct to reflect the use of AI and fintech tools and applications. They need to be transparent to the extent in which these will be used on all stakeholders, directly or otherwise, as well as all through the corporation's departments and supply chains (Wood, 2010). The plans, ethics, values, and behaviors accepted should be widely circulated. Sharing the corporation's stance across the entire network of the company and not just among senior leaders and non-executive directors' matter. Given AI's complexity, creating directional clarity is important (McKinsey, 2017b), but then it must be embedded within the culture of the banking corporations through continuous education. An AI board committee should be formed and must lead all AI legal, corporate governance, and responsibility issues (Cannon, 2012). All financial corporations should, in light of this, review and publish their AI values and codes of conduct openly in their annual reports mandatorily, so as to be held publicly accountable for board and management failures of noncompliance. There should be a whistleblowing hotline for internal purposes so that employees can address fears and concerns anonymously without fear of repercussions or job losses.

Global AI Alliance – Banks should help set up and fund the 'Global AI Alliance' bringing all stakeholders together. Some stakeholders to be involved should include bank employees and their customers; financial technology firms; start-ups in regtech, fintech, and insurtech; NGOs; researchers; developers; human resources personnel; IT; unions as well as clerical/non-managerial employee representatives together, with particular focus on the strategy and policies on the governance issues around ownership and responsibility in AI. This approach may improve stakeholders' outcomes and advocate for a fair, well-governed, and responsibly implemented AI. The banks coming together to fund this may mean a symbiotic relationship that will help the banks in particular but society in general, opening up banks to a superior pool of global resources with the capacity to design principles across AI and fintech with contributions of diverse stakeholders.

TIAAI – The International Agency for Artificial Intelligence (TIAAI) – Finally, the creation of an international agency, modelled after the European Agency of Robotics and AI ('the Agency'), is recommended. This Agency may use the responsibility measures advocated above to deliver on the challenges and concerns highlighted as well as questions raised (Scherer, 2016). It will help to provide legal and ethical expertise and support to banks and other AI and fintech stakeholders, pulling together work done by other agencies as already established in the US, China, South Korea, and Japan (Allen and Chan, 2017). The French government led by President Emmanuel Macron, for example, recently advocated the open availability of all AI algorithms made for the use of government, wanting all of the society to help in the verification of AI's correct application. Bank boards and managers may need to emulate this approach. Though there may be claims of security and competitive advantage being compromised, there may be the need to juxtapose this against the overall advantage for all stakeholders, not only shareholders, for the good of all. This approach will audit, and bring to the fore, the rationale used in decision-making processes of AI and fintech tools and their potentially detrimental consequences within banks. In setting up this international agency for AI, collaboration of financial institutions and government as well as the third society will be key. They should work together quickly to ensure all aspects of deploying AI and fintech tools from inception to design and testing are thoroughly scrutinised for any impacts and decision-making that may have adverse unintended imports upon society.

Without the implementation of governance and responsible strategies at a commensurate pace in the establishment of AI and fintech tools within banks, the risks of the commodification of human labour could be taken to an extreme, which could then lead to the demolition of society (Polanyi, 2001). Therefore, banks must ensure that they seriously assess AI from the point of view of considerations for the #AIFearFactor, client and employee safety, well-being, and financial inclusion as well as privacy and personal data protection. If the boards and management in banks are not knowledgeable themselves and therefore ill-equipped to manage responsibly, fears may be stoked that the AI-led initiatives, applications, and fintech tools are being applied without relevant corporate governance (Arjoon, 2005), ethical, and responsible considerations. Hence, the reputation of some banks, which may not have fully recovered from the financial crisis of a decade ago (BIS, 2018), may be damaged further. Consequently, public trust in AI and fintech might decrease further.

Finally, modern banks and their managers need to go beyond any governmental regulations by following well-laid-out, transparent legal, governance, and responsible strategies as advocated above. Since bank managers could be said to be AI's moral agents and in AI decision-making accountable positions, they should be obligated to go further than just taking the right action (Gunkel, Bryson and Torrance, 2012). Bank should inculcate responsible, ethical, and legally agile governance into their daily activities with "adaptive, human-centered, inclusive and sustainable policymaking" (WEF, 2018). This will guarantee loyal customers and motivated employees who will be able to work alongside AI enhance AI's reputation and that of banking institutions with all their stakeholders (FSA, 2010). The cost implications of adopting these strategies though may be high at the start because of the regular advancements in AI. This will reduce eventually, as the responsible strategies will be fully integrated and embedded as part of the daily routines in banks. This approach will make banks better for their clients, reduce staff attrition rates, and may help them avoid the proliferation of the #AIFearFactor in society.

6 Conclusion

AI will impact banking and its future in significant ways. Board members and management of modern banking institutions around the world will need to embrace transparency and responsibility as the minimum requirements necessary to minimise the effects of the AI disruptions to their customers and employees and the communities they serve. This will help to eliminate what I have identified in this chapter as the #AIFearFactor.

AI's use will increase and drive change in banks all over the world. The priority for them will be to safeguard their customers and employees and, by extension, all of society, by thoroughly understanding the AI and fintech systems, tools, and applications to be deployed in their banks. They will need to be open and transparent, as well as responsible in adopting the recommended governance, legal, and responsibility strategies as proposed herein. They need to ensure that they have the platforms such as TIAAI and insights like TEA and ACTWISE to do this responsibly and etching these robustly into place within their organisations. This chapter informed modern banking institutions on new ways of doing business, helping to prepare their customers and employees for the future of banking. It focused on how banks can relate with new AI technologies, with the support, openness, and transparency of other stakeholders. I am hopeful that the strategies on AI and fintech within banks will change, not by just writing new lists of conduct to show compliance and obeying the law, but by the emulation of the effective governance, ethical, and responsible solutions discussed in this chapter. That being said, this chapter is designed to educate on the use-cases of AI and fintech in banking, on #AIFearFactor, and how managers and boards of banks may be able to ameliorate the consequences that may arise in their adoption and deployment. This chapter is a means of sparking conversations rather than being the final word and aims to encourage further research in social sciences that are required on the responsible use of AI in banking.

References

Allen, G. and Chan, T. "Artificial Intelligence and National Security" (2017) Belfer Centre for Science and International Affairs. <https://www.belfercenter.org/sites/default/files/files/publication/AI%20NatSec%20-%20final.pdf> accessed 3 August 2019.

Arjoon, S. "Corporate Governance: An Ethical Perspective" (2005) 61 *Journal of Business Ethics*, pp. 343–352. 10.1007/s10551-005-7888-5. <https://www.researchgate.net/publication/227329914> accessed 10 August 2020.

Autonomous Research. "Augmented Finance and Machine Intelligence" (2018) <https://next.autonomous.com/augmented-finance-machine-intelligence/> accessed 3 July 2019.

Bank of England. "Will There Be Another Financial Crisis?" (2018) <http://edu.bankofengland.co.uk/knowledgebank/will-there-be-another-financial-crisis/> accessed 3 August 2019.

Barclays Bank. "Financial Institutions Embrace Artificial Intelligence" (2018) <https://www.barclayscorporate.com/content/dam/corppublic/corporate/Documents/tech_digital_innovation/Financial-institutions-embrace-artificial-intelligence.pdf> accessed 3 August 2019.

Big Brother Watch. "House of Lords Select Committee on Artificial Intelligence – Big Brother Watch Response" (2017) <https://bigbrotherwatch.org.uk/wp-content/uploads/2017/10/Lords-Select-Committee-on-Artificial-Intelligence-Implications-of-AI-Submission.pdf> accessed 23 July 2019.

Bird, G. "Managing Global Money: Essays in International Financial Economics" (1988) 1st ed., Hampshire: Macmillan Press Ltd.

BIS. "Volatility Is Back" (2018) Quarterly Review of BIS. <https://www.bis.org/publ/qtrpdf/r_qt1803a.htm>. For further reading, see also Alex Brazier's warning of risks building in the mortgage market- <http://www.cityam.com/284329/bank-england-official-warns-risks-building-british-mortgage>.

Bossmann, J. "Top 9 Ethical Issues in Artificial Intelligence" (2016) World Economic Forum. <https://www.weforum.org/agenda/2016/10/top-10-ethical-issues-in-artificial-intelligence/> accessed 3 July 2019.

Bostrom, N. and others. "The Cambridge Handbook of Artificial Intelligence" (2014) 1st ed., Cambridge: Cambridge University Press, pp. 300–364.

Bryson, J. and Wyatt, J. "Artificial Intelligence" (1997) <http://www.cs.bath.ac.uk> accessed 3 August 2019.

Buolamwini, J. "Facial Recognition Technology Is Both Biased and Understudied – MIT Media Lab" (2017) <https://www.media.mit.edu/articles/facial-recognition-technology-is-both-biased-and-understudied/> accessed 3 July 2019.

Cannon, T. "Corporate Responsibility: Governance, Compliance and Ethics in a Sustainable Environment" (2012) 2nd ed., Harlow: Pearson Education Limited, pp. 12–19.

Centre for Data Ethics and Innovation (2020) <https://assets.publishing.service.gov.uk/government/uploads/system/uploads/attachment_data/file/894170/CDEI_AI_Barometer.pdf> accessed 10 August 2020.

Crosman, P. "AI Is Augmenting Morgan Stanley's' Advisers Not Replacing Them" (2017) The American Banker. <https://www.americanbanker.com/news/ai-is-augmenting-morgan-stanleys-advisers-not-replacing-them> accessed 4 July 2019.

DBEIS, Department for Business, Energy and Industrial Strategy. "Industrial Strategy: Building a Britain Fit for the Future" (2017) p. 37. <https://www.gov.uk/government/uploads/system/uploads/attachment_data/file/664563/industrial-strategy-white-paper-web-ready-version.pdf>.

Deloitte. "Global Human Capital Trends – Rewriting the Rules for the Digital Age" (2017) Deloitte University Press. <https://www2.deloitte.com/content/dam/Deloitte/global/Documents/About-Deloitte/> accessed 5 July 2019.

Economist (The). "Machine Learning Promises to Shake up Large Swathes of Finance" (2017) <https://www.economist.com/finance-and-economics/2017/05/25/machine-learning-promises-to-shake-up-large-swathes-of-finance> accessed 5 July 2019.

Ferran, E. and Goodhart, C. "Regulating Financial Services and Markets in the 21st Century" (2001) 1st ed., Oxford: Hart Publishing.

Floridi, L. and Taddeo, M. "How AI Can Be a Force for Good" (2018) Science. 10.1126/science.aat5991. <http://science.sciencemag.org/content/361/6404/751.full> accessed 3 August 2019.

Freeman, I. and Hasnaoui, A. "The Meaning of Corporate Social Responsibility: The Vision of Four Nations" (2011) 100(3) *Journal of Business Ethics*, pp. 419–443. <https://link.springer.com/article/10.1007%2Fs10551-010-0688-6> accessed 3 August 2019.

Friedman, M. "The Social Responsibility of Business Is to Increase Its Profits" (1970) New York Times. <https://www.colorado.edu/studentgroups/libertarians/issues/friedman-soc-resp-business.html> accessed 3 July 2019.

FSA (The). "Effective Corporate Governance" (2010) Consultation 10/3. <https://www.fca.org.uk/publication/consultation/cp10_03.pdf> accessed 10 August 2020.

Füller, G. "Reading the Readers: The Role of Semiotics in Visitor Research" (1997) XII (3–4) *Visitor Behavior*, pp. 30–31.

Gunkel, J., Bryson, J. and Torrance, S. (eds). "The Machine Question: AI, Ethics and Moral Responsibility" (2012) A symposium proceeding published by The Society for the Study of Artificial Intelligence and Simulation of Behaviour 3–5 July.

Hambrick, D. "Upper Echelons Theory: An Update" (2017) 32(2) *Academy of Management Review*, pp. 334–343. <https://journals.aom.org/doi/abs/10.5465/amr.2007.24345254> accessed 3 July 2019.

Hodgson, C. "HSBC Rolls out Facial Recognition for Mobile" (2018) Financial Times. <https://www.ft.com/content/acc823c0-52a6-11e8-b3ee-41e0209208ec> accessed 3 August 2019.

HSBC. "Artificial Intelligence – The Ghost in the Machine?" Game Changers (2018) London: HSBC Global Banking and Markets, pp. 1–11. <https://www.gbm.hsbc.com/insights/securities-services/artificial-intelligence-the-ghost-in-the-machine> accessed 3 July 2019. Photo of Pepper taken by Owen Beard on Unsplash – License | Unsplash. <https://unsplash.com/licence> accessed 14 December 2020.

KPMG. "Forging the Future: How Financial Institutions Are Embracing Fintech to Evolve and Grow" (2017) A Global Survey of Fintech Activities in Financial Institutions. <https://assets.kpmg.com/content/dam/kpmg/xx/pdf/2017/10/forging-the-future-global-fintech-study.pdf> accessed 3 July 2019.

Margaris, S. "Machine Learning in Financial Services: Changing the Rules of the Game" (2017) 1st ed., Margaris Advisory. <https://www.MargarisAdvisory.com> accessed 14 July 2019.

Marous, J. "The Use of AI in Banking Is Set to Explode" (2017) The Financial Brand. <https://thefinancialbrand.com/63322/artificial-intelligence-ai-banking-big-data-analytics/> accessed 22 February 2019.

Martin, S. "Stephen Hawking: AI Will Be the Worst Ever Invention and Could Destroy Us All" (2017) Express. <https://www.express.co.uk/news/science/876550/stephen-hawking-end-of-the-world-artificial-intelligence-ai-university-of-cambridge> accessed 3 August 2019.

Mayer, C. "Reinventing the Corporation" (2016) 4 *Journal of the British Academy*. <https://www.dropbox.com/s/n0pug2xo9k3h3tm/Journal%20of%20British%20Academy%20article%20%2800000002%29.pdf?dl=0> accessed 3 August 2019.

McKinsey Global Institute. "A Future that Works: Automation, Employment and Productivity" (2017a) McKinsey & Co, pp. 1–148. <https://www.mckinsey.com/featured-insights/digital-disruption/harnessing-automation-for-a-future-that-works> accessed 3 July 2019.

McKinsey Global Institute. "Jobs Lost, Jobs Gained: What the Future of Work Will Mean for Jobs, Skills and Wages" (2017b) <https://www.mckinsey.com/featured-insights/future-of-organizations-and-work/Jobs-lost-jobs-gained-what-the-future-of-work-will-mean-for-jobs-skills-and-wages> accessed 15 August 2019.

Polanyi, K. "The Great Transformation the Political and Economic Origins of Our Time". Foreword by Joseph E. Stiglitz, Introduction by Fred Block. (2001) 2nd ed., Beacon Press, pp. 71–80. "To allow the market mechanism to be sole director of the fate of human beings and their natural environment indeed, even of the amount and use of purchasing power, would result in the demolition of society". AI could easily fit into "market mechanism" in today's world hence the need for urgent conversations on AI.

Russell, S. and Norvig, P. "Artificial Intelligence: A Modern Approach" (2003) 2nd ed., Upper Saddle River, NJ: Prentice Hall/Pearson Education International, pp. 947–975.

Scherer, M. "Regulating Artificial Intelligence Systems: Risks, Challenges, Competencies, and Strategies" (2016) 29 *Harvard Journal of Law and Technology*. <https://heinonline.org/HOL/Page?collection=journals&handle=hein.journals/hjlt29&id=375#> accessed 11 March 2020. Also see discussion paper by IPPR which recommends an "Authority for the Ethical Use of Robotics and Artificial Intelligence". Read pp. 37–39: IPPR Commission on Economic Justice, "Managing Automation: Employment, Inequality and Ethics in the Digital Age" (Institute for Public Policy Research 2017). <https://www.ippr.org/research/publications/managing-automation> accessed 28 July 2019.

Schwab, K. "The Fourth Industrial Revolution: What It Means and How to Respond" (2017) World Economic Forum. <https://www.weforum.org/agenda/2016/01/the-fourth-industrial-revolution-what-it-means-and-how-to-respond/> accessed 23 July 2019.

Son, H. "Bank Staffing Branches with Humanoid Robots" (2018) <https://www-cnbc-com.cdn.ampproject.org/c/s/www.cnbc.com/amp/2018/06/26/this-bank-is-staffing-branches-with-humanoid-robots-that-dance-take-s.html> accessed 23 July 2019.

Thaler, R. and Sunstein, C. "Nudge" (2009) 1st ed., New York: Penguin Books, pp. 1–30.

Thompson, J. "Regulating the Robots: Key Principles for Framing the Future of Artificial Intelligence" (2017) <https://www.georgetownlawtechreview.org/regulating-the-robots-key-principles-for-framing-the-future-of-artificial-intelligence/GLTR-11-2017/> accessed 13 July 2019.

Winfield, A. and Jirotka, M. "Ethical Governance Is Essential to Building Trust in Robotics and AI Systems" (2018) *Philosophical Transactions A: Mathematical, Physical and Engineering Sciences*, pp. 1–19. <http://eprints.uwe.ac.uk/37556> accessed 24 August 2019.

Wood, D. in Visser, W., Matten, D., Pohl, M. and Tolhurst, N. "The A-Z of Corporate Social Responsibility" (2010) London: ACCA.

World Economic Forum. "New Physics of Financial Services" (2018) Future of Financial Services Series. Canada: World Economic Forum, pp. 1–154. <http://www3.weforum.org/docs/WEF_New_Physics_of_Financial_Services.pdf> accessed 24 August 2019.

Zlatev, J. "The Semiotic Hierarchy: Life, Consciousness, Signs and Language" (2009) 4 *Cognitive Semiotics*. <https://www.degruyter.com/view/j/cogsem_cogsem.2009.4.issue-spring2009_20140116150000/cogsem.2009.4.issue-spring2009/cogsem.2009.4.spring2009.169/cogsem.2009.4.spring2009.169.xml> accessed 10 August 2020.

Appendices

Appendix 1 Terms used in artificial intelligence

Terminology	Meaning
#AIFearFactor	#AIFearFactor is defined as the scale of the feeling of apprehension that is determined by any individual in or out of a corporation towards the corporation's use of artificial intelligence usually viewed as a reason not to engage, grudgingly engage, or even to overreact to artificial intelligence. Formulated by Lola Ololade Durodola 2016.
Algorithm	A series of instructions for performing a calculation or solving a problem, especially with a computer. They form the basis for everything a computer can do and are therefore a fundamental aspect of all AI systems.
Expert system	A computer system that mimics the decision-making ability of a human expert by following pre-programmed rules, such as 'if this occurs, then do that'. These systems fuelled much of the earlier excitement surrounding AI in the 1980s, but have since become less fashionable, particularly with the rise of neural networks.
Machine learning	One particular form of AI, which gives computers the ability to learn from and improve with experience, without being explicitly programmed. When provided with sufficient data, a machine learning algorithm can learn to make predictions or solve problems, such as identifying objects in pictures or winning at particular games, for example.
Neural network	Also known as an artificial neural network, this is a type of machine learning loosely inspired by the structure of the human brain. A neural network is composed of simple processing nodes, or 'artificial neurons', which are connected to one another in layers. Each node will receive data from several nodes 'above' it and give data to several nodes 'below' it. Nodes attach a 'weight' to the data they receive and attribute a value to that data. If the data do not pass a certain threshold, they are not passed on to another node. The weights and thresholds of the nodes are adjusted when the algorithm is trained until similar data input results in consistent outputs.
Deep learning	A more recent variation of neural networks, which uses many layers of artificial neurons to solve more difficult problems. Its popularity as a technique increased significantly from the mid-2000s onwards, as it is behind much of the wider interest in AI today. It is often used to classify information from images, text, or sound.

Source: Adapted from DBEIS (2017).

Appendix 2 Principles of robotics and AI published as at December 2017

	Principles	Number of principles	Year of principle
1	Asimov's Laws of Robotics	3	1950
2	Murphy and Wood's Three Laws of Responsible Robotics	3	2009
3	The EPSRC Principles of Robotics	5	2011
4	Future of Life Institute's Asilomar Principles for Beneficial AI	23	January 2017
5	ACM US Public Policy Council's Principles for Algorithmic Transparency and Accountability	7	January 2017
6	Japanese Society for Artificial Intelligence (JSAI) Ethical Guidelines	9	February 2017
7	Draft principles of The Future Society's Science, Law and Society Initiative	6	October 2017
8	Montreal Declaration for Responsible AI draft principles	7	November 2017
9	IEEE General Principles of Ethical Autonomous and Intelligent Systems	5	December 2017
10	UNI Global Union Top 10 Principles for Ethical AI	10	December 2017

Source: Adapted from Winfred and Jirotka (2018).

Index

Note: Bold page numbers refer to **tables**; *Italic* page numbers refer to *figures* and page numbers followed by "n" refer to notes

Accenture 71
access: to data 78; issues faced by people in the UK 67–69; to user testers 78
ACTWISE 270–271, 273
Affordable Credit Loan Fund (Scottish Government) 66
agent 27, 28, 37, 41
AI, computer, technology, wearables, internet, sensors, email (ACTWISE) policy *see* ACTWISE
AI-based discrimination: anti-discrimination laws 221–223; Apple credit card 215–216; case analysis 223–225; caused by algorithmic decision-making 214; facial recognition 216–217; GDPR 219–221; lack of transparency 217–218; legal safeguards helping to tackle 218–225; Microsoft and IBM 216–217; UK A-level results 2020 214–215
AI(D) as tools 232–233
Airbnb 145
AI systems: bias within 212–218; legal safeguards and tackling AI-based discrimination 218–225; overview 211–212; risk of discrimination in 211–226
Albion Capital 265
algorithmic decision-making: examples of discrimination caused by 214; and transparency 218, 225
algorithmic discrimination: challenges posed by 221; current legal safeguards tackling 211–226; and lack of transparency 212
algorithmic trading 264

Alice Corporation Pty. Ltd. v. CLS Bank International 242–243
Alliance for Financial Inclusion (AFI) 55–56, 58
Amazon 147, 159, 214
Analytics-as-a-service (AaaS) 34
animals and AI 233
Ant Finance 28, 37
anti-discrimination laws 221–223
anti-money laundering (AML) 129, 134–135, 137, 139, 177, 184–185, 265
ANZ 265
Apple 137, 159
Apple credit card 214, 215–216
Aristotle 23
Arner, W. 17
array of stakeholder ABC 35–37; agent 37; business 36–37; customer 35–36
array of technological ABC 30–35, *35*; artificial intelligence (AI) 34–35; big data 32–34; cloud computing 30–32
Article 22, GDPR 220–221
Article 29 Data Protection Working Party 221
Artificial General Intelligence (AGI) 232, 246
artificial intelligence (AI) 34–35; animals 233; authorship 238–240; candidates for ownership 252–254; copyright and moral rights 236–240; DABUS 249–250; defined 262; ethical, governance, and responsibility strategies for banks 270–273; and implications for intellectual property 230–257; as invention 240–248; inventions in current IP system 235–255; as

280 *Index*

inventor 248–254; inventorship and ownership 250–252; legal person 233–235; originality 237–238; patents 241–246; responsible use in modern banking 262–273; role and status of 231–235; special regime for AI within IP 255–257; terms used in 277–278; trade secrets 246–248; UK Government defining 198
Artificial Super Intelligence (ASI) 232, 246
Association for Financial Markets in Europe (AFME) 91, 100
Association for the Protection of Intellectual Property 240
Association of Banks in Italy (ABI) 170n4
AstraZeneca 256
authorship 238–240; and AI 240
automation: and value 13–25; and virtualisation 13–25

BaFin 5
Bailey, Andrew 183
Bank for International Settlements (BIS) 100, 173n10
banking: algorithmic trading 264; credit decision-making 264; customer engagement 264; employee surveillance 265; fraud detection 265; insurance 265; legal and sentiment/news monitoring 265; portfolio management 265; security/verification 266; transactions 266; use cases of artificial intelligence in 264–266; use cases of fintech in 264–266
Bank Negara Malaysia (BNM) 48, 53
Bank of America 263
Bank of England (BoE) 128, 137, 170–171, 172n7, 172n8, 173, 186–187; central bank digital currencies 169–187; design principles set out by 175–178; genre of CBDC being projected by 178–182; native digital pound and regulatory aspects 169–187; regulatory considerations 182–186
Bank of International Settlements (BIS) 173–174
Bank of Tanzania (BoT) 55
banks: ACTWISE 270–271; Global AI Alliance 271; The International Agency for Artificial Intelligence (TIAAI) 271–273; TEA (transparency, education, and accountability) 271, 273

Barlow Clowes International Ltd v Eurotrust International Ltd 153
Barrdear, J. 93
Bartlett, R. 4
Beijing Internet Court 238
Berg, T. 4
Berne Convention 236, 240, 252, 255
bias: within AI systems 212–218; described 213–214
big data 32–34, 160–161; and blockchain technology 160–162; defined 32; Gartner on 32; as "information assets" 32; visualisation of big data definition 34
Bitcoin 85, 88–89, 107–109, 112–113, 115, 116, 119, 125–129, 135, 146
Bitcoin Cash 109
Bitconnect 116–117
blockchain technology 7, 146, 153, 160–161, 176, 266
Blurb Inc. 239
Bowman v. Monsanto 255
Brautigan, Richard 20
British Patient Capital 265
Brummer, C. 146
BTC-e 126, 130, 138
Buolamwini, J. 216
business 36–37

Cambridge Centre for Alternative Finance 129
candidates for ownership 252–254
Carney, Mark 170
case analysis: AI-based discrimination 223–225
case study: Open Banking for Good (OB4G) 71–78; social-purpose FinTech 71–78
central bank digital currencies (CBDCs) 7, 93–94, 169–187; core ledger 179; *vs.* crypto-assets 94–97; defined 175–176; genre being projected by Bank of England 178–182; Koomhof on 175–176; Noone on 175–176; Payment Interface Provider (PIP) 179–182
Central Bank of Canada 93
Charter of Fundamental Rights of the European Union (the Charter) 222
chatbots 264
Chaum, D. 107–108
cheating, public revenue 151–152
Chen, C.C. 37
Chernobyl disaster 266
Chikalipah, S. 4

China 170; civil law jurisdictions 253; increase in the internet insurance market in *30*; insurance industry 29–31
closing the gap: and financial exclusion 4; in FinTech 4
cloud computing 30–32; defined 30–31; services **33**
co-creation: aim of 76; collaborative learning through process of 76; defined 76; examples of 76
collaboration: digital financial services ecosystem 58; key tool for a FinTech's success 58
collaborative learning through process of co-creation 76
collateralised debt obligations (CDO) 13, 17
Committee on Payments and Market Infrastructures (CPMI) 88
common law offence: cheating the public revenue 151–152
community finance development institutions (CDFIs) 65
Companies Act 2006 156
COMPAS recidivism tool 214
Competition and Markets Authority (CMA) 203
Computer Misuse Act 1990 131, 134
connect database 155–156
Consumer Empowerment and Market Conduct Working Groups (CEMCWG) 53
Consumer Protection for DFS (CP4DFS) framework 53
Consumer Rights Act 2015 119
copyright: AI 236–240; moral rights 236–240
Copyright Design and Patent Act (CDPA) 239
core ledger 179
corporate offences of failure to prevent tax evasion 151
Council of Europe Union 204
COVID-19 pandemic 50, 56, 85–87, 214
creating time and space for innovation 75
Creative Adversarial Networks (CAN) 236
Creative Machines (CM) 249–250
credit decision-making 264
Credit Union Investment Fund (Scottish Government) 66
crime: and cryptocurrency 125–139; financial 7, 48, 59, 126–127, 130–136, 139, 144–145, 148, 157;

indirect cryptocurrency 132–133; and technological innovation 160–162
Crime and Courts Act 2013 155
crime threats and ICOs 116–117
Criminal Finances Act 2017 151, 158
Criminal Law Act 1977 132, 133
Crown Prosecution Service 131, 133
crypto-assets 85–86, 128; *vs.* CBDCs 94–97; definition and features of 88–90; definition and situation in EU 86–88; financial inclusion 86–88, 94–97, 101; and financial stability 97–98, 101; latest EU crypto-asset initiatives 92; legal situation in EU 90–92; option of central bank-issued digital currencies 93–94; regulation of crypto-assets in EU 98–101
Cryptoassets Taskforce 118
cryptocurrencies: Bitcoin 107–109; creating new realms for TE 147–148; and crime 125–139; definitions of 127–130; overview 105–109; reasons public investing in 113–114; role in financial crime 130–136
cryptocurrency crimes: indirect 132–133; individual activities 137–138; jurisdictions 138–139; micropayments 137; possible flaws 136–139
customer 35–36
customer engagement 264
customs and excise duties, evasion of 150
Customs & Excise Management Act (CEMA) 1979 150

data: decentralised 161; trainers 253–254
Data-as-a-Service (DaaS) 34
Data Protection Act 2018 132, 219
Dawn Capital 265
Dawson, C. 129, 138
Dean Armstrong QC 130
decentralised data 161
Deep Learning (DL) 232
deferred prosecution agreements (DPAs) 158–159; influence of technology on 158–159
de la Feria, R. 155, 160
Deloitte Consulting 266
Depop 146
designing social-purpose FinTech 64–79
Devanny, J. 162
Development Agenda (World Bank & OECD) 65

282 *Index*

Device for the Autonomous Bootstrapping of Unified Sentience (DABUS) 249–250
Devlin, J. 194
devolved nations and financial inclusion 65–66
Digi Bank 263
'digital assets' 128
digital currencies (DCs) 85, 128, 128n13; central bank-issued 93–94
digital financial services ecosystem: avoiding hindering FinTech ecosystem 57–58; collaboration 58; financial technology (FinTech) 46–47; FinTech and financial inclusion 49–50; FinTech regulation and financial inclusion 55–57; implementing sandbox environment 58; issues 47–49; objectives 52–58; regulators and FinTech companies improving 46–59; regulator's perspective and responsibilities 50–52; regulatory bodies and regulation supporting FinTech development 53–55; regulatory overview 52–53
digital financial services (DFS) environment 46–53
Digital Financial Services Working Group (DFSWG) 53
digital insurance 29
direct unlawful activities 131–132
disclosure and black box effect 244–245
discrimination in AI systems 211–226
dishonesty 153–154
distributed ledger technologies (DLTs) 88, 126, 170, 199–200
Dogecoin 109, 115
'double your Bitcoin' scams 125

eBay 145, 147, 156
ECB Crypto-Assets Task Force 88
e-commerce: breakthrough for 161–162; technological innovation 161–162; and VAT evasion 146–147
Edelman Trust 113
Edelman Trust Barometer 3
El Erian, Mohamed 16, 25
E-Money 47
'e-money token' 129
employee surveillance 265
Engelhard, Antje 239
Engert, W. 171n6
Enyi, J. 109
Equality Act 2010 8, 212, 219, 222, 223–224

'Eternal-Blue' 125
Ethereum 109, 113
Etsy 146
EU Committee on Legal Affairs 232
European Agency of Robotics and AI ('the Agency') 271
European Banking Authority (EBA) 89–92, 100
European Central Bank (ECB) 86, 90, 105–106
European Commission 6, 91, 194, 201, 219; Action Plan on Fintech ('the Plan') 91, 100
European Convention on Human Rights (ECHR) 8, 212, 219, 222, 223
European Parliament 90, 204
European Patent Convention (EPC) 241
European Patent Office (EPO) 242–243, 250
Europeans Commission High Level Expert Group on Artificial Intelligence 204
European Securities and Markets Authority (ESMA) 88, 91, 100
European Supervisory Authorities (ESAs) 90
European Union (EU) 85, 87, 144, 170; crypto-asset initiatives 92; definition and situation in 86–88; Fifth Anti-money Laundering Directive (AMLD) 90–91, 128, 146; financial inclusion 86–88; Financial Intelligence Units (FIUs) in 138; Fourth Money Laundering Directive (4MLD) 148; legal situation in 90–92; regulation of crypto-assets in 98–101
European Union Agency for Law Enforcement Cooperation (Europol) 130, 134
evaluation of investigation-centric instruments 157–158
evasion: of customs and excise duties 150; of income tax 149; of VAT 150
Expert Group on Regulatory Obstacles to Financial Innovation (ROFIEG) 91, 100

Face ++ 214, 217
Facebook 89, 159
facial recognition: Microsoft and IBM 216–217
FAFT categories of virtual currency *106*
Fair4AllFinance 67
Fairer Scotland action plan 66
Fang, K. 36

Federal Bureau of Investigation (FBI) 125, 137
Federal Reserve 128
Feedzai 266
Felzmann, H. 218
Fifth Anti-Money Laundering Directive (5MLD) 90–91, 128, 146
Finance Act 2011 156
Finance Act 2018 149
finance industry 16–17
Financial Action Task Force (FATF) 53, 105–106, 134–136, 139
Financial Conduct Authority (FCA) 113–114, 117, 118–119, 128–129, 183, 196–197, 202–205
financial crime 7, 48, 59, 126–127, 130–136, 139, 144–145, 148, 157; direct unlawful activities 131–132; indirect cryptocurrency crimes 132–133; money laundering 133–136; role of cryptocurrencies in 130–136
Financial Crimes Enforcement Network (Fin-CEN) 138
financial exclusion 194–198; closing the gap in 4
financial inclusion 194; crypto-assets *vs.* CBDCs 94–97; defined 86; definition and situation in EU 86–88; in devolved nations 65–66; FinTech and 49–50; FinTech regulation helping bridging gap in 55–57; market stability and 85–101; World Bank on 86
Financial Inclusion Commission 195
Financial Reporting Enforcement Panel 5
financial services: impact of policies to improve access to 66–67; UK government policy around access to 64–66
Financial Services and Markets Act 2000 118
financial stability: and crypto-assets 97–98, 101; and inclusion 101
Financial Stability Board (FSB) 92, 97–98, 100, 101
financial technology (FinTech) 46–47, 69–70; access issues faced by people in UK 67–69; closing the gap in 4; data 20–22; designing social-purpose 64–79; finance industry 16–17; and financial inclusion 49–50; FinTech revolution 18–19; gaps in 5–6; impact of policies to improve access to financial services 66–67; Open Banking for Good programme 71–78; overview 64; practical reasoning 22–24; regulation and financial inclusion 55–57; regulation and supervision 5–6; responsible use in modern banking 262–273; social-purpose FinTech 71–78; social-purpose FinTech initiatives 70–71; standard view of value 14–16; UK government policy and access to financial services 64–66
Finck, M. 217
FinTech development: monitoring 51; regulatory bodies and regulation supporting 53–55
FinTech ecosystem: and DFS 51; regulators doing to avoid hindering 57–58
FinTech revolution 18–19
Flash Boys (Lewis) 18
Fletcher, William 234
Forgery and Counterfeiting Act 1981 131, 132
Fourth Industrial Revolution 235, 270
Foxglove 223–224
fraud detection 265
Friedman, B. 213
Friends Provident 194
Fukoku Mutual Life Insurance 37
Fung, B.S.C. 171n6
The Future of Money speech 170
"A Future That Works: Automation, Employment and Productivity" report 264

Gartner 32
Gates, Bill 125
Gebru, T. 216
gender-based discrimination 215
Gender Shades project 217
General Data Protection Regulations (GDPR) 8, 212, 219–221, 223, 269; Article 22 220–221
Global AI Alliance 271
global pandemic of 2020 3; *see also* COVID-19 pandemic
Goldman Sachs 216, 264, 265
Good Translate 216
Google 159
Gorfine, D. 146
government-backed challenge funds 70–71
Grab 48
Green, Curtis 130
grounded innovation 72–73; operationalised in OB4G programme 74

Haines, A. 147
Hari, O. 110
Harper, Richard 73
Hawking, Stephen 262
Heinemeier, David 215
Her Majesty's Revenue and Customs (HMRC) 144, 147, 149, 155; Connect 145; data-gathering powers of 155–156; providing false documents and information to 150; tax evasion investigated by 155
HSBC Bank 263, 265, 268
HSBC Private Bank (Suisse) 144, 158
Hugo, Victor 256
Human Rights Act 1998 222
Humanyze 265, 268
Hyde, Dan 130

IBM 214, 217, 266; facial recognition 216–217; Watson Explorer AI 37
inclusion: and crypto-assets 101; and financial stability 101
Inclusive Economy Partnership (IEP) 71
income tax evasion 149
indirect cryptocurrency crimes 132–133
indirect discrimination 216
Infrastructure as a Service (IaaS) 31–32
initial coin offerings (ICOs) 95, 109–111; advantages of 111–114; crime threats 116–117; cryptocurrencies overview 105–109; disadvantages of 114–117; investors 112–113, 115–116; issuers 111–112, 114–115; overview 105; reasons public investing in cryptocurrencies 113–114; UK regulation 117–119
innovation: creating time and space for 75; grounded 72–73
'innovation cage' 75
insurance 265
InsurTech 27–41; array of stakeholder ABC 35–37; array of technological ABC 30–35; overview of 29–30; taking the lead 37–41
intellectual property (IP): AI as the invention 240–248; AI as the inventor 248–254; AI(D) as tools 232–233; AI inventions in current IP system 235–255; artificial intelligence and implications for 230–257; copyright and moral rights 236–240; liability 254–255; role and status of AI 231–235; special regime for AI within 255–257

Intelligent Voice tool 265
The International Agency for Artificial Intelligence (TIAAI) 271–273
International Banking Federation 183
International Monetary Fund (IMF) 129
International Tax Compliance Regulations 2015 156
internet insurance 29
invention: AI as 240–248; 'conception' of 245; patentable 242; and 'technical effect' 242
inventive step (nonobvious) 243–244
inventor, AI as 248–254
inventorship and ownership 250–252
Investec 265
investigation-centric instruments 157–158
investors 112–113, 115–116
IOTA (DLT firm) 134
IR35 and RegTech 149–150
Irwin, A. S. M. 129, 138
Ivey v Genting Casinos (UK) Ltd t/a Crockfords 153

Johnson, K. 199
The Joint Council for the Welfare of Immigrants 223–225
Jones, Matthew 130
Joseph Rowntree Foundation 194
JP Morgan Chase 264

Karafiloski, E. 161
Kardashian, Kim 125
Kempson, E. 194
Kinetica 265
Kocsis, O. 32
Koza, John 249–250
Ku, R. 128
Kumhof, M. 93, 175–176

Land Registry and Driver and Vehicle Licensing Agency (DVLA) 155
Law Commission 157
Law Library of Congress 129
legal: and policy 200–205; and sentiment/news monitoring 265; situation in EU 90–92
legal person 233–235
Lewis, Michael 18
liability 254–255
Libra 89
Lin, L. 37
LiteCoin 89, 109
Loomis v Wisconsin 217

machine learning (ML) 231–232, 241, 244, 251, 254, 263, 264, 270
Macron, Emmanuel 272
Magnuson, W. 17, 64, 69
Mann, M. 222
Marian, O. 145
market stability and financial inclusion 85–101
Mastercard 3
Matzner, M. 222
Maya Declaration 55–56
Mayer, Colin 270
McKinsey Global Institute 264
micropayments 137
Microsoft 214, 217; facial recognition 216–217; Socio-Digital Systems group 73
Mittelstadt, B. 221
Mizgier, K. 32
modern banking: #AIFearFactor 266–267; AI should be for good 270–273; challenges for artificial intelligence in 266–270; challenges for fintech in 266–270; employee surveillance fears 268–269; governance and accountability fears 269; journey so far 263–264; overview 262–263; privacy rights and data protection fears 267–268; proposed ethical, governance, and responsibility strategies for banks 270–273; responsibility and knowledge fears 267; responsible use of AI in 262–273; responsible use of fintech in 262–273; use cases of AI and fintech in banking today 264–266
money laundering 133–136
The Money Laundering, Terrorist Financing and Transfer of Funds (Information on the Payer) Regulations 2017 148
Money Laundering and Terrorist Financing (Amendment) Regulations (MLR) 2019 118, 148
Monzo 146, 266
moral rights: and AI 236–240; copyright 236–240
Morgan Stanley 270
Mossack Fonseca 144
M-Pesa 57
MTN Mobile 57
MyCash Online 56

Nadelmann, E. A. 139
Nakamoto, Satoshi 107, 128
'Napster' 128
National Banking and Securities Commission (CNBV), Mexico 54
National Health Service (NHS) 125
National Security Agency (NSA) 125
Nationwide Building Society: Open Banking for Good (OB4G) programme 7, 64, 71, 78
Natural Language Processing (NLP) 263
NESTA 71
New York State Department of Financial Services 215
The Next Rembrandt 236
Nissenbaum, H. 213
Noone, C. 175–176
Norton Rose Fulbright 129

Obama, Barack 125
'OccupEye' 268
Ofcom 113
OneCoin 116
open banking 71–78
Open Banking for Good (OB4G) 7, 64, 71–78; access to data and user testers 78; collaborative learning through process of co-creation 76; creating time and space for innovation 75; grounded innovation 72–73; grounded innovation operationalised in 74; lessons for the future 76–77; organisational remit 77; overview 72; real and grounded challenges 74–75; resource 77–78
organisational remit 77
Organisation for Economic Co-operation and Development (OECD) 32, 129; Common Reporting Standard (CRS) 145, 156
originality 237–238
Ormerod, D. 151
ownership: candidates for 252–254; and data trainers 253–254; inventorship and 250–252; and programmers 253–254; and users 253–254; work-for-hire doctrine 252–253

Panama Papers 152
Panetta, Fabio 187
Panigyrakis, G. G. 195
Park Jin Hyok 125
Pasquier, U. 110
Patel, Priti 224
patent eligibility 241–243

patents: AI 241–246; disclosure and black box effect 244–245; eligibility 241–243; inventive step (nonobvious) 243–244; skilled person or machine 245–246
Pay as You Earn (PAYE) scheme 149
'PayMe' app 264
Payment Interface Providers (PIPs) 178, 179–182, 180–183
PayPal 146, 270
Peng, Y. 35
People for the Ethical Treatment of Animals (PETA) 239
Ping An Group 39
Ping An Insurance 37, 38–39, 40
Plaid 21, 24
Platform as a Service (PaaS) 31–32
PlexCoin 116
PlusToken 116
Police and Criminal Evidence Act (PACE) 1984 155
Police and Justice Act 2006 131–132
portfolio management 265
Poshmark 146
power of technology 198–200
practical reasoning 22–24
Pratchett, Terry 14
Privacy and Electronic Communications (EC Directive) Regulations 2003 132, 134
Proceeds of Crime Act (POCA) 2002 119, 131, 134, 155
programmers 253–254
prosecution and technology 158
public-private innovation partnerships 71
public revenue, cheating 151–152

Quantexa 265
quantum computing 200

Randall, Charles 201–202
RAVAS (Retailers Against Vat Abuse Schemes) 147
reasoning: means–end 23–24; practical 22–24
regulation of crypto-assets in EU 98–101
regulator's perspective and responsibilities 50–52
regulatory bodies and FinTech development 53–55
The Rent Recognition Challenge 70, 202
reporting standard and beneficial ownership registers 156–157

resource: Open Banking for Good (OB4G) 77–78
Revolut 146
Rowe, B. 196–197
Royal Bank of Scotland (RBS) 270
Royal College of Nursing v Department of Health and Social Security 157
R v Barton and Booth 153
R v Charlton and Ors 152
R v Cross 150
R v G and another 150
R v Ghosh 153
R v Hudson 151
R v Less 151
R v Montila 152
R v Neal 150
R (Business Energy Solutions Ltd) v Preston Crown Court 157
R (Hart and others) v The Crown Court at Blackfriars and HMRC 155

Salter, D. 153
sandbox environment, implementing 58
Schwab, K. 262
Schwarz, S. 5
Securities Commission of Malaysia 53
security token offerings (STOs) 95
Sellen, Abigail 73
Serious Crime Act 2007 131, 132, 133
Serious Fraud Office v Rolls-Royce Plc and Another 159
Shadow Brokers 125
Shift Technology 266
Shih, R. 128
Shrestha, Y. R. 213
Silk Road 125, 130
Sinclair, P. 119
Singh, N. 48
skilled person or machine 245–246
Slater, David 238–239
small and medium-sized companies (SMEs) 94, 98
social investment 71
social-purpose FinTech: designing 64–79; inclusively designed 71–78
social-purpose FinTech initiatives 70–71; government-backed challenge funds 70–71; public-private innovation partnerships 71; social investment 71
Software as a Service (SaaS) 31–32
Sonnad, Nikhil 216
Southall, E. 107
Specialist Fraud Division of the Crown Prosecution Service (CPS) 155

Spunta Project initiative 172n8
standard view of value 14–16
StatusToday 268
structural discrimination 216

Tanzania Communications Regulatory Authority's (TCRA) National Transfer Interoperability Agreement 54–55
Taxes Management Act 1970 149
tax evasion (TE): corporate offences of failure to prevent 151; cryptocurrency creating new realms for 147–148; prevention of, and technological innovation 160
tax evasion offences 148–154; cheating the public revenue 151–152; common law offence 151–152; corporate offences of failure to prevent tax evasion 151; dishonesty 153–154; evasion of customs and excise duties 150; evasion of VAT 150; income tax evasion 149; IR35 and RegTech 149–150; key elements of 152–154; knowingly concerned 152–153; providing false documents and information to HMRC 150
Tax Journal 158
Taylor, A. 119
Taylor, M. 107
technological innovation: accompanying effects 162; assessment of prevention of TE in light of 160; big data and blockchain technology 160–161; breakthrough for e-commerce 161–162; decentralised data 161; as façade for crime facilitation 160–162; feasibility 162; as indispensable helping hand 160–162; pre-emptive strategy 162
Technological Singularity 232
technology: an indispensable helping hand 154–159; beneficial ownership registers 156–157; common reporting standard 156–157; connect database 155–156; cryptocurrency and TE 147–148; detection, investigation, and technology 155–157; e-commerce and VAT evasion 146–147; a façade for crime facilitation 146–148; influence of technology on DPAs 158–159; investigation-centric instruments 157–158; power of 198–200; prosecution and technology 158; and tax evasion in world of finance 144–162
Tesco Supermarkets Ltd v Nattrass 151

Thaler, Stephen 249–251
theft, defined 131
Theft Act 1968 131, 134, 151
Theft Act 1978 131, 134
Thomas, Sam 130
'Too Big to Jail'(TBTJ) policy 149, 158
Toss 48
trade secrets 246–248
Trade Secrets Directive 246
TransferWise 21
TRIPS 252
Turin, Alan 230
Turner, Adair 16, 25
Twitter 125

Uber 28, 145, 217
UK A-level results 2020 214–215
UK Animals Act 1976 255
UK Patents Act 1977 250
UK Sanctions and Anti-Money Laundering Act 2018 135
UK's Intellectual Property Office (UKIPO) 250
UK's Money Laundering and Terrorist Financing (Amendment) Regulations (MLR) 2019 148
UK Strategy for Financial Well-being 66
Unfair Contract Terms Act 1977 119
United Kingdom (UK): CDPA 253; contemporary access issues faced by people in 67–69; Cryptoassets Taskforce 118; FCA 118–119; financial inclusion in devolved nations 65–66; government policy on access to financial services 64–66; Information Commission's Office (IOC) 204; National Crime Agency (NCA) 134; regulation of initial coin offerings (ICOs) 117–119; South East Regional Organised Crime Unit (SEROCU) 134
United States (US): Government Accountability Office 108; National Institute of Standards and Technology 30
US Copyrights Office Compendium 239
US District Court for the Northern District of California 239
US Dodd–Frank Act 19
users 253–254
US Patent Office (USPTO) 243, 246, 249–250
US Securities and Exchange Commission 117
US Supreme Court 238, 242, 244, 255

value, standard view 14–16
Value Added Tax Act (VATA) 1994 150
value research through an array of ABCs 27–41
VAT evasion 150; e-commerce and 146–147
VATFraud 147
Venmo 21
Vinnik, Alexander 126, 138
virtual currency 105, 128; Bitcoin as 107; cryptocurrencies as category of 105, 127; defined 105; European Central Bank (ECB) on 105; FAFT categories of 106, *106*; FATF on 105; structure and convertibility of 106, *106*
Vocalink Analytics payments 270
Von der Leyen, Ursula 91

Wachter, S. 221
Wagner, S. 32
Wall Street Journal 117
WannaCry ransomware 125, 133
Wheatley, M. 31

Whyley, C. 194
Wiggins, David 23
Wikimedia Foundation 239
Wirecard scandal 3, 5
work-for-hire doctrine 252–253
World Bank 85, 86, 88
World Economic Forum 175
World Health Organisation 53
World Intellectual Property Organization (WIPO) 232, 235, 245, 252, 257
Wozniak, Steve 215
Wyman, Oliver 183

Xcelerit 265
Xianghu Bao 28

Yang, Y. 213
Yorke, C. 152, 153

Zest Finance 264
Zhong An Insurance 39–41
Zlatev, J. 264

Printed in Great Britain
by Amazon